Pedro R. Portes

Dismantling
Educational Inequality

A Cultural-Historical Approach
to Closing the Achievement Gap

D0187814

PETER LANG
New York • Washington, D.C./Baltimore • Bern
Frankfurt am Main • Berlin • Brussels • Vienna • Oxford

Library of Congress Cataloging-in-Publication Data

Portes, Pedro R.
Dismantling educational inequality: a cultural-historical
approach to closing the achievement gap / Pedro R. Portes.
p. cm.
Includes bibliographical references and index.
1. Educational equalization—United States.
2. Academic achievement—United States. I. Title.
LC213.2.P67   379.2'6'0973—dc22   2004020884
ISBN 0-8204-7606-4

Bibliographic information published by **Die Deutsche Bibliothek**.
Die Deutsche Bibliothek lists this publication in the "Deutsche
Nationalbibliografie"; detailed bibliographic data is available
on the Internet at http://dnb.ddb.de/.

Cover design by Lisa Barfield

The paper in this book meets the guidelines for permanence and durability
of the Committee on Production Guidelines for Book Longevity
of the Council of Library Resources.

Dismantling
Educational Inequality

PETER LANG
New York • Washington, D.C./Baltimore • Bern
Frankfurt am Main • Berlin • Brussels • Vienna • Oxford

To Helio and Eulalia;
and Trish, Sebastian and Lev

Table of Contents

Part III: Transforming the Education of Educators and Policy Makers

Figures

Figures

Text Boxes

Tables

Prologue

The daunting task of closing the achievement gap at the national level requires much more than new slogans or a mishmash of insufficient and fragmented reforms. This task is formidable largely because the evidence—over the decades following the declaration of war on poverty and the call for civil rights—suggests that we are on the wrong track and can do much better. What the present educational system offers Students Placed At Risk (SPARs) is insufficient to balance the massive inequalities found in our system. The No Child Left Behind (NCLB) act has set into motion many disjointed strategies and efforts to address the gap that stems largely from mandating higher standards and accountability systems without the necessary changes to close the gap perpetrated in our system of education for the public. This change is not only economic but is also based on empirically supported strategies grounded in a human development theory that maximizes our investments.

The contributions stemming indirectly from many researchers' work—and particularly those included in this book—need to be acknowledged early because they helped advance a new policy direction in education. This direction is marked through numerous theoretical lenses and inter-cultural disciplines that buttress a general proposal for changing the structure, as well as the goals, of the present educational system. It is based on many of the voices heard from communities of scholars and educators in our field during a late modern zeitgeist of rapid transitions toward greater social injustice.

The fields of teacher and counselor education, educational administration, and policymaking are struggling to address the achievement gap by responding separately to current educational reform. This book describes a new model that provides a course for integrated actions that progressively shrink the ethnic gap at the national level. The change must be comprehensive and will take time. Through a synthesis of the major ideas and approaches attempted thus far and an extension of a cultural-developmental approach, a bold, comprehensive strategy is proposed. While not immediately viable, such change can serve as a beacon for the educational community. However, for a systemic perspective, it is necessary to understand how social inequality is sustained by educational policies and practices today.

First, a basic foundation is presented to help the reader understand how inequality in both processes and outcomes are organized in our public education system, which is currently under attack. A historical understanding facilitates the development of a plan that takes into account how children are socialized. At the group level, the present system produces both excellence *and* unequal opportunities for student learning. The central difficulty in closing the gap is reflected by disproportionate statistics on student learning. These statistics result from a conglomeration of social and economic practices, which operate at different levels and are structured to place additional burdens on the least advantaged. What is needed is a way to reverse the mechanisms that have produced the academic achievement gap, which serves as a barometer for the health and ethical nature of any democratic system.

The achievement gap in education has become an increasingly debated issue, and two major writings have recently emerged concerning this topic. The first is a thorough sociological analysis of the problem by Jencks and Phillips (1998) that summarizes the main explanations and problems associated with this gap. While it proposes that we employ several of the avenues suggested in this book, their analysis fails to offer a developmental framework for addressing what is, essentially, an intercultural and developmental problem. Such framework is needed for eradicating inequality at the group (ethnic) level. Recent writing by Thernstrom and Thernstrom (2003) summarizes much of the same data as here but for a different purpose that focuses on racial gaps. They propose a solution based on vouchers and charter school recommendations. These solutions, however, cannot dismantle the mechanisms that produce and sustain inequality because of a flawed analysis of the problem.

This book aims to help educators (school counselors, teachers, school administrators, and policymakers) understand the focal problem facing the nation's educational system. The academic achievement gap remains unresolved and is directly connected to the social and economic problems confronting our society. Unfortunately, educators and policymakers seem to clearly understand only parts of the problem. In order to define it, specific goals and SPAR populations need to be considered and defined, along with an examination of why various approaches to reducing the achievement gap have failed. In effect, educators may need to develop a broader cultural and historical understanding of the achievement gap in relation with the cycle of poverty and its intertwined effects.

To avoid the fragmented approaches stemming from pressures exerted by higher standards, educators as professionals need to have a reasoned conceptual framework to guide their practice. This is a major problem that indirectly prevents SPARs from being "well" educated in the present system. It is not difficult to understand why, as both educators and non-educators often misconstrue the problem of closing the gap. Amidst a series of slogans, discourses, and rhetoric, educators now learn to guide their practice based more on myths than on proven methods.

Different ways of assessing educator and student performance need to be considered, particularly for SPARs. Programs that prepare professional educators still need to focus, analyze, and evaluate the various reasons why the achievement gap remains intact, reform after reform. The gap in test scores essentially reflects how different social conditions that have been organized inside—and outside—education affect socialization practices and SPARs' development over time. This gap is a social phenomenon, defined by the fact that children from historically oppressed groups are provided with inferior education and thus fated to be over-represented in poverty or the underclass and exposed to inter-related categories of risk. The current educational system is the primary means for perpetuating this cycle. How the educational system helps produce and reproduce inequality—and the extent to which it may be able to avoid creating part of a larger social problem—is the major concern of the first section. Given that our culture has perpetrated an unfair educational system, the issue lies in finding a feasible way to restructure the system into a win-win context.

In the second section of this book, a new conceptual framework is presented as a starting point for transforming a system that still places the most vulnerable students at risk. An exposition of how the problem of inequality is socially constructed helps provide a framework for a multilevel transformation. It is not sufficient for teacher education alone to tackle the problem through multicultural and social justice ideological training, although a "badly needed" transformation in counselor or teacher education may be pivotal in closing the gap. As well, single-bullet approaches like leadership, multiculturalism, curriculum, Head Start, charter schools, summer reading programs (Kim, 2004), or small schools (Klonsky & Ford, 1994) and classes cannot independently shrink the achievement gap by even a single grade level.

Rather than criticize particular initiatives and approaches, an attempt to integrate current initiatives within a comprehensive, long-term plan for restructuring the educational system is needed. Once the problem of structured inequality becomes understood within a developmental framework, primary prevention practices with accurate assessments of progress of various SPAR populations—and other means to assist SPARs—become essential for progress, particularly after decades of failed reforms. Systematically reducing the gap between groups in terms of grade level academic performance then becomes the goal. While this is only one of a variety of ways that might be used, it is the most instrumental in assessing progress and in holding the system accountable for SPARs' learning. Simply arguing against testing is therefore shortsighted.

The concept of primary prevention is also important to help readers understand its great potential for addressing the key risk factors adversely affecting those subject to status inequality (De Vos & Suárez-Orozco, 1990) and the achievement gap. In order to become effective agents of change and to lift standards of professional development, we need to share a common knowledge base founded on learning and development in their social contexts. Only with a unified long-term plan for SPARs can a large-scale effect be expected and sustained.

Educators play an essential, strategic role that can play a major part in preventing the achievement gap from being perpetuated in future generations of children. However, a number of important intermediate steps are necessary before their effect can be maximized. This approach calls for an important curricular change of secondary education based on development of critical, logical thinking in the area of life skills for adolescents. This is a key to cultural development for SPARs and society. Not only are new roles and functions needed for educators but also new structures that can empower our youth and remove the gap for good.

In sum, the problem of educational and social inequality is delineated from a sociocultural perspective. Assessment and mediated learning are important in promoting development Kozulin (2003). Primary prevention and adolescent development of logical reasoning are important keys to educational reform, equity, and excellence. An unambiguous, multilevel strategy to eliminate educational inequality is presented here which aims for all SPARs to be educated at grade-level within a coordinated national strategy. The intention is to provide a "must read," thought-provoking, and possibly contentious book that offers educators and policymakers a fundamental understanding of how the achievement gap is not only organized and maintained, but how it can be evenhanded at the group level.

Acknowledgments

It was soon after the Westinghouse Report announced the failure of early childhood interventions in closing the gap that the seeds for this book were planted. It seemed then that the top research priority was designing one that would be sustain early gains. *As the Twing is Bent* soon followed and that seemed to end the bold efforts inspired by the War on Poverty to achieve equity in education. The search for the perfect intervention soon ended after realizing what was happening to poor kids in school. It was then that the promise of a cultural psychology appeared in the contributions of Mike Cole, Jim Werstch and J. Valsiner as they shared a different paradigm in psychology and education.

Around that time The Fulbright Program afforded me some time to think and learn abroad. While in Peru, one of so many educational reforms was underway. The book can be traced to that time when for the first time, my opinion was valued at the policy level while wearing the American academic garb and questions were fired by locals about their reform's potential for success. I remember not feeling prepared well enough to respond wisely and authoritatively but this left a mark in 1987. It took years to learn more about learning and development at the individual as well as the socio-cultural level, and about failed efforts in intervening in others' culture. Around 1996, a second serendipitous opportunity was extended to connect ethnicity and culture to psychology and education, a task that required years of apprenticeship in areas foreign to my training. Calfee and Berliner's Handbook was to be the next knowledge base for education since Wittrock's in 1986 and I had to step up. I again was privileged to review many of the fine ideas found in books competing for the Grawemeyer Award in Education. I'd like to also acknowledge many a scholarly critic, some of them friends for their hard questions and encouragement. They include George DeVos, Roland Tharp, Michael Cole, Henry Trueba, Ursula Casanova, David Berliner, Robert Gagne, Luis Moll, Richard Duran, Joseph deVitis, Kris Gutierrez, Peter Smagorinsky, Olga Vasquez, Robert St. Clair, Alex P. and students who helped (M. Sekhon & D. Oatley). Finally, I dedicate this book too to both my parents who were lifelong educators and kept the faith through numerous hardships and so many equity-minded individuals working to promote greater justice. Without them, this work would not see the light of day. Perhaps this synthesis and idea will help future generations in some measure.

Part 1

Defining the Problem

Equity *and* Excellence *in* Education

Understanding the Achievement Gap

"It is a wise man who said that there is no greater inequality than the equal treatment of unequals."

—JUSTICE FELIX FRANKFURTER, DISSENTING,
DENNIS V. UNITED STATES, 339 U.S. 184 (1949)

Introduction

The main obstacles to excellence and equity in education depend, in great part, on grasping the complex nature of how social inequality is socially organized and sustained. Educators today need a common knowledge base to help dismantle a system that reproduces inequality and hinders excellence. Too few know that the longer SPARs stay in school, the further they fall behind. Without a common game plan and clear set of goals, a new tower of Babel is built, filled with ideological conflicts and misunderstandings.

While the states of America are united, its people are not, and the nation remains at greater risk today than decades ago. The main reasons include a tradition of inequity in our history and inconsistent values, but, most important, the lack of a conceptual and practical understanding of how to eradicate the gap in learning outcomes. Without the latter it is difficult to create the will necessary to restructure the educational system and its related principles and policies.

As the twentieth century ended, wealth and privilege reached an all-time high in terms of the small proportion of the population that enjoyed most of it. Meanwhile, the achievement gap in school did not decrease for students living in poverty. Today's massive inequality persists in a struggling economy that will doom over 20% of the most prosperous nation's children to the underclass, in a manner that is unfairly distributed by ethnicity (P.R. Portes, 1996). The future that is thus being created guarantees Third World conditions for the nation.

Children are placed at-risk long before they experience many of the consequences associated with group-based inequalities in education. The cycle of poverty is unjust because it takes perfectly competent children—our nation's most valuable resource—and underdevelops their potential by maintaining a series of barriers[1] that most families living in poverty (Rank, 2004) are unable to overcome. A troubling fact is that after thirty years of compensatory programs for "at-risk" students and reforms, the achievement gap remains intact. In fact, attention paid to the instrumental role of schools in widening the gap for some groups of students has placed our nation's educational system under increased scrutiny (Bourdieu & Passeron, 1977; Bowles and Gintis, 1976; Oakes, 1990a, 1990b). We have yet to see how high stakes will affect the gap. SPARs receive the equivalent of only a middle school education, while the majority graduate with a high school education, based on meeting proficient standards for grade level performance (P.R. Portes, 1996). This serves as a definition of the achievement gap.

Prior to the 1960s, the problem of inequality and intergenerational poverty was regarded mainly as one of race-based segregation for some minorities and women, which was then linked to a lack of effort, ability, or both. It was an uncomplicated time compared with today, when nominal fallacies abounded. Instructivism[2] and logical positivism also reigned. An ethnocentric educational system and curriculum operated well within the prevailing norms of oppression, and the demographic trends of the time exerted minor pressures to change the prevailing caste-like system that was stable prior to the 1965 change in immigration policy and Civil Rights actions. In the decades that followed, a cultural revolution transformed society, as many more voices became included and began to demand change along a whole spectrum of human rights. While the issue of excellence in education had been paramount after the launching of *Sputnik,* the issue of equity began to compete for attention as the nation faced two interrelated threats. The external threat was then, of course, the threat to capitalism posed by the Soviet Union, communism and its socialist approach to equity. After the 1962 Cuban missile crisis threat, the federal government launched social programs to reduce the impact of poverty and the development of disempowered groups, particularly at home.

The internal threat concerned the Civil Rights movement and the Vietnam War, as the nation was shocked into appreciating the nuances of social justice and the links between poverty and violence, which competed with—and undermined—the social equity agenda of President Johnson's "Great Society" after Kennedy's assassination. The federal government also began to keep a record of educational outcomes in 1971 for the three major national ethnic groups, after Johnson's War on Poverty only a few years earlier. Not only was inequality found to be quite disparate in education, but education was deemed to be the principal mechanism to either sustain or reduce group-based inequities in both educational and, eventually, economic outcomes. Unfortunately, after the collapse of the socialist bloc in Eastern Europe, the commitment to social equity at home diminished, as evidenced by the lack of equity-related progress during prosperous economic booms in the years before 1999.

In the following chapters, it will become clear that the achievement gap has not been reduced in terms of educational and consequent social outcomes. This begs the following questions: What are the principal reasons for the persistence of glaring inequity in educational outcomes for a society that is so keen on equal educational opportunity in its definition of democratic values? Are schools less effective for children from certain cultures? Can better teaching close the gap? Is it mainly a social class problem in a society that requires a certain level of poverty, or unemployment, for supply-and-demand reasons? Or, could it be related to how poverty shapes cultural practices that then interfere with school learning? These represent some of the questions that are addressed throughout this book and that lead to other related issues. For example, could it be that educational policy is just not well informed by social science? Or, is our 'science' adequate or sufficiently advanced to improve education or to level the unfair distribution of poverty?

Perhaps education is informed about teaching and learning for some but has yet to find more effective practices for some groups that, unfortunately, are still regarded as the problem itself.[3] Here an essential problem is central to this book. This problem focuses on the ethical dilemma—now found in social justice discourse—of keeping some minority groups in poverty at *three* times the rate found for the majority. Conceivably, we may be on the right track, but the implementation of new policies and practices needs stronger support for dissemination throughout the educational research community. Perhaps we simply do not yet have the scientific know-how[4] to improve education and dismantle educational inequality. From a critical perspective, it is possible these are not even the right questions given the role of education in a market-oriented economy. Although we are at a crossroads in education that demands excellence, there is still the blatant fact that a failure to educate some student groups is an established cultural practice. The system is designed, financed, and organized to tolerate educational practices that leave certain groups or populations of students forever behind. As will be argued, social science simply has not found the best solutions or a unified model. Single-bullet solutions such as Head Start, vouchers, multicultural education, family or teacher education programs, and others fall short. Perhaps education cannot and never will move beyond these crossroads, because it cannot transcend the social, political, and economic constraints that govern it.[5] Fortunately, a cultural-historical perspective considers social change as possible when grounded on the (re-)organization of mediated actions and concerted goals. A quest for a solution, or at least a direction for measured improvement, may be designed by reversing the direction of the key structures and practices that now still reproduce between-group inequality (P.R. Portes, 1996). The problem's very sustenance may be understood through mediated actions from institutional and economic agencies in relation to cultural changes and their organization. The latter actions may occur on a range of levels, such as various types of desegregation, mainstreaming, standards-driven instruction, bilingual and preschool education, teacher education, or changes in allocating educational resources, in leadership, or new curriculum content.

Explaining the Gap

It has long been known that success in school is predictive of success in life overall, particularly for students placed at-risk (SPARs). For Bowles and Gintis (1976), success in school is greatly influenced by the child's socialization in and out of institutions, cultural programs, and informal learning contexts. In low-income areas, in particular, a range of factors contributes to youth's lack of opportunities to succeed academically. According to a study by the Carnegie Corporation (1996), it is estimated that up to 40% of the time of children and adolescents is "unstructured, unsupervised, and unproductive" (p. 10). It is believed that during these time periods many children undertake activities that lead to problems in their lives. Structuring alternative activities and creating new contexts for human development—such as after-school programs—might reduce some of the consequences of inequality. However, minimizing the gap in educational outcomes requires a much deeper approach to understanding human development in relation to schools, society, and family life. Superficial approaches such as vouchers leave the current structures fairly intact.

A tendency to oversimplify this historical problem[6] still prevails, blaming the achievement gap on the culture of origin, the community, teachers, or the family. Of all the current accounts for the achievement gap, insufficient parental support has enjoyed the most empirical support and is often seen as the main cause for the gap. Others point to the key role of early childhood socialization and the need to "catch-up" low-income children to middle-class norms in school readiness. After years of quasi-experimental research, Head Start and early interventions remain without positive long-term effects on student achievement as a whole, although some exceptions may apply. This may be because the critical period model, which served to guide such initiatives, is flawed when applied to human cognitive development (see Chapter Three). The first and least tenable explanation for the ineffectiveness of early childhood programs and schools concerned hereditability of IQ-related genes, which is based on the misnomer of race. Because serious and conscientious experts in both genetics and human development (see Nisbett, 1998) have already debunked this argument, it will not merit further attention here. Secondly, the school-constructed argument for the achievement gap remains popular today (<u>Singham, 1998</u>) and will be elaborated in the next chapters. Thirdly, empirical data documenting successful preschool to elementary school transitions exist, though generally these are the exception (see Ramey et al., 2000; Weikart, 2002). Most SPARs enter school already behind and proceed with less and less support from home. This situation may be largely a result of subtly institutionalized socialization processes that tend to be more compatible with middle-income, than with low-income, families. Also, we must consider that perhaps only effective Head Start programs, which pre pare SPARS for school, serve only a fraction of eligible children. Even fewer children have access to Even Start programs or after-school academic assistance. From the Head Start "in-house" view, the achievement gap only becomes significant after participants enter public school, and the longer they stay there, the more their performance parallels low-income children not served by Head Start. This evidence suggests that Head Start is only part of the solution.

From the school's perspective, the gap exists because children have not been prepared well, and their families are not involved in the child's education. The gap—or problems of teaching and learning—only becomes more severe as task demands increase in the upper grades in schools. If the bar is raised, children in poverty become at greater risk unless corresponding changes, such as higher levels of school-based, community and government support, are restructured and organized. As Singham (1998) notes, SPARs are truly like the canaries in the coalmines, the experimental birds that serve to alert us about pedagogical threats and opportunities as new market-driven demands force the system to adapt. While current programs to support family literacy and to develop parent involvement abound, they show insignificant effects on school achievement. Differences in resources between schools have been identified as accounting for the gap (Darling-Hammond, 1996), but these have been minimized only in some cases. Tracking practices have hardly been reduced in recent decades (Jencks & Phillips, 1999; Oakes et al., 2000), and the gap remains significant. The effective schools movement (involving leadership and organizational factors) has been largely ineffective in closing the achievement gap. Today, America Reads, family literacy, mentoring and peer tutoring programs, and after-school programs are reported in the literature as helpful in closing the gap. At the secondary level, school-to-work and school-to-college programs can be found, along with different schedules and grouping patterns, for instruction. In sum, a fragmented landscape filled with well-meaning efforts is salient today in a climate of stress resulting from reform and accountability. Yet still the gap still remains unaffected.

Understanding of the elements required for a success in school and for any effective, systematic approach centers on activating parental involvement (Funkhouser, Gonzales & Moles, 1997; Epstein, 1991), extending learning time and bridging research and practice (Donovan, Bransford & Pellegrino, 1999; Tharp et al., 2000). However correct these elements are, they call for new practices to be integrated in restructuring an educational system that places too many students at-risk. Some key leadership practices are now promoted by higher standards that guide instruction towards test outcomes (Waters, Marzano, & McNulty, 2003).

There is considerable evidence that reduced teacher-student ratios and developmentally sensitive interventions are important in improving school achievement, for SPARs in particular. Relative to middle-class children, at-risk students have less access to after-school assistance in terms of the quantity and quality of guided academic activity necessary to thrive in school. McCollum (1996) notes that where student achievement gains have been documented, much of this effect is attributed to low adult-to-student ratios—and thus greater individual attention and more quality time spent guiding the child. Snow, Burns, and Griffin (1998) note, "The association of poor reading outcomes with poverty and minority status no doubt reflects the accumulated effects of several risk factors, including . . . access to literacy-stimulating preschool experience" (p. 4). One might see that it is the relative difference in learning experiences before and after school that are strongly linked to academic achievement gaps.

These authors agree that while many at-risk children become successful in school, most do not (Snow, Burns, & Griffin, 1998, 131). In effect, much of the current research on the achievement gap concerns a standard deviation from the norm across a variety of multidimensional factors. These factors include literacy practices and reading readiness activities; parental education and involvement in the educational process during the formative years; assisted or meta-cognitive support/exposure by peers and adults; time on task related to school achievement (i.e., reading, modeling, attitudes, values, motives); peer and adult support of academic and social competence; access to educational tools and activities found in technology, museums, and travel; and responsive in-school education.

According to a recent RAND report, lowering pupil-teacher ratios for students in "lower grades in states with low SES [socioeconomic status] . . . have very large predicted effects" (Grissmer et al., 2000, xxvii)* They also note that preschool has much stronger positive effects for at-risk students with respect to student achievement, which would also seem to support extended learning time programs. Such findings provide us with vital clues regarding the subtle and pervasive differences in socialization that gradually structure massive inequalities in development.

A two-year gap is generally constructed in elementary school for one in five students living in poverty. In general, achievement differences in first grade are not as correlated with SES in terms of measured standardized performance as they are in the higher grades. But at-risk students who complete high school generally do so with three- or four-year gaps in reading, science and math (*Condition of Education,* 2002)* Low-income groups generally obtain a middle school education from the education system while the rest acquire a standards-based twelfth-grade level of education or more. This is the risk that structures future poverty on certain groups of children, particularly those underrepresented.

When over 20% of school-age children are stranded in a cycle of poverty, little hope exists of overcoming the barriers imposed by the increased literacy demands of a global economy and high-stakes reform unless the present system is overhauled. And yet, we raise performance standards and hold educators accountable, as if the higher scores produced by more test-driven instruction will somehow mysteriously close the ethnic achievement gap. This is forcing many educators to teach to particular tests without addressing the roots of the problem at a deeper level. For most African, Latin and Native American children, the proportion of those living in poverty (see Table 1–1) is over three times that of poor non-minority children (14%). Familial poverty tends to be underreported and shows great disparities. In sum, a 13-year-old mainstream student performs at the same level as a 17-year-old African American or Latino student from at-risk backgrounds (*Condition of Education* 2002). This probably holds true for a vast number of poor non-Hispanic white and Native American students whose levels of achievement can't be discerned from nationally commissioned reports.

From a sociocultural perspective, addressing group-based inequality (GBI) in educational opportunities and outcomes should lie at the center of the excellence and equity education agenda. The factors that contribute to improving student performance across a variety of school districts serving low-achieving students remain a crucial topic in education. As demographic changes reflect an ever-increasing concentration of poor minority students at-risk for educational failure, pressure mounts to find ways to improve learning and teaching for SPARs. Public pressure for accountability and excellence

Table 1–1. Poverty Rates by Ethnicity 1970–2001

	1970	1975	1980	1985	1990	1995	2001
Black	34	32	33	31	32	29	22.7
Hispanic		26	25	29	27	30	21.4
Asian & Pacific Islander	0	0	0	0	13	14.8	10.2
White	10	9.9	10	12	11	11.3	9.9
Non-Hispanic White		8	7	9	8.5	8	7.8

at the other end is fueled by international and national comparisons of student achievement (Stevenson and Stigler, 1992). Both situations demand heightened visions of a nation at-risk in a competitive global and technologically oriented future. At the heart of the matter lies the track record of a traditionally mono-cultural, public educational system that has failed to meet either old performance standards or new pedagogical challenges posed by diverse students socialized in poverty. The inadequacies of our educational system are exposed most gravely in poor urban school districts and classrooms where students' ethnicity is almost synonymous with poverty. When our educational structures and practices fail to prepare students from certain expanding populations to minimum grade-level standards, risk conditions are reproduced and galvanized for all groups in a democratic society. The system's outcomes result from the gaps imposed on poor children's development in and out of school despite their ability to learn. We label and often mistakenly construe the achievement gap in terms of color, lack of work-ethic values and similar "explanations" such as blaming teachers, genes or deficits in others' culture (Berlak, 2001). From an ahistorical, privileged standpoint, it becomes easy to be persuaded by a "no excuses" rhetoric that insists on higher-level performance without as much attention to higher—or at least more equitable—levels of support.

Contemporary Issues: Excellence in Relation to Equity

The questions before the educational research communities remain focused then on understanding and synthesizing the essential factors in institutional reforms that actually serve to reduce the achievement gap, are cost-effective, and are scalable.[7] The National Research Council (1999) report discusses the idea of a Strategic Education Research Program that includes certain crucial features (i.e., collaborative, interdisciplinary work, and a plan that is sustainable and has an overall cumulative structure to build on previous steps). Decades of fragmented and underfunded educational experiments and evaluations seem to call for an empirically grounded interface of developmental theory and best practices (Mosteller and Boruch, 2002). The public is calling on the educational research community to clarify what it does know about the "multi-edged" equity-excellence problem.

Excellence is operationally defined here in terms of the proportion of children who meet or exceed educational performance standards. Improvements in the latter raise the rank of the United States in international comparisons. Yet, in the final analysis (that is global by definition), the proof of excellence for any one system boils down to various indices of economic productivity and quality of life for all of its citizens. Higher test scores for the nation do not necessarily serve as a guarantee of progress toward equity.

Equity may be defined in terms of all groups of citizens having (proportionally) comparable school learning outcomes regardless of cultural history, gender, or ethnic background, particularly at different quartiles of a normal distribution. Equity is thus a relational term by definition that must be understood carefully and historically. It concerns the issue of whether one group has comparable access and outcomes in education relative to another group. Progress in equity, on the other hand, can guarantee progress toward excellence. The proportion of SPARs escaping from intergenerational poverty indicates one criterion. Such proportion fluctuates for majority and minority groups as some regress to poverty and others surmount it, depending on the economy, and social and educational advances.

We must also examine some of the rare successes across the nation in those few locations (mostly elementary schools) that perform particularly well in spite of serving high numbers of SPARs. What works—and why—still needs to be addressed. Such exceptions need to be examined, particularly in terms of what roles and practices school administrators, counselors and teachers play. Before attempting to replicate and disseminate programs across a variety of contexts and populations on the basis of exceptional situations, certain hard questions must be addressed.

One question concerns the analysis of current reform movements across states as higher standards guide instruction and define the attainment of excellence. More information must be taught and learned in the time allotted to schooling. Teacher effectiveness, measured largely by content expertise (Robelen, 2002), is an important factor for selection but is neutralized by teacher shortages, low salaries, and a neo-behaviorism in defining the purpose of education in terms of high test scores. Educators are pressured to produce higher test scores by whatever means necessary in a shotgun approach.

When success occurs in some schools some of the time—generally elementary—the idea of cloning what seems special is a tempting quick fix for a national problem where legalized segregation remains the norm. On one end of the spectrum, we find a handful of exceptions where various programs have made a difference, such as in Texas, Maryland and in particular districts that employ rather different models and practices. These were reported by what may be regarded as the positivist camp representing the government's No Child Left Behind (NCLB) policy, the Education Trust, and Regional Educational laboratories (see Reynolds, 2002; Haycock, 2001). On the other hand, we find that despite a few exceptions, the NCLB Act of 2001 is not addressing the enormous disparities in the quantity and quality of resources expended on those left behind. When students are trapped in classes and schools with low-achieving peers and/or less-qualified and motivated educators—with per-pupil expenditure differentials of over $25,000 per decade of schooling—the argument for emulating the few rare exceptions as the basis for closing the gap seems misguided, if not dishonest.

As educators are forced into test-driven instruction practices in some areas to address the crisis, an impact analysis of this trend seems essential. A systematic approach to achieve excellence through equity is one aim of this book. It provides educators, policymakers, and the public with a conceptual framework from which to gauge current and future efforts to improve education and intercultural conditions. While major tools such as desegregation, Title I, PL94 accountability, and other means are necessary; they clearly are not sufficient in dismantling GBI.

Epistemological Concerns

In this new millennium, the research community finds itself still caught in a modern crisis that concerns epistemological issues such as "How do we really come to know?," as well as the issues of "How do we define what works?," "For whom does it work?," "Whose evaluation?," and, most importantly, "What is the purpose of such evaluation?"

Various aspects of constructivism and related deconstruction-oriented critiques of social practices, along with resistance from a tradition of social science positivism, make it difficult to define what works and what is valued. Questions about the internal validity of any single approach places improvement-oriented efforts themselves at-risk for what may be regarded as a general malaise in recent times. However, a pendulum swing has occurred recently in the field of public education where scientific positivism (e.g., Slavin, 1998, 2002b; National Research Council, 2002) is again determining practices with high-stakes testing that expose equity issues. Federal funding for educational research now requires that the best evidence support treatments that contribute to a general knowledge base.

Part of this crisis in educational research is based on the sense that educational policy and practices are not necessarily driven by scientific knowledge (Towne, Shavelson, & Feuer, 2001). A sense of futility afflicts many educators in attempting to change prevailing norms. Some are convinced equity in education is unlikely, if not impossible, for a variety of reasons that may include social class, entrenched privileges, ethnicity, ability and effort. Issues about the relativism of power are of concern when intervening in other cultures or with other people's children (Delpit, 1995). Different views of the problem contribute to the gridlock of today, because most reform efforts are doomed by preemptive criticism of those who see the dominant culture as malevolent and intervening in other cultures for self-serving reasons. Regardless of outcomes or potential for meaningful, democratic change, these forces tend to discourage any top-down change and question the very definition of success. Top-down change in education is very difficult, in particular, because this system, unlike the defense, tax, or postal systems, is financed locally. Hence, change at the national level is constrained and influenced by "mutual consent," reflected in the use of standardized tests, federal aid, and what can be defined as the political economy of education.

As we enter the new century with an immense level of social inequity, we find the social science research community divided and in endless reform crises. Whether it is reflected in the production, utilization, or evaluation of findings, or with philosophy of knowledge issues, or with discussion regarding the very goals and purpose of education in a democracy, these quarrels reflect interactions of class, power and education. Amidst these lofty yet significant concerns, the day-to-day business of schooling proceeds as usual at the front lines. We continue to prepare educators to play more or less the same roles and demand more and more of them while providing them little assistance and support.

An analysis of inequality in the United States points to its debilitating role in a democracy and the uneven functioning of its institutions from family and community to schools. Globalization, population, and immigration trends are making the problem of group-based inequality (GBI) even more acute than in the past. What can be learned about dismantling this type of inequality may carry implications for other developing parts of the world. It seems indispensable to specify different categories of inequality by socio-economic status (SES) and cultural history in order to define a clear course. It is not just a minority or race problem, as many think. To eradicate today's caste-like society, sustained educational and socioeconomic practices and/or structures have to be organized in a new architecture, thus transforming the educational system and society itself.

State and district efforts to close the achievement gap are most visible today, yet they seem confined to specific school-based activity. Since the largest part of the problem extends beyond schools and the educational system, closing the achievement gap requires a radical shift in these efforts to reorganize education precisely for equity and excellence. Progress must be evaluated in terms of the proportion of students performing at grade level across the least advantaged groups. At present, it is only known that achievement varies by ethnicity, and this information must be extrapolated from free-lunch data to learn about the progress of SPARs indirectly. Approximately one third of African Americans are in the middle class. Estimates for Latin Americans vary due to variance in definition. It should be made clear from the beginning that the focus of educational reform is not the elimination of poverty in the present economic system (as desirable as that might be) but the elimination of inequality in school outcomes based on group or ethnic membership. Of course, learning outcomes themselves are instrumental in sustaining the present social order and poverty cycle. As noble as this goal might seem, it is impossible to alter the present economic world order without significant social upheaval. However, if the proportion of families in the middle class or students graduating with standards-based twelfth-grade education were comparable across groups, the ethical and moral dimensions of the problem would be much less perturbing.

The aim then is to explore a win-win situation to end the disproportionate rate of poverty and school failure for the least advantaged populations. SPARs are defined so because they are overly represented in poverty and below the twenty-fifth percentile on standardized school achievement tests (also in some special education classes and similar categories). In striving for equity and fairness, a way is also found for improving the achievement of the majority of students who constitute the largest group at below grade level.

A systematic reorganization of structures and practices can eliminate the over-representation of some ethnic groups at the bottom of that distribution. This might easily lead to higher scores for the school. Educators need to understand why this happens, how GBI is reproduced, and what can be done to foster equity across groups, and consequently, more opportunity for further learning. This knowledge is a precursor to effective collaboration. Unless, and until, this type of inequality is identified and curtailed, excellence in education will remain elusive and subject to endless political exhortations and slogans of limited substance. Since this type of inequity in academic (literacy) outcomes reproduces subsequent poverty and perpetuates social injustice, this not only undermines excellence in education but also places society at-risk for violence. Along with a host of related social and health problems that contribute to the achievement gap, this link must be addressed in any sound reform.[8] A strategy for breaking the intergenerational chains that bind children's cultural development due to family and community membership, and the historical consequences of structuring group-based cultural and educational deficits is thus part of the proposed framework in Chapter Four.

Gaps and Needs Assessment

The main limitations of current initiatives for closing the achievement and literacy gap need to be more fully examined by educators and need to be grounded in the analysis of the problem of excellence (or lack thereof). A multidimensional approach to eradicating the inequality being imposed on perfectly capable children needs to be integrated into the nation's educational agenda. Educators need to become experts not only in teaching or guidance, but also informed about their role in the context of broader sociocultural processes. Their professional education needs to include not solely practical skills but a broader understanding about the genesis of various interrelated social problems, and the role of class, power and history rather than just stereotypical concepts in multicultural education. Understanding the problem that is manifested by the gap is far from sufficient, although it is necessary for professional educators as it helps avoid ineffective action driven by mindless slogans such as No Excuses, No Child Left Behind.

The transformation of professional education must be included in national and state strategies to achieve and sustain equity and excellence in educational outcomes. Today, many educators enter the field without the necessary tools, training, or understanding of development in relation to context activities or practices. Relative to how medical doctors are trained to deal with the main problems of the human body, how well prepared are educators to address the problems of schooling today concerning the role of culture in human development? Few educators graduate and enter the field understanding the significance of a primary prevention focus in educational policy and practices. The ethical dilemma and consequences of high-stakes testing and new reforms also need to be considered. Education reform initiatives and their evaluation, instructional methods, dynamic assessments and impact analysis of various strategies to close the gap need to be prioritized and integrated by those who will educate and socialize our students in the future. Changes in higher education are critical in transforming the present system and will be addressed in the latter parts of the book.

Defining Gaps: Types of Group-Based Inequality (GBI)

A key concept in this book for understanding the origin and prevalence of the achievement gap is GBI. The term was coined (P.R. Portes, 1996) to denote a particular type of inequity affecting groups disadvantaged by the effects of cumulative interactions in past and current societal practices. Without it, closing the gap becomes vague conceptually and in practice. It is useful to distinguish among the types of communities living in poverty that actually define the achievement gap. This concerns not only class-related inequality but also group memberships that vary as a function of ethnicity, inter-group relations, gender, capital, and cultural history. Cultural history refers to a particular past of inter-group relations that denote power differentials over time that are ingrained intra-culturally. It is a more precise term than race, color, or minority. As a result of such inter-group histories, a mutual set of relations is set in motion at the societal level that constrains the development of some families, children, and communities relative to each other in spite of major federal initiatives. Those constraints become structured and institutionalized in subtle ways that continue to limit perfectly competent children.

The problem of inequality is not based on color or minority status per se (De Vos & Suárez-Orozco, 1990). Yet, many perceive all minority students as being at-risk, which is not necessarily correct. For example, we can expect an achievement gap for children of immigrants initially that gradually disappears in many of the following generations, as can be generally documented for some groups. Some immigrant students may be aware of discrimination and still not be at-risk, scoring above the norm in standardized achievement tests (A. Portes & Rumbaut, 2001). Still, other children of immigrants may gradually assimilate into the cultures subject to GBI in what has been termed "segmented assimilation." It is important to distinguish first- and second-generation students from those in groups remaining outside the mainstream across many generations such as African, Mexican, and Native Americans.

The rate at which the achievement gap disappears for ethnic groups after immigration or invasion in relation to a mainstream norm is a problem that can be divided into two general categories. The first concerns recent immigrant groups that vary in their adaptation and positioning in the dominant host society. The second concerns groups that have endured subordination historically by the dominant groups and have been left behind. They are described as "involuntary" or "caste-like" (see Ogbu 1992, 2002). Figure 1–1 attempts to show the various types of groups based on cultural history.

The problem of inequality in educational achievement concerning immigrant groups is not the central problem here. The construct of GBI helps define issues of equity and ethics from a historical standpoint. It can be defined by the prevalence of differential rates of school failure and poverty imposed on perfectly competent children based on their family's group membership or cultural history. A semiotic, caste-like phenomenon has been constructed that hinders the educational and socioeconomic progress of students subject to GBI. It is played out interculturally across institutions and communities beyond the first few generations of immigration or adaptation. While educators today play more sensitive roles, the types of activities and practices that promote inequality tend to remain the same. In the following figure, we see that the type of group is not necessarily static over time.

In the past, subordination and structured inequality were intentional and explicit. As more democratic practices and values began to take hold in the twentieth century, efforts to reverse status-based inequalities were observed in the suffrage and civil rights movements. In education, documentation of the consequences of GBI has evolved into various models that attempt to

Figure 1–1: Group-Based Inequality Categories in Relation to Numerical Proportions

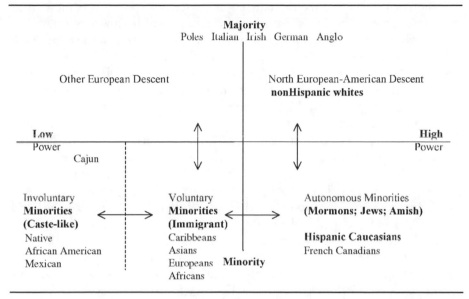

account for the persistence of the achievement gap into the new century after opportunity structures have been created. In a sense, the problem can be viewed in varied ways from a sociohistorical lens. We have progressed from the low-literacy stage prior to the twentieth century to a segmented-literacy period where established group differences are maintained. For example, in the case of gender, one might ask how many generations and structural changes it takes to eradicate GBI in income or in literacy outcomes such as achievement in reading, math, and science. Two main indicators can be used that are interrelated in answering the question in terms of ethnicity. Closing the achievement gap is really about those SPARs in caste-like groups.

The first indicator concerns the educational progress of students subject to GBI. How long before (non-immigrant) students from various minority groups are educated in comparable fashion? Attention to grade-level performance in relation to age is important to note across groups in this regard.[9] The second concerns representation in poverty. How long before the proportion of students living in poverty is comparable across ethnic groups? Is it only a question of time and know-how before equity goals can be achieved? Are the best ways to expedite a historical process that depends on culturally mediated actions actually being organized? Is proportionality a good way to define equity and ethics?

The prevailing view is that equity in educational or economic outcomes is not realistically possible in the present system. Equity in access to optimal teaching and learning conditions is yet to be structured socially, and so we must define equity more precisely. Surely there will always be variability in academic achievement within groups, due not only to class but also motivation, family involvement, and other contextual factors. The central issue is whether we can reorganize the educational system so that low achievers are not mostly from historically subordinated groups and high achievers are not mostly from the dominant majority in the national test distributions. Although GBI in educational outcomes is not likely to be eradicated under present conditions, this need not be so. In particular, proficiency in grade-level performance as measured by current standards is not only possible but also a necessary step toward both equity and excellence.

Some current reform initiatives appear promising but struggle without a solid, strategic plan or conceptual framework to achieve a significant change. For example, evidence exists that shows that although all children placed at-risk benefit from preschool education, those benefits do not persist for poor minority children in elementary and secondary school. It would seem then that effective early education should be established for the most needy and that school and instructional practices need to be improved to bring about equity in learning outcomes in spite of unequal economic and social supports. Students below grade level can no longer be socially promoted because of chronological age. The questions raised above may thus vary in answers around issues of a group's intent, ideology, and cultural values. Nevertheless, a sound theory linking development and culture is needed to undergird a major shift in policy and practice.

Types of Group-Based Inequality (GBI)

Inequalities in opportunities to learn are structured for some children by virtue of the group they belong to, their status in society, and social capital. These are different from individual differences and involve the cultural history of some groups that make children's success under current school conditions difficult. There are two types of GBI in education that place children at-risk for disadvantages in school learning. The first type involves students from groups that have been historically oppressed or disparaged (caste-like) and, as a result, still remain overrepresented in the culture of poverty. The second type of inequality is just defined by class or SES differences in educational performance as a result of political and economic oppression and its long-term consequences. The rate of poverty for students in our society hovers at 20% when all groups are aggregated, masking the differentials shown in Figure 1–1. For most European American mixed groups, the rate is a third of that from involuntary subordinated groups.

The first type of GBI is a measure of inequity that is disproportional and affects children from caste-like groups although they are as able to develop and learn as others. Children and families from these historical backgrounds may not share the values, resources, and practices expected in public schools. They have less developmental support to assist their children to perform well in school relative to the middle class. This first type of GBI (GBIa) is of greatest concern because children from those ethnic, low-income groups are three times more likely to live in poverty and be doomed practically at birth to be unsuccessful in school, facing a host of risk factors. The resulting social costs are great in terms of health, crime, violence, neglect, abuse, and prison.

Since these children are more likely to grow up in poverty relative to those from the majority group (14%), they also show disproportionate rates of risks related to low income and education. This becomes a critical ethical problem for a democratic society. As with massive gender disparities in education not long ago, the problem of disproportionate rates of poverty and its many forms are anti-democratic. The moral fiber of a society is tested given the slow progress achieved since the War on Poverty of the 1960s. That initiative produced a myriad of programs that sustain huge bureaucracies yet has produced few gains in academic achievement. At the collective level, education remains the principal means for evolving from poverty to the middle class. The poverty rate, as with the divorce rate, has been stable in recent years. While 10–12% of all families live in poverty, as generally estimated, the actual rate is much higher (Gans, 1995; Rank, 2004; Turner, 2000) when considering the affected children from ethnic groups subject to GBI. This is where the gap is largest and defines the problem of the achievement gap directly. Here we see the problem is not just about increasing academic learning through leadership, smaller classes, or diversity training for educators. Culture, status, power, and context must be considered in "proofing" standards-based education from GBI.

The achievement gap is one of the most telling and important indicators of the extent of social injustice and at the same time, a prognosticator of future social conditions for all. Our social progress might be defined by the extent to which the gap between these groups is closed. The limitations faced by children from poor family contexts constrain children's future unfairly and become part of the political economy of education. In sum, the second type of inequality (GBIb) places children at-risk mainly because of class and not ethnic membership. If all cultural groups had comparable rates of poverty, equity would be mostly defined by socio-economic factors.

Historically, poverty was ingrained in caste-like cultures in ways that became normative relative to the dominant population. This still causes many of the incompatibilities that exist today between schools and family/community cultures. GBIa and GBIb represent two different yet interrelated ethical problems that handicap perfectly capable children and waste our cultural potential. Children, as the most important resource for society, are socialized in ways contrary to society's best interests. Children are the most critical source of capital for a culture (Rauch, 1989). If disproportionate numbers of children (from the three main involuntary national subcultures in particular) are not invested in, we assure the perpetuation of group-based inequalities that will continue to be reproduced in the future disproportionately.

A historical analysis of the problem is critical to understanding what course to take in any future change of policies and practices. Of the two types of inequality, the first appears as the most pressing for a democratic society. In addressing and reducing it directly, a way to diminish the second type of inequality for the whole of society is found. This also facilitates excellence in education. That is, by targeting ways to promote the development of those most in need, the whole system benefits. Not only can the average scores for schools and the nation improve relative to other countries, but also the work of educators and students as a whole improves gradually. A host of social problems can be prevented as the nation's human capital is developed. In short, assisting those least empowered is in the best interest of society's current goals.

Of course, this argument may be considered less important in time of war or if one believes poverty inevitably will always afflict some groups more than others. That is, there are those who believe that education is a limited resource for the few or that it should serve as a filter or those who believe there is no further obligation to promote further equity-related opportunities for groups subjected to exploitation in the past. Some might contend that a national campaign to end GBI or change the current economic conditions and their correlates is unrealistic. Many social scientists believe poverty rates are part of a political economy shaped by those unwilling to risk losing certain advantages that allow some groups to enjoy and develop more capital at the expense of others. Finally, it may be argued that the present proposal is too radical, naïve, or both since eliminating GBI requires a social transformation and upheaval. These and other cultural beliefs affect the extent to which changes occur. A growing movement today focuses on social justice and holds that greater equity is in the best interest of the nation. Yet, it appears a historical fact that in order to maximize economic or political advantages, keeping certain groups disempowered is necessary. Consequently, gaps in literacy and other cultural tools must be created and sustained to ensure stability in/for an educational system that mindlessly responds to a market economy.

In limiting access to opportunities to learn and work, a caste-like society is easily established. Expanding, instead of limiting, those opportunities for a period in history can help to undo the inequities that confront children because of their group membership. Equity at the group level with regard to educational outcomes is not only a goal but also a primary means for promoting a fair distribution of capital across groups.

A strategy to reverse years of inequality within a society driven by market forces would hinge on ensuring that greater proportions of the underrepresented citizenry have access to equal opportunity structures. An allusion to a Marshall Plan type of investment at the domestic level is instructive. There may be several motives for developing a plan or architecture of this nature, although such an endeavor may be critiqued as a form of social engineering. Yet a strong counterargument lies in the fact that such plan development has already occurred and is grossly unfair whether we would like to admit it or not.

Proof of whether a new plan may actually work can be examined historically and by the extent to which the educational outcomes for students subject to GBI improve relative to the norm each year. In the past thirty years of deliberate efforts to narrow the gap, billions of dollars have been spent. The (four-year) gap noted in 1971 has not been narrowed even one-half of a year in spite of past and current reforms. So even if a better strategy is not utilized, it is far better to have developed one than not. It can also serve to guide and integrate current efforts and policymaking. In the best case, it may help guide and bring about steady progress.

A body of knowledge may be eventually developed that could integrate the various socialization initiatives that lie fragmented in the educational field. Rather than continue providing costly remedial or social services to youth once they are already behind or in trouble, primary prevention can help mediate development at the institutional level. A restructured educational system provides for a demographic, equitable shift. That is, after one or two generations, group inequality in academic learning might be progressively reduced.

Designing a Fair Future?

Wise orientation of our cultural history is essentially what is needed, not just high test scores, vouchers, or college admissions. Can a new history be organized in the future to counter the damage caused by previous generations? Oppression and exploitation have short- and long-term consequences, whether they occur at the individual or the group level. The current system or plan acts through family, community cultures and socioeducational structures to place children not only at-risk, but to guarantee lifelong disadvantages for some groups. A new one is needed that spans from preschool to college.

The economic gap is directly and indirectly related to the gap in literacy and related outcomes. Students placed at-risk for familial poverty graduate not only years behind in basic skills but also are less likely to develop life skills as a result. This means that blaming the family, students, or the school is futile. It begs the critical question of how best to transform our shared cultural history as a nation.

Ethical Concerns

As a result of group membership, the level of literacy necessary to escape poverty is so disproportionately low for some that the very ethics of the nation's educational system are called into question. Some schooling practices have influenced the cultural adaptation of disempowered and dominant groups differentially. The long-term effects of structured practices constrain the development of literacy-based tools and skills in a cumulative fashion. From a cultural-historical perspective, constraints on the development of any group, through gaps or uneven acquisition of these tools, limit full participation in a multicultural world. From a sociogenetic analysis, certain practices have been restructured and have improved conditions for women. However, the overrepresentation of some groups found in the depths of poverty suggests that the critical mechanisms that would counteract past activity patterns still remain in place for other groups. Those mechanisms continue to produce different outcomes in literacy tools embodied in standards-based performance. These are instrumental to the development of economic and cultural capital.[10] Even when these are applied equally, they do a disservice to those already behind.

The issue then is not whether the achievement gap can be closed, but whether the constraints employed to create the prevailing gap can be reversed. The issue is to discover the best ways to reorganize cultural conditions to produce comparable educational outcomes in school at least in meeting basic standards. This is a first step in equalizing access to college and related professional and economic options.

A New Rationale for Why Education Needs to Be Reorganized

Given the fact that past and current strategies have failed to close the gap, the plan calls for a new approach to be formally integrated in middle and secondary schools. This plan advocates that educators help develop and implement a spiral curriculum that extends life skills content into a broader primary prevention and promotion plan. In focusing on development and learning for adolescents—and their families in the future—the plan promotes and targets parental involvement in future generations of SPARs. This is most critical, particularly for those placed at-risk. This curriculum is not to be reduced to civics, home economics, social studies, or carrying eggs around all day. It is a curriculum for breaking the cycle of poverty by empowering future parents with critical knowledge and thinking skills. Our society is not likely to redistribute wealth equitably, but perhaps it might allow learning and teaching opportunities to become more equitable. While all students may be served by this new restructured spiral curriculum, the aim is toward SPARs who would

Text Box 1–1: Not an Issue of Majority or Minority Status

Cultural history can influence power relations such that a minority, as well as a majority group, controls conditions that favor one group over others. In the United States, Australia, and similar contexts, members of the majority culture tend to enjoy more advantages than some other groups, not because of ethnicity or majority status but because of a history of sociopolitical relations, acts, and practices. In Andean and Central American contexts, the minority culture enjoys and reproduces such advantages while it is the majority's children that remain placed at-risk. Is this a question of Western versus non-Western culture or color, language, religion and other similar common-sense contenders that determine the gap? History would tell us otherwise. But the one thing we know that holds true, regardless of whether it concerns the quick fall of the Inca Empire[11] or the present situation in the United States is a familiar common denominator. It is the relative edge in literacy, in mediated action or functional skills and tools, that one group holds over another.

otherwise remain at-risk under the present sociopolitical system. While this new curriculum may not be regarded as academic enough or necessary to close the literacy gap that is driven by tests that assess only certain academic areas, its need and relevance may be described in terms of a standard needs analysis:

- American working families today need help in carrying out their traditional socialization functions. They need to be strengthened in carrying out the social, emotional, and overall socialization of children. For over the last half-century, there has been a frontal attack on the American family as an institution. With more women in the labor force and resulting changes in gender roles and rates of divorce, parent involvement for SPARs has been particularly compromised. Since the baby boom, the extended family has disappeared. The traditional socialization practices that once conserved cohesion and quality time and supported children's socioemotional development have been undermined. Many parents today live under constant stress. They have not had solid models for effective parenting, and they often lack the time and expertise to provide the kinds of involvement that support children's development. This sets the stage for intergenerational learning or socialization problems now manifested by new modern phenomena (e.g., school violence).
- Schools also need help in socializing children as families adapt to the new economic order. Economic and personal constraints mount as we observe an increase in time demands.

- The nation's economic policy has changed toward the poor since 9/11. Two incomes have become necessary for most families to survive before this era. Children's socialization suffers under an unfriendly family policy, particularly affecting children with low-income single parents. One in five children is placed at-risk economically, as many experience neglect, family conflict and dysfunction and are further disadvantaged in school by tracking. Thus the learning gap and poverty reproduced in the academic failure of one generation compromise the next, exacerbating the problem of an education system bent on higher standards reforms. Ironically, when schools do not assist the education of SPARs or provide the conditions and contexts for their development, other institutions end up dealing with socialization failure. The juvenile and penal system, social work alternatives, and health and justice care are far more costly and ineffective alternatives. When those whose development and socialization remain at-risk too long, a double risk is produced, first for them and also for others.

- To break the cycle of poverty and low achievement, family involvement practices need to be promoted and modeled effectively. Yet these are not fostered even close to the level that we promote sports, physical education, and other non-academic activities at school. Before adolescents attend high school, we have one last opportunity to reach and lend the know-how necessary to help future generations of children. Teaching them to think more critically and develop a future orientation and abstract thinking as a viable alternative to drilling those already left behind several grade levels.

- We cannot continue to blame families and the culture of the child. To blame the victim for circumstances that have been largely determined, imposed, and structured historically is irresponsible. Schools are already being called upon to do more and more beyond academic instruction. Yet they cannot succeed under a system focused on only part of the problem: accountability in test scores. Nonetheless, schools still offer the only—and last—window of opportunity for primary prevention and building a knowledge-based support system to strengthen families in future generations. Some of them work incredibly well.

- Just as families need assistance, schools also need help in reorganizing their functions. As they organize to carry out new functions, the type and the level of preparation for educators also require change. Educators are expected to do more with less than is actually required to do it well. They lack the means (preparation, structures, and skills) needed to close the gap. We still maintain a system that

favors those with a priori advantages and that unashamedly undermines the potential of those most impoverished.

■ Schools need to be better organized to promote SPARS' development directly. Rather than only focusing on what tests measure, a
rethinking of curriculum structures, goals, teaching practices, financial allocation decisions, and mission is required along with new practices and new roles for educators.

■ These new roles require a new type of preparation in higher education if the personnel in schools are to actually close the gap.
Counselors, teachers, and principals need to first understand the
problem and then have comparable knowledge of how to jointly
carry out concerted actions to demolish the gap.

■ In sum, we need to go beyond single-dimensional tactics such as
vouchers into a comprehensive plan for preparing all students and
educators for success. Once key strategies are coordinated and sustained, a sufficiently large effect on a population level can be
produced.

The above ideas illustrate how primary prevention and promotion
principles can become part of a culturing plan that extricates the educational
system from contributing to inequality. It is clear that to promote greater
parental involvement we must empower adolescents as future parents
with a new knowledge base and aim higher than producing higher test scores.
This transformation needs to be embedded in higher education. There
may always be an achievement gap just as there may always be poverty.
However, the main issue here concerns the disproportional and massive,
unethical inequality for millions of children who are disenfranchised because
of their group of origin. The gap between groups in meeting minimum
standards of performance is critical. SPARs are doomed to fail or be
failed by the very ways schooling has been organized. To reverse the historical conditions that place populations at-risk inequitably by ethnicity,
it is necessary to think outside of the box and to be willing to consider
reversing mediated actions collectively from a developmental perspective.

Can Federal Funding Generate Educational Equity?

Social class is unevenly distributed in multicultural societies in ways that
reflect power differentials that are then reenacted and enforced in educational
practices. Unless a nation is willing to reinvent itself and provide equal opportunities for all of its children—regardless of their history at the group level—
educational policies and practices are unlikely to close the gap. Yet here lies
the first and most fundamental problem that inhibits large-scale change

efforts toward equity in educational outcomes. Education remains locally funded with resource allocation constraints that impede effective strategies to help the less advantaged nationwide.

This gap is relative as programs that target groups other than those subject to GBI are unlikely to be supported. Any effective technology or pedagogical innovation is generally adopted first by the most advantaged. The latter are already receiving what is being proposed for SPARs. Hence, the likelihood of SPARs prospering or catching up is unlikely unless we draw the line at minimum proficiency standards. In the past four decades, students subject to GBI, even when they graduate from high school, remain 3–5 grade levels behind the norm (*Condition of Education*, 1998, 2002). This gap is sufficient to reproduce inequality in adulthood and subsequent generations and to sustain the poverty cycle with all its attributes. In order to stop this cycle, certain institutional practices and policies must be reorganized and new ones created to reverse the current patterns. Reorganization implies adding as well as subtracting or reducing practices. The resulting conditions stem from changes in mediated action. Some types of action are mediated legally and institutionally while others are initiated locally. Some actions are mediated through laws and statutes at the state level while others are local and more difficult to scale at the district level. Some may be classified as gap reducing (class size reduction for SPARs) while others are essentially neutral (school uniforms) or harmful to learning (tracking based on tests). How the achievement gap is being maintained requires careful analysis before educators engage in new roles and practices.

The Gap as a National Problem

Certain paradoxes may be noted in actual practice(s). The federal government only helps fund local programs partially and temporarily, yet it controls the practices and outcomes of many others such as national defense, the INS, IRS, and homeland security. The federal government contributes often less than 10% of the costs associated with educating a child in public school. Hence, the responsibility for maintaining or eradicating GBI is mostly up to the states and local school districts. One might wonder what would happen if schools, like the postal service and the military, were mainly funded by the federal government with its larger power to level discriminatory practices (see Department of Defense [DOD] schools). Imagine if states and districts organized and funded the defense or internal revenue system. The historical record suggests that equity and social justice require strong federal support and direction for major restructuring to be realized. Yet, under the present climate, resistance to bigger government threatens any form of centralization as busing for desegregation becomes increasingly unpopular and internal school segregation practices have become standard (Orfield & Yun, 1999).

Given that structural limitations are unlikely to change, one must then ask what other methods might serve to eradicate the achievement gap for these groups of students in locally financed schools. How may we alert policymakers to an effective solution for reducing the massive inequality that prevails in one of the most wealthy and democratic diverse societies in history? How can different states and districts get on the same page in closing the gap? While federally funded public schools may not be a plausible solution to the majority of voters, neither are vouchers or charter schools that tend to favor only a few. Perhaps past experiences in establishing more fair learning environments for underserved groups should be reconsidered. Since states vary in wealth and support of education, greater equity may be promoted by assisting the least advantaged in more systemic fashion than Title 1 and related programs have done in the past.

Summary

This chapter integrated key insights and new ideas in addressing population differences related to the achievement gap that pose risks for both students and society. This integration serves educators in sharing a common knowledge base that includes primary prevention and cultural change principles. These are extended within a cultural-historical framework elaborated in the next section. The framework is needed in forging a restructuring plan to reverse inequality in education for those least advantaged. Such a plan can incorporate many single-problem approaches such as those noted earlier. The model calls for transforming the role of educators and the current structures of education in establishing equity in learning outcomes, particularly for those now most underrepresented. It calls for new way of conceptualizing one of the most important missions of the educational system. Finally, the chapter also detailed different types of inequality, defined the gap and considered the role of the federal government in local and state reforms. A comprehensive plan for eliminating the gap in achievement and a common knowledge base in developmental theory is outlined next in advancing educational, family, and social policy.

Endnotes

1. For example: class size, tracking, an age-graded system, resegregation (Orfield et al. 2003), teacher expertise.
2. In contrast to constructivism, it is associated with direct instruction.
3. Here I refer to the theoretical knowledge and proven practices and "tools" that can help level the playing field for SPARs. Resource allocation is regarded often as a separate matter in terms of having either the tools or the resources needed. As with

NASA's space projects, both elements need to be organized and deployed systematically.

4. This view is prevalent in some areas of social science, particularly sociology. It may be argued, for example, that any innovation or technology found to help low-income groups would be adopted by the middle class, leaving the achievement gap untouched in relative terms.

5. There is no absolute solution but perhaps only an approximation of that democratic ideal. The constant is the dialectics that sustains relative differences in power, acquisition of tools, capital and/or skills.

6. I define the problem as that of educational "outcomes" in relation to equity across ethnic groups. The problem is defined by conditions that produce low achievement overall and significant group difference. The worst problem is resolved when all groups are at or above grade level and continuous progress is made over time.

7. For an educational program or method to be truly effective and reliable, we should be able to reproduce it on a larger scale from one class to the whole school or from the school to the whole district and sustain the progress made.

8. A conceptually well-organized plan to close the gap in the current reform efforts remains to be seen.

9. As discussed throughout the text, this type of equity is defined by comparable proportions of students from various groups that perform at or above grade level. This is a minimal, incomplete form of equity but one that can serve as a temporary goal in the process of dismantling inequality and promoting excellence for all.

10. This would include both social and economic capital (Coleman, 1987; Bourdieu, 1987).

11. When only a few hold the keys to literacy and technology, the risk for the whole culture increases.

The Construction and Persistence of Inequality in Educational Processes and Outcomes

A Primer for Educators

2

"Children in the United States do not have equal
opportunities to succeed."

M. DONALD THOMAS AND WILLIAM L. BAINBRIDGE
(PI II DELTA KAPPAN, MAY , 2001)

Overview

The goals of public education have evolved over time, reflecting various corresponding sets of noteworthy values, functions, and results. From a critical
perspective, public schooling is designed with purposes remote from reducing educational and socioeconomic inequality. Historically, two of its primary
functions are to prepare the workforce and to instill a shared national identity.
Schooling focuses mostly on academic learning, literacy, and learning how to
learn. It has yet to serve as a mechanism for reducing population differences
in academic and subsequent economic outcomes—except for gender, to a relative extent. Public education or school remains unchanged, in spite of the
perception that it serves as the great equalizer in social outcomes related to
power. Social scientists generally agree that public education cannot eradicate
the massive socioeconomic inequality that persists between dominant and less
powerful groups in U.S. society (Coleman, 1990; Bowles & Gintis, 1976;
Bourdieu & Passeron, 1977). The question remains whether it can reduce
the academic achievement gap still manufactured today.

Today's system of public education thus not only indirectly reflects, but also reproduces, inequality. The principal causes for the present caste-like society, however, stem from other long-standing historical socioeconomic relations and factors outside of school. The educational system of the United States is organized around primary and secondary sets of functions, goals, or purposes. Economic and political survival play a key role that has both inter- and intra-national dimensions, from *Sputnik*-driven to higher-standards reforms. Citizenship, democratic values, and a collective identity remain essential goals alongside the transmission of culturally valued knowledge and beliefs. The other primary functions center on preparing youth for present and future workforce demands with respect to literacy skills in academic areas generally linked to higher education.

Although progressivism and democratic inclinations made public education appear as the single most peaceful instrument for reducing inequality in the twentieth century, it might be argued that this function is still not primary even after the Civil Rights movement. World wars and intergroup conflicts have contributed significantly to concerns about social and educational equity. The voices of women and outsider groups in the United States heard in this late modern period (Giddens, 1992) fade before the importance given to global economy risks, opportunities, and national security.

Education's role as a tool for liberation (Freire, 1993) or for social stratification (Apple, 1989; Bourdieu, 1987; Giroux, 1980, 1983; Nieto, 2000b) is part of a new discourse of social justice in education. After the nation declared war on poverty in the 1960s, the measurement of educational outcomes by race (as a proxy for social inequality) became salient in national reports such as *The Condition of Education* series. With an age-graded, segmented educational system in place, middle-class students generally develop a four-year literacy edge over those from the least advantaged ethnic backgrounds. Hence, the paradox of a system of public education lies in its instrumental role that stratifies society by constructing a huge gap between groups each generation. How can it also close the gap? The contradiction appears blatant when the purported reform goals and actual outcomes of the educational system remain inconsistent.

Gender and Immigrant Clues in the Puzzle

During the post-industrial period following President Lyndon Johnson's Great Society, deliberate compensatory early childhood programs attempted to achieve greater equity in education between social class and ethnic groups. The gender gap in mathematics was later eliminated. Unlike the ethnic gap that disproportionately associates high rates of poverty with black and most Latino groups, this gender gap does not get compounded. That is, while women still earn less than men, the gender gap has closed because most women belong to the dominant majority group. Ethnic groups are not balanced by social class. Much can be learned by studying social change across groups as a function of their history, immigration policies, and social practices. After costly educational investments in compensatory education, group-based achievement gaps remained in spite of school desegregation efforts.

Class differences are compounded by ethnicity and cultural history. In spite of the prevailing belief that schools are incapable of compensating for the effects of the cycle and culture of poverty, changes in immigration policy after 1965 allowed for an additional category and phenomenon to be observed. Many ethnic children of immigrant groups—who are also subject to poverty and language differences—can and do overcome the achievement gap and in some cases outperform average mainstream students' school and subsequent economic performance (P.R. Portes, 1999; A. Portes & Rumbaut, 2001).

The above phenomena may help clarify some key points in determining the extent to which a reorganization of public education is required to reduce the achievement gap. First, it is clear that changing certain sociocultural conditions (i.e., beliefs, ethics, values, expectations, knowledge) can eliminate some forms of group inequality (e.g., gender based). This type of change has been the staple for schools. Mathematics, for example, concerns an essential cultural tool that serves as a gateway to a variety of professional and economic options for families. A gender gap remains in other areas such as science, technology, and engineering. Is it because schools have greater influence in determining learning in math than other content areas? Is the power exerted to bring about gender equity greater relative to that of closing the gap for some ethnic groups living in poverty?

Second, equity was achieved in spite of a biological group difference based on sex, and a gender difference based on culture and history. Given the general intellectual capacity and potential of the human species, this problem reflects the influence of major historical developments that are of interest to cultural psychology (Cole, 1996) and social science. The example shows how a new history can be forged through social agency, through the restructuring of access, and the practice of literacy-related tools and the encouragement for acquiring them.

A third point that is relevant to the closing of the achievement gap stems from the concept of GBI. While not all immigrant students manifest an edge in the first or second generations over non-immigrants, evidence exists that poverty alone is not always the cause for school failure or the achievement gap. There is evidence that severe poverty is not as intergenerational as before. It can be surmounted when several efforts are concerted in and out of the home. In explaining why some immigrant groups living in poverty outperform poor non-immigrant minority and majority group students, it appears that many immigrants have a different sociopsychological frame of reference (Ogbu, 1992) that can be lost with cultural assimilation in subsequent generations. Immigrant minority groups are generally not only poor but also experience a sense of optimism regarding opportunities for development that appears greater than that found in many alienated groups of students in this country (Steele, 1997). Motivation and belief systems are different for non-immigrants from some cultures that, in turn, vary by social class and historical conditions. While it is harder for the first generations of immigrants to achieve a comparable level of upward social mobility relative to the majority middle class, it is more common for them to surpass the level of low SES ethnic minority groups that are more likely to be unemployed, imprisoned, undereducated and poorly motivated in public schools. If it were not for the high prevalence of poverty in the nation's lowest SES groups, it would be impossible to argue against the (majority) notion that "poverty alone is not the primary cause for school failure." Otherwise, the lot of immigrants in the United States would be more limited and similar to Third World immigrants in more homogeneous and developed European nations that remain lower in status attainment.

Many immigrant groups bring their own social capital and have the support of their ethnic enclaves, making for more successful adaptation (A. Portes & Rumbaut, 2001). Yet, not all immigrant students—including some Asian groups—adapt to school well, show "effort optimism," or perform at or above grade level (P.R. Portes, 1999). Some experience "downward assimilation" and manifest patterns described as "resistance" or "learned helplessness" (Erickson, 1993; Ogbu, 2002) that sometimes characterize students subject to GBI. Hence, a complex picture emerges in contrasting immigrant students and involuntary minority students (from groups subject to GBI). We do not yet know if the majority of SPARs actually exhibit learned helplessness or resistance any more than alienated majority or immigrant groups. Some lack academic motivation as a consequence of intercultural treatments, regardless of ethnicity or gender. Others become subject to stereotype threat (Steele, 1992, 1997). Clearly, the construction of the achievement gap, in relation to the economic gap, is interactive and mediated structurally over time and by different types of social and psychological factors. The gap is driven by significant variations in literacy outcomes that are the product of schools' co-construction with students and their communities.

The gap is a problem of culture rather than of color. Intercultural differences in socialization practices are generally related to a history of inter-group relations and power. The latter can produce pedagogical problems in the treatment of children from some historically oppressed groups. They can also influence social and psychological development. For instance, South Africa or Andean nations serve as interesting cases that show the relation between minority status and academic development. On the surface, color and minority status appear as causes for achievement and a variety of other gaps. However, cultural history accounts for differentials in status and power across ethnic groups. Some groups have developed cultural practices that are geared toward survival, often reacting to subordination and disparagement from the dominant mainstream culture (De Vos, 1993). Such cultural accommodations may result in a gap in educational outcomes, yet may also safeguard some groups' self-esteem. Unfair structures and practices have changed only relatively, keeping such differentials in place. When students are unfairly placed at-risk depending on group membership, American society places itself at-risk. In some countries—as noted above—poverty rates are considerably higher for majority group members, so explanations by color or minority status are inadequate. The largest ethnic minority groups find their children below average—or rarely above grade level—while the risk of perpetuating a caste-like society and cycle of poverty is increased.

The gap in school achievement is not a minority but rather an intercultural issue. Worldwide, examples such as South Africa, Andean countries, and similar contexts show how majority groups lag behind a dominant minority group economically and educationally.[1] These examples show how literacy levels co-vary with development at both the individual and group levels. The social organization established by colonialism, and later by the industrial age, left norms that are still institutionalized in a variety of ways. Even with a new period of enfranchisement for disempowered groups, great disparities prevail in opportunities to learn in school. How long it might take to reverse the effects of past unequal treatment to empower future generations is perhaps not the most pressing question related to educational change. Rather, the question is how far is leveling allowed to take place. We also need to know if there is a strategy capable of closing the gap at the collective level, and secondly, how far might such a strategy be allowed to go in producing a new set of norms.

The factors that helped close the gender gap and that allow some immigrant students living in poverty to perform above grade level relative to other SPARs would be important in forging such a strategy.

Inter and Intra-Cultural Expectations

As the public becomes increasingly aware of the achievement gap and related reform efforts that define it, the short- and long-term goals of current policies remain unclear. We must wonder how narrowing the gap is defined in the current "No Child Left Behind" agenda. Is a reduction of the gap to be defined in relation to school-based norms for test performance relative to last year's achievement test averages or learning outcomes? For some, equity requires mainly having more students meeting standards or improved scores on tests. For others, this is just a first step. We assume narrowing the achievement gap is the primary means toward achieving greater equity in economic outcomes and political power. Educators, social scientists, and the public remain unclear and divided in this regard.

Some seem convinced that schooling cannot reduce the gap in relative terms. At this time, we are not clear if modest improvements in meeting new minimum standards in academic performance are sufficient or if reform efforts truly aim to narrow or abolish the gap between groups at some point in the future.[2] Educators and the public differ considerably on how the achievement gap is defined and on how the goals of current efforts are to be prioritized.[3] The gap has not been reduced after several decades of interventions. However, let's assume for a moment that test scores had improved for every group in the last decade. The evidence, of course, is to the contrary (Lee, 2002; Jencks and Phillips, 1998). How would this improvement actually address equity and the achievement gap?

Do we define "closing the gap" to mean:

a. Any low-achieving group gains while others remain the same or gain less?

b. Specifically SPARs from minority groups subject to GBI gaining in standards-based tests, relative to others?

c. Specifically SPARs from minority groups subject to GBI gaining ground, regardless of others' performance?

d. SPARs from any group (majority and immigrant) gaining ground, relative to non-SPARs?

e. SPARs from any group (majority and immigrant) gaining ground, regardless of others' performance?

The above differences are important yet subtle. Current reforms in education and books on this topic (Thernstrom & Thernstrom, 2003; Williams, 1996) do not specify or make their objectives clear. What exactly are the priorities, intentions, and goals of current reform efforts? These goals determine the extent to which new resources can be mobilized and new practices sustained. It would seem that a relentless approach toward ensuring all groups are comparable in meeting minimum grade level standards is the first priority.

Defining the Achievement Gap

The literature suggests a variety of indicators for assessing the gap. Reduction in dropout rates and school persistence are important and influence actual test scores but not necessarily in a positive direction. This is because the exclusion of low-performing dropouts could actually raise the school's average. School attendance, teacher expertise, and class size all influence engaged learning time in academic areas of development. Perhaps completing high school—regardless of test scores—could be regarded as a measure of achievement as well as honest citizenship regardless of class or income. For example, dropout rates for African Americans have been drastically reduced and are almost comparable to the majority. But is this sufficient in closing the achievement gap? This group, like others, has actually lost ground with respect to poverty, in NAEP score performance (National Assessment of Educational Progress), or the percentage completing college. Perhaps finishing high school, or at least attending it long enough, defines success for some. Comparability in at least basic educational performance outcomes is most critical in defining equity and closing the gap—for example, having comparable proportions of students performing at grade level from ethnic groups overrepresented in poverty. Over time, this criterion could be upgraded to focus on proportions above grade levels.

Standardized test scores (SAT, ACT, NAEP or similar measures) serve as essential criteria not only because grade-level data can be derived in comparing groups. Grade point average is a less reliable measure but is useful as an indicator, although alternate assessment criteria can often be advocated.[5] Other criteria—such as advanced courses—appear relevant in admission to colleges. The percent of students completing college is another important indicator that would again have to be defined according to groups to be included in the definition of the gap. A host of other indices serve to estimate the extent of educational inequality. It would thus seem that one clear way to define the gap is in terms of the percent of students who meet minimum performance standards as a function of the teaching they receive in school. Regardless of background, students can be taught and assisted (Tharp & Gallimore, 1988) to meet minimum grade level standards.

Measured academic literacy outcomes serve to hold accountable the political economy that governs the educational system in reducing GBI. The outcomes produced by schools are the critical indicators of progress in the system with respect to ethics and democratic values. In assessing progress toward closing the achievement gap, at least four types of gap may be discerned:

1. The gap between the United States and other developed nations.
2. The gap between US ethnic and majority groups.
3. The gap in scores that after decades of reforms show insignificant pre- and post-gains over time.
4. The gap in terms of the percent of SPARs who actually meet the minimum performance standards across groups.

How the achievement gap problem has been constructed and understood is complex. Educators, as well as the public in general, need to be clear about what defines success if we are to establish greater equity than in the past. Surely several indicators are clearly interrelated and need to be monitored. What is the case against using standards-based tests? Are they not also tools for oppression? Perhaps, but a more important issue lies in how they are used for their ultimate purpose (see Portes & Vadeboncoeur, 2003). All groups of students should be challenged regardless of grade level or test scores. However, as in war, we must have measurable objectives. Grade-level performance in relation to standards-based test scores represents a useful way to determine the effectiveness and fairness of school reforms. Without such data, the extent to which equity in education is being achieved cannot be monitored. As Smith (2001) notes, "The speed of a convoy is determined by its slowest ship . . . during hostilities, an emergency solution might be to abandon . . . the slowest ship" (p. 574).

This analogy is telling in today's reform climate. In this convoy (or educational system), we have various ships or groups, each with its own intercultural history. Consequently, some can't keep up with others. The emergency is possibly related to competition in a global economy where we must be positioned to "win" or to at least preserve a high-level quality of life. Abandoning the slower vessels may be achieved by raising standards—for example speeding up those well outfitted in the convoy without first refurbishing the vessels that may have been sacrificed in past service to the fleet. Perhaps what is needed is an overhaul of the system that, once in place, would allow all vessels to achieve a minimum rate of speed (or development). This would allow optimal functioning for all. The survival of the military system is also based on this premise.

To know when equity in education has been achieved is important, yet it is still a relative question given modern world history. It may be that education cannot produce equity in economic outcomes nor reduce the level of poverty in a nation.[4] However, it may help reduce poverty cycle-related problems. The question is whether education can produce more equitable outcomes at some minimum level regardless of students' social background. It is this strategic means that can have a significant effect and outcome although the end result is as yet unknown. The data selected, along with reports from the *Condition of Education* series, may be criticized for whitewashing the gap. Until recently, few noted the four-year gap between groups because the reports focused mostly on within-group gains in NAEP scores. The issue is whether the present reform in education is likely to restructure or regulate resources, which seems unlikely:

a. Until minimum grade level performance standards are met; that is, when groups were to master basic functional literacy standards. Otherwise, why continue developing standards that some students cannot meet? The question is how well prepared are we to do so?

Will a national effort be organized so that the least advantaged are provided with the continuous support needed to *not* fall behind in grade-level performance? or,

b. Until each ethnic group is comparable in the distribution of educational outcomes; that is, in the proportion of students performing above or below the national average or completing college? A major problem is that we do not have a national system but rather school districts governed by different state norms, which respond to politically disparate population characteristics. The federal contributions are generally designed to ameliorate inequality but have yet to achieve this end. Does this suggest that the reorganization of the educational system might require greater equity in financing? Does the IRS or the military provide viable models? Is the structuring underlying the gap a national problem?

In sum, the nation's system of education, which also includes (access to) preschool and college, poses a formidable challenge that has resisted every equity-minded reform in recent history. The above questions require attention in any thorough treatment of this subject.

Defining the Closing of the Gap

It is important to address the above issues as part of the knowledge base educators share in their professional training. Even if a common definition of the problem remains to be established, we can come closer to a consensus by delineating central aspects of the problem. A developmental approach in which various phases of progress are achieved programmatically seems useful.

Let's assume that instead of the actual gap (see Figure 2–1) of four grade levels in reading, math or science, we would have reduced the standard 1971 score/grade level gap to two grade levels or more. This may be sufficient to claim success relative to the lack of progress in the past thirty years. It would definitely be a sign of intermediary progress. Sustaining this rate of success is critical not only for policymakers but also for SPARs gaining grade levels. We would know the costs as well as the practices involved in producing this measure of improvement.

If a programmatic reduction of GBI occurs, the educational community would have at least met the professional and ethical obligations to educate students in public schools.[6] We would have met the goal of gradually achieving equity in comparable educational outcomes across groups. The minimum performance standards level defines both the essence of the problem and the goal. It would be up to colleges to sustain and extend the progress made, much as it is up to K–12 schools to sustain the gains made by effective preschool programs such as Head Start. It may then be up to business and

Figure 2–1. Estimate of the Gap by Group

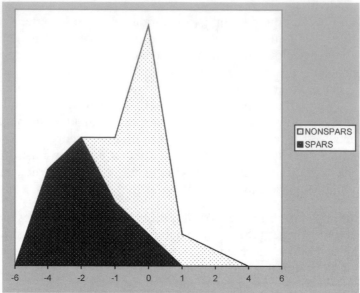

NONSPARS
SPARS

-6   -4   -2   -1   0   1   2   4   6

Gap in Grade Level Performance in General

industry to provide a decent wage, jobs and advancement opportunities, and reduce the proportion of families living in poverty. Unfortunately, family policy, while impacted most by the economic system, is not its direct concern. Even if the moral issue of poverty (Haberman, 2002) for working people were not addressed fairly, educators could feel that they had met their professional ethics within the constraints of the system. Ironically, the most effective way to support a coherent family policy is indirectly through a restructured educational system.

The current criterion of continuous progress for low-performing schools that tend to serve the majority of SPARs (Orfield, Frankenberg, & Lee, 2003) is gaining ground across states. Schools and educators need the most support in assisting SPARs. Their load should be shared with the more affluent schools that have fewer SPARS. Affluent school districts operate in ways regulated differently than those laden with SPARs. Somehow, we have yet to coordinate our efforts and resources within a national framework or plan that can produce an effect size sufficiently large to reduce GBIa. It is not that reducing GBIb is unimportant. Rather, the main argument here is that in addressing GBIa we also lower GBIb. In a nutshell, only when we find reliable, systematic ways to promote the development of children subject to GBIa will we begin to establish greater compatibility between school-based learning and SPARs' development overall. In failing to distinguish between the two or in focusing on GBIb, the relative gap found now will still remain.

In effect, while we know much about the origins of inequality, the bottom line is that reforms in education have failed in terms of improving the outcomes of school for impoverished groups reaching minimum grade level standards. Without this step, many other avenues are thwarted. Does a democracy require such fairness? Would we allow a corporation or the military to continue for forty years when it fails to meet its objective 20–40% of the time? Is education so intertwined with power and wealth that a massive learning gap can be ignored? Groups placed at-risk by the dominant culture develop cultural practices geared toward survival that become interactive and problematic. Culture is in flux as it comes in contact with new tools and practices. Groups placed at-risk disproportionately develop their own subculture as they adjust to the institutionalized practices of dominant groups. Such patterns of interaction and activities help co-construct enduring characteristics for each group, often regarded as learning styles, attitudes, expectations, values, and communication characteristics that surface and transform themselves in schooling and other institutionalized activities. Some tend to co-produce compatibility problems that result in motivational and value gaps in academic learning and educational outcomes. Today 20% of students are placed at-risk not only because of the 11% rate of poverty endured by families but also by virtue of adaptation patterns resulting from the above historical situation.

Placing Competent Students at Risk

Students and educators in general tend to believe that "at-risk" is synonymous with culture of origin (ethnicity). The terminology is part of a discursive story. We constantly hear veteran educators associate school failure with the lack of parental involvement, chaotic families, poverty, and cultures that do not value and support education. Children born to parents living in poverty—whether the parents are employed or not—are at risk at conception. Yet, educators need to ask how and why this situation exists and the extent to which it might be changed for future generations. Students are placed at-risk largely because of historically determined constraints and conditions that continue to affect the development of poor families and their ethnic culture. Living in poverty affects the development of attitudes, beliefs, values, and practices that are not only different but also instrumental, in school adaptation. Poverty has not decreased in spite of consecutive years amidst economic growth. It did not diminish significantly during the economic boom of the early to mid-1990s.

Educators also need to be aware of the language game regarding terms such as "disadvantaged" and "at-risk." By truncating the term (students placed at risk vs. at-risk) without reference to the underlying causes, we observe educators often limited in their thinking by the term as if the label were the cause for learning difficulties. Those students at-risk are often regarded as having a "built-in" disability that is viewed as independent of societal practices. "At-risk" is a term or concept that denotes an effect, or result, of a developmental process more than the cause of the problem. "Placed at risk" contains reference to both cause and effect. The labeling found in this language game is problematic not only in blaming the victim but in perpetuating a fallacy. We would not respect a medical doctor who thought scurvy was due to the patient's color or other symptoms rather than not having vitamin C or an adequate diet. Similarly, educators need to be educated in depth about human development in relation to culture. The point here is that the main reason the child is placed at risk through familial poverty is not only because of the prior unjust treatment of the culture to which parents belong. More precisely, the risk (of not learning in school or not having the social support required for success) is also due to interactions in beliefs and actions, in knowledge and strategic skills learning concerning both the schools designed by the dominant society, and SPARs and their community. In other words, it is because in the course of social adaptation (e.g., poverty in relation to tracking or to school safety), certain patterns of activity tools, motives, and knowledge remain constrained or disconnected, thus undermining academic development (for students subject to GBI). Meanwhile, other tools, skills, and aptitudes have evolved in adapting to society that may be positive, neutral, or negative depending on the context. It is quite possible to be poor and still have tools, motives, and values that are instrumental in succeeding not only in school but also in other contexts. How the achievement gap problem is constructed in and out of school is thus important.

Text Box 2–1: Discussion Questions

For those using this book with students, a discussion question may be centered on "What are some of the ways risks are produced for both groups?" or "Why is the present 'at-risk' discourse situated on one group only?" The history of mainstreaming serves as a didactic example. A public law was required to end the harmful segregation of special education students. We may be close to a similar scenario with the high stakes and accountability discourse, yet the latter is problematic with regard to equity. Would a new public law be necessary to end the achievement gap? Is the No Child Left Behind initiative enough? Why or why not? Do SPARs constitute a new special educational category?

Basic Concepts in Constructing the Gap

We know the public school culture is not compatible with most cultures that have been subjected to oppressive, intergenerational poverty. The observation that color or skin pigmentation is often correlated with poverty and status inequality does not mean that color causes lower achievement in a school. Nor is the cause for the gap due to teachers, practices, or beliefs alone. Caste-like groups are placed at risk primarily because their development is imperiled by poverty, and secondly by how ethnic characteristics are aligned with the very ways schools organize learning and teaching. For example, the way the educational system structures homework, instruction timelines, and prepares and allocates human resources has a differential effect on students. For most non-SPARs, such organization works well enough to meet and even surpass standards. For the least advantaged students caught in the middle, it is not sufficient. The current system seems still based on a lockstep industrial-age production line model aimed toward producing a predictable set of results: students who enter the labor market, those who are prepared for college or specialized training, and those for whom schools play essentially an academically-enriched custodial role.

As Smith (2001) notes, the school day and year are organized in a tightly structured way so that there is really no extra time available to catch up because this would mean less time for the student to learn and master other performance standards. Standards are useful but not when they are to be met in a limited amount of time regardless of how difficult the task might be for educator and student alike. Given the Goals 2000 types of recipes for educational reform and higher standards, it is estimated that high school students would achieve mastery of all the required areas at age 22! We compound the problem by tracking educators as well in the political economy of education. Kozol (1992, 2000) has more than documented the tracking of economic resources across schools in his classic description what he calls "savage inequalities." Unfortunately, even if academic learning time could be increased effectively, this carries a lesser impact after grade level gaps have been created.

Even after desegregation ordinances were implemented in the 1970s, and prejudice reduction and multiculturalism were infused in education in recent decades, the learning and teaching gap prevails. In spite of the fact that teachers are working hard to educate children from these groups (mainly African, Latin and Native American) and that most educators try their best, they still must work under an outdated, autocratic system that has clearly failed to get the job done. Educators deal with local situations as best as they can, according to how the problem is situated locally. They generally seek to negotiate the best learning situations for the less privileged in the very system that places them at risk. Under district, peer, parental, and professional pressures, educators are caught in a catch-22 situation.[7] Few schools have the resources and/or know-how to increase the achievement of SPARs given budget pressures and competition for resources. There are only so many expert educators at each level, and they are also sorted according to local pressures. Further sorting occurs in terms of access to college. In June, 2004, *USA Today* reported college costs were significantly higher for high school students, keeping underrepresented groups so. Other groups less subject to GBIa that achieve poorly in school also require attention. There are poor non-Hispanic whites and immigrant students from various countries. The latter gradually tend to adapt fairly well in school after some initial difficulties related to language and poverty, although some experience downward assimilation into the caste-like groups. Poor Euro-Americans, on the other hand, also tend to experience intergenerational poverty but to a less severe degree than minority SPARs. In sum, even after a quarter century of a most progressive era, nine-year-old African American and Hispanic students' reading proficiency today is still significantly below the 1971 level exhibited by non-Hispanic white students. (See table 10–1, *Condition of Education,* 2004).

In 1971, the government began to keep track of school performance by race/ethnicity and distinguished non-Hispanic white Caucasians from a new pan-label category of Hispanic. Since then, it has again become popular to view the achievement gap in relation to the pseudo-concept of color and race, even in sophisticated academic circles. Viewing the gap as a problem predominantly of students of color is misguided and conceals the role of cultural history, particularly limitations in access to tools—which is the main cause for the problem. We find some groups over-represented at the lower end of the achievement distribution and thus seriously underrepresented in the higher achievement ones for two interrelated reasons (intergenerational poverty and their group's cultural history). Either way, the goal of increasing the number of students of color at the higher levels of proficiency in science, math, engineering and technology (SMET), for example, is problematic. The "at-risk" label misrepresents the real problem and disguises the "doer," the causal agent for the problem, leading new generations of educators to situate the problem as others' problem. This is a subtle form of mis-identification at the institutional level that fails those most in need by allowing the issue to be colored with minimal attention to social class. As a result, the most needy remain so in a growing multi-ethnic underclass.

Since current statistics are appalling, programs focused on improving the achievement of underrepresented groups focus on preparing the high-achieving minority students on the basis of color (rather than history) for advanced classes and college. Unfortunately, this is a band-aid type of strategy that is not aimed at the root of the problem. The National Science Foundation finds 0% of African, Hispanic, and Native American twelfth-grade students scoring at the advanced level of proficiency in mathematics on NAEP scores *(Condition of Education,* 2002). In 1989 non-Hispanic white students outscored black students by ninety-four points, but by 1999, the gap increased to 106 points. So few African, Hispanic, and Native American students have access to or take advanced coursework such that they comprise

25% or more of the student population but only 8–9% appear in AP courses (Oakes et al., 2000).

The gap is not about test scores but rather the massive inequality that is situated in some groups. There are several types of subpopulations under the SPAR category. Understanding their characteristics is important in addressing the ethical aspects of group inequality.

a. Students are placed at risk by virtue of membership in ethnic minorities subject to GBI, or immigrant groups in poverty, and also by belonging to the majority group's underclass.

b. The problem needs to be understood developmentally and historically to "see" what we are really doing in the present era. Students from African, Latin and Native American groups are placed at risk by virtue of systemic limitations imposed upon their cultures decades and centuries ago (GBIa).

c. Unlike in immigrant and mainstream student populations, the gap in achievement is more extreme and affects a larger proportion of the GBIa populations. This is a known fact to some, and yet, most are unclear about this concept.

Anthropologists such as De Vos and his students (De Vos & Suárez Orozco, 1990; Ogbu, 2002) have examined underclass populations in terms of status inequality or as being caste-like in terms of inter-group relations. Because of such treatment and status, students develop certain reactive characteristics and identities (Steele, 1999) in response to the social context. As a result, certain incompatibilities emerge between the schooling made generally available and students' development. These characteristics are actually co-constructed or co-developed since two parties (or more) are required to produce educational failure. It is a semiotic relationship between the two. Such failure occurs when the same teaching has different consequences on students because of their prior knowledge, development, cultural context, status, and power relative to others. The ethical aspect of the problem of inequality thus has layers to be analyzed. It is more severe when we examine carefully the different constituencies within the SPAR category and find that not all groups have the opportunity to develop equally in some areas, even if in terms of capacity they are created equal.

Situating the Gap

Casting the problem in terms of color is thus problematic for a number of reasons. The term 'racial gap' (Thernstrom & Thernstrom, 2003; Miller, 1995) is a misnomer. Not all SPARs are "of color." An undetermined number of Caucasian students from Latin America do not classify themselves as

Hispanic. Even if they do, many do not present an achievement gap (P.R. Portes, 1999). Many are from immigrant groups that adapt in ways different from those Spanish-speaking SPARs who have lived in the United States longer. The larger subgroups of Hispanics have roots in the United States as deep as many majority group and black students. Their roots in the West can often be as much Native American as they are Spanish, as both groups attempt to adapt to areas governed and regulated by the dominant group. Some SPARs have not mastered standard Spanish although they are classified as Hispanics. As with many Native Americans, fluency in the native language is being lost, making their identity and communication with the elders in the family and educators muted in a diffused society.

Middle-class African American students, who are also not at-risk, generally are lumped with those who are because of the way many (mis)conceptualize the problem. Over half of these students perform at grade level or higher, reflecting a major error in those who conceptualize the problem mainly in terms of color. Yet, GBI is most severe in the above groups because they are three times more likely to live in poverty than the majority group. For decades, middle-class African Americans have been faced with stereotypes, low expectations, and have employed the few opportunities available.

Poor, non-Hispanic white children represent about 15% of the majority group culture and the largest group of SPARs overall. As the largest group of SPARs who remain below grade level, a class issue may be distinguished here that is of analytical relevance.[8] They remain less visible than others when the discourse attends to the problem in terms of color and because of how the outcomes in schooling are reported by the government. By using race/ethnicity without indicators of SES, reports such as NAEP—which reports on the progress of the educational system periodically—we remain without sound data to directly monitor the progress of the reforms and of any of the above groups of SPARs.

Educators and policy-makers need to understand the finer details of how the concepts of at-risk and resiliency have been socially constructed and what they refer to in precise terms. At-risk membership refers to poverty status in groups that have a high rate of school failure. Schools tolerate a certain level of failure to learn from a given amount and quality of teaching. Since the "clock" is important to the dominant culture for economic reasons (Smith, 2001), so much has to be taught by a certain time to have the majority of students at grade level. This is part of the political economy of schooling. Some school districts have been able to recognize this and require extra days of schooling for students below grade level. However, more of the same (retention or summer school) does not allow those behind to catch up. The "production line" keeps moving forward. Higher standards are now required even when equity could not be achieved with lower ones and through the educational practices and structures that still prevail today. The current accountability focuses less on equity than overall test scores that may be raised in a variety of other ways.

Higher standards reforms are speeding the clock for struggling SPARs without a corresponding change in the ways teaching and learning are organized and supported. In rushing forth to compete with the standards set in other world cultures (Stevenson & Stigler, 1992), we again continue to structure the achievement gap without assisting educators to succeed with those students left behind. We want more for less without investing in equity sufficiently. For many, that is the way it is and has been, so why would one expect any change in the future? Students and their low-income parents seem to know this; educators know it too. So why try to alter a system that is aligned so well with a segmented society? SPARs resist in adolescence, and seem to know—at a collective level—that trying harder is not enough to break through the carefully coded system. Teachers know they can only do so much given the constraints on time, and demands from non-SPARs whose development and motivation are much more compatible with the schedule, content, and practices of the system. Homework and projects allow advantaged parents to flex their capital. Even modest levels of failure can be compensated with special tutors or financing of alternative colleges and programs later on. The few exceptions where SPARs succeed seem to be invariably used to validate the fairness of the present system as it incorporates higher standards.

So, perhaps the kids are right—why try to buck the system? It is easy to understand why so many SPARs stop identifying with their role as students and why teachers tend to others who do (Varenne & McDermott, 1999). The current teaching practices do work for the majority and for some minorities and immigrant groups who generally achieve at grade level or above and those whose parents already have the capital necessary to ensure success regardless of education (P.R. Portes, 1999).

The longer SPARs stay in school, the less they catch-up or want to learn and the less teachers want to teach them. Obviously those who do not want to learn are separated from those who do. Advantaged parents see to this, usually through their class-differentiated involvement, or through advanced, gifted, and performing tracks. Even though most students seem to start similarly in kindergarten, the system gradually places a load on the support system (outside the school) that gradually produces a robust gap. In effect, we provide faster and slower trains to go through a number of graded learning stations. Those who are slow to start to learn, don't "want to" learn, or those whose parents can't compete with others' educational or social capital, experience a different menu of options at each of the twelve stations. They come out of the K–12 race with less, expect less at the next one, and, in fact, do get less. Before long, it only seems to make sense that those who are obviously not ready not to work as hard at some tasks, and, in turn, should get less in life. Educators learn this reality gradually in the field and know they can't do much about it. This informal, field-based curriculum prevails even in the ivory towers of higher education programs. Meanwhile, the above situation is often rationalized along individual factors such as self-efficacy, achievement motivation, or locus of control, which are employed to explain low achievement overall.

From this view, educators don't appear to require special training in teaching, since it does not seem to make a difference, as some have argued (Ohanian, 1996). History tends to support the view that educators are generally not among the top students in college, so their low status and lack of efficacy make them easy targets. The special pedagogical training found in certification programs may not contribute beyond the content expertise teachers may have as math, science, English, or similar undergraduate majors in predicting how well K–12 students perform in school. However, there is now evidence that certification or professional education matter even more now as equity and excellence agendas exert great influence. Teacher competency testing may be regarded as a response to concerns that the achievement gap may be due in some part to the low quality of teaching offered to SPARs in most public schools. Singular approaches to the gap respond to oversimplified analysis of the problem.

Deconstructing the Gap

What can educators learn that would make a difference? Does it matter? How have some managed to make a difference? Does it seem as though educators don't want to try any more than the majority of students long placed at risk?

The interesting point here is that invariably we construct our reality. If we can end segregation, place humans in outer space, and eradicate lethal diseases, perhaps we do need to begin by learning more about this problem and its various characteristics in a systematic way. We need to know what needs to be addressed first, how best to do it, and with what resources. We also need to assess our current goals and priorities. The question today is how badly we want to eradicate an institutionalized source of injustice and mediocrity in mass education. The system can and does provide excellent schooling for some without much cost to those who usually succeed. And this, perhaps, is the crux of the problem. We address it and tinker with it, but we don't want to change it, because we are afraid of destabilizing a pyramid of privileges. If it is not affecting the majority that much, why change it? We can try and seem to try as long as it doesn't really change structured privileges. And for those who it affects unfairly, they may also suspect things will always remain so. They exert the least political pressure and are aware that they remain less educated or cultured in some ways. Why try to run the race starting from behind and with a less resourceful team? This challenge seems more attractive in sports and entertainment. So as long as we think this way, we are trapped and uncomfortable with the win-win prospect of eradicating the last vestiges of a system that structures inequality.

The first grand step in educational change was perhaps the eradication of illiteracy. Today, in a complex world, the second step would be to eradicate GBI in basic educational outcomes measured at least by grade-level performance skills. Just as a number of technologies emerged from space travel or the threat of military defeat, we believe this mission in education would not only heal and liberate but also carry several positive by-product effects for societal wellness. This problem falls squarely in that category of things that have always been so, still are, and will be until a reversal occurs through a willing informed generation(s).

As with the healthcare industry, we find it tolerable for some children to obtain better care than others depending on the insurance their family can buy. Equity in financing comparable to that of other social institutions such as defense, access to national transportation, security, and other domains related to quality of life may be part of the solution. We allow some schools, their educators, and their communities to struggle in some districts with high proportions of SPARs while others in the same district thrive with fewer problems and more (social) capital. It is not uncommon to find school districts with more than 70% low-income students in the student population (Orfield, Frankenberg, & Lee, 2003). In these settings we find turnover of educators, impoverished families we blame for "low involvement," and the lowest national test scores. It appears that as a society we value equity in some sectors but not others. The next chapter will examine some current myths that claim equity is being established in education.

More Statistics

Below are some startling findings for those who believe equity is being gradually established. One should be mindful that ethnic breakdowns underestimate the real plight of SPARs since the average includes the performance of each group's middle-class populations that are not proportionately distributed. In 1999, by the end of high school:

a. only 1 in 50 Latinos and one in 100 African American 17-year-olds can read or gain information from specialized texts, such as the science section in the newspaper (compared to about 1 in 12 whites);

b. fewer than one-quarter of Latinos and one-fifth of African Americans can read the complicated but less specialized text that more than half of white students can read;

c. about 1 in 30 Latinos and 1 in 100 African Americans can comfortably do multi-step math problems and elementary algebra, compared to about 1 in 10 white students;

d. only 3 in 10 African American and 4 in 10 Latino 17-year-olds have mastered the usage and computation of fractions, commonly used percents, and averages, compared to 7 in 10 white students; and

e. African American students are only about half as likely as white students to earn a bachelor's degree by age 29; Latinos are only one-third as likely as majority students to earn a college degree (US Census Bureau, 1998; Haycock, 2001).

The reason a lower proportion of these students complete college or advanced courses is due to at least two obvious factors. First, while fewer than 25% of majority students are scoring below basic levels—in what is generally regarded a normal distribution—two to three times that rate of failure persists in groups affected by GBI. No wonder it is rare to find students from those populations scoring at the advanced levels of proficiency on NAEP scores. These statistics suggest that in order to end the severe under- representation of students from these three groups at the top, we must find ways to transform educational practices strategically so that their overrepresentation below basic levels of proficiency is leveled. Secondly, coloring of the problem (i.e., viewing the problem as based on race) is counterproductive because it covers up the roots of the problem. Students "of color" scoring above basic grade level performance are mostly those from middle-class backgrounds and families that have not lived in poverty for some time. If we distributed the race category by class, the proportion of students from groups subjected to GBI could actually be larger than reported here. Many students from immigrant, sometimes professional, families are lumped in the above statistics that tend to adapt well to school (P.R. Portes, 1999).

Thirteen-year-olds from the majority group are as proficient in reading, writing, and science as seventeen-year-olds from the two poverty-laden minority groups (*The Condition of Education,* 2002). SPARs often do not understand basic information, nor can they learn from specialized reading materials. Younger students, from less marginalized groups achieve such understanding and can learn largely due to the cultural compatibility found in schools and their social capital at home. This multiplies their edge in learning during the last and most important years of public education.

Conceptual Issues

It is important to understand that there are no at-risk students per se. There are only at-risk conditions that have been organized and these continue to be imposed to place certain groups of students at risk for educational failure. The current discourse on this topic continues to confuse cause-and-effect for lack of a cultural-historical understanding of the problem. Social conditions, rather than superficial markers, account for the robustness of the gap. In effect, we have myths based on a tautology (or faulty reasoning):

a. At-risk conditions for human development produce vulnerable, at-risk individuals, and at-risk conditions obstruct human development and have been imposed more severely on some groups than others.

b. The most negatively affected groups are students of color since they are underrepresented at the higher levels of proficiency on tests, income, and higher education. The educational system has not been able to educate them effectively.

c. Therefore, color causes the gap and students to be at-risk, learn less, to be less able, and have different learning styles and less motivation in school. Higher standards can close the gap, because the problem is due to low standards. Raising test scores at each school is the way to deal with the gap (and other corollaries).

In sum, by lumping causes together and confusing them, the problem remains poorly defined and understood. That is, the root causes for why some students become "at-risk" are left out in reforms aimed at treating some of the symptoms. This faulty logic reigns in education reform, resulting in a host of pseudo-solutions ranging from blaming teachers and parents to vouchers. Most educators and policy makers take it for granted that "risk" is synonymous with certain ethnicities and that children "of color" are naturally at-risk because of their culture, families, and lack of effort. This ingenuousness impedes progress by defining the gap in terms of color (race) rather than what is actually cultural history (P.R. Portes, 1996). Minorities not at-risk (already middle class) are often regarded and treated as if they were underprivileged because of this superficial analysis. Students of Asian background, on the other hand, are automatically regarded as superior to whites because of their features. The main risk immigrants from Spanish-speaking countries or "look-alikes" face is that of being treated as native involuntary groups who are still placed at-risk because of a history of deprivation and unfairness. However, while some immigrate and share a history of their country of origin, others do not. In sum, the empowerment of groups subject to GBI remains well outside the understanding and arms of the educational system.

Keeping Score: Understanding the Subtleties of Inequality

School persistence widens the gap for SPARs as higher standards for math, science, and writing proficiency (for grades four, eight, and eleven) become required (Gamoran, 2001). By focusing almost exclusively on within-group improvements—which are statistically significant for five–ten point changes—between-group differences, which remain generally well over twenty points, tend to be ignored in many national reports. Thus, many conclude that the gap has been dealt with or has been narrowed in spite of evidence to the contrary (Blank and Langesen, 1999). While the rate of children subject to poverty has remained at 20% during the prosperity of the 1990s, over twice that rate prevails for historically disempowered groups. Given the poverty rate for non-minority students drops lower than 15%, statistics generally fail to monitor the progress of groups subject to GBI or their current levels of progress specifically. Since they are aggregated with established middle-class minority and immigrant families on the basis of color or language, the levels of inequality remain underestimated. Murky indicators in the educational sector obscure the interaction of class and ethnicity as well as the effect of any new policy. While hopefully not intentional, one recommendation for closing the gap is to ensure the development and use of accurate indicators for learning outcomes within pan-ethnic labels (i.e., social class). Although low SES remains quite prevalent in some ethnic groups, the improved scholastic achievement reported for non-mainstream students might conceivably be explained on the basis of the performance of minorities (native and immigrant) not living in severe poverty and mediating their adaptation differently.

GBI reproduces poverty, not the other way around, although a few exceptions apply. The few that escape from the cycle of poverty and inadequate public education are labeled "resilient." They are often used to serve as examples for others trapped by poverty. The problem is that low probability phenomena, per se, cannot be used to produce high probability norms over time. This critique applies to similar arguments founded on the few schools where SPARs have thrived. We can surely learn from successful anomalies, yet the cloning implication here can actually deter structural changes necessary for bringing about significant improvements at the population level.

Other types of inequality would remain even if GBI in education were to be eliminated. However, the ethical aspect of a historically produced inequity would at least, in great part, be resolved[9] by reversing many of the means used to produce it. Continuous progress in achieving proficient levels of literacy for all students remains as the first hurdle in reducing GBI in education.

Constructing the Gap in Educators

So far we have analyzed how a knowledge gap is structured for SPARs. Educators have a knowledge gap as well and are often led to presume that equal opportunities have been—and are being—established in American society. They are taught that equal opportunities to learn exist for all students

Text Box 2–2: The Glass Remains Half Full

The packaging of the problem into the cultural categories provided by the government does not inform the public about how well schools educate increasing numbers of poor students from diverse cultural contexts. Even after the removal of repressive practices such as segregation, it is clear that proficiency levels for at-risk students in general have not improved as much as government reports (by ethnicity) would suggest. Also, the educational achievement of immigrant children since 1965 is generally fused with that of larger national ethnic minorities with whom they are classified. While considerable variation in achievement exists with immigrant student groups (Gibson & Ogbu, 1991; P.R. Portes, 1999), it would seem that this aggregation of data in most reports is problematic in addressing the problem.

Believing that the problem is being addressed satisfactorily leads, unfortunately, to "more of the same" practices in funding educational policy and literacy-oriented interventions. Critical analyses seem to be discouraged today in an unfriendly political climate where budget cuts for compensatory programs threaten to strip the meager gains achieved by past interventions. Thus, a triple-edged problem has seemingly emerged; one identified as:

- a policy that may not be well founded on developmental theory and the criterion of best practice.
- the institutionalization of nugatory practices and a prevailing fear that critiques such as this one may lead to dismantling of the limited assistance mechanisms that "poor" students receive at present. Poor students often receive inferior education and the least effective teachers, pedagogy, and conditions necessary for effective learning.
- the prevailing GBI issue is muted by political campaigns with frequent, well-publicized claims that focus exclusively on such secondary gains as lower dropout rates and within-group test scores.

In sum, the achievement gap was far from being narrowed as we entered the new century. Significant poverty and population trends place the nation as a whole at-risk. Educators need to understand this reality as they prepare to integrate more effective means (e.g., primary prevention) in public education. Human development takes on new meaning when it is promoted as part of the "culturing" or curriculum that might be made part of public education (see Chapters Four and Five).

and that falling behind is the students' own responsibility or that of their parents. Educational psychology classes teach future educators that low-achieving students lack achievement motivation and high expectations and need to improve their self-efficacy along with similar individual characteristics. Unfortunately, the latter are only correlates of low achievement and the ways teaching and learning are organized. The massive educational gap cannot be explained by individual factors alone.

Most educators are taught that the actual causes for the inability of schools to teach whole groups of children to levels comparable to those achieved by other groups are cultural in origin. This is taken to mean that the problem lies in the culture of SPARs. The meaning that is often shared from the dominant view is that the culture of SPARs needs fixing to be similar to ours. Educators take more courses to become culturally sensitive and responsive (Villegas and Lucas, 2002) and since they are not really expected to close the gap, this is regarded as sufficient preparation. The premise here is that by learning about students' cultures, they can become more sympathetic and encouraging. Counselors are educated in similar fashion. Both are often taught to promote self- (behavior) management and resiliency skills since many of the students become behavior disordered in adapting to the present system. Sports, music programs, and other options are organized that compete with academic learning time, although these educational activities are not part of accountability testing or critical to the achievement gap. Perhaps a large part of the problem in closing the gap is that there is something drastically wrong with the ways we prepare educators to reenact traditional roles that sustain the achievement gap. It would seem such preparation and practices ought to be more closely focused on eradicating GBI and promoting excellence in education. Educators are taught the problem is individual or familial. They are also led to believe the causes are cultural, which may be correct but not in the way cultural is defined here. The problem is cultural, but it is not just about SPARs; it is also about a dominant culture and how it interacts with other cultures (Murrell, 2001; Wenger, 1998).

A more accurate view is that the problem is intercultural since learning and teaching obstacles involve past and present interactions between groups. Intercultural differences make it hard for some to learn and for educators to teach even basic skills. The problem does not seem to be centered on those skills as much as how their acquisition is structured. We must delve deeper in discovering why this is so if we are to transcend superficial solutions. How is the lack of continuity in learning established that makes learning and teaching in school difficult? What is the most effective, respectful way to bridge the cultural divide? How is academic learning time structured so that those with the least support fall several grade levels behind? If that divide is defined by differences in wealth, knowledge, tools and skills, values, goals, and expectations, how can education be transformed to allow all students equal opportunities to learn? Educators who are taught to believe the reason for the achievement gap is cultural need to understand another meaning of this term. From a cultural historical perspective, cultural does not necessarily refer to ethnic or dominant groups. As Van der Veer and Valsiner (1994) note:

> The 'historical' portion of the label cultural-historical refers specifically to the developmental nature of all psychological phenomena. Note that in this context, the term has little in common with the more traditional meaning related to past events. In cultural-historical thinking, historical implies the connection between past, present, and future. . . . In cultural-historical thinking, individual human beings are considered to play an active role in their (as well as others') psychological development. Previous psychological schools attributed causality to the environment ("nurture") or inborn and predetermined "essences" in individual persons ("nature"). In either case, the person was believed to play a passive role—as the target of environmental stimulation in the first case or as the "vessel" within which nature's causal essences unfolds in the second case. In contrast, cultural-historical thinking emphasizes the instrumental function of the person, who, by acting upon his or her environment with the help of tools or signs, changes his or her development. Note that in this case cultural means "instrumentally created" and is different from the way in which the term is used in contemporary cross-cultural psychology—that is, meaning "specific to a certain group of people who make up a culture." (p. 60)

For the educational system to produce comparable academic outcomes across groups, it must first establish comparable opportunities to learn and benefit from the teaching and resources offered in school. For comparable conditions to be co-constructed, we must understand the relations among diverse elements that define the cultural divide. It is not just about the early stimulation or socialization of children before entering school. Nor is it just about financing huge bureaucracies to promote family literacy and parent involvement programs. Nor is the divide likely to be narrowed by hundreds of after school programs that presently do help SPARs. The great divide is based on the interaction of these and other key factors. Together, these produce differences in values, goals, expectations, and other cultural traits. Wealth is produced by privilege and power, as much as by knowledge, motivation, and mastery of tools. Education can't do much about the former but is in business to promote the latter factors.

Equity in Access to Tools

We must carefully distinguish among opportunity structures, access to them, and equality in educational outcomes for children from historically exploited and marginalized cultures. This raises an important question. Must comparable rates in poverty precede or follow comparable distributions in educational outcomes? That is, should the disparity in poverty rates first be reduced through employment, job training, reparations, and similar means outside public education? Some may argue that fair wages, healthcare supports, and building decent housing may be more effective than educational reform insofar as the achievement gap is concerned. With lower levels of children living in poverty, educators would be able to increase the educational effectiveness of schools and improve the academic performance of SPARs. From a political and economic standpoint, it may be more difficult, if not impossible, to alter the wages and jobs of workers whose families produce SPARs. With the public's approval, business and industry have long resisted "socialist" reforms. Hence, it may be more feasible to pursue equity by improving the "human capital" produced by education. An increase in the number of competent, well-educated persons that will enter the economy may bring about societal changes that would perhaps reduce poverty. That is, by achieving comparable educational outcomes for all groups that are standards based, the economy may grow and excellence would follow. The question is how willing may a nation be to change its educational system in order to address the ethical problem of GBI in minimum performance standards?

While this first step may promote excellence across the system and gradually reduce poverty, the position here is competency or tool oriented. The first step is "doable," realistic, and necessary yet educators do not decide rates and distributions of poverty for society. They have some control however for that portion of poverty that is the consequence of low academic performance. Literacy is a commodity or form of capital that helps define SES.[10]

How the Gap Is Maintained

The prevailing gap in educational outcomes is relative and instrumental in sustaining other aspects of inequity. The gap is organized and maintained in ways that extend way beyond the end of segregation and placement of students in low-track classes. The problem persists in terms of pedagogical differences, in the allocation of resources, instructional practices across schools, family involvement, and expectations. Classroom discourse patterns and content, teacher expertise, early education, parent involvement, and peer norms appear to vary systematically across schools and classes with high proportions of SPARs. In spite of the attention given to these critical aspects of schooling, the gap has not narrowed in spite of reported gains in academic achievement (Jencks & Phillips, 1998; Lee, 2002). Therefore, a new approach is needed to guide and enrich the development of SPARs across districts and states.

Other structures remain in place that exacerbate the gap further, such as inflexible within-school tracking or an age-graded curriculum that fits the developmental "sequence" imposed by middle-class curriculum and assessment experts. Such structures and practices lead to a rigid educational

**Table 2–1: Typology for Assessing Reform Actions
and Their Consequences**

New Practices *Added* and Their Effect on the Achievement of SPARs	Old Practices *Removed* and Their Effect on the Achievement of SPARs
Reduced Class Sizes +	Special Education for Bilinguals-
Teacher Content +	Age-graded Classes for Elementary
Teacher Testing (PRAXIS)—unknown effect	Grades—unknown effect
Head Start—unknown effect	Emergency Certification—unknown effect
After-school Programs +	Phonics in Reading—unknown effect
Effective Schools +	Direct Instruction—unknown effect
Multicultural Education—no effect	Busing for Desegregation +
Resource Centers—unknown effect	Segregation +
Technology—unknown effect	Uncertified Teacher +
Itinerant/Resource Teachers +	Discovery Learning +
Same Gender Schools +	
School Uniforms—unknown effect	
Adopt a SPAR +	
Ungraded Primary—unknown effect	
Whole Language—unknown effect	
Mainstreaming—unknown effect	
Constructivist Practices—unknown effect	
Affirmative Action—unknown effect	
Test-based Instruction—unknown effect	
Resegregation -	

timetable where an initially small gap becomes impossible to bridge in secondary school. Differences in access to higher education are thus created and complete the cycle of educational inequality. The delay in "performing at grade level" that requires mastery of tools and knowledge causes irreparable damage (in terms of self-efficacy, motivation, identity, and self-esteem) in the formative years to students involuntarily placed at risk.[11] Along with differences in teacher capital, coursework, and resources, the system maintains subtle gap-producing practices that are later reflected in test scores. Some structures have been left in place that may help document and reduce the gap, such as standardized testing—which in spite of much criticism, allows for reliable and valid assessments of variations in the quality of education. When new practices or reforms are introduced, many have not been proven effective in improving SPARs' learning outcomes. Many of the initiatives to close the achievement gap can be seen in Table 2–1. The current trend in high-stakes assessment, based on Goals 2000, has led to a generally narrow approach to a broad-based problem.

The above table shows some examples of what may be regarded as mediated actions to improve education. Many of the applied practices are not systematically evaluated in terms of their effect on students' development. Some initiatives can serve to build a significant positive effect or to remove various long-term constraints when sustained over time. They may or may not impact directly on the school achievement of SPARs. However, except for a few research studies, such impact is seldom known in evaluating the above practices.

The educational outcome-based reform has yet to make a case for equity and reorganize its own means and resources to achieve it. The distribution of educational outcomes for children subject to GBI would seem to be as critical a concern as raising the average standardized test scores for all students.[12] Mandating the latter without providing a reliable set of supports for the first concern is shortsighted.

Today we are faced with the paradox that in spite of many positive changes since the 1960s, the gap remains intact in the key areas of school outcomes that index literacy skills essential for adaptation to today's society. Yet, the gap is only a reminder that the mechanisms that produced inequality (intentionally) before have yet to be fully reversed at the group level. It is also a reminder that the present discourse aimed at helping students left behind is moot unless we transform not just teaching but rather the system itself.

The Social Origins of the Gap[13]

At the individual level, a gap does not exist in the "head" initially, but rather, is developed externally. Gradually, the gap is co-constructed in proximal social contexts, relative to conditions found in other contexts. The gap is situated (at the micro-level) around children before it becomes amplified by schooling. This gap, or relative index of over- or underdevelopment in academic-related areas, can be generally predicted early in terms of what their parents have, know, and do. The child will only be placed at risk when external mediated activities or forces converge to orient development sufficiently in a different manner that, in this particular case, makes schooling practices become ineffective and inefficient. While other forms of success have been regarded as evidence of progress, academic outcomes remain the principal target in testing our own savvy and mettle as educators and researchers. If reparations to populations oppressed earlier were a concern, the real coin of compensation might be sustainable and equal opportunities to learn today. Can it be done without further oppression and deculturalizing others? Yes, it is not that other outcomes are unimportant, but that so much depends on basic academic success. Schooling remains the main battleground for reducing inequality at the group level. Anything else tends toward the diversionary and iniquitous, regardless of political benefit or intent.

A Review of GBI [Types A, B & C]

GBI was defined earlier in order to identify children, who by virtue of their caretakers (here we mean both dominant and minority cultures), are destined to experience significant constraints in their development. They are, in effect, placed at risk for educational and economic disadvantages that result from a literacy gap that becomes cumulative. Differences in the acquisition of cultural tools, in turn, reproduce a complex disadvantage each generation. Economic and other outcomes that tend to place future generations into a vicious cycle of poverty eventually become "normative" or accepted inter-culturally. Such caste-like groups (De Vos, 1967) in turn must adapt in ways that accommodate relative disadvantages that are structured culturally, often in a negative, anti-social fashion.

When groups subject to poverty share the ethnic characteristics of the dominant group and its national history, group-based inequality is essentially the same as SES. This case may be called GBI (b), with respect to class and how some groups' children are destined for poverty. Other types of inequal-ity may be identified where the dooming of perfectly capable children occurs in terms of historical constraints imposed on the basis of ethnicity, gender, or religion.

Equity and social justice, insofar as education is concerned, require care-ful analysis of class, ethnicity, and gender in relation to power and the control of tools affecting development. A central concern in this book concerns GBI which is situated in the intersect of class, ethnicity, and cultural history. African, Latin, and Native American children are subject to intergenerational poverty with an intercultural history of oppression that plays a major role in producing cultural differences or incompatibilities, and they are placed most at risk. This triple interaction of ethnic minority, intergenerational history, and past oppression produces the greatest incompatibility for educators. In effect, the risk for students in these groups may be distinguished conceptually from that of immigrant and mainstream groups living in poverty (Ogbu, 2002). I refer to this type of integration as GBI (a), although both types are lumped together in the at-risk discourses of today.

I differentiate between these two types of GBI because we have tended to underestimate how (inter-)cultural history influences the very characteris-tics of a given culture. When a group is oppressed, conquered, and treated differentially for centuries by a dominant group, a number of adaptive char-acteristics result that are not necessarily intra-culturally produced.[14] These are referred to as secondary or acquired characteristics that reflect an adaptive response to a set of circumstances imposed from the outside (see Ogbu, 2002). Over time, characteristics that originally served a purpose or had a functional motive evolve and seemingly become a defining characteristic of the culture even when external circumstances change. Later, when these are regarded as if they belong to a particular ethnic group, few consider the interactive origins or causes that were involved in the adaptation to certain conditions and the appropriation of specific tools, patterns, or traits that such interaction produces. For example, some minority students appear disinterested in academic learning; in fact, they may show resistance or apathy. From the majority perspective, this is attributed to cultural differences that reflect how some values, expectations, attitudes, and behaviors vary from one group to another. Ogbu (1997b) has observed a form of "learned helplessness" in (black) inner-city adolescent students that differs from other minority students who are also living in poverty and seem more motivated to learn. From his interviews he finds that a lack of effort in academic study stems from a history of prejudice that taught many in that community that such efforts do not pay off—and that the system does not operate fairly—so that no matter how hard they try, the results will remain poor. Erickson (1993) describes student resistance while Steele (1997) focuses on stereotype threats. Many youth feel that compared to others who are grade levels ahead, they do not have much of a chance to compete for good jobs or college.

Educators are taught about such differences and learning styles (multicultural education/counseling) with ethnic stereotypes. Educators need to understand these are learned styles or patterns of adaptation to a set of circumstances that stem from a collective history. The solution is not to adapt our practices in ways that validate and reinforce those circumstances. A primary prevention approach would not accommodate practices to the symptoms of a larger problem. It would address the problem at its roots, in light of the conditions that produce that pattern of learning or similar characteristics. Evidence exists that poor immigrant students manifest "effort optimism" that is grounded on a different cultural belief system that links effort with success. It reflects the collective experience of other groups over time. Beliefs and collective experiences vary across, as well as within, groups. Inequality tends to be concentrated most in groups that have endured it, been conditioned by it, and been subject to a system in which certain expectations are fulfilled.

Other types of inequality should be noted at this point that require attention since they are qualitatively different in nature. Class-based inequality (GBIb) may be observed, as noted, for members of the dominant majority (European-American ethnicities) who are subject to poverty at one-third the rate of the minority groups generally. Poor "white" children are doomed early by virtue of class and constitute 14% of the student population. They may very well represent the norm of the present political and economic system and provide a baseline for assessing our progress with the other groups. The 14% poverty rate may be reduced in years to come if the home-school cultural compatibility structures and instructional practices can be improved.

Another type of inequality that raises equity concerns is perhaps less pressing but still noteworthy. GBIc refers to a more recent development, one that is controversial today. As noted earlier, the problem of inequality has been traditionally understood in terms of race, class, minority status, and cultural history. The majority, dominant culture has attempted to compensate for past inequities through desegregation, affirmative action, and similar programs in a variety of areas. A result has been that the beneficiaries of such programs are sometimes not those subject to GBIa (thus creating reverse discrimination, the c type of inequality). Some of those who qualify were not poor intergenerationally but were the ones most prepared to take advantage of equal opportunity structures. Few had to overcome educational barriers, since they were children of ethnic middle-class groups. As a consequence, considerable backlash has been felt in some states that challenged college admissions due to membership in minority groups. GBIc is complex to understand since it addresses one aspect of GBI. By attending to equity solely based on "race" or ethnicity, it does not address the needs of the most needy (those subjected to GBIb) yet is often regarded as doing so.[15] This practice is problematic for efforts that attempt to orient policy and educational reform directly toward reducing the production of GBI. Affirmative action strove to reduce inequality for those few who survived public education and achieved well enough. Unfortunately, this policy is based on the pseudo-concept of race rather than cultural history. To a large extent, this serves as an example of how fuzzy conceptualization of the problem can lead to superficial social actions that may be necessary but are not sufficient to end GBIb (see Figure 2–2). In this figure, the top part represents various student populations as they are influenced from below by the system and some of the actions available.

On the other hand, it did create opportunities without which members of GBIa would not have been likely to succeed. It also addressed the problem of discrimination in the larger sense since evidence abounds regarding prejudice regardless of the education or class of the minority involved.

Equity in Academic Outcomes

Schools and society could focus on quality and equity in educational outcomes so that differences between groups become insignificant while individual differences remain within groups. The public and educational community must decide the extent to which restructuring is to be aimed at a

Figure 2–2: The Problem Is Deeply Rooted

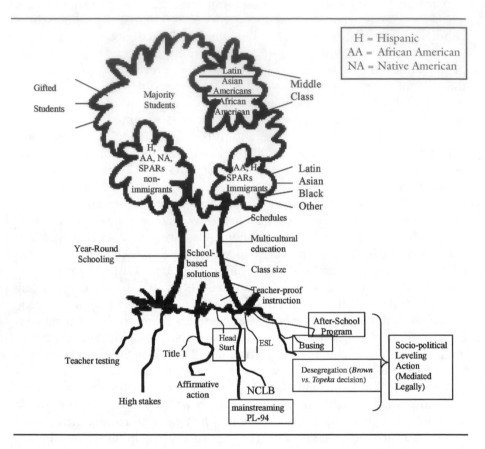

H = Hispanic
AA = African American
NA = Native American

Gifted Students

Majority Students

Latin
Asian Americans
African American

Middle Class

H, AA, NA, SPARs non-immigrants

AA, H, SPARs Immigrants

Latin
Asian
Black
Other

Schedules

Year-Round Schooling

School-based solutions

Multicultural education

Class size

Teacher-proof instruction

After-School Program

Teacher testing

Title 1

Head Start

ESL

Busing

Desegregation (*Brown vs. Topeka* decision)

Socio-political Leveling Action (Mediated Legally)

High stakes

Affirmative action

NCLB

mainstreaming PL-94

historical correction, delivering perhaps more support to groups that have had their cultural development restricted intentionally by the dominant culture or geared toward the poor in general. This is not what is occurring now. Affirmative action practices may appear as an example of this strategy on the surface, but they have had different purposes and consequences (Bowen & Bok, 1998). The momentum of affirmative action has faded precisely because its focus was not clear and was mostly based on giving access to underrepresented minority groups regardless of class-based inequality. Affirmative action policies alone are ineffective in reducing the achievement gap unless they are integrated within a more complete strategic plan. While such action benefits many who have already surmounted basic literacy gaps, it does little to improve the literacy outcomes of schooling, thus placing the cart before the horse in some ways. However, the economic benefits from the leveling of educational opportunities have helped in reversing past discriminatory practices and increasing the representation of excluded groups in politically important ways.

The Literacy Gap Again

A noteworthy issue with respect to literacy is that math shows a lesser gap for students subject to GBI. This may be explained by the fact that math is less dependent on verbal skills than reading and related areas. A different symbol system is involved that includes non-verbal reasoning. Math also reflects the effects of school-based instruction more than other subjects where the home has leverage (Murname & Nelson, 1984). This suggests that rather than making instruction teacher proof (Hirsch, 1996), it can be and should be improved so that class differences are lessened.

We can learn much from the eradication of the achievement gap for women in the area of mathematics. The suffrage movement preceded the civil rights movement by about fifty years. How was the gap closed? When greater attention to gender bias was brought into teacher education, expectations changed as educators and society in general dismantled barriers in educational and job opportunities. While male students tend to score slightly higher than females, the difference is slight (Blank & Yangesen, 1999). In 1982, the gender gap in NAEP scores was forty-three points and by 1999 had been reduced to thirty-six points. At the "superior" level of performance, 3% of boys are found compared to 1% of the female student population. While current reports suggest the gap in math has now been eradicated, we can appreciate how slight differentials in educational outcomes relate to participation in advanced levels or select activities. However, comparable participation rates in advanced, upper-level high school math and science courses (calculus, chemistry and biology) are now about the same, except for physics and computer science. Female students are now more likely to major in physical sciences (40%), mathematics (45%), and biological sciences (64%). Unlike students subject to GBI, the majority of female students score as having a basic knowledge of science and math on NAEP tests. They also tend to be more advanced than boys developmentally in terms of maturity and verbal skills in childhood. An important difference between the gender and GBI gaps is also related to the fact that most women in the United States are of European descent and enjoy the conditions afforded by their husbands' class, power, or capital.[13] Desegregation and equal opportunities to learn appear to have been sufficient to close the gap since gender is balanced equally across class and ethnicity. Unfortunately, the ethnicity of students subject to GBI is not so balanced. If, like gender, SPARs were 50% from the majority group, the situation would be different today. In sum, it is no wonder that so many misconceptualize the problem as one of race or color given the correlation between SPARs and ethnicity.

The proportion of children sacrificed each year to poverty's concatenated effects, as noted, remains perplexing. The nation's uneven educational record appears biased towards highlighting positive trends, particularly in recent years, in the presentation of educational outcome data.[17] It might be argued that achievement levels in the early part of the 1970s for minority students were depressed due to years of segregation and lamentable educational conditions. When educational achievement data are examined developmentally, it can be seen that the gap is far from being eradicated despite the compensatory educational practices that have been in effect.[18] However, the facts show that even after more than a quarter century of the most progressive US era, seventeen-year-old black and Hispanic students' reading proficiency is still below the 1971 level exhibited by non-Hispanic white students finishing middle school.

Poor non-Hispanic white children do not fare much better and remain less visible because of how these outcomes in schooling are classified and reported by the government. Thirteen-year-olds from the majority group are as proficient in reading as seventeen-year-olds from the two minority groups (*The Condition of Education,* 2002). This means that even after staying in school an additional four years, at-risk students do not understand relatively complicated information, nor can they learn from specialized reading materials. Younger students from less marginalized groups achieve such understanding and can learn largely due to the cultural compatibility found in schools (Tharp, 1989).

Why does school persistence seems to widen the gap for SPARs? A pattern holds true for math, science, and writing proficiency (for grades four, eight, and eleven), particularly at higher levels of complexity. Educators know that to succeed in math, science and technology, reading at grade level is a must. Current estimates show that 60% of jobs in the future require skills that only one in five students will have when entering the job market. In a few years all jobs will require significant technical skills, and most of those jobs do not yet exist (Moses, 2001, 8–9).

Although low SES remains highly correlated with some ethnic origins, the improved scholastic achievement reported for non-mainstream students may be explained largely on the basis of the performance of those not living in severe poverty. The packaging of the problem into the cultural categories provided by the government does not inform the public about how well schools educate increasing numbers of poor students from diverse cultural contexts. Even after the removal of repressive practices such as segregation, it is clear that proficiency levels for at-risk students in general have not improved as much as government reports by ethnicity would suggest. Also, the educational achievement of immigrant children since 1965 is generally fused with that of larger national ethnic minorities with whom they are classified. While considerable variation in achievement exists with immigrant student groups (Gibson & Ogbu, 1991; A. Portes & Rumbaut, 2001), it would seem that this aggregation of data in most reports is problematic in addressing the problem of equity.

Believing that the problem is being addressed satisfactorily leads, unfortunately, to more of the same practices in educational policy, funding and literacy-oriented interventions. Critical analyses seem to be discouraged today in an unfriendly political climate where budget cuts for compensatory programs are threatening to strip the meager gains achieved by current interventions.

Summary

This chapter examined the extent and manner in which the achievement gap is constructed unevenly for some groups. Various practices were reviewed that have been linked to closing the gap. The achievement gap is a most instrumental indicator of group-based inequality for it serves to maintain differentials in information, knowledge, strategies that reflect the "culturing" of individuals collectively. Different types of GBI were noted. Part of this chapter aims to provide a knowledge base for education that explains how students are placed at risk. The conditions that sustain inequality were reviewed as the primary obstacles to the success of current practices. The relation of equity and reforms focused on higher test scores was also examined. How educators are often persuaded to view the problem of SPARs in terms of group membership remains a concern for the field.

Endnotes

1. Peru is an example of other Andean countries where "whites" are a minority.
2. That point begins with comparable percentages of students performing at grade level, at least at a minimum level of proficiency, regardless of background. This might be called the first level.
3. This observation is based on the review of the literature cited in this book, which shows divergences in this regard (e.g., The Education Trust Fund literature and critical pedagogy).
4. Poverty is outside the scope of the model proposed in this book.
5. For example, when academic achievement expectations are "imposed" on those placed at risk, it would seem that from a subjective stance, those labeled so are now being oppressed further by using standardized tests. Consequently, several scholars advocate the use of other developmental criteria or indicators (Luis Moll, Peter Smagorinsky). The argument against relying mostly on test performance is that the tests have been misused historically to segregate, allocate resources, and sustain group-based inequality. They play an essential role in certifying the outcomes of a system designed to educate some students better than others.
6. From an ethical view, gaining equity in basic, minimum standards of performance is a necessary step in a long road toward greater parity at higher levels.

7. Catch-22 is a set of contradictory mandates for actions and a term made popular by Joseph Heller's novel of the same name.

8. Here we introduce the notion that a first step toward equity lies in the opportunity for students to develop and learn to some standard level or measure. That measure is initially to be based in grade level performance or measured by standards-based tests (see Popham, 1997).

9. Historically, literacy has been regarded mostly as an all-or-nothing dichotomous variable regarding the capacity to decode symbols or letters. Being literate or cultured meant knowing how to read and write and was associated with higher status. Over time, as public education established minimum levels of literacy, how literate one became in certain areas became increasingly predictive of access to certain opportunities and lifestyles. Today, a proficient level of literacy and skills is as crucial as the difference between being literate or not in earlier times. Deliberately raising the level of literacy, while addressing inequality in achievement outcomes, can serve as means to excellence. These two agendas can be organized to work against or to cancel each other. Or, they could be reorganized (structurally) to work well together. For example, impartial accountability can serve as a means toward assisting the least advantaged in any school.

10. This is exactly where a ceiling effect has been created that prevents public universities from graduating sufficient numbers of qualified (e.g., SAT scores) minority students. In California and other states, colleges and universities are under pressure to make their student bodies more diverse. They encounter difficulties in attracting sufficient numbers of academically competent minority students. Some have gone as far as recruiting and preparing average and high-achieving SPARs in high school to fill their quotas. This practice of recruiting the few SPARs performing at or above grade level is called "creaming" off the top. This is a quick-fix approach that is shortsighted and does not contribute substantially to the eradication of GBI. Because of the various definitions of SPARs, many of those recruited may not be SPARs from groups subject to GBI. Nevertheless, this type of action from higher education sets a good precedent for future collaboration in our estimation. Some improvements in structures surely have been established in some schools but not necessarily the critical ones that would programmatically reverse years of disadvantage for some groups. Several aspects of inequality have been addressed more efficiently than others. Whether the glass is half empty or half full depends on the understanding of the problem and various groups' social construction of what the achievement gap means.

11. These are characteristics resulting in great part from structural constraints. This identification and student resistance are both adaptive social psychological reactions.

12. Here we draw attention to the fact that there are many different strategies available for improving the average student test performance. Aptitude-treatment interactions often occur where a new educational change advantages agroup with certain characteristics over another group(s). The latter may remain the same or perform below as a result of the innovation.

13. The analysis here presumes a healthy child and excludes organic conditions such as Down's Syndrome and biologically based mental retardation.

14. Intercultural contact alters the culture of each party and is positioned as a developmental principle for the sociogenetic component of cultural psychology.

15. The point here illustrates the difference between an approach that is ethical (aimed at the least advantaged and a satisfactory one.

16. That is, the gender gap would not be eradicated as rapidly in South Africa where most women (and men) are poor.
17. For example, in *The Condition of Education* (1994, 2002) reports, positive findings are generally noted by contrasting the current achievement levels of students in various groups relative to each group earlier. This is done without noting the corresponding fact that between-group differences remain quite significant and unaltered at both practical and statistical levels of significance.
18. Although most official reports have begun to recognize the widening of the gap during the 1990s, most insist that there has been great progress (Jones, 1984; Lee, 2002; National Center for Education Statistics, 1994b, 2000b).

3 Current Approaches to Equity

"As long as egalitarians assume that public policy
cannot contribute to economic equality directly but
must proceed by ingenious manipulations of
marginal institutions like the schools,
progress will remain glacial."

JENCKS ET AL., 1972, P. 265

Overview

Social inequality is established to a great extent by sustaining group differences in academic learning. This process is often subtle and multilayered. This chapter analyzes how efforts to end inequality in educational achievement, the "key" indicator of literacy, are curtailed by the limited understanding that has guided educational policies, models, and practices over the latter quarter of the last century. The conceptual underpinnings of educational policies in force today aimed toward the elimination of group-based inequality (GBI) in school achievement are questioned, along with some contextual political factors and recent statistical trends. The evidence concerning the educational achievement of students placed at risk (SPARs) shows that the 1971 gap in literacy (reading, math, science) remains about the same after decades of efforts to address inequality in education.[1] Several conjectures are advanced with regard as to why current policy remains unchanged insofar as inequality is concerned. These concerns involve basic conceptions about mental development, culturally perceived ability, and power. They may also relate to the fear that a critical analysis of current policy might be used politically to slash the already meager, insufficient educational assistance allowed by the political economy of education to upgrade the opportunity structure for SPARs.

Introduction

One major premise is that while poverty and inequality may be inherent in capitalist societies, they need not be reproduced disproportionately in capable children. Ethically, they should not be reproduced by virtue of the cultural history that some students bring to school or by how literacy is generally promoted in some groups relative to others. Literacy, like money, is a commodity as well as a vital tool that is co-constructed in and out of schools. It is dependent on social class. Variation in the quality of this tool is influenced directly by schooling and indirectly by the political economy of the present society and the characteristics of children's home culture. Few interventions seem capable of neutralizing or reducing the influence of students' socioeconomic status and cultural background in schooling. As a result, present efforts may be understood as generally having played rather small roles in closing the achievement gap although each contributes in some way to a general strategy focused on higher standards without equity as a central concern.

Fundamental Questions

Some preliminary questions asked in this chapter are

a. Is there actually a comprehensive and explicit strategy today to reverse or reduce the inequitable conditions that produce an achievement gap in learning outcomes?
b. What exactly do educational policies and reforms offer today that might arguably alter the practices and structures that reproduce both inequality in educational outcomes and group-based poverty?
c. What changes in culturally organized activities would be needed in attaining a "level playing field" for children trapped by GBI?
d. How may educators become better informed and more effective in connecting individual, group, and inter-group relations and development in their roles and practices across schools and communities?

The first question is rather easy to answer. No, there is no cogent, comprehensive strategy in place that is founded on a sound developmental approach to equity and excellence. At best, there is a modest strategy of supporting randomized field experiments in education (see Mosteller and Boruch, 2002) beyond the usual recycling of educational reform. There is a trend for evidence-based projects to build on a knowledge-base in raising test scores and to improve education. Yet, a longstanding gap between that trend and policy change remains that requires change in higher education. Another group of researchers (Tharp, 1997; Tharp & Gallimore, 1988; Tharp et al., 2000) have identified and confirmed essential pedagogical and organizational factors that can improve education. Another strategy concerns lesson-study media technology (Hiebert, Gallimore, & Stigler, 2002) to improve teacher practices and instruction. Yet another focuses on leadership training (Waters, Marzano and McNulty, 2003). The above are major initiatives with great potential that promise new directions for the educational system. Other less effective, political strategies rely on rhetoric more than actual data, such as No Excuses (Thernstrom & Thernstrom, 2003), which fails to alter the present structures that produce GBI. A main purpose of this book then is to formulate and articulate a broader, systematic approach that begins to tackle some of the main reasons why a progressive reduction in the academic learning gap has not yet been accomplished.

Today's educational landscape is jam-packed with reform movements focused on higher standards and accountability. Undeniably, the main agenda nationwide is fueled by state legislatures and political campaigns focusing directly on school productivity. Because of this trend, equity has again become a concern in the implementation of high-stakes reform. This new rhetoric emerges without fundamental changes in the educational system—except that of increased accountability (no child or school left untested). For example, the Education Trust literature exhorts educators to close the gap without the deep restructuring necessary to assist those left behind (Haycock, 1998; 2001). The bad news is that the gap in educational achievement has not been reduced even with past standards. It has recently increased, and the proportion of minority students placed at risk remains alarming (Miller, 1995). It is unlikely that as higher standards are woven into the curriculum, the teaching and learning problems that have made the educational system ineffective in the past will somehow magically be resolved. Efforts to weed out unprepared teachers with increased testing are countered by a teacher shortage that often requires emergency certification and substitutes. The testing pressures to identify underachieving schools—generally those with high proportions of SPARs and underprepared teachers—have led to a new phenomenon. The newspapers report instances of teachers cheating and helping students on standardized high-stakes testing. It is found that schools that fail to make progress must issue vouchers so that students can transfer to better schools, utilizing Title I funds earmarked for education (not transportation). If all the students who are behind grade level were to move to "better schools" as some argue, a mass exodus of SPARs would result that would overwhelm those few schools so that they would be unlikely to retain their exceptional status. Under a political siege, educators are forced to teach to the tests that reflect the higher standards. Higher standards can mean moving skills and concepts formerly considered above grade level to grade level expectations. This represents a speed-up effect that, like higher taxes on the poor, compromises ethics and students living in poverty. While most would like to see higher standards and better teaching and learning, this comes at a time when the achievement gap in basic skills is yet to be addressed and an effective developmental approach to compensation remains unaddressed.

The relatively good news is that accountability, as a pillar of the new reform trend, will inevitably put into clear focus the problem of equity. While supporting higher standards, it is argued that these should be founded first on meeting the conditions that mediate effective learning and teaching that are found both in the classroom and outside of it as well. The educational system needs to be restructured and aligned with well-established developmental principles in order to address both internal (in-school) and external (social context) conditions. The relativity of the achievement gap as well as current conceptions that seem to guide current reform policies must be understood. It should be noted that, although excellence is the most challenging problem of American education in recent decades, it is relative in nature. This (relativity) implies a number of problems in actual practice. Excellence depends both on higher standards and equity. Let's examine one problem regarding students historically subject to GBI and poverty and those more advantaged in the majority population.

Generally, when one attempts to rectify an unfair situation, compensation on one side is necessary until equilibrium is achieved. In education, it is nearly impossible to employ a new technology or effective set of practices for SPARs without others also extracting the most benefit. A scientific approach is necessary to clarify exactly what would be required to dismantle GBI. This is the first step. The second step is to test the new model empirically before attempting yet another reform. When adequate evidence becomes available, the better model or scientific paradigm can become established (Kuhn, 1962). However, in education, a third step is needed to determine if there is a sufficient power base to restructure the system and alter the status quo. To know whether the status quo has been changed is not difficult, since a reduction in GBI serves in evaluating new educational outcomes. Gender equity in education and status provided a good frame of reference here.

A second set of problems concern educational compensatory programs that are defended staunchly and primarily on the basis of secondary effects. These effects, related to competence (Zigler, 1986), may be questioned in terms of reflecting an acquiescent, compliant response that is adaptive to accepting inequality. The competence discourse, originated decades ago to defend meager gains by federally funded early age interventions, draws attention away from the underlying system that produces GBI and the policy changes needed for progress. An example may be the focus on reducing the drop-out rate for minority students without reducing the four-year gap in test scores at the end of high school for these SPARs.

It might be argued that establishing secondary effects may have become a goal of current policies that accept GBI in principle but attempt to affect some of the more blatant indicators (e.g., completion, retention, or suspension rates). Once educators settle for second-order benefits such as better attendance or graduation rates and limit their advocacy for effective grade-level instruction, they may reinforce the very system that structures inequality in learning outcomes.

Success in the second-order effects poses a twofold problem. First, it gives the impression of actively pursuing and achieving the goal of establishing equal educational opportunity in terms of comparable rates of grade-level performance across groups. Secondly, it suggests that truly effective strategies are being employed for the eradication of structural obstacles in children's development. The problem is that while both are false, both myths still prevail today!

There are considerable political considerations concerning the extent to which early, in-school, and after-school educational interventions ought to impact the GBI problem. If interventions socialize SPARs in ways that eliminate the school performance gap, the means employed might become suspect for some who would see them as enforcing the values of the dominant culture. The absence of intervention seems not a viable alternative either. Yet, interventions that are culturally sensitive and responsive but fail to eliminate the achievement gap appear to have become the default option in education. Except for some rare well-funded, unsustained or under-mobilized experiments (Tharp & Gallimore, 1988; Comer, 1990), most public schools do not catchup SPARs. The canon of multiculturalism or cultural relativism favors tolerance and celebration of differences yet leaves the GBI problem relatively untouched. Any attempt to hold the educational system itself accountable for imposing a growing gap in learning outcomes is subject to a political double-edge sword.

The Imperialism Trap

Politically correct views suggest that the end (eliminating GBI in educational outcomes) does not justify the means. The means may be regarded as imposing dominant group rules, tests, knowledge base and standards.[2] Accordingly, dominant group standards and tests on minority cultures should not be enforced. They only make the educational experience of SPARs more painful and damaging. This is because in relative terms, culturally different children will tend to be overrepresented in the bottom tiers of the achievement distribution even if grade-level performance differences were comparable. This is a compelling argument, but one that must be rejected. While the conceptual part of that argument may appear accurate, its current ramifications and suggestions for practice leave SPARs still disempowered and well behind the mainstream. Yet, another position is that the current NCLB policy is probably as good as it gets. This position may be associated with the celebration of diversity movement that seems accepting of achievement differences as part of culture along with accountability.

A cultural-developmental approach rejects all of the above positions by synthesizing a transcultural perspective of development. It does not view the end of GBI as an end in itself but rather as a means toward cultural development and higher societal standards in a broad sense. Dismantling GBI opens the doors for achieving excellence in education. A historical analysis of GBI suggests that until the intergenerational cycle of limited access to literacy-based tools for some groups is ended, cultural development will be retarded and society fragmented. An ethical policy founded on children's rights to a fair system of education is needed. It needs to be one that can also shrink between-group differences in academic achievement and tool acquisition.

Avoiding the Liberal Criticism Trap

The model delineated in the next chapter must respond to the above traps, particularly to those who might view the approach as cultural imperialism. The model involves cultural change for all parties involved, expanding cultural development for both those placed at risk and those placing them there. To regard this approach as an imposition of dominant cultural values seems inconsistent given the fact that past and actual practices and values are being imposed already and regrettably sustain GBI. Denying SPARs the means through which they can participate fully in the general sociocultural field on the basis of "preserving cultural differences" surely compromises development and equity intergenerationally. Some of those cultural differences originated in reaction to oppression, poverty conditions, and inequalities that have been learned. Poverty tends to preclude the construction of any culture, whether mainstream or not.

Let's examine more closely some of the assumptions and positions inherent in present practices. While the educational community in the United States is facing considerable pressure from international comparisons of student achievement, it appears that the issue of inequality in education is regarded as a separate, if not a somewhat related, encumbrance in striving for educational excellence. Unfortunately, few appear to understand that a particularly effective way to promote educational excellence for all lies precisely in addressing the teaching/learning problems found in educating poor students from different cultural backgrounds. To frame the question differently, to what extent can twelve years of standards-based education be reliably delivered to all students regardless of ethnic background once grade-level gaps in student learning are prevented at the group level?[3]

Conceptual Problems in Current Policy

What has been defined here as current policy is actually a conglomeration of reform strategies and practices to foster children's development, particularly those from lower-income backgrounds. These may be found in federal entitlement programs, Head Start, state-mandated reforms, district and local efforts, specific programs such as AVID, Accelerated Schools, Upward Bound, Success for All, or Gear Up consisting of initiatives, activities, and strategies to influence both the processes and outcomes of schooling (see those cited in Borman for these and others; Slavin, 2002b). Some are based on rather ethnocentric, ahistorical, or erroneous assumptions (Sizer, 1992). Others work and make a difference as long as they are sustained (Adams & Englemann, 1996; Hopfenberg & Levin, 1993; Comer, Haynes, Joyner, & Ben Avie, 1996; Schweinhart, Weikart, & Lerner, 1986; Tharp & Gallimore, 1988). Most today focus more on raising performance than reducing the achievement gap.

Preschool educational interventions and current entitlement and privately funded projects originated initially from a "cognitive deficit" model. After Bloom's (1964) finding that by age four, a child's intellectual performance level at age seventeen is largely accounted for, a number of compensatory education programs were launched to reduce the deficit early which was located (conceptually) in the child's understimulated mind and culture. In other words, the lower educational level at home is less beneficial to the child relative to that of the class groups that are more educated or cultured. During this time, Hunt's (1961) work challenged beliefs concerning fixed intelligence and behaviorism still reigned. A new social climate was emerging that concerned civil rights, social justice, and the man in the moon. Early childhood education programs were funded as a way to bring about a change in the "culture of poverty" with one fell swoop.

The theoretical underpinnings of early childhood educational interventions were largely based on the notion of a critical period, an idea loosely borrowed by psychologists from ethology (Lorenz, 1952). The notion of critical period in mental development was considered an important explanatory principle that justified the millions of dollars spent on the War on Poverty in the 1960s. Programs were launched to inoculate or treat the "problem" early, stimulating children to avoid mental underdevelopment. This effect would then be presumably evidenced in the subsequent educational success of disadvantaged children in school. The initial boost in IQ then was expected to be sustained by the treated participants without assistance, except for that of families participating in such programs (P.R. Portes, Dunham & Williams, 1986). These social scientists hypothesized comparable distributions in intellectual performance would be sustained upon school entry and even later in life.

This view is based on several faulty assumptions. For example, the reasoning is that early intelligence is quickly fixed. It explains and predicts future academic performance. Individual intelligence might be boosted by intense stimulation. In this narrow psychometric approach, once the child's individual intelligence is boosted experimentally, it remains stable since it is viewed as a fixed individual trait. The boost was considered sufficient to be sustainable in future grades in school.

These programs generally produced modest short-term gains in achievement for some participants initially (see Lazar & Darlington, 1982; Dunham, Kidwell, & Portes, 1995a and b; Schweinhart & Weikhart, 1998; Zigler, & Muenchow, 1992) but the academic gains were "washed out" over time. Some produced positive non-intellectual gains for participants such as reduced retention and dropout rates. Some focused on parent education, the child, or both. Unfortunately, the "critical period" premise that guided those programs was only partly correct, yet still prevails today in Head Start. As a result, an educational handicap continues to be institutionalized for most children subject to GBI since the majority thinks Head Start closes the gap in public K–12 education when it actually does not.

In retrospect, educational policy has been hard pressed to show that it has contributed directly toward the leveling of GBI. It seems that before the promise of equal opportunity can be achieved, aiming for comparable distributions across groups in educational outcomes is essential. However, another dimension to the educability puzzle is from Alexander and Entwisle (1988) and Dreeben and Gamoran (1986) who have failed to find significant group differences in achievement prior to first grade. If the conclusion to be drawn from the literature (e.g., Oakes, 1990a ; Oakes et al., 2000) is that achievement differences are produced and amplified through schooling, practices such as tracking—the logic behind educational policy today and schooling practices in particular—warrant careful attention. In the next sections, a closer look at the critical period and the main frameworks that undergird compensatory educational practice is provided. Various approaches to achieving macro-level changes through education are examined in terms of the means each one emphasizes, the location of the problem, and the supporting evidence.

A Developmental Perspective of a Critical Period in Early Childhood: Two Positions

Soon after Hunt (1961) and Bloom (1964) pointed to the role of early experiences in development and the idea of a "critical period" in human development was accepted, the solution to the gap was conceptualized in terms of normalizing differences in early experiences through preschool interventions. The target and location of the problem were conceptualized to be in the head of the child living in poverty and in parents' deficits in knowledge and socialization patterns. Ever since then, many innovative in- and after-school programs for at-risk children have been developed. Most have neither been effective in sustaining academic gains nor critically examined for their potential effect on school and work outcomes. "We should bear in mind that no educational project has shown the ability to consistently deliver a one standard deviation improvement in test scores" (Levin, 1997). Today there is a lack of research on the long-term effectiveness of the Head Start programs. In all fairness, many who are served by effective Head Start programs do show significant benefits upon completion. The current Head Start position is that "these programs do work" at least until the gap is constructed later in the educational system. Thus, the main problem is cumulative and lies in public schooling practices where a gap is created and enlarged. Others believe that they can't work well enough without comparable emphases on family processes (Hart & Risley, 1995; Portes, 2002).

So what is known about these programs in public schools? Again there is evidence that when educators and students receive assistance, the gap is lessened or closed. The KEEP (Tharp & Gallimore, 1988) and Comer (Comer, Haynes, Joyner, & Ben Avie, 1996) programs provided important gains and information about what may be required in and out of classrooms. As noted, the literacy gap among students subject to GBI may appear to be slight or non-existent at first grade, particularly for Head Start children. There is evidence from scores of studies that SES accounts for little more that 5% of the variance in achievement (White, 1982). However, it seems plausible that subtle school practices and structures gradually impose and sustain the achievement differences. Key indicators of inequality in scholastic performance still reflect an enormous lag, even after a quarter century of direct anti-poverty educational interventions and programs at the national level. Teaching and learning in school account for 50% of the variance in student achievement, (Seashore, 2004) when factors such as parent involvement are excluded.

Schooling, seen as a cultural program that organizes specific competency areas, requires or at least presumes certain conditions or linkages be established (e.g., a partnership between the family/community culture and school-based teaching and learning). There appear to be at least two major ways of understanding the problem of successfully educating students from different sociocultural backgrounds. Each concerns the many reasons why schools are unable to narrow or prevent achievement differences between groups of competent students.

The first position holds that a massive gap between social class groups is largely language mediated (Hart & Risley, 1995) and occurs quite early. These authors documented a three–one ratio differential in the linguistic-based measures observed between low and upper-middle SES groups within the first three years of life. Socialization differences persist and become evident later in school through a one-standard deviation difference in academic achievement, regardless of pre-, after- and in-school programs. But why consider the first three years of life as critical? It may be that performance differences appearing later during the elementary school years are largely a function of differences in early language-based interaction patterns (Hart & Risley, 1995; White, 1975) socialization practices and values that co-vary with the development of brain structures.

A second position on the problem holds that this lag can be, and has been, narrowed by some early interventions including some Head Start-like programs that seem particularly intense and comprehensive. From this view, the problem originates early in children's development, and the gap can be prevented with top-notch early interventions from pre-K–12. This is accomplished by preparing children to develop strategic mental structures, attitudes, knowledge, and routines that are compatible with middle-class learning environments and later acquiring more capital through college-level preparation.

Preschool alone cannot eliminate the gap since it is constructed again when children leave effective programs to enter school. By fourth grade, the effects of Head Start and other early interventions are negligible with respect to academic outcomes. Since the actual gap is regarded as minimal and even insignificant between social class groups at first grade, later differences are attributed mostly to schooling practices and structures that are most compatible with middle-class groups' values and their literacy-related practices.

Most positions fail to recognize a misconstrued concept that remains popular yet misunderstood. The alternative explanation to the individually oriented "critical period" hypothesis is that cognitive development is mediated mainly through rather stable communication and activity patterns in the family environment. The latter act as filters as well as purveyors of cultural experience. Family interaction patterns evolve intergenerationally, are consistent, and are also constrained by poverty, parents' education, social competence and child/family relations. Family interaction or childrearing patterns are related to social class and show some susceptibility to change (P.R. Portes, Dunham, & Williams, 1986; P.R. Portes & Vadeboncoeur, 2003).

The gap, as a difference in development, is also generated from before birth. This is because parental beliefs, practices, and interaction patterns endure intergenerationally and through social learning. They have a semiotic[4] relationship with the individual child's development since the developmental context coexists with the person's growth. This context is generally set early and remains present during and after school and after assisted performance in special programs is terminated. The child's cognitive development and school competence is then determined jointly by the interaction of school and family environments, each of which have a determining capacity and jointly interact over time. As school begins to increase literacy demands tied to performance standards, the delivery capacity of low-income, often single-parent homes is pitted against that of a middle-class group norm. It is this capacity that is recognized today as social capital (Bourdieu & Passeron, 1977), which, from an activity-oriented model, forms the mind that the child brings to school for schooling.[5] SPARs' parents have the capacity but often have less know-how regarding the ways schools are organized. This type of capital is thus not simply a function of parental income but knowledge that can be constructed systematically (see Chapter Five). In short, the more co-dependent a child's academic learning in school is on the support lent in the home, the greater the discrepancy in learning outcomes between groups. In short, to reduce the gap, school learning needs to depend less on SES mediated parental support.

A historical or developmental perspective is critical in dismantling or compensating for the mechanisms that reliably produce the achievement gap. At present, the gap that is constructed early compromises middle and high school education efforts among low SES students and also teachers' sense of efficacy. By middle school, the chances of schools and teachers to help such students to "catch up" become smaller given the disparate tracks programmed for high-achieving students. As schooling is now generally organized, it cannot be considered independent of students' learning and development outside school. Rather, it is intimately connected with class and the conditions it governs in the classroom over time. Schooling is organized in ways that explicitly and implicitly impose demands on the home and student. Much of what schools and educators can accomplish in educating students, however, depends on how the home has organized and sustains the student's development. Very little of the know-how is shared with low SES adolescents before they form families.

Efforts to reduce GBI directly are non-existent. Most of the current approaches aimed to reduce the achievement gap target some students at risk in some areas some of the time. Since Head Start and subsequent entitlement programs such as Title I and Even Start, numerous projects have been initiated, including some in elementary, middle and secondary school. These are not sustained over time or integrated nationally. These efforts need to be examined in terms of how they aim to close the achievement gap. In sum, contemporary approaches can be sorted into several types: those that emphasize early childhood (critical period); those that focus on providing vigorous academic assistance in school (see Borman, Overman, & Brown, 2002); and those that focus on providing academic assistance after school. Let's review some of their assumptions:

Preschool Education

This area is often debated in policy circles and ponders such questions as what types of preschool are appropriate and to what extent are preschool and daycare effective or what types of staffing, curricula, and physical environments work best (Comer, 1980; Osborne & Milbank, 1987). The reigning belief is that adequate methodologies based on cognitive developmental theory have been proven effective in enabling at-risk children to compete successfully with mainstream children (Levin, 1988; Schorr, 1988). The success of early age interventions in producing long-term effects in non-intellectual domains (see Lazar & Darlington, 1982; Schweinhart, Weikart, & Lerner, 1986; P.R. Portes & Dunham, 1988) is often (and erroneously) associated with closing the educational gap. The main problem with early age intervention strategies may be that the policy does not go far enough in protecting any gains made by corresponding changes in and out of school. By focusing on "fixing the at-risk child," this policy initiative becomes just a revised cultural deficit model (see Baker, Piotrkowski, & Brooks-Gunn, 1998; Jordan, Snow, & Porche, 2000; Shaver & Walls, 1998; Starkey & Klein, 2000).

School-Based Reorganization

This framework is concerned with effective school practices and reform. That the scholastic achievement gaps stem from deficiencies in educational systems that "operate to place some children in an inferior status" throughout the schooling process and which limit the aspirations of disadvantaged children is a long-held public belief. Those deficiencies are associated with low expectations by school personnel, tracking, testing, and inadequate curricula and teaching strategies. Today many believe that effective schools (Lee, Bryk, & Smith, 1993; Stedman, 1987) can establish equality in educational opportunity. However, leadership approaches (Waters, Marzano & McNulty, 2003) are limited mostly to school-level factors that are not well defined, such as school climate (Lee, Winfield, & Wilson, 1991), administrative leadership that often leaves out contextual factors, and instructional or cultural practices. Coleman (1966, 1990), among others, has found that the home environment accounts for inequality in scholastic achievement far more than a host of school variables. While school organizational factors may explain only a small part of the school achievement gap, renewed efforts to influence variables related to school learning abound. Levin's Accelerated Schools have produced valuable results that also call into question Coleman's methodology and conclusions (Goldberg, 2001).

In sum, a rich literature exists in education that points to school-based inequality (see Good, 1987; Heath, 1983; Kozol, 1992, 2000; Phillips, 1983) in accounting for the GBI problem. They document how certain practices present obstacles that place children at risk. Some improvements have been made experimentally and have produced positive results with at-risk groups (Comer, 1980; Levin, 1988; Marshall, 1996; Tharp et al., 2000) under special conditions, many of which can be assimilated into the mainstream of education. However, the sustainability of effective programs remains in question and will require historical analysis much along the same lines of early age interventions that proved successful initially. Other initiatives have attempted to reduce class size (Achilles, Finn, & Bain, 1998). The organizational structure of schools or "school cultures" (Goodlad, 1983) seems resistant to change from the inside (Parish & Aquila, 1996) as well as from the outside (Soder, 1996). Efforts to change students' beliefs or classroom learning arrangements or grouping also seem insufficient to keep SPARs from falling behind.

Political Influences

Some efforts that aim to maximize academic learning time have centered on accountability, new performance standards, and vouchers when schools fail. The latter remain controversial since only some parents can use them to avoid low-performing schools and move their children to better, often private schools. While the argument is appealing insofar as children's right to a sound education is concerned, two counter arguments persist. One is that while middle-class parents can supplement vouchers with their own resources to have children attend private schools, low-income parents' options will remain limited. Secondly, this new market economy of schools and movement of students undermines public education without reducing GBI.

Sociobiological accounts of GBI by many conservatives (e.g., Herrenstein & Murray, 1994) have been dismissed in most intellectual circles due to serious conceptual and methodological flaws. Yet, influential groups in our society persist in equating intellectual ability with IQ and believe race and heredity offer the most valid explanation for why the gap cannot be closed. Such pseudo-scientific views are distracting and deter forging a coherent educational policy.

Multicultural Pedagogy

New waves of multicultural pedagogy are crashing at the classroom door, suggesting that the GBI problem can be fixed by culturally sensitive curricula and activities (Sleeter, 1996). Multiculturalism has oriented policy toward a "cultural therapy" mode that builds identity, self-esteem, and mutual accommodation without equity. It is based partly on a cultural difference view, in which value judgments about the worth of a given culture and its members are avoided (Cole, 1990). Little evidence exists now to suggest that, even when joined with school-based reforms, multiculturalism in our schools will end GBI in academic success unless the very criteria employed in defining educational progress are altered as well. While multiculturalism in education may be deemed necessary in raising teacher expectations, it is hardly sufficient to end GBI. A growing concern about educational outcomes has been felt with respect to practices that do not empower "other people's children" (Delpit, 1995) with methods and policies that are unlikely to bridge the gap. Also, there is little evidence to support claims that teaching to students' learning styles is effective as advocated by this literature. Teachers cannot accommodate the variety of purported learning styles. The latter appear as a misnomer that may be associated more precisely with learning *sets* (Bruner, 1966) that children acquire developmentally across cultural contexts. The issue is, thus, that learning is situated (Lave & Wenger, 1991), and predispositions can be influenced by how the social context is organized. Critical race theory takes many of these factors into consideration, particularly after the *Brown* decision (Ladson-Billings, 2004).

Bilingual Education

This framework has proven successful for teaching mostly poor, English-limited students. In this framework, schools need to accommodate to the student so that meanings can be co-constructed efficiently rather than wasting years of schooling on the basis of language. The data are clear (Krashen, 1996) that bilingual education is an effective compensatory strategy for this subgroup of students subject to GBI. However, many immigrant children are not as subject to GBI as their US-born, English-limited counterparts who represent caste-like minorities. The school achievement level of children of immigrants appears to be due to many factors of which proficiency in English plays only one part. This puzzle suggests that cultural history (P.R. Portes, 1996) requires further consideration at the policy level for children subject to GBI that extends beyond social class. Moll (1992) has shown how bilingual education students' social capital and competence are generally ignored in public schools. In many cases, SPARs' competence is ignored and wasted in instructivist approaches that are not student centered. English-only policies can serve to maintain and expand the achievement gap by placing large number of vulnerable children further behind.

Macro-Sociological Models

Macro ethnographic approaches consider schools as the enforcers of the American caste system, which ensures continuation of the educational gap and inequality in opportunity (Ogbu, 1992). Ogbu's model attempts to show how often schools are organized as agents that promote a caste-like system. It has been regarded as a model of "cultural dominance" described by Bereiter (1994) and discussed by Giroux (1980). This view combines a reproduction model made popular by Bowles and Gintis (1976) with deficit-like types of recommendations (see Ogbu, 1992). He suggests SPARs subject to GBI should emulate their more successful Asian counterparts and desist from some of the culturally different values and behaviors. Macro-sociological models generally tend to remain wanting in terms of outlining specific pedagogical, organizational, or other changes in practice (see Jencks & Phillips, 1999). In line with Thernstrom & Thernstrom (2003), effective schools can only do so much when SPARs' culture fails to follow that of the "Asian model minority" groups. A "be-like-Mike" mentality is implied by this approach as if cultural change could be designed from atypical cases as suggested by Ogbu (1992).

After-School Initiatives

After-school programs represent another strategy to reduce the gap in academic achievement. Although not all of these programs provide academic support, many do and have shown positive effects for SPARs. The main variable they appear to influence is increased time on academic learning through mentoring activities before or after school and motivation through positive models and expectations. Extended learning time initiatives and year-round schools also represent strategic initiatives that appear important in reducing the achievement gap. Some school districts in the nation have extended the number of school days for all students in attempting to meet the new standards. Others have focused their summer programs on SPARs, in particular those students who tend to regress during vacation.

Other Approaches

Class size reduction, student and teacher attitudes, self-efficacy, motivation, cooperation or mastery learning, and peer group influences represent other sources of variance in student achievement that are also hypothesized to help in closing the gap. For example, current research attempts to link

Text Box 3-1: Discussion Questions for Educators

Taking into consideration that sociohistorical conditions appear to:

- determine the selection of children for placement at risk from certain groups, and
- that public education is somehow expected to extricate itself from the very practices it has organized to produce inequality.

What would be required to transform the educational system toward the ideals of a meritocracy, fairness, and excellence?

Consider the following:

- First, would the "haves" share capital with the "have-nots" to end GBI? Would they share if it meant "gradual horizontal radiation," that is, reversing the underrepresentation of various groups' children in the middle and upper tiers of economic and political power? Would they have to gradually lose their political and economic edge? If so, why would they want to? Or, could the "haves" eradicate GBI in education without sacrificing their status and power? Would they commit to the transformation of schools as we know it, having them become a means for advancing toward a more equitable society where between-group variation would be insignificant? Do we have the means and know-how to accomplish this task even if the will existed?

The problem of finding an effective approach that responds to GBI requires a developmental model that can integrate successful practices within new structures. What is meant by developmental? How can it address the cultural incompatibility stemming from home and school settings? How would it reorganize actual institutionalized structures that govern teaching and learning processes?

character and environmental education and similar programs with school climate in improvements in academic achievement. However, like many other initiatives noted above, a developmental, systemic approach is needed for reducing the academic gap and sustaining educational outcomes. Even the combined effort of a few of these approaches such as single-gender classes, small schools, uniforms, and the like seems unlikely to level massive inequalities in opportunity to learn.

None of the above models can level persistent group differences in academic performance. Overall, these are increasingly common in most developed, multicultural nations. The approaches outlined have one problem in common. Each one fails to specify the means through which children's development of mind is constructed differentially. The influences of cultural contexts, language, and history are recognized at best as part of espoused theories (Argyris and Schon, 1992). Each model appears useful in some ways for some students some of the time. Educational policy today remains limited then to maintaining an impoverished, ahistorical view of the important links between cultural conditions and human cognitive development. Since the interdependent, cultural nature of the GBI problem is not understood developmentally, current policies continue to institutionalize "at-risk" conditions and seem designed to leave children behind.

Some Common Myths

Several myths exist today that deter taking a proactive approach to the ending of GBI. It seems that some of the concern about the achievement gap is primarily due to the obstacle gross population disparities present to the higher standards agenda or perhaps the basic principles of a democracy. Rather than focusing on the ethical problem of ending group-based inequality, first, the stakes are centered around the interplay between higher standards and test scores.

Myth one: Current educational policy is working and gradually eradicating GBI.

This is based largely on selective interpretations of educational trends reported in the literature (NCES, 1994b; OERI, 1991; *Condition of Education,* 2002) and recent political speeches (e.g., G.W. Bush in 2004). Dropout rates have decreased for African Americans, as indicated by higher high school completion rates. The reading gap has been cut in half for older minority, Spanish-speaking students. Small overall achievement gains, relative to each group's previous levels, are often highlighted (see Ekstrom, Goertz, & Rock, 1986). While the good news is that school persistence is up, inequality in student achievement has not changed. During the 1990s, the gap increased (Lee, 2002).

An overemphasis on the positive prevails in current government publications and related reports. For example, statements that achievement gains are up for at-risk students (Applebee, Langer, & Mullis, 1986; Ekstrom, Goertz & Rock, 1988; Koretz, 1987) are based on the fact that there has been less of a decline for these groups than for non-Hispanic white students. The gains associated with Chapter I funding appear significant when compared to the reading scores of non-Chapter I students (Lee, Winfield and Wilson, 1991) although a between-group disparity persists and becomes accentuated as a function of the number of years of schooling (see Lee, 2002). For many, this seems like an issue of whether the glass is half full or empty. Yet, if dropout rates have decreased partially at the expense of lower academic standards and social promotion practices, and the reported gains are mainly based on the criterion of a lessened decline in academic achievement (rather than the criterion of performance at grade level without group differences), then a reasonable question might be from whose perspective is the glass half full? Is it from the perspective of groups whose children continue to achieve significantly above the norm or from groups whose children are left behind each year in the present educational system?

After decades of policy initiatives, the question is obviously why the glass remains half full after decades of programs and reform policies. Why has the gap between groups not been reduced for four decades? There will always be upper and lower quartiles in any test distribution, and more likely than not, there will be group differences related to social class. The more important issue, however, is why maintain an outdated system that ensures a disproportionate number of SPARs subject to GBI will fall behind and finish well below grade level? Why raise the "production" quota (e.g., higher standards) when the old one could not be met and the system remains resistant to change? The ideas that guide current educational reform may be regarded as problematic, yet ironically they do shed light on an unresolved problem.

Myth two: A primary goal of post-Civil Rights educational policy is to establish equal opportunity to learn with regard to academic outcomes of students from different groups.

If the end of GBI were indeed the goal of modern educational policy, current financing and practices would require a judiciary investigation. The overwhelming evidence that reveals a massive inequality in educational achievement remains significant after decades of equity-minded policy is irrefutable. As government documents explain, those who score lower in school are generally students who live in and remain in poverty.

Myth three: The proportion of children living in poverty has been reduced significantly since the War on Poverty.

Poverty remains as a primary reason for the educational disparity and problems educators face daily (Rank, 2004). School reforms attempting to improve the educational performance of SPARs may be futile, costly, and aggravating until familial poverty is reduced significantly. In effect, many believe schools and their outcomes are determined by the economic order and that the educational system cannot transcend or change that order. Reform may not be able to make educational outcomes comparable across groups until poverty rates are leveled. The chances of reducing the gap are unlikely since the poverty rates for students at-risk have not decreased significantly in relative terms much since Coleman's 1966 report on inequality

(Gans, 1995, Lee & Burkham, 2002). As Jencks noted in 1972, society, rather than education, must be restructured to end inequality.

Between 40–65% of children living in single-parent homes in the United States live in poverty with changing family forms that are headed primarily by women or belong to certain minority populations (Grissmer, Flanagan and Williamson, 1998; Office of Educational Research and Improvement, 1991). For example, the average black family's income increased less than $800 from 1970 to 1990. The gap between black and non-black family income in 1970 was $17,518 while in 1990 it was $18,477 in 1987 (Grissmer et al., 1998). These authors note that in terms of NAEP mathematics and reading scores from 1971 to 1996, "Even when black gains were largest, they never came close to eliminating the gap. The largest reduction was for seventeen-year-olds' reading scores. In 1971 (when students had been segregated), the median black scored between the tenth and twelfth percentiles of the white distribution. By 1998 the median black scored between the twenty-sixth and twenty-eighth percentiles of the white distribution. For other age groups, the gap remained even wider" (p. 187).

While the rate of poverty for non-Hispanic white children under eighteen years of age is 14%, 43% of black children must learn to endure it and develop alternative literacies.[6] The poverty rate for Hispanic children has actually increased from 28% in 1973 to 35.5% in 1989 (US Bureau of Census, 1990). Literacy levels and rates shadow the economic rates. The rate for Native Americans is not any better.

Because they are born into disempowered groups, these children encounter limited educational and socioeconomic opportunities before entering and during school (Good & Marshall, 1984; Oakes, 1990a, 1990b). They are bound by a context that produces economic and cultural deprivation in key literacy areas. Consequently, each generation's literacy development, their motivation for achievement, is progressively limited, thus lowering children's probability of benefiting from formal schooling (P.R. Portes, 1996). Increasing per-pupil expenditures at school is no guarantee that SPARs will receive the academic assistance they need since those costs are averaged. Increasing school funding does not guarantee that SPARs' developmental needs are met since the money can be spent in various, and less efficient, ways.

Myth four: Head Start, school reform, and after-school programs are closing the gap. The current models that guide these practices are correct. What is needed is more support in reaching more eligible SPARs.

The theoretical model(s) that underlies entitlement and local intervention programs warrants attention in today's complacent climate. Educational policy may be limited in understanding the relation between mental and cultural development. The links between individual and sociocultural development are generally not evident or explicit in today's educational policy. Today's approach to a host of social programs is to compensate, in small measure, for complex conditions that place most poor children and their intellectual development at risk. The reaction by many to criticism regarding the disappointing results of early education and school-based programs is that more funding is needed before significant changes can be achieved (see Levin, 1997; Schorr, 1997).

Head Start programs have been generally declared successful, although they are clearly insufficient to close the gap in academic achievement by themselves. The model of early educational and nutritional compensation is incomplete. Such is obviously necessary but not sufficient in ending group inequality. While modest benefits may be attributed to Head Start, Title I, and dropout prevention programs, the "more of the same is needed" argument is deceptively counter-productive. In reading, writing, and math, the data still reflect a significant, one standard deviation gap in performance that remains after decades of educational experimentation. Data from 1992 NAEP scores in reading, math, and science still show a familiar pattern when broken down by ethnicity—an indirect measure of inequality. The gap is illustrated in the achievement of students from poverty-laden groups that average below the thirtieth percentile of white, non-Hispanic groups. Some Hispanic groups tend to be well above the 50th percentile, while most do not (P.R. Portes, 1999). The College Entrance Examination Board's National Report (1993) shows that SAT scores of college-bound seniors remain significantly lower for children of the above groups and that this pattern pertains to black students in particular. The pervasiveness of the problem can be seen much earlier in the lifespan, where over 40% of majority children attend pre-kindergarten, while less than a third of African American and 21% of Hispanic children do so (*The Condition of Education*, 1994; 2004). Actually, an alternative explanation to the modest within-group gains reported from 1971 reflect a rebound effect after the most suppressive segregation practices were removed by the Civil Rights movement. The majority of SPARs graduate with only a middle school education.

Myth five: Current efforts to improve teacher standards, hold schools accountable, and raise standards will abolish inequality in educational outcomes.

High-stakes accountability is essentially guided by a black box approach that leaves the basic structures that produce group differences in academic achievement untouched. Pressure applied by the state on education in raising performance standards and assessing student performance more closely resembles a collective contingency management model based on behaviorism. The main change is to hold schools accountable as they attempt to adapt instruction to performance objectives any way that works. Those that do are rewarded. Schools that draw more difficult sets of constraints (in terms of students', families', and educators' characteristics) are penalized. Many new practices are test score driven. New "hands" are eventually dealt, shifting students, families and school personnel around. Amidst a teacher shortage, as the ineffective educators are weeded out, students can become eligible for vouchers to try their luck elsewhere without addressing the resulting gap.

One wonders about the fates of those SPARs who are kept below grade level for years before a school is declared in crisis—or an educator is fired—and the student is moved to a new environment. The current approach reacts late to problems that already exist in a revolving system that reliably fails those it leaves behind. It attempts to disperse and penalize the bottom distribution of educators, students, and communities already in high-risk contexts. Rather than acting proactively in helping prevent impediments to learning and promote SPARs and educators' development in a systematic fashion or reorganize the conditions that place the least advantaged at risk, the current approach reproduces failure before lending assistance. The most vulnerable are identified and pressured without catching up SPARs sacrificed in the process. Without altering structural barriers such as class size, the preparation and professional development of educators, and similar actions, vouchers play "musical chairs" with those most in need of assistance. An impact statement has yet to document the consequences of moving SPARs from failing schools. It is not difficult to see that the vouchers are a shortsighted strategy, along with charter schools.

A Cultural Developmental Approach Is Needed

From a developmental and cultural perspective, a systemic approach based on best practices helps reduce the gap now resulting from schooling. Secondly, a concerted effort has yet to be made, but such effort must be made at the national, state, and local levels. From a cultural-historical view, development can be improved by cultural means, such as those underlying tools in school literacy. Interference and obstructions in the development of crucial tools or means at the individual or group level produce quite different futures. Cultural and social capital can be defined as those means that enable development. Such means can be part of a new policy in education, a new software for the system, in addition to other actions. The theories themselves that inform educational policy also represent means from a cultural-historical perspective. It helps understand how the organization of mediated action and strategies jointly influence individual and societal development.

Incompatibility between the home and school contexts can quickly transform various cultural differences into performance deficits in academic areas (Tharp, 1989). Homework and projects indirectly serve to amplify the effects of differences in the delivery capacity of the family and their capital investment. Discourse and learning/teaching patterns also reveal discontinuities that place low-income minority children at risk for educational failure.

Even with early intervention (Schweinhart, Weikart, & Lerner, 1986; Zigler & Styfco, 1993), far from all at-risk children are served. Of those served, too few develop sufficient school readiness to produce a significant effect. Culture-based differences interact with SES and result in pervasive effects that are generally founded on a sustained divergence in delivery capacity (Dunham, Kidwell, & Portes, 1988) regarding factors such as those inherent in parent involvement, time on task, adult-child ratio and mediated activity (Black & Logan, 1995; Davis et al., in press). Schools' effects on human development are not independent of the family/community culture. In fact, their interdependence grows over time and before long, the consequences become further etched via tracking programs, expectations, identities, and a host of non-academic factors.

In sum, even if the most effective early interventions were to be delivered to 100% of children placed at risk, the gap would only be constructed later in school. In response to the position that schools are then "to blame," a number of initiatives have been launched. We see a number of efforts across the nation's schools to reduce the gap that work when a sufficient number of factors are brought to bear to increase the learning rates for SPARs. Yet, this rare synchronization of conditions needs to be organized nationally and sustained under a general model that can benefit all children within state and local districts.

A major problem with any vigorous campaign to end GBI, then, is that an informed conceptual framework is needed in coordinating and expanding current efforts. The rationale for ending GBI is not to impose the values of a dominant or majority culture but, rather, to transform society as it now exists in ways that allow a greater freedom of movement for all students. Whether the elimination of GBI has actually been a priority in educational policy is debatable. But even if it were a priority, to what extent are educational policy and its agents informed well enough to effect and guide this type of cultural change? Whether it currently is a priority may seem a moot political question. A more interesting one concerns how new practices may be organized in ways that would reduce the correlation between children's cultural background and success as indexed by school achievement.

Summary

In closing, major questions remain concerning whether GBI has to remain distributed so by ethnicity. If educational policies and practices serve to organize, sustain, and reproduce GBI, could they not then be restructured to level basic learning outcomes in the present system across cultural groups? How could education be reconfigured to produce ethnic as well as gender equity[7] in educational outcomes, at least as a first step in reversing a cultural-historical phenomenon? Do we know how? Obviously not, unless one would think a collective malicious intent is prevailing, and one would hate that to be the case. Yet the issue of whether the dominant groups actually want to eradicate this source of social injustice totally remains open because the question of intent is relevant if a clear path to excellence and equity were clear. As long as it is unclear, it remains irrelevant.

Some reduction of GBI, rather than eradication, characterizes current goals. Even so, that is not the key problem since reduction precedes eradication historically. The problem is then that we don't know how to reduce the gap programmatically, either in educational or economic terms. GBI prevails in prisons, schools, and the professions while population gaps remain in learning and teaching outcomes.

This chapter ended with popular myths that serve to underestimate inequality. In order to address social inequality, a reliable, sustained, developmental approach is needed. Establishing gender equity in learning outcomes has taken decades and came about gradually. When developmental outcomes are measured, what tends to be critical in determining outcome variations is/are the context(s) of socialization and how they are affected by policies such as taxation or desegregation. In spite of affirmative action or support for early childhood and other compensatory programs, the ethno-cultural gap in learning outcomes has yet to narrow between groups.

Text Box 3–2: Problem-Finding Questions

- What are the principal reasons for the persistence of glaring inequity in educational outcomes for a society that is keen on equal educational opportunity?
- Are schools less effective for certain cultures?
- Is SES the primary problem, or poverty's shaping of certain cultures?
- Is it primarily just a question of the social class-literacy connection?
- Could it be that educational policy is not informed well by social science?
- Or, that it is well informed about teaching and learning but that the implementation of these policies (practices) needs further assistance and dissemination?
- Is it that social science has not had the answers and is not even on that course?
- Or perhaps that even if it were on the best course, education cannot eradicate the achievement gap between groups because it cannot transcend a political order based on a modern oligarchy?

Endnotes

1. Some reports appear to minimize the extent of the gap, as if ten–fifteen points were indicative of the gap. As noted earlier, a thirteen-year-old non-SPAR performs at a level similar to a seventeen-year-old SPAR. This gap is sufficient to reproduce poverty intergenerationally. The misleading aspect is that it artificially reduces the true extent of the gap by adding and averaging the scores of middle- and upper-class Latino and African American students. Oriental groups, mostly immigrants—like Jews and European Americans—have larger proportions of middle-class representation and, like the majority, average around 14% of SPARs. The point here is that the problem is cast in terms of race and ethnicity when it really needs to be assessed in terms of a national population of multicultural children placed at risk for not being educated to grade level in a system that is outdated and unethical. This is the other class argument, for which equity is a moot issue here. We assume that there will always be group variations in income and literacy, and those lowest across groups are joined together as the low-status group in any society. Our argument is different and concerns a more pressing equity issue—that is, that historically exploited ethnic groups present the most grave of ethical dilemmas and require assistance to become comparably literate. Until parity is reached in educational outcomes for these groups, the ethical problem cannot be resolved. This is not to say other groups—immigrant or majority—do not deserve consideration and assistance. Some Latino immigrants, for instance, are of Native American heritage and come from historically oppressed groups in Central America or the Caribbean and face regimented assimilation (A. Portes and Zhou, 1999).

2. I do not concede political, analytical, or scientific correctness to this camp here but recognize my perspective may be regarded as too conservative by this academic circle and too radical or socialistic by conservatives. I reject a cultural deficit view but also the smug critique of privileged academics who purport to speak for SPARs subject to GBI. Those belonging to the latter group who "make it" academically and are successful exemplify the win-win situation. They master the literacy standards required in school and retain their cultural heritage and values. More than bicultural competence (Ramirez and Castaneda, 1974), I suggest that regardless of cultural origin, the acquisition of cultural tools leads to a transcultural identity. Further, these cultural tools do not "belong" exclusively to one dominant culture but are the product of many cultures over time. I reject the "us" and "them" mentality that suggests that any educational intervention is chauvinistic and robs others of their culture. The culture of poverty does not belong to SPARs only but to those who have co-constructed it and benefited from it. While it is true that many dominant group interventions have been devastating to native cultures historically and are quite ethnocentric, I do not believe in discarding the educated baby with (the malpractices in) the water. Further, I believe that the interventions inherent in the present educational system, including those based on critical pedagogy or cultural literacy, are much more imperialistic, unethical, and deficit motivated than my approach. In effect, the problem is not of educational interventions but how best to intervene and from whose perspective it is to be carried out and evaluated.

3. Note that the target is equity at grade level as the key step although group differences for the proportion of those above grade level would remain.

4. Semiotic in this sense denotes symbolic.

5. Labor and capital analyses point to the structural aspects of inequality, particularly in economic terms regarding distribution, transfer, and production. It is frequently argued that the educational system cannot transcend the economic one and that the latter uses education to sustain and reproduce itself.
6. Alternatives such as hip-hop, sports, and other subcultural patterns and activities that promote other social identities.
7. Women continue to earn a quarter less than men for every dollar.

Part II

A Cultural Approach *to a* Historical Problem

Overview

This section presents a comprehensive model to promote the development of poverty-bound children who are left behind by the present system. It is based in part on some existing approaches that are integrated within the components of a new developmental framework. Because SPARs are already disadvantaged before they enter school and fall further behind, the problem must be understood developmentally and requires concerted actions within and outside schools. The gap originates long before schools create glaring gaps in achievement or grade level performance. SPARs are placed behind in our educational system in great part because schools are class dependent. It is not that the system is failing in general, but it is failing those students who are in a class/culture different from that for which it was designed and for those who remain in power.

Class and culture interact in ways that are inseparable. Low-SES involuntary minorities learn and develop in qualitatively different ways from their middle- and upper-SES counterpart groups. The educational system works for some better than others, even within cultural groups. For the system to work effectively and more fairly, greater compatibility, flexibility, and assistance with students' level of development, home environment, and culture needed. Part of this problem has been resolved by advanced and gifted programs that challenge advanced students or those in special education. However, at the heart of the current crisis in education lies an inability to educate SPARs, at least to grade-level standards, thus creating 3–4-year gaps. Using a computer analogy, we may explain the problem in terms of a CD-RW incompatibility issue. The SPAR is initially like a program (on a CD) that is being co-constructed as it encounters different (cultural) systems. SPARs go back and forth across settings (home to school to others), interacting and programming themselves with what is culturally available and compatible. The interactive programs offered at school generally are less compatible with SPARs', producing cumulative errors that compromise future instruction and learning in later grades. SPARs are labeled and assessed below proficient by a school system not itself proficient in educating SPARs.

Schooling also may be regarded figuratively as sponsoring a race to a goal (graduation). Students participate in age cohorts, are trained, educated, tracked, and assessed. The educational system expects each student to willingly be guided by educators who provide attitudinal, affective, motivational and academic efforts. To close the gap, differential factors external to schooling would have to be neutralized to allow SPARs to gain ground relative to others. Placing already disadvantaged students, many of whom have not had adequate preschool, into elementary schools that fail to organize extra assistance sustains the reproduction of GBI in educational outcomes. Once this gap in grade level performance is created, it is widened programmatically upon entry into middle and high schools, where the system offers less and less sensitive instruction while raising the bar as peer influences reign.

Schools employ tests to assign students into high, medium and low tracks so that their predictive validity is indeed fulfilled through the learning environments offered. Involved parents ensure their students obtain the best and most challenging treatments within schools. They advocate for better programs and teachers, or they are willing to move their children towards better schools and districts. SPARs may be as intelligent and competent yet attend classrooms where instruction, content, and class-effects constrain academic progress. By fourth grade, the original small gap in first grade is much wider, compromising subsequent efforts and fulfilling the prediction (Entwisle, Alexander & Karp, 1992).

In order to benefit from current educational opportunities and compete educationally, the failures to promote not only individual learning but improve the context surrounding future SPARs need to be eliminated in and out of schools. The achievement gap is not the fault of schools, teachers, students, ethnic cultures, or families. It is a complex problem that has been constructed in and out of school over time. Therefore, any effective approach must target the root causes for group differences in compatibility. It must include strategies for mutual social change not only through multicultural education but also new ways to maximize home, community, and societal structures that require us to think out of the box. What would happen if the resources now employed for sports in school were to be channeled toward SPARs' academic learning? What if sports were left up to communities to sponsor? The time, space, and activity now devoted to promoting national pastimes might be prioritized differently as long as SPARs remain undereducated. A national investment may also be called for in assisting SPARs' need for a special or more effective education.

4 A Multilevel Plan for Eradicating Inequality in Education

Primary Prevention Promotion as a Lynchpin for Sustaining Academic Success

"All this will not be finished in the first one hundred days. Nor will it be finished in the first thousand days, nor in the life of this administration, nor even perhaps in our lifetime on this planet. But let us begin."

—FROM THE INAUGURATION OF JOHN F. KENNEDY, JANUARY, 20, 1961

Introduction

One way to approach the achievement gap from a policy standpoint is to ask the following question: What changes in current structures and practices might lower the correlation between children's ethno-cultural and economic history and their school achievement? Given that the achievement gap has been historically determined by virtue of compounding poverty, lesser educational opportunities, and expectations with ethnicity—and, in many cases, long periods of oppression—what might the best strategies be for reversing the cultural incompatibility that has been created? We know this incompatibility between school culture and low SES increases over time for students placed at risk. The plan offered here outlines a new direction for guiding reform efforts to reverse many of the mechanisms that concentrate the gap in some populations.

Figure 4–1: How Poverty Is Associated with the Gap[1]

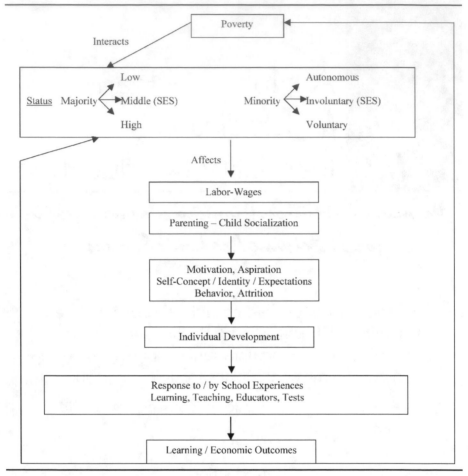

The three most important predictors of school success remain parent involvement, adult-child ratios, and academic learning time, as noted earlier. These are no accident since they are quite interrelated. All three maximize learning activity related to what schools expect, teach, and value and are directly related to social class and tests. The adult present or level of assistance in the home and school available for tasks and experiences valued at school seems, in fact, to account for how parental involvement is defined. Of course, other variables exist that are also important in determining achievement differences that vary in their susceptibility to change (Portes, Dunham, & Williams, 1986). What is needed then is a brainy, reliable way to ensure that combinations of factors are maximized and integrated in the lives of SPARs from underrepresented groups at multiple levels. We need to understand the reasons why some variables such as teaching characteristics (content and instructional expertise), leadership, collaboration, and similar school factors differ from others structured socially from a multifaceted view.[2] It cannot be expected that interventions focusing on individual level factors such as self-esteem or character can close the gap any more than vouchers or high expectations at other levels. A comprehensive plan must direct strategies toward a common purpose and anticipate the social impact and costs of altering learning or economic outcomes (see Figure 4–1).

The plan centers on restructuring our system of education so that the usual groups of children are not disproportionally those left behind. The issue of the gap revolves around the quality of educational outcomes. A smart restructuring effort needs to tap the main factors that account for school success. For it to be reliable enough to reduce the gap in achievement, the effort must become an integral part of the system of education, at least until group-based differences in achievement become negligible. There will always be poverty and a gap in terms of individual differences in intellectual performance as well as income. The crux of the problem is inequality reproduced by the relative differences sustained by our educational system's segregation (Orfield, Frankenberg & Lee, 2003).

Current high-stakes reform plans do not target directly the massive, between-group inequality in educational outcomes as a primary concern. It is not an equitable reform at all because exhorting educators to do more (of the same) cannot possibly narrow the present gap where it is most needed. Delivering a variety of add-on programs intermittently, usually when extra funding is sporadically available, does not provide the necessary supports for SPARs' journey through the system. The reforms' attempt to produce higher test scores relies mostly, if not completely, on a school-based analysis of the problem. Yet, the problem of inequality in school achievement extends well beyond schools.

Requirements of a Reorganization Plan in Education

Educators and policymakers need to think and function more like engineers, designing and implementing a system locally that consistently educates SPARs at grade level from preschool preparation to college. The plan and strategies require support across districts and states for group differences to be minimized. What a preschool or elementary grade(s) initiates at one level must be sustained later at other levels. As those students enter secondary school, the activities and goals of the restructured system may change but what has to remain consistent is a commitment to equity as test scores are raised. The plan must include ways to advance parent education proactively to maximize intellectual and social development.

The model is based on a simple question: What would be required to attain the goals of equity and excellence? It is not based on what is now most likely to occur but what would be progressively required to eradicate a four-year gap in grade level for those groups now left behind. The model serves as a prototype to correct the inequities that make the current educational system unfair to some disempowered groups. A system that is fair to some does not have to be unfair to others. It can be redesigned to meet new specifications and produce outcomes that allow SPARs to participate more fully in a meritocracy. The strategy must extend beyond school to other social contexts that place the child's academic or literacy development at risk over time in seamless fashion. Participation in social activities often results in tools for development[3] being forged that, in turn, depend on activities over time. These tools are amplified over time and govern future development. Unless new, strategically timed educational activities involve SPARs across various contexts, SPARs will not benefit similarly from schooling.

Timing and Development

The rate of development is largely determined by the quality of supports available during periods of rapid change in the individual's growth. The formative years are critical since development proceeds at the rate at which it is started and sustained. To minimize the effects of poverty on academic development, a parallel system of support needs to be applied so that schooling becomes more meaningful, fair, and effective. The direction and extent of support activities are linked with the schedule present within and across grade levels in school. Therefore, it is of utmost importance to ensure that SPARs' development is not delayed for lack of preparedness and meaningful learning in the school. The delivery capacity in the home of high-achieving students needs to be approximated for SPARs at some levels and at some times.

Our society has agreed on a schedule based on chronological age that sets minimum standards for when the learner should acquire certain knowledge and tools. Students performing outside the regularly scheduled cultural program[4] eventually require special education. Schools attempt to do this by speeding up or slowing down instructional content standards and pace in ways that now affect SPARs' potential for development. Most schools have not found effective ways to meet the special education needs of SPARs for whom schooling becomes aversive and difficult. They often adopt counter-identities, feel threats, resist, or learn to accept the status quo. In sum, school will continue to penalize the student at-risk unless educational processes are reorganized to generate assistance for comparable grade level performance across groups in terms of minimum standards.

Time management is a particular cultural artifact so related to cultural values and goals that it becomes almost invisible as a sorting tool. The educational system runs according to a clock that is imposed on all students on the basis of chronological age, presuming learning conditions outside are equal when in fact they are not. Unlike golf, there is no handicap for the three- to five-year gaps found when most SPARs graduate. Imagine a K–12 system where more advanced students leave one to two years early, and SPARs stay one to two years longer. Failure to keep up with scheduled tasks is blamed on a variety of factors, mainly those pertaining to the individual, educators, or the parents' community. The latter are blamed for learning conditions outside not being equal, yet little is being done on a national scale.[5] Even when help is provided, SPARs as a group cannot catch up sufficiently to reap the benefits of a high-standards education. Time devoted to meaningful academic learning and guided social skills must be increased for SPARs before motivation and optimism wane. Only after a network of new opportunities replaces extant conditions can a sufficient number of SPARs begin to capitalize on them. Only then might the gap begin to close for underrepresented populations to level and embark on a course of excellence. Another option is to place less emphasis on chronological age and more on criterion-referenced performance.

One option for adolescents already lagging behind in school, at the very least, is learning how to become more savvy, socially competent parents of future SPARs during this period. Effective parent involvement with respect to schooling ensures children have models, extra encouragement, and time for academic learning or guided participation to compete and collaborate in school. These are attributes of middle SES and generally of a college education. Regardless of students' current home situation, however, certain seeds for change[6] can be planted in activating this most crucial out-of-school factor during secondary school. If poverty constrains certain types of knowledge that affect learning and adaptation, a more concerted effort to share such knowledge directly seems fair and essential in a graded system that is unlikely to change.

Primary Prevention and Time

Primary prevention is a means for attacking a negative condition before it compromises development and becomes increasingly difficult and costly to treat. It is a strategy used in medicine through which healthy development can be maximized economically and effectively. It is essentially a cultural tool that remains untapped in educational policy and practice. Ironically, it is education that provides the most powerful means for (social) change through prevention and promotion activities in schools.

Educational primary intervention represents the most powerful means in activating "the missing half" of the equation for narrowing the one standard deviation gap in scholastic performance noted earlier. No approach has yet proven effective in accomplishing this reduction. This missing half concerns family socialization patterns (P.R. Portes & Vadeboncoeur, 2003) that favor children's development. It concerns a broader understanding of what parent involvement really means and is by far the most important factor in determining academic success. Transforming the goals and content of secondary education to promote change in the next generation of parents, particularly of SPARs, is necessary. Modifying the ways we educate SPARs from K–12 is also essential. Unfortunately, major initiatives focusing on families and schools (see Epstein, 1995) have not reduced the gap significantly for efforts come too little and too late in secondary level interventions.

A historical, mediated action approach would focus on altering various contexts through which incompatibility is constructed between SPARs' home and school life developmentally. It would help prevent and reverse many of the processes that currently place low SES students at risk before they actually become risks. For example, some argue that the gap is due to tracking and other unfair school-based practices (Oakes et al., 2000). However, from a sociocultural perspective, this amounts to confusing cause and effect. Tracking is a "within-school" response to a deeper-seated (out of school) problem that has yet to be addressed nationally. As noted earlier, what happens before and after school is equally, if not more important, than what happens in school insofar as the establishment and maintenance of cultural incompatibility is concerned. Schooling (and its effectiveness) is so intertwined with the sociohistorical context as to have baffled the social science and educational community for decades.[7]

A Developmental Approach to Transformation

A lifespan-developmental model calls for a set of concerted actions in mediating the development of children from cultures placed at risk (see Figure 4–2). It consists of organizing action at four levels (better preschool preparation for all SPARs, elementary school supports, a life-skills adolescent curriculum, and higher education transformation in preparing educatiors and decision-makers). This model is interactive; all four components are designed to work together to have a significant population effect. It is economical relative to what the present system is costing our society in terms of uneven educational outcomes and their social consequences. It can also be extended beyond the United States.

First, education can be employed preventively for planting the seeds of a sociocognitive support system for SPARs. The home environment has been the most difficult factor to tap and remains a top challenge ever since inequality became an urgent social issue in our society. Targeting adolescents as future parents is a new strategy oriented towards promoting the growth of a future generation of children (who would then be assisted through the other

Figure 4–2. A Developmental Lifecycle Model for Primary Prevention: Preparing Parents, Educators, and Children

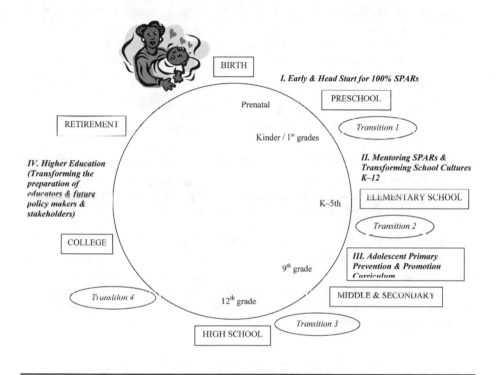

components). Once the parents of future SPARs, who are now adolescents in our schools, learn and participate in the proposed curriculum workshops, they become more knowledgeable and likely to engage their family in the future with skills (see Chapter Five). First, the component helps adolescents directly to some extent, but it mostly helps the next generation. This first component consists of sponsoring the maximum development in a double stimulation approach. This cultural/culturing change promotes critical child socialization concepts and practices as part of the standard curriculum of secondary schools. This approach to education helps build comparable "cultural models" (Gallimore & Goldenberg, 2001) in educators and peers in and out of school. A cost-benefit analysis can easily justify the economic resources to be expended for prevention. The other components build on the adolescent life-skills omponent with:

a.   All young, poor, competent children having access to effective Head Start and other preschool programs (see Chapter Six).

b. Once in elementary school, they would encounter a new set of supports in and out of school to stay at grade level each year (see Chapter Seven). It also calls for college students and retired personnel to participate in the plan by serving as mentors in after-school programs.

c. As adolescents, they would continue to have extra academic support as they complete the first generation cycle. In secondary schools, they would complete the cycle and participate in human development workshops to be structured as an integral part of the educational system. In addition to providing SPARs full coverage or support as they grow, direct academic supports in and out of school would be sustained to prevent the gap from emerging.

d. The last component requires transformations in the professional preparation of educators and other college students in higher education. They need to be prepared with a more complete knowledge base of the gap and primary prevention.

Once the full system is in place, a more level playing field can begin to be established and free children from many of the constraints now imposed by poverty and GBI. Society may also become more ethical through a system of educational practices powerful enough to reproduce less inequality. Excellence would be more easily attained since eventually all groups would perform at grade level.

Coordination of Components: Rationale and General Description

If one were to understand that K–12 education serves not only children but also future parents, secondary schooling would be recognized readily as a golden opportunity to influence SPARs' (future) social context. The latter is so often criticized (the home environment). Figure 4–2 sketches how the four major components would alter the educational system in the life cycle of SPARs. A primary reason why current preschool and school-related programs are unable to close the gap[8] is precisely because constraints existing in the home culture or outside context remain essentially unaffected, and efforts are disconnected. In these activity settings, the personnel available to the child differ from those who are not being placed at risk. They have different scripts and routines, values, and expectations (Whiting & Edwards, 1988; Weisner, Gallimore & Jordan, 1988). They place different demands on the child and interact differently around different goals (Lareau, 1989). How best to make the home context more compatible with school and less constraining for the child that is otherwise placed at risk? A preventive, historical approach thus calls for policy changes in the ways that secondary education is presently organized.

Everyone must understand that education is about culturing (Goldenberg, Reese and Gallimore, 1992). Culturing involves the teaching and learning of tools and concepts that facilitate adaptation. It is empowering in different ways and for different purposes. To be cultured, one must learn to master certain tools that promote, in turn, access for further development. They tend to be symbolic and depend on certain types of social activity. Since social class mediates different types of activities, the focus for change centers on those most influential in preparing children for school. Not only in terms of the basic curricula and content areas but also in more subtle ways, what is taught or not taught matters for each generation. Most high school youth will eventually become parents and engage in social and parenting practices that are rarely (closely) examined. Children may or may not be served by Head Start. Only a few that enter elementary school will receive the support necessary to reach or exceed grade level performance. Of those, only a few will complete college. Hence, a comprehensive plan must not provide only food and health care. It must go much further to eradicate GBI in knowledge, skills, and opportunities. It must strive toward developing a seamless support system for external socially mediated activities alongside those offered in school for SPARs. This compensatory assistance must be timed and based on a lifecycle, cognitive-developmental approach at least until equity in educational outcomes is achieved for SPARs subject to GBI. The trajectory from preschool, elementary school and adolescent periods must be coordinated with contexts and activities that promote academic and social development. At present, some of these activities exist but are considered extracurricular (e.g., boys and girls clubs, Big Brother/Sister programs) and are happenstance. The effect on SPAR groups is negligible.

Among the first patterns that contribute to students being placed at risk is that of timing in relation to resources. In terms of understanding the origins of disadvantage, there is probably not a more powerful means to place children at-risk than this type of asynchrony. The manner in which the pace is set now allows 80% of non-SPAR students to learn at grade level (Haycock, 2001). By having most SPARs performing below grade level early, the whole system acts in a way that castigates them. Byproducts of this situation can be observed in the adolescent population. For example, resistance, disidentification (Steele, 1997) or low-effort optimism (Ogbu, 1992) help account for the lack of motivation in SPARs. Immigrant SPARs tend to have higher achievement motivation yet not all of them (P.R. Portes, 1999; A. Portes & Rumbaut, 2001). By the same token, not all black and Latino students react with resistance, low-effort optimism, or receive less parental support.

Timing is a critical issue when adolescents reach cognitive maturity and, for the first time, can develop abstract formal skills. This capacity is not tapped outside of academic areas. These skills are promoted in academic areas mostly, in classes for the more advanced students. Considerable evidence exists of tracking that leaves SPARs busy mastering concrete basic skills for the most part (Oakes, 1990). This is then reflected not only by test scores that serve as barriers to entering college but also in other pervasive ways that leave SPARs not knowing how far they have been left behind.

As SPARs become disenfranchised from economic opportunities to advance, they adapt once again as a new generation that reconstructs what has been termed the culture of poverty, low culture, the underclass and similar terms. Some attempt to strike back,[9] while others find alternative ways for breaking out of a cycle that unfortunately confines most SPARs. Adolescent SPARs and others could benefit from activities that promote social development, particularly when they learn to think abstractly as future parents and citizens. Yet the formal operational thinking that is required for understanding the ways that intergenerational poverty and the market-economy works is rarely a topic in the schooling these students receive like so many others. Social justice, character education, life skills, conflict resolution, and other psychoeducational activities are loosely linked with the academic gap. What then might adolescents learn in high school that would help them understand adolescent and young adulthood issues, effective parent involvement, and a host of issues related to health, economics, and human relations? A change in curriculum introduces new competencies in SPARs' present development in reliable fashion. When logical reasoning skills are promoted in key social and economic areas, SPARs become empowered and are more likely to guide their children out of poverty.

What Is Needed and Why

Pre-parenting education is not being explored systematically as a technology or tool for cultural change in high schools. Yet, it is this tool in particular that promotes key factors that are associated with academic success (e.g., time on task, adult-student ratio, modeling). Each year large cohorts of future parents leave the school system without the needed "supplies" (Caplan, 1964) or the sociopsychological knowledge and skills to:

a. Break out of the cycle of poverty, or at least,
b. Nurture their offspring's sociocognitive development so they do not fall behind.

Primary prevention has yet to be infused in our system of education for this purpose, particularly for those who do not have the informal curriculum prevalent in middle-class homes. Educational policy is missing a most powerful and strategic opportunity to influence the cognitive environments of children before they become "at-risk." Few have thought of activating this field deliberately and systematically to prevent the host of social and psychological problems that eventually cost millions to society. It is a fertile area for loosening the grip of poverty and optimizing sociocultural change pluralistically. In fact, it seems critical that parenting skills based on a multicultural foundation be developed. Once in place, this would contribute to the long-term success of pre-school and elementary compensatory education programs.

Poverty constrains development of knowledge and reasoning skills. So do schools for SPARs. Educators need to understand that while many fine programs are "out there" that focus on different problems and levels and that succeed from time to time, a comprehensive approach is still needed to integrate and guide change. With a common knowledge base and strategy, collaboration at various levels can prevent students from remaining below grade level.

Educators in general and pre-service teachers in particular need to know more about how effective collaboration can emerge with equity as a primary goal. Since educators already come together for various purposes in local schools, we must distinguish how this model is different from current practices that remain ineffective. Continuous improvement of student outcomes appears as the common goal that is regularly assessed by educators. This requires a different type of collaboration from the more typical top-down meetings often observed. Surely the latter are useful, but we must ask, "How different is the collaboration found in schools that produce dramatic improvements in the school achievement of SPARs?" How do meetings with teachers focusing on SPARs and content areas such as math, reading, writing, integrated curricula, cooperative learning, and grade-level teacher discussions differ across schools? What types of theoretical and applied knowledge do educators need in transforming education? Subsequent chapters attempt to provide a partial answer.

It is much more effective, efficient, and economical to influence development early. This principle applies not only to SPARs but those being prepared to educate them. Most of the literature on outstanding schools where SPARs thrive stems from elementary schools, suggesting changing the school culture is more difficult later on. It is not difficult to understand why. First, teachers vary more for students in secondary school. Under this new plan, SPARs subject to GBI might be grouped with others in cohorts with educators who have succeeded before with keeping SPARs at or above grade level. Second, once SPARs enter the middle grades, most are already behind grade level since only a few elementary schools prevent the gap. Middle schools generally draw students from different elementary schools. The gap is instrumental in constraining middle and high school teachers' effectiveness or probability of helping students catch up. Third, collaboration across elementary, middle and secondary teachers that focus on the SPAR is practically nonexistent and infrequent across grades. Fourth, discontinuity in school cultures focused on the learning and teaching of SPARs across (and within) schools is common. Hence, an integrated approach is required.

Other Aspects of the Model

Counselors and principals can assist teachers more if they were all prepared early in:

a. Helping create a school culture where professionals come together regularly to assist struggling students; Year-round schools in areas with high SPAR concentrations seem a must. Other means to maximize quality learning and teaching exist.
b. Finding assistance for those students by capable others in the community; something that assists teachers to work more effectively; After school programs that serve all SPARs effectively can employ college and community mentors.
c. Monitoring student progress across classes and helping SPARs to avoid falling behind in grade level through regular dynamic assessments; and
d. Promoting shared learning among school faculty in support of shared goals.

When educators are assisted in their instructional role, students benefit the most. There are several ways to maximize the conditions for learning in the classroom externally. What educators can accomplish in the classroom remains the critical factor in closing the gap, yet much can be done in ensuring that SPARs benefit as much as others in this regard. In Chapter Eight, we address a way to meet some of the needs and content for preparing educators as prevention specialists for closing the gap. With advanced preparation, the myth and reality of educators as disempowered or co-opted agents in an unfair system can be addressed. With a common knowledge base and strategy, collaboration at various levels can prevent students from remaining below grade level. This component offers multiple advantages.

A more comprehensive preparation for educators that focuses squarely on closing the gap helps provide overdue professional respect and empowers educators to work together effectively. There is no reason for front-line educators to be uninformed or undereducated about these key issues concerning equity and excellence. Field experience is surely necessary but need not compete with higher professional knowledge that might make teaching and learning more effective and equitable.

At the instructional level, approaches grounded in learning theory easily outperform empirical, traditional ones (Karpov & Bransford, 1995). Similarly, practices informed by well-supported theory can bring about significant gains as shown by reciprocal teaching (Palincsar & Brown, 1984), cooperative learning (Slavin, 1990) and well-designed instruction (Gagné, 1977). Educators require greater understanding of these human development and learning principles, and students' and schools' cultural models. For rooting out GBI, content and pedagogical knowledge are crucial.

Educators need to know, as part of their preparation, about how to transform their local practices and structures in ways supported by research. For example, a collaborative model helped reduce the achievement gap in a predominantly minority school (Goldenberg & Sullivan, 1994). How this was achieved required those educators to collaborate more than usual, based on shared goals, with performance feedback to guide their new practices, assistance from capable others, and a leader who provided support and helped maintain a steady course. Rather than having teachers work mostly as isolated professionals in a cellular model, closing the gap requires professionals to work together regularly as part of developing a learning community. But how can educators change from working mostly alone in the classroom to a collaborative model aimed at improving students' learning? This requires a change in the culture of the school and a sense of common purpose. In contexts where conditions change to promote such collaboration, at least four elements are involved. These appear closely related to what we have found in the exceptional schools where the gap has been dramatically reduced. Educators collaborate first when they share the common goal of assisting those generally left behind. Secondly, they seek multiple indicators to guide their practices. Thirdly, in these working conditions, a culture of mutual assistance emerges where support is lent at every level; from principal and counselor to teacher, from teacher to volunteers and from more advanced students to other students. A fourth factor in this model is that of nurturing leadership where both support and modest pressure is exerted on all participants. Principals assist educators, and educators assist students in a loop focused on closing the gap and dynamic assessment.

In sum, how the gap has been closed in some sites and how some schools beat the odds, producing unexpectedly high educational outcomes, remains a mystery to most. A new knowledge base is emerging in this area that is yet to be integrated with that found in higher education. Changing the culture of school where SPARs remain below grade level requires educators to collaborate more strategically, based upon shared goals that serve to organize their daily practices and routines. Unlike typical meetings where members often feel discussions don't lead to improvement, performance feedback regarding SPARs is an important staple in collaborative meetings focused on goal-directed actions. Feedback to guide and readily adjust practices leads to organizing mutual assistance from capable others. Leadership provides support and helps maintain a steady course within a collaborative framework. Educators in general, and pre-service teachers and counselors in particular, need to understand how effective collaboration (Goldenberg & Sullivan, 1994) emerges with equity as a primary goal and leads to exceptionally powerful schools. The latter are generally part of the explanation for successful schools that in spite of obstacles succeed in helping SPARs achieve at or above grade-level standards. Community partnerships and technology support can also help. In many cases, schools reach out and involve the community in ways that make education more effective for children (Maeroff, 1998b; Rose, 1995; Slavin, 2002a). Sometimes they manage without extra funding and, seemingly, through sheer determination.

Conclusions and Potential Drawbacks

Current policy is too fragmented and fails to coordinate support efforts directly or consistently for SPARs. Its narrow focus on test scores does not result in academic nor social progress. Re-thinking how secondary schooling can be organized to minimize the effects of poverty in future generations is essential to a developmental approach. Thus far, efforts to impact SPARs' parent involvement have been unsuccessful because not only are too few available, but they come too late. The SPARs who would most benefit from parental support in academic work are the least likely to obtain it. There is little evidence that parent involvement or parent education programs are effective in closing the gap. An ideal timing would be before and during the time a family is first forming. Unfortunately, a primary prevention approach entails intervening before susceptible groups are affected as a whole, and effects require time to document. High school is the only time when whole groups of future parents are gathered and can develop formal reasoning with respect to family life and child development. It is during this time that the academic curriculum attempts to promote abstract reasoning in math, science, and other academic areas. Yet, this is the only time when those who most need to know about principles of human development in relation to family life might receive it. We know that it is generally during early adolescence that formal operational or higher-level thinking skills begin to be learned.

Two potential criticisms must be considered before the model is presented in greater detail:

a. The proposed changes are too much like (Big Brother) "social engineering." Even if it were to produce more comparable distributions in academic achievement across groups, it would be imperialistic and politically incorrect to intervene in others' culture to promote academic-support values.

The response to this point requires noting interventions that are actually in effect already do place large proportions of students at risk and in poverty. The cycle of poverty that results and engulfs some groups is largely the cause of practices in the home and school that place students in peril or have caused cultural incompatibilities. Hence, why not recognize the effect of past actions and reverse the most damaging ones until equity is achieved?

The other critique is more problematic:

b. Closing the achievement gap may remove one of the last obstacles for advancing equity in our society but does not guarantee an end to intergenerational or low status poverty. Even if all SPARs were at grade level, relative differences would remain that would still leave SPARs behind in many other (economic) areas.

The response to this point is that while poverty is likely to remain associated with ethnic membership, it need not be produced directly by this system to cause a disproportionate segment to perform below grade level. Perhaps the real problem here is the immorality of poverty itself for those who actually do work (Gans, 1995). As Noddings (1996) cogently argues, "Poverty is a moral problem, not an educational one. No person who works at a legitimate job should live in poverty" (p. 287). The aim in proposing the above framework is based on the belief that intervening for greater equity in learning outcomes is better than not intervening more proactively or accepting past and current approaches that remain ineffective and unfair to SPARs. The belief here is also that a great part of the problem has been the lack of an alternative approach and historical perspective of the problem. Reducing GBI offers a straightforward, more equitable strategy towards achieving excellence and promoting higher test scores and competencies.

A Lifespan Plan for Promoting SPARs' Development

This multilevel plan calls for a major reform of how middle and high school curricula and educational activities are now organized. A space and time for a life skills curriculum needs to be constructed in schools for adolescents to gain life skills before they graduate from high school. This calls for a curriculum extension at a time when most SPARs are already very much behind. Those who focus only on test score gains and accountability might well oppose it since academic learning time might be threatened. This view is contested as being narrow and against a broader perspective of the goals of education. It misses the target because it ignores the root causes for the gap and the value of critical thinking. Adolescent SPARs are generally so far behind that a very limited effect can be expected from the high-stakes movement alone. They are also capable of developing critical thinking if adequate conditions are introduced. While it is important to support SPARs' potential for learning academically, a broader scope in assisting the next generation's development seems worthwhile.

In the proposed spiral curriculum, many of the current occasional[10] efforts for life skills development, service learning, home economics, school to work, and prevention programs could be integrated nationally. This would create opportunities for active discussion of problems facing teens today and in the future. Problem-solving and decision-making skills are but a few of the skills that need to be promoted. Fostering cognitive strategies and higher-level thinking in context with adolescent issues is critical for strengthening the family as an institution. The contention here is that SPARs' development can be assisted most effectively before birth and without imposing a particular viewpoint or set of values. What is important is that various actions and their possible consequences are regularly considered during this time of transition. Adolescence offers the greatest opportunity for promoting cultural change, particularly if a strategy is well coordinated before and in higher education.

A Multiple-Focus Curriculum Change

School districts focus mostly on academic learning and sports. How might they be persuaded that other, "less" academic content knowledge in human development is important and can be used to foster higher level thinking skills, and an equity to close the gap? School-based programs[11] can be directed at future parents in ways that maximize their involvement as well as providing youth with life skills in a variety of areas. A spiral curriculum would also foster critical thinking in other areas of current interest to school programs (e.g., safety, health, drug prevention, conflict resolution, mentoring, character education, test-taking skills, parenting, sex and economic education). In housing under one roof a variety of initiatives to impact positively on SPARs at different points in their development, greater political support may be found.

Loops of Collaboration

The transformation of education being proposed in this book, while focused squarely on closing the achievement gap, can also impact positively on a number of interrelated factors that promote excellence. The question, however, is complex at the application level. For example, in the secondary school component, "Where do we begin? What exactly is in the new curriculum? What are the best social learning methods? How are the personnel roles to change?" In this next part, a guide to transformation is presented. In

Figure 4–3: Promoting Collaborative School Cultures and Assistance to SPARs

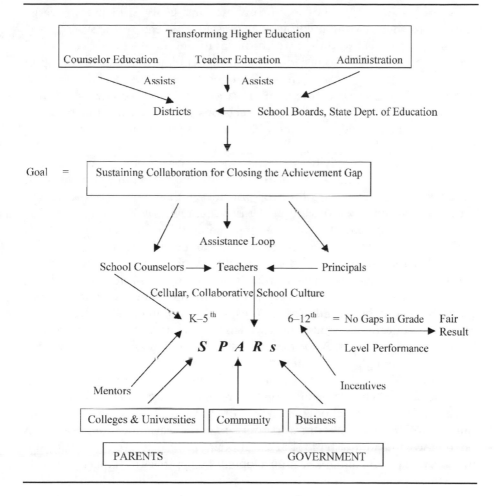

Figure 4–3, the focus is on three types of educators who, at the molecular level, must collaborate to change school cultures. They each need the others' assistance in order to educate students effectively as students and future parents. There is need for a common knowledge base and set of goals in order to close the gap. The base can be, in great part, constructed by transforming the way higher education prepares educators. That, in turn, requires changes at the university level.

Figure 4–3 shows how different needs are distributed. The principal needs to respond to the superintendent, PTA, and community in general and ensure compliance with school district policies. District personnel respond to school boards that may vary in their willingness to close the gap with decisions such as school or class sizes (Klonsky & Ford, 1994). The teacher needs assistance from above to teach effectively a variety of students and to rouse their interest and learning of specific instructional goals. Students with large gaps in prerequisite content knowledge present problems to the system, particularly to teachers who deal with unfavorable student–teacher ratios and learning histories. The counselor or school psychologist attempts to help in decisions concerning the assignment of students to teachers, dealing with students' needs and those of the administrator. Routines become established each fall that concern thousands of decisions that set in motion how the school will operate and determine what the most important goals are collectively and individually.

Amidst the many activities of each school and classroom, we must ask key questions. To what extent do our frontline educators view the elimination of the achievement gap as one of the top priorities in their work? To what extent is this goal the common thread and motive that regulates decisions? To what extent is there an understanding that in pursuing this goal relentlessly, a facilitation of other important educational goals can be effected?

Rather than focus on only one community of educators such as school counselors, principals, or teachers, transformation of the professional training of all educators is deemed necessary within the conceptual framework reflected in this book. Educators must have a common knowledge base regarding educational equity and excellence, of cultural history and related concepts and principles. A sociocultural approach allows for changes at various levels. Although transforming the roles and functions of schools is a principal aim, it is clear that all educators must be involved in closing the gap.

The cultural change being proposed here is perhaps as radical as ending segregation between schools, tracking, or imposing higher standards. Not only do we propose that educators reorganize the way education is, and can be, defined and administered, but we also aim to restructure the curriculum in reflecting prioritized goals. A developmental approach is required to close the achievement gap in a reliable and democratic fashion. Ending GBI in educational outcomes through this approach might replace the NCLB and No Excuses slogans. It serves as a primary focus and as an organizing principle for public education. On its coattails, challenging education for students at all levels becomes the modus operandi regardless of age. College education and income are still predicated on how much learning a school produces or facilitates in a set number of years. Unless we are willing to level learning activities and opportunities to learn for children regardless of their background, inequality will hound our sense of ethics. The gap cannot close when SPARs fail to be prepared by age four and when they are allowed to fall behind grade levels before secondary school. The gap presents us with the foremost of scientific problems of our times in education and social science. It inextricably links tools, the family life, culture, and time as determinants that mediate development both individually and at the group level.

Defining Success

Thus far, solutions have been advanced to improve schools through particular models (effective schools, accelerated learning, vouchers, and multicultural educators) that call for the active manipulation of certain variables believed to affect achievement. Regardless of how successful they have proven to be in some districts or how they may have increased academic learning time and meaningful learning, we must ask why have not all the others followed suit? Can they? Why has there not been a general approach that once proven effective, can be implemented across the board with similar success (see Goldenberg & Gallimore, 1991)? Furthermore, how do we know that the primary prevention, developmental approach in this book will be any different?

In order to address these issues, it is essential to first define how success is defined. Improving a school's overall achievement average relative to the years prior depends on what happens at the classroom level, the types of students, teachers, methods used and levels of external (parent) involvement.

The achievement gap concerning international or interstate comparisons must thus be distinguished from the GBI gap in achievement before going any further. It may be argued that by closing the former, the nation is less at risk and that in any case, part of the effect benefits those affected by GBI, although they will remain significantly below the mainstream. This is the excellence without equity position that seems to be in vogue today (Thernstrom & Thernstrom, 2003). I argue that significant improvement in our educational system must be based from the start on reducing the gap related to students placed at risk by GBI. Further, the argument here is that this can be achieved without degrading the system for those at or above the achievement distribution.

In this book, it is argued that where miraculous or exceptional improvements have been recorded (aside from insulated, segregated private schools), the effect has been achieved by practices that unlock the learning potential of students at the bottom of the distribution who are those that most schools place at risk. The improvement is situated locally and will not be likely to be easily exported unless we understand and harness the fundamental aspects of the problem. The improvement indexed by higher test scores is generally reflective of a host of coordinated actions constructed locally in the school culture by a critical mass of educators. They share certain beliefs, collaborate toward a common purpose, and are fortunate to have support from outside the school. As with "gifted students," these exceptional school cultures rarely emerge (i.e., 3–5% of the time). They have student bodies with a high proportion of students placed at risk and outperform those with similar proportions. In these school cultures, a pattern is formed by interactions, decisions, and practices responsive to feedback long before others notice the anomaly in the school's average performance on standardized tests. The intersecting of several key factors that keep being noticed in the literature produces the anomaly that may or may not be sustained.

While the rare occurrences appear serendipitous, they need not be so. In this book, what is proposed is a restructuring of the educational system so that rare successes with SPARs become the norm nationwide, so that we can have a system that educates all students, regardless of background, in ways that produce grade-level performance. The parameters of the present system are redefined, as are its functions. The components of the proposed model are discussed in greater detail next. Their joint effects are regarded as necessary and sufficient in closing the gap as defined by grade-level performance standards at the national level. Once that is achieved at the elementary level, it will be easier to sustain later as adjustments made become more economical.

Summary

The present reforms in school are inadequate for SPARs who are already behind. They allow most to graduate, but few actually benefit as much as those who finish at or above grade level. At this level, the damage is already done, and raising test scores a few points is not as meaningful as preventing this situation from reoccurring en masse. The problem also needs to be considered in context to the gap in college.

The adolescent component needs to be pilot tested, and gradually implemented with the older teens (first). Long-term evaluation is needed programmatically. It will require changes in the ways that we prepare educators to work collaboratively at various levels of the plan. Other components have already proven effective in closing the gap and require broad scaling. In the second component extending effective Head Start to the remaining eligible SPARs who are now left behind is easiest. Programs such as the Abecedarian project (Ramey et al., 2000; Weikart, 1995) clearly show the persistent effects of effective preschool when subsequent support is provided. Their long-term follow-up evaluations show their preventive value for advancing SPARs' development.

After-school programs in elementary and secondary school can then more easily prevent the gap with parental and community support of academic development. When the above actions are combined with transformations within the school culture that prioritize the academic development of SPARs, a new secular trend moves both equity and excellence forward. The remainder of the book is focused on detailing these actions and their implications more specifically. For example, in Chapter Seven, some of the within-school practices that have proven effective in closing the gap are considered. The following chapters address higher education and transforming counselor and teacher education. They include leadership with an excellence through equity agenda.

In sum, a new pedagogy to construct higher-level thinkers is needed for maximizing parent involvement as the adolescent component restructures the educational system. The pre-parenting and life skills workshops in high school need to focus on family functions that are in peril in a postmodern era that hinders the socialization of competent children. The strategy includes assessment of current opportunities in and out of school, short- and long-term goals and changes in curriculum design. A new pedagogy constructs formal operational or higher-level thinking with adolescents but remains to be developed in ways that are not offensive to a variety of stakeholders. Finally, a primary prevention approach that promotes social competencies serves multiple purposes in education and is an essential tool in disarming GBI and strengthening the other components.

While the plan seems to be organized from the earliest roots of the prob lem before and soon after SPARs enter the world, a top-down approach is also important at the policy levels that govern pre-school and K–12 education. This is because the problem of the gap is so robust it must be attacked from several directions simultaneously. The model calls for a unified approach to higher and early childhood education, including how parents are prepared indirectly to support all children's development. This joint preparedness is focused squarely on the elimination of GBI and its instrumentality in establishing educational excellence. The gap was defined operationally in terms of standards-based grade-level performance, for the nation's SPARs.

An important part in the current reform movement is the professional preparation of all educators and policymakers. A shared knowledge base to attack GBI must be integrated in higher education. All future lawmakers, principals, counselors, teachers and stakeholders need to know the score in more ways than one. The roots causes and effects of GBI on SPARs call for a national strategy of inclusion and specialized skills to eradicate inequality based on group membership.

Ethically public education is for the good of the nation and should have comparable effects on literacy development regardless of the child's cultural background. Not only must we learn to deal with time-related practices now in force but also with others that advantage one group over another. For example "homework" and "technology" are still used as sorting mechanisms. It is not that homework per se is bad; it can surely aid development. How it is used, intentionally or not, along with projects and how such activities are valued in academic scorekeeping do matter. Scorekeeping, tests, and grades per se are not bad, but how they are used in the academic socialization process can help reduce inequality and risks for academic failure. Particular grouping arrangements for instructions and development are not, as such, good or bad but how and why these practices are used can be. Finally, our educational goals, and curricula must attend to both the academic and socioemotional development of all student populations over time. In effecting cultural changes through education, ethical dilemmas emerge that serve to question the motives, goals and consequences of any new agenda or innovation. Our response to their question is unequivocal in nature. Given that current policies and interventions have proven unfair and ineffective, bold means for achieving equity in learning seem justified now more than ever.

Endnotes

1. A child born in poverty may fall into the majority or minority groups that vary in terms of how ethnicity and social status interact. Depending on the latter, the child is socialized by different activity patterns that vary in terms of how parenting and socioeconomic variables are associated. In turn, the development of the child is shaped and responds differently to schooling and leads to substantial differences in school learning and development of cultural tools. Thus, poverty may be reproduced in the next generation more often than not within groups according to status.

2. This is why reducing gaps at one level without similar effects at other levels is not an effective strategy for achieving significant reduction of the gap at the population level.

3. In cultural historical theory (Vygotsky, 1978), tools mediate or serve in learning how to learn as the human mind develops and constructs internally various dimensions of the outside world. Literacy in math and reading is a basic mediational tool that allows for adaptation to complex cultural environments. Mentors also serve as resources by guiding the learner through activities such as learning a cognitive strategy to solve a problem. The strategy or formula too is a tool that the learner may acquire during standard instruction at school or outside.

4. Meaning the dominant group's culturing or school-based socialization program defined in terms of academic preparation for work or higher education. The problem is then not only tracking the middle and upper class for college as a sorting function, the issue of equity is even more urgent at the basic level of functional literacy. The massive inequality to first be addressed lies in ensuring minimum standards are met by all groups as measured by grade level or performance standards data. This is the first of many battles or stages that remain in gradually attaining equity in the representation of SPARs by GBI in college, the professions, and similar areas.

5. Clearly programs such as Success for All, Accelerated Schools, Fifth Dimension, and others are helpful but cannot serve the majority of SPARs at present.

6. By change, we mean socialization strategies that would promote greater compatibility between children's development and school-based academic learning.

7. We use the term decades rather than centuries because it took the Civil Rights era to gradually convince the public that quality education is a human right in our society. Today there are sectors proclaiming that all students have a right to learn physics or other areas generally programmed for the few.

8. While some programs (e.g., Success for All, the Abecederian project) have produced significant effects, they have not been scaled broadly or closed the gap as defined by national norms as a consequence. Their effectiveness centers on comparisons with

untreated control groups that place experimental groups at an intermediate level when middle-class students are included (Dunham et al., 1988)

9. "School violence is up" (*USA News,* June 28, 2001, 1).

10. "Occasional" here refers to the fact that many of the aspects of life skills or human development programs are already available and in effect in some schools some of the time for some students. Often they are extracurricular although some regular courses include some of the topics.

11. In making this component school based, we avoid many of the limitations that deter the effectiveness of after-school programs for youth in closing the gap. The latter may be helpful, but like Head Start, are limited to a few and of limited scope. Programs such as those studies by Heath & McLaughlin (1993) are positive but represent a band-aid that is unlikely to change the status quo for most. Yet, much can be learned from such activities in adapting them for primary prevention in school.

The Adolescent Component

New Roles for Educators in Secondary Schools

"All who have meditated on the art of governing
mankind have been convinced that the fate of empires
depends on the education of youth."

—ARISTOTLE

Overview

This chapter outlines a new strategic curricular plan for eradicating the achievement gap that goes beyond current higher standards to help prepare future parents. What is being proposed is that well-prepared educators organize and deliver a human development and life skills curriculum as part of the requirements of a high school education. Through activity-oriented workshops and group work during adolescence, teens can be prepared for critical thinking in parenting and life-long skills in addition to traditional academic/career orientation. The adolescent component is presented before the preschool component because from a primary prevention framework, adolescents are the first direct source of SPAR populations who will be served in pre-K–12 grades. This is a new deliberate plan to activate an essential parental involvement element in a primary prevention strategy to offset major social and economic constraints.

Competencies to be developed in this human development component may be eventually driven by a requirement for graduation. There would be reading, performance, and writing requirements, but the focus would be on activity and group discussions to promote critical thinking about the future and choices about family and work. These activities extend beyond those now offered by educators. Community-based experts, projects, arts, modeling, and similar means can be incorporated. The new curriculum might be offered once per week to all students over a period of years or more often. This "class" might help replace and subsume other psycho-educational, infrequent non-academic interventions. The skills and knowledge co-constructed with adolescents can be connected with community-based after-school programs and service learning to promote development.

The strategy implies a cultural change that is different and more ambitious than current reforms. In influencing youth's social and cognitive development deliberately in specific social competency areas, the preparation of tomorrow's parents is maximized. A basic argument is that even with full pre-school and after-school components; the gap is unlikely to be eradicated because the most important predictor of academic achievement has been left out. Parental involvement cannot be promoted collectively with the current offerings of brief parent involvement and family literacy programs (e.g., Jordan, Snow, & Porche, 2000; Epstein, 1995; National Center for Family Literacy, 2003).

Risk behaviors are often fueled by risk conditions that are difficult for teens to avoid. At-risk students often receive the least challenging education in areas for which they have little motivation once they have fallen grade levels behind. A comprehensive life-skills curriculum approach is outlined and integrated with a "needs assessment."[1] The task is comparable to what is required in physical education in terms of resources. The goal however, is to foster critical thinking skills in adolescents as future parents, who can gain ground in spite of low incomes. As a result, better choices can be made in guiding their children and their future.

This secondary school curriculum centers on a primary prevention treatment for all adolescent students in public school. The goal is to cultivate strategic knowledge about human development and family competencies needed for smart decisions. A socio-dynamic, spiral curriculum promotes the development of effective parent involvement practices for future generations of students. While this human development curriculum involves adolescent students as future parents, the actual targets of primary prevention are children born after high school students become parents. In order for future generations of SPARs to avoid the gap[2] they need knowledgeable parents to lend support. A different set of socialization options is proposed as part of developing critical thinking with adolescents.

Critical knowledge that is generally constrained by poverty forms much of the content for this initiative. Only an outline of what may be included in the new mission of schools can be elaborated or described here in terms of the content and procedures for this human development curriculum. This is an open-ended proposal, in effect, that can serve multiple purposes—of which closing the gap is of foremost importance. It is presented first in the model since it begins with a treatment before the birth of the actual target generation of SPARs. That is, in order for the next generation of SPARs to stay at grade level, parents must be empowered to maximize children's development more than they are today.

Introduction to a Basic Problem: What Is Parental Involvement?

The achievement gap is a multifaceted problem co-constructed in school, in its larger societal links, and at home. Historically intertwined structures and practices are located in the educational system. The latter operates according to the characteristics of the students in ways that are largely segmented. The students' home environment, regardless of culture, can support or disrupt the adaptation and success of students in school. Parental involvement is a key mediating factor that accounts for school achievement more than any other single variable because it reflects the interaction of a host of less visible factors: childrearing practices, parental beliefs, achievement motivation, interaction patterns, and values and aspirations in the context of class and culture. The latter accounts for a significant amount of between- and within-group differences in academic achievement.

Thus far, parental involvement has been a fuzzy, poorly understood notion that gains new meaning from a sociocultural perspective. It actually stands for different types of socialization processes and activity settings that orient development (Portes and Vadeboncoeur, 2003, 1986) and that serve as a type of sociocultural DNA through which certain beliefs, motivations, and attitudes—not to elaborate on other cognitive and affective characteristics—are coded and transmitted from one generation to the next (Dunham et al., 1995a). Parental involvement is a key feature of the home activity setting, in which individuals interact with various concepts, knowledge, and skills indexed by SES and culture. Social competencies can be developed a priori for stimulating and sustaining a new gap-free generation of underrepresented students.

Although parent involvement is known to be by far the most important variable in predicting school achievement (Iverson & Walberg, 1982), it remains largely fossilized by class and culture. Traditional approaches (e.g. Shaver and Walls, 1998; Brand, 1996; Burns, 1996; Epstein, 1991) to activating this variable for SPARs consists of providing rather brief, one-shot programs to a few when it is perhaps already too late to make a significant difference in children's school outcomes. An optimal way to involve parents is to educate them before they form families by raising concerns:

a. about how best to assist children's literacy development through a variety of practical means
b. about how children learn and develop attitudes and aptitudes over time, and
c. about how guided activities help extend new learning valued in school.

A curriculum for parents of at-risk children would need to incorporate clear, basic examples of assisted performance principles (Tharp & Gallimore, 1988) to optimize the child's cognitive supports. It includes a basic understanding of various aspects and stages of human development and also the role of caretakers and environmental factors. However, to impact an entire generation, it needs to be delivered when at least two basic conditions are met. First, the learner must be mature enough to be able to develop higher-level thinking, which begins during adolescence. Second, the concepts and skills must be presented at a time when the whole future generation is available for the primary prevention trial—that is, while in school.

One implication for new curriculum is that formal, school-based, well-sequenced curriculum units be delivered reliably with the explicit aim of developing social competencies—particularly skills and concepts for future parenting. Such curriculum would center on areas that support children's future academic development. It might begin in eleventh or twelfth grade, although it could eventually spiral into earlier grades. Public universities and schools would work together to develop, improve and evaluate the new curriculum. They would also help apply theory-based strategies in ways that have already been shown to be cost effective.

Savings in terms of reducing future retentions, special remedial services, delinquency and other current social costs have been documented and can be employed to support the application of this social policy. With the above collaborations in research and development, social policy can be informed by a sound conceptual base and brought to bear on specific problems such as dropout rates, teenage pregnancy, and the school performance gap. The best examples from community-based, after-school, temporary school-based programs, or "add-ons" to education can be incorporated into a new curriculum formally.

The Challenge

How this most critical factor (parental involvement or home environment) might be tapped proactively is still to be fully understood in the field of education. Current approaches (e.g., National Center for Family Literacy, 2003; Epstein, 1995) cannot close the gap because they are insufficient and belated. Family literacy and parent education programs have failed to demonstrate a significant effect size in closing the gap for rather obvious reasons:

a. First, the connection between parent-child interaction and development is generally absent from programs that vary considerably in "what" is being delivered. Even when such connection is established, it is not sustained with subsequent assistance.
b. When information about how socialization patterns affect development is not clear or prioritized, most programs end up providing simple tips that are insufficient in reducing the gap.
c. Parents living in poverty need to better understand how they can optimize their children's development regardless of SES. Reaching them while yet in school is essential.
d. Not only is the internal validity of existing programs unknown, but they are delivered to only a small fraction of those who would benefit from such preventive education.

It is believed, nevertheless, that these programs are important, and some parts can be incorporated into a primary prevention approach. Information and conceptual knowledge are indeed powerful means that help mediate and promote development.[3] In ways similar to the problems of developing and sustaining effective preschool programs (Early and Head Start), programs of this type generally fail to attract those who most need them.

The concept of primary prevention is still unfamiliar to most educators and policymakers.[4] Generally, attempts to promote parental involvement and remediation are launched only after SPARs are already behind. As long as only a fraction of those who might profit from such interventions is served, the gap cannot be eradicated. This is because problems related to parenting begun long ago, and young poor parents today (long ago placed at risk themselves) are unlikely to be involved effectively in their child's academic development.

Even when low-SES parents participate in parent education programs, there is limited scientific evidence that these programs make a significant difference in children's subsequent school success unless they also include extra assistance in preschool (Portes et al., 1986). Yet there is a continued heavy investment even when it is too late, and too few are served across the nation. There are already curriculum programs in related areas with emphases on the environment, peace, and character education among others. An educational curriculum is yet to be aligned with the mission of providing for competent caretakers and functional families.

Middle-class educators take for granted that the family will educate everyone in non-academic areas that involve skills development and parenting in general. It is assumed that the child-centered focus found in our late-modern society carries with it guidelines for effective parenting and that all sectors of society somehow know how to support children's academic development. Only over a half-century ago, ironically, most children were not expected to be educated as they are today. They had to work and education was a luxury. In 1920, only 16% finished high school while in 1960, 63% did. Today, education remains behind in addressing two criteria: societal expectations for higher standards and equity in educating all sectors of society. Discerning which types of information and skills are most important for our future generations to have in integrating both types of criteria remains a problem. Beyond academic learning, there is little consensus as to what needs to be included in the curriculum and as to methods in secondary school that would help promote equity and greater parental involvement when higher standards are pursued.

Why we miss the opportunity to educate parents and strengthen families during this critical time in particular centers on the need for educators and the public to better understand:

a. The potential of primary prevention, fully and across generations.
b. How formal operational thinking and cognitive skills are socially constructed and ready to be mastered in adolescence. The proposed curriculum of life skills is most likely to have a permanent impact after concrete thinking paves the way to more abstract reasoning. The maturity level necessary for students to understand sociopsychological, economic, and relationship issues is during adolescence. Critical thinking skills transfer across formal and informal areas when dynamic, group-work methods are utilized. Adolescence is a critical period that remains to be tapped.
c. How to combine a and b above. The education of adolescents in this critical area of human development has not been fully appreciated nor recognized as a means to prevent not only the achievement gap but also many of the evitable concomitants of poverty.
d. The political constraints that deter attempts to educate the whole student outside tested academic performance areas.
e. Lack of well-prepared educators and preparation programs.
f. Lack of a clear formal curriculum in this area along with well-prepared educators.

g. Failure to include "f" in the mission and assessment of educational outcomes.

In sum, an important opportunity to empower SPARs' home life is missed because of the above interrelated reasons and a longstanding tradition of not valuing human development content before college. It remains a controversial issue (Delpit, 1995), particularly in a high-stakes reform climate. In the long run, we also miss an untapped opportunity for establishing and sustaining excellence in education.

Critical Thinking as a Prevention Lynchpin for Teens

Over a hundred years ago there was not a sound knowledge base when the present curriculum was designed, particularly before it was known how cultural influences impact on school adaptation (P.R. Portes, 1996). Different concerns existed at that time.[5] However, today it is known that higher-level thinking and reasoning skills are learned socially by having students participate regularly in guided activities. Formal operational thought— that is, the most advanced stage of logical reasoning—depends on education and social interaction (Cole, 1996; Piaget, 1971; Vygotsky, 1978). This aspect of higher level intelligence does not emerge independently of others but through education and mediated learning (Kozulin, 2003). But it is crucial for prevention and effective parenting.

Just as scientific reasoning is promoted in chemistry labs and classes, logical reasoning can be fashioned to promote sound decision-making skills, avoid child neglect, and promote effective parenting practices as part of a mandatory life skills curriculum. Why limit this knowledge to those few who attend college, and why constrain that area of development for those who most need it? There is no reason why those skills and content areas cannot be "seeded" and cultivated in the public educational system, particularly when the family, as an institution, needs help. The premise is that resiliency can be promoted and that the few exceptions who beat the odds are those who develop many of these skills and concepts. What is being offered today in consumer, economic, and life skills programs is insufficient.

A dual role is served by promoting such critical thinking skills. First, these are a legitimate part of any education. Logical reasoning in one domain can generalize across other domains. In fact, most educational reforms attempt to promote creative and higher-level thinking regardless of content area standards. These skills transfer from one area to another more easily once they have been developed meaningfully in one context. Generally, the conditions necessary for their attainment have to be provided (Gagné, 1977). Part of the reason is because there is a tendency to equate academic achievement and success solely with current standardized tests. These tests tend to measure mostly lower level-thinking and basic content, which, of course, are often the foundation for advanced, abstract thought. However, exposure to activities that promote higher-level thinking is important nevertheless because these activities may motivate SPARs to grasp key concepts for themselves.

The curriculum is currently designed and implemented in ways that leave SPARs with the most basic content and knowledge. It is often presumed they are not as capable in dealing with abstract or critical thinking. The system offers sports and less demanding tracks, thus leaving SPARS behind. The latest accountability reports find a shocking proportion of Florida schools failing to meet the new standards set by the 2001 No Child Left Behind Act, while many other states show a similar pattern. The problem lies not with the new accountability system that uncovers how far behind some SPARs are being left. It lies in not fulfilling an important past of our educational mission, in failing to construct knowledge and skills important in mediating and sustaining SPARs' academic success.

Adding this new curriculum to secondary education may be regarded as unrealistic and yet another burden on educators. Yet without it, the cycle remains and a true reform is avoided. An opportunity to educate the whole population in ways that will eventually help educators in the future is also missed. Without it, most SPARs will not have other opportunities to obtain critical knowledge and skills (unlike more advantaged students). Many are thus destined for secondary and tertiary services that are most costly to society consequently. These skills eventually impact on the quality of future SPARs' home environments and level of parental involvement in just a few years.

Primary prevention and promotion of social competencies within the mission and practices of school, over time, might be economic and sustainable relative to increasing violence, healthcare costs, prisons, and safety. The proposed workshops and activity units under a new curriculum represent a type of social science knowledge, the sharing of strategic social capital. The latter is part of what has been termed hidden curriculum in the middle class. It operates alongside the school and other informal formal curricula that constitute the socialization process. The argument is then that key facets of such capital may be more fairly distributed through primary prevention embedded in a new school curriculum. This task will require changes in higher education and school policy.

Practical Issues

The proposed curriculum can be most meaningful when it focuses on issues that are relevant to adolescents and require their active participation. As an integral part of high school, successful participation in and completion of the human development curriculum activities might be required units for graduation. Students would participate actively in joint-learning activities.

In sum, a most cost-effective strategy to mediate the relation between parental involvement and school achievement remains untried, nationally, or even locally. To have a more significant effect on parent involvement and developing the necessary know-how, it is important to think ahead. The preparation of adolescent students as future parents can have a large-scale effect when all SPARs become empowered in the secondary schools. Specific aspects of our human development knowledge base must be considered as the most important to share with the student population while still in school. For example, what types of knowledge, experiences, and skills might adolescents co-construct through this curriculum that could make learning in the home environments of future at-risk students more compatible with that in schools? What types of information and research findings can help prevent obstacles in children's early development?

SEER

The State Education and Environment Roundtable (SEER) based in San Diego, California, provides a framework for education that is in some ways relevant to that proposed in this book. Both frameworks aim to close the achievement gap by transforming curricula and instruction. However, profound differences can be noted that may help to better understand this proposal.

SEER employs an approach based on using the environment as the organizing principle for improving learning. Using the Environment as an Integrating Context for learning (EIC) means that standards-based content areas are taught using pedagogy that integrates natural and social environments. Diverse natural and community contexts are integrated with reading, math, science, social studies, and writing in ways that are interdisciplinary and rely on team teaching and project-based activities. Educators define the environment locally in adapting to instruction to individual needs across forty programs operating in thirteen states. Students construct their knowledge using a school's surroundings, using proven educational practices with the guidance of teachers to promote general and disciplinary knowledge, basic life skills, interpersonal communication, and thinking skills. Evaluation of these programs is based on contrasts with traditional program students who show better performance in reading, writing, math, science and social studies, reduced discipline problems, and more motivation and engagement by participants (www.seer.org).

This model serves as an example for other initiatives found in the literature such as character education, social justice, multiculturalism, or school-to-work programs in secondary schools. Few offer hard evidence in closing the gap. The question being raised here is whether the SEER model, as an example, is based on a thorough problem analysis of the achievement gap. The achievement gap will not be closed unless a much more systemic transformation occurs at other levels besides that of a single organizing principle. In this case, making teaching and learning more meaningful is clearly part of the solution but, as argued repeatedly, not sufficient.

The aim here is not to criticize every single model that purports to close the gap but rather show how each may contribute in some way toward a comprehensive model. In this case, SEER is valuable in pointing us to some of the groundwork necessary in organizing a human development curriculum indirectly. The focus on the environment could be replaced or complemented with human development/parenting life skills. Yet it illustrates how critical the analysis of the problem is in determining the content, process, and the likelihood of attaining stated goals in any proposal for change. Other approaches exist that are most promising, such as the one advanced by the National Council on Economic Education (grades 9–12). While the NCEE curriculum is not aimed at closing the achievement gap, it has developed units, student (workout) practical skills, educator guides, and group exercises that capture much of what still needs to be done in the area of human development. Many of the units founded in the teacher's guide *Financial Fitness for Life* (Morton & Schug, 2001) are directly relevant to what SPARs need to know when thinking ahead about family life. Because adolescents are looking forward to living on their own, basics such as how income is determined, why some jobs pay more, the impact and cost of babies, budgeting, credit, and many other concepts can be made meaningful through group work and as adolescent-oriented pedagogy that is "with-it." For example, teens would learn not only about millionaires, the impact of divorce, and remarriage but also facts such as the chance of getting rich the easy way. The average person who plays the lottery every day would have to live 33,000 years to win once (one chance in 12 million). The chances of being struck by lightning are much better (one chance in 1.9 million). In sum, much is already available and could be adapted to the model, not only from similar programs but also from college-level courses in human development, health, and family that generally exclude SPARs.

Envisioning a Spiral Curriculum: Applying Human Growth and Development

Pre-parenting and life skills education in high school seems a most realistic means of mobilizing key resources not tied structurally to SES. This type of education would be designed to provide scaffolds mainly to low-income youth that concern smart planning and parenting. As greater compatibility is established between home and school, low-income students may be placed less at risk in the future. The knowledge and awareness produced by this "non-academic" curriculum are valued educational outcomes that will take time to justify. It is already known that SPARs perform better in school when parental support is established. What is still to be known is how best to increase the probability of parental involvement through activity-based workshops in schools. To what extent will such knowledge be applied when adolescents become parents? In fact, the direct contribution of this component will not be known directly since it is its interaction with the other components that can produce the effect size required to close the gap in years to come.

The human development curriculum would also target knowledge, skills, attitudes, and values clarification in forging critical thinking skills for adolescents. While the content is primarily social and developmental, the fact that it may not be regarded as academic does not rule out its value in promoting motivation and thinking skills. The latter are part of most educational goals at the state level. The actual goals are to provide knowledge and skills in social, economic, and psychological areas to help adolescents make sound decisions and plans. Since the organizing principle is that of planning for family life, critical, higher-level thinking can be promoted through activities related to economics, career planning, health, education costs, expectations, identity development, and similar areas that may serve to consolidate and expand learning in math, social science studies, writing, and reading.

The philosophy behind this curriculum is largely constructivist and information driven. It is not about imposing a set of middle-class standards and values but providing opportunities for youth to explore and simulate authentic solutions and problems. For example, the objective in a unit may be to analyze wages for typical jobs in relation to costs involved in raising a child. It may include discussions with new parents, police, ex-convicts, and role models of various ages and backgrounds. However, rather than direct the process towards the teaching of abstinence or a particular set of character values, the focus would be on information, skills, and value-clarification interactions where the group leader encourages multiple perspectives and provides guidance in processing and evaluating consequences or problems.

At this junction, it is suggested that the new curriculum be organized precisely around relevant problems or social issues with increased student input. The methodology may vary and include finding problems as well as attempting to resolve them. Adolescents might, after an orientation, be presented with the problem of the week and form expert panels that extend beyond most consumer education courses. Other group techniques would be used to explore and utilize existing resources. Each student would write in their electronic log or portfolio what they are learning, realizing, or wondering about. They would invite community resources and also participate in service learning such as mentoring younger SPARs. They would learn about the gap and help toward its reduction. However, the organizing principle behind all actions would be connected with closing the gap and GBI in school achievement for the next generation of SPARs.

General Focus of Objectives

The objective is to encourage adolescents to consider various issues and problems from a variety of perspectives, engage in cost-benefit analyses, be exposed to different issues, and develop preliminary stances based on data, resources, and group discussions. The proposed curriculum integrates various types of developmental knowledge that may be first divided into various areas. In Table 5–1, workshop units that concern adolescent development and pre-parenting relations are separated from those concerning child development, smart parenting, and skills for prevention and promotion of children's potential. Some parents have advantages in this area from informal learning that serves to establish readiness for school long before school begins. Others have less or even participate in children's development in ways that are incompatible with the school success of their children. While this area is well known in some aspects of educational research and social policy, surprisingly little has been done to promote this knowledge in schools (systemically) except for partial exposures in home/consumer economics, health, or after-school programs.

The first barrier to restructuring the present educational system is that this is not a valued area. It is invisible or seen as unnecessary since the public is convinced that such skills are not really part of the educational mission. From a needs assessment perspective, before this curriculum becomes part of the official socialization program of schools, students will tend to reproduce the parental involvement patterns they are exposed to at home. For groups over-represented in poverty, this becomes a double disadvantage. Not only do they graduate grade levels behind in the formal content areas but also without the know-how to guide their future children out of poverty. Part of the answer to this problem lies then at the educational and social policy levels. To influence the latter, the higher education component to be discussed later becomes relevant.

The proposed activities may be also connected with academic courses or used to reinforce them. While the curriculum lends itself to integration with these areas, as well as social and physical sciences, a separate identity and accountability system is important to establish and maintain.[6] It is important not to fall into a trap of infusing the human development curriculum into the regular program. Rather, this curriculum needs to be delivered independently although integration with other courses is encouraged and probably inevitable.

Table 5–1: Proposed Topics for the Curriculum: A Spiral, Outcome-Based Prevention Program to Build Family Strengths

- Adolescent Development and Dealing with Adults
- Conflict Resolution
- The Social Origins of Critical Intelligent Thinking
- Activity-based Workshops: A Performance-Based Pedagogy for Teens
- Service Learning as Part of the Curriculum
- Teen Pregnancy Consequences, STDs
- Violence Prevention and Conflict Resolution
- Eating Disorders
- Gangs and Peer Pressure
- Neglecting, Smothering, and Spoiling Your Child
- Economic Pressure on Young Couples
- Drug Abuse and Families
- How the Mind Is Formed
- The Role of Music and Arts in Learning
- Verbal Stimulation
- Stress Management
- Why Values Work and What Happens When They Are Missing
- Bullying, Self-respect, and Esteem
- Exploring Roles and Identities in Adolescence
- How the Media Affects Us
- Divorce and Single Parents
- Depression
- Parenting Styles
- Resilient Persons
- Teaching Strategies
- Social Learning
- Self-Efficacy

Much more relevant than the content taught in the curriculum is what SPARs students may be ready to learn next as young adults. In laying the foundations for family competencies, knowledge, and skills in support of children's development (in the future), education takes on a double purpose. Strategic support in science, math, language, and other content areas is not excluded by this strategy. Learning by doing gains new meaning. Teaching SPARs how to teach their children and how they learn or use mnemonics and similar skills seems worthwhile.

The new curriculum would call for a non-traditional adult-like pedagogical approach. Workshop units based on group work and general objectives described below can serve to co-construct a variety of competencies with an assortment of activities. Some examples of topics for clinics and workshops are noted in Table 5–1..

New roles for educators are called for which extend beyond current practices. They require training as primary prevention experts and guides. The model differs from others that have begun to focus on the gap because both academic and socioemotional competencies are central goals. Regardless of academic level, it seems wise to invest in developing family, social, and work competencies as many SPARs become parents.

Beginning in the eleventh grade, the first phase of the human development component would be initiated and later spiraled unto the lower grades. The adolescent component may be exported well beyond some of the health and life skills classes that are available now in some districts. One hopes that the present accountability-oriented reform community can recognize that to sustain higher school achievement, a systematic investment must be made in development as a whole. Focusing only on test performance for SPARs is shortsighted, particularly in secondary schooling, where large gaps have been already established. To close the gap and eradicate disproportional rates of school failure, developmental processes must be focused on as early as possible. What is being suggested is that it is not an either (academic)/or (holistic development) issue. Meaningful reform requires a holistic approach that impacts on future SPARs as well as their contexts. An educational system is not needed solely to sort students for the economic order by producing segmented outcomes based on group membership. What is needed is a system that educates well enough to meet standards and bridge gender and ethnic gaps in learning outcomes. The sorting functions that sustain status inequality (De Vos and Suárez-Orozco, 1990) will still operate above levels of proficiency at each grade level. However, educators need not be part of operations that reproduce GBIs based on ethnicity and cultural history. Rather, they need to be part of ensuring all students learn at grade level.

Rationale of the Adolescent Component and Content

If the effects of poverty on children's socialization produce gaps in educational outcomes at home and school, the impact of reform must be directed at both to promote development *in spite of* poverty. As long as poverty remains a constant (Lee & Burkham, 2002), the mission of education is not to simply ensure a supply of labor at various levels, since that is achieved by other means than school outcomes (e.g., immigration policy). A preferable mission would be to preserve the democratic ideals, practices, and conditions for freedom in society and to reduce inequality in access to learning as much as possible across populations. In doing so, what is found, ironically, are ways to improve learning and teaching for all so that the correlation between poverty and lack of knowledge about human and economic development can be reduced.[7] In sum, the secondary school component must attend to both academic and human development areas. To the extent that the home mediates SPARs' response to schooling, reform must help attenuate the effects of poverty on children at more than one level. Raising test scores alone is only part of the solution. For example, there is evidence that sound parenting reduces and prevents violence (Orpinas, Murray, & Kelder, 1999). A positive home environment not only facilitates learning but can be promoted.

The good news is that efforts to support SPARs' academic development are gaining attention with some modest initial results. Unfortunately, only a small segment of the SPAR population benefits sufficiently to stay at or above grade level and escape poverty. The gap thus remains (collectively) unless the conditions that cause SPARs to struggle in school are also restructured. SPARs can lose motivation and adopt alternative values (see Fordham & Ogbu, 1986).

Those who are already behind in academic areas might be successful in the proposed curriculum areas. This is actually something that might result under the proposed plan. A positive identity and social competence can be promoted as primary prevention strategies unfold. Group work can help reduce prejudice and its effects, such as stereotype threat (Steele, 1997, 1999). Topics concerning learned helplessness, self-efficacy, and locus of control could be part of a "checking your beliefs out" curriculum unit that connects with child development. Adolescents could also discuss Erikson's (1968) psycho-social model and others as part of active discussions about identity issues. Supervised service experiences, tutoring others, early child care encounters, conflict resolution, and confidence-building activities can help make today's adolescents more responsive parents in the future. They would learn how important early stimulation is, about attachment styles, effective teaching interactions, how development proceeds at the rate it is started and sustained, and how motivation and initiative can be promoted. Workshops on conflict resolution, stress management, establishing trust, and the effects of abuse and neglect may not improve test scores immediately but could do so in later generations. For those already behind academically, the curriculum offers an avenue for success while still in school since none would be grade levels behind.

Dilemma or Opportunity? Making Room for Both Missions

An analysis of the problem suggests that to reduce and close the gap in standards-based achievement—a massive and multifaceted problem—one must find ways to also address the primary mediators that operate outside the classroom. Family or parental involvement is one difficult, paradoxical mediator. At one level, it seems taboo to meddle in education that extends beyond academic areas, even if the intent is to promote them. It seems that education on subjects that traditionally come under family functions, such as sex, drug, and character education, will remain controversial unless it is value free and secular. There are already parental involvement and family literacy initiatives operating across the nation precisely to support literacy and academic development. What seems to solve the paradox is the idea of educating adolescent students as competent future parents. The idea that a human development, life skills curriculum for adolescents may serve as a legitimate mechanism or tool with which to accomplish higher test scores, improved learning and teaching, and greater equity remains a policy option and requires thinking out of the box.

The main educational goals are, of course, equity and excellence. They might include the development of both academic and socio-emotional areas as the central mission of education.[8] The good news is that there is no need to start from scratch in launching the human development component, part of which is designed to promote parental involvement for SPARs in the future. A number of life skills-oriented programs are already in operation. Most of the political and social content is already available from college and needs to be adapted for SPARs. The challenge lies in synthesizing what is presently available with what is needed in strengthening family socialization functions and promoting parental assistance and involvement in future generations. This curriculum serves everyone but is particularly important to those to be placed at risk. The least the educational system can do for a high school student population that is already grade levels behind in academic development is to promote humanistic aspects of development strategically. This requires envisioning the problem as cyclical and shaped at various levels during different points of the lifespan and across a number of settings. The approach has to be invitational.

To choose between investing in the "non-academic" primary prevention strategy that aims for academic gains later en masse, and the present initiatives found to help few SPARs in school now to meet standards and some to enter college presents a dilemma. The position being presented is that the academic supports being explored by programs such as AVID, CRESPAR, and others[9] are important and necessary to maintain as education is being restructured. Such programs allow higher proportions of SPARs to break out of the cycle of poverty. They invest in SPARs who are most likely to survive the present system. However, what has been termed "creaming"—taking the students from underrepresented groups who are performing competitively to the next level in college—may at times include some minority students who are not necessarily at risk. This will remain a problem as long as SPARs are defined by other than GBI.

Many universities are concerned about the lack of diversity and are seeking minority candidates, many of whom are not SPARs. In the long run, this strategy alone is not sufficient to establish and sustain equity and excellence yet remains necessary in the overall plan. The AVID model provides an effective means for lending assistance to SPARs. It is argued that if equity and excellence were, in fact, the main goal, then all the means necessary must be integrated into a strategic plan until GBI is eradicated. Consequently, the academic supports structured for the elementary school level (Chapter Seven) must be sustained with the human development component at the secondary level simultaneously for primary prevention. After effective preschool education for all SPARs, the plan calls for academic support from K to 12th grade. However the component proposed in this chapter deals with what might be regarded as non-academic skills in the social, emotional, interpersonal realm that might support competent adults and families. It does not have to be a dichotomy. Table 5–2 suggests how this adolescent initiative can move the distribution forth in non-academic competencies even when SPARs have remained and ended behind several grade levels. In other words, given that adolescent SPARs have, in fact, already been allowed to fall behind by the present system, a reasonable alternative lies in a preventive component aimed at what underlies the observed gap in test scores.

This double load might seem unreasonable to place on the shoulders of struggling SPARs and educators. Educators would rather use the time solely for academic remediation. However, remediation is not primary prevention. The two agendas need not compete with each other.[10] The risk of failing to achieve sufficient competence in either is lower test scores and poverty. The goal is not just to produce higher scores for an international academic (TIMMs-like) Olympics[11] but rather, greater rates of escape from poverty for groups overrepresented in it. Accountability and standards-based reform are viewed not as deterrents to closing the gap but rather as instrumental in a deeper restructuring of the educational system in the near future.

For new educators, this the gist of the primary prevention approach. As important as it is to help SPARs in our schools through programs like AVID, Big Brother and Sisters, and so on, in the long run primary prevention can pay a higher dividend. It can decrease the proportion of SPARs subject to GBI by impacting on the social conditions that produced the gap. By pinpointing assistance to those for whom educational inequality is greatest, resources are deployed most efficiently across the lifespan. Over several generations, group differences may be less significant because of the conditions that have been organized. This endeavor also teaches how excellence may be promoted in the overall system.

Building a Knowledge Base for Educators in the Secondary Schools: A Lynchpin for Success and Sustainability? Methods and Personnel Issues

In addition to developing a curriculum in human development for adolescents, further consideration must be given to what will be required in delivering it (methods). A new type of educator is needed who understands the problem well enough to coordinate the most effective activities within the proposed framework. While school counseling appears as the ideal profession to lead the adolescent component, all educators can be prepared in primary prevention and leadership. This is important because collaborations among counselors, principals, and teachers are crucial in closing the gap. Partnerships that include members of the community are also helpful in organizing learning activities for adolescents. Higher education offers the logical learning environment to begin seeding collaboration and leadership to promote meaningful partnerships.

There are now a number of initiatives in teacher education that attempt to close the gap, including improvements in content knowledge, teaching, multicultural education, class size reduction and professional development for leaders in instruction. Changes are needed in transforming the school culture in K–12 that require corresponding changes in higher education programs for educators. The roles and activities that might actually serve to close the gap require all educators to become better prepared. So what are some of the requirements for delivering the adolescent component and the principal obstacles? Let's examine a few:

a. Educators generally remain uninformed about the origins of "at-risk" students although they are instrumental in changing or maintaining the achievement gap (see Kozol, 1992, 2000; Erickson, 1993; Spring 2001; Varenne & McDermott, 1999).

b. The professional preparation and roles found in degree programs are not aligned with promoting equity and excellence directly. Their training is limited to developing lesson plans and individual content-related competencies rarely connected with an overall strategy to reduce the massive inequality and the problems it produces for both educators and students.

c. It seems as if the premise that is being currently worked under is that if educators are certified and do their job well, both excellence and equity will be automatically achieved. Unfortunately this is not the case. Reform after reform has failed largely because of interrelated limitations in knowledge, structure, tools, roles, and power.

d. A theory-based approach must define the roles and functions of educators in launching a sustainable and cost-effective approach.

Educators need a more complete and powerful education in reorganizing our educational system and its practices.

e. Educators need institutional support in transforming their school culture and practices.

f. They need to provide effective assistance to adolescents in elaborating key experiences and conceptual knowledge based on a human development curriculum in secondary school.

g. Most graduates entering the field are taught indirectly that if they are committed and work hard enough and are culturally sensitive that the problem can be solved with the present system. They don't see how the present system structures and reproduces the problem largely by the ways education and professional roles are organized. Prevention requires knowledge and concerted action and leadership or agency.

Tackling Other Problems

Let's assume for the sake of the present argument that most school districts in the nation were willing to work toward equity in educational outcomes beyond the limited reforms that still fail to significantly improve SPARs' lot. What would this mean? If social justice and equal opportunity to learn for all were truly desired and if inequality as maintained and reproduced unfairly at the group level were known, what might the educational system begin with? A strategy that initiates simultaneously we components appears best.

The school culture is often at odds with the adolescent culture for at-risk adolescents. Adolescents' identities generally are formed in peer cultures that strive for differentiation from adults. This is a period of crisis, and teachers' goals are generally not those that concern students placed at risk. Educators are often called upon to help when it is too late for SPARs to catch up academically. To prevent future generations of children and adolescents from being placed at risk is critical in advancing any comprehensive approach. Yet educators' professional education generally does not address prevention of the achievement gap but rather deals with many of its consequences. For example, most of the literature in this field is limited to traditional types of interventions that are unlikely to affect the gap in the long run (Kim, 2004). In some cases (Brown, 1999; Chubb & Loveless, 2002; McGee, 2004; Snipes & Casserly, 2004) sound strategies are offered to improve achievement within schools that should become a standard for internal school reform. Brown (1999) assembles useful strategies to be considered for a new curriculum that can help guide the preparation of educators and the adolescent curriculum. Its compilation of strategies falls within a framework that, unfortunately, is not sufficient to close the gap.

Conceptual Issues Need to Be Understood

When individuals participate in a common endeavor, it is useful to understand the goals as well as the reasons or factors that constitute the problem. If the problem is closing the achievement gap, the question to be asked is, "What are the essential concepts that might contribute to effective collaboration in attaining that goal?" The literacy gap is produced in great part by schooling and its very consequences. Schooling is often viewed through rose-tinted glasses as democratic and as the Great Equalizer. It is only democratic for the middle class and organized to be compatible with certain class-based cultural experiences. Is there an unintentional complicity between schooling and the ways learning and development impact outside schools? Counselors, teachers, and principals, as well as their university educators, have yet to develop and apply a common strategy to make a difference. They need to be prepared more efficiently in addressing the gap as a cultural and developmental problem along with future policy makers.

Why is the creation of a human development program of studies for adolescent students necessary in dismantling this structured inequality? What should it include besides sound decision-making and parenting skills? The gap is primarily produced and sustained by economic poverty. However, it is not only poverty but also the differential effects of the power and knowledge it constrains. These are related but are separate categories. Poverty has a direct impact on families and thus on how children are socialized before and after school. Economic status also has a direct influence on the quality and quantity of actual education afforded by schools. They are the two primary pillars upon which poverty sustains the gap.

How cultural history accounts for why poverty has remained higher for some ethnic populations in the United States has already been addressed. Educational reforms have not decreased the correlation between social class and academic achievement by improving school instruction based on standards. These two pillars interact in producing a gap in achievement that becomes instrumental in fueling the cycle of GBI. In sum, to reduce the gap, strategic knowledge must be shared to establish comparable distributions in grade-level achievement for SPARs and non-SPARs. Surface-level approaches are simpler but do not work. The complex nature of the problem requires a systemic approach.

Educators often think in terms of one dimension that situates the problem in the school, parent education, the student, teaching, or in early childhood. Most tend to think that the purpose of education is to prepare youth for college and the working world. Educators fail to realize that these youth will soon be socializing new generations of students, often without the understanding of what is necessary to be successful in today's world. While youth may be learning so much more now than in the past, there are also some gaps in important areas in which assistance is needed. Access to key social, psychological, economic, and political knowledge may only be found through public education for many students, particularly SPARs.

The Correlation Between Social Class and Parental Involvement Is Not .99

A significant part of what are generally considered social class differences in parental involvement and other factors are not necessarily dependent on parental income or occupation. Many of the differences that impact children's development stem from knowledge, skills, beliefs, and related practices that are learned both formally and informally. Much of what middle-class parents know and do derives from their formal education, which is a form of capital, a resource that is limited and has a cost. Having "it" (e.g., a college degree) not only implies predictable differences in preparing and supporting children's schooling. It also buys power and influence, since educated parents are socially on equal (or higher) footing with educators. However, the present context is limited to the knowledge, skills, and related practices that stem from the benefits students have (non-material) by virtue of parental education, capital, and involvement.

Whatever "it" is seems to make a huge difference in how compatible school learning is to students, how well they learn, and what educators expect of them. Children's socialization has been carefully studied (see Bourdieu & Passeron, 1977; P.R. Portes & Vadeboncoeur, 2003; Hart & Risley, 1992) in terms of language processes, achievement motivation, beliefs, interaction patterns, identity development and activities. The question before us then is rather academic at first glance. It concerns the extent to which some of the advantageous knowledge or capital—including not only how to best socialize children for school success but also how best to "work the system" to their children's advantage—can be unpacked, harnessed, and shared with those who are the least well served by the educational system. Assuming that there is the willingness and ability to do so, what would be the most cost-effective means to share the advantageous knowledge or capital educated parents have with those who most need it? If knowledge is power, what type of knowledge can be shared with adolescents that is not governed by family wealth and contribute to achievement motivation?

In rethinking the current system and its goals, adolescents in secondary school offer a timely educational window to promote effective parental involvement and family life-skills. Strengthening families begins before adolescents become parents. Adolescent students also are cognitively ready to develop a future orientation that extends beyond vocational guidance if an activity context is offered. Outside of economic redistribution from the wealthiest to the poorest, an alternative is a different type of capital (social) transfer, which may be of strategic value in helping youth who otherwise have limited access to it. For example, what could the parent of a motivated SPAR do to prevent the school from tracking her into lower standards instruction? Can certain types of social knowledge help a future generation of SPARs?

Implications

As promising as this component appears from a theoretical and empirical standpoint, it has yet to be envisioned, developed, and tried. Because it is complex and long term, this component is unlikely to receive much political support. Unless schooling is rethought carefully and re-mediated (or re-tooled), more than 20% of the top resource—children's potential—will continue to be wasted. Children-as-capital is an idea classified by Rauch (1989). As a consequence, a host of social problems and costs are being faced that fuel the cycle of intergenerational poverty and inequality and that undermine excellence in the education of all. This is basically a human development problem, not just an academic achievement issue. Not only must SPARs work hard, but also schools and all of society.

Success in schools is a sociocultural problem that demands multicultural analyses of both individual and societal development. Socially constructed gaps can be reversed if development is understood. By preparing the minds and skills of those on the frontlines, theory can begin to be put into practice and evaluation into more useful, equity-driven practices.

Actions that are executed in the social plane carry significant implications for how individuals or groups are socialized and for the direction and extent of their development. The *Brown* decision in 1954, the Civil Rights Act, gender equity legislation, Head Start, and similar actions mediated the development of various students. Much of the social progress witnessed in the last half-century has been centered on providing greater access to tools and education for those challenged by disabilities and groups within the special education domain. Other such actions defend the development of the gifted and talented students. Until now, unfortunately, there has been little done to defend SPARs against grade compression and to promote a set of mediated actions to dismantle GBI in learning outcomes. SPARs are considered for mainstreaming special education (PL94) more than skill streaming. SPARs thus present a special case before society and education. The basic question concerns the extent to which to reorganize the educational system by leveling ethnic barriers to achieving minimum grade-level performance. Secondly, how could the change be best accomplished? The achievement gap is thus an intercultural problem that requires a historical understanding of development and a lifespan perspective.[12]

A multilevel plan would need to be supported by a critical mass of society and by educators before the adolescent component would be accepted politically and become established policy. Enacting this type of mediated action at the collective level may take some time. Until a grade-level education becomes a basic right, perhaps a first step is to examine some of the main components for multilateral change and begin to weave them into the educational system that prepares tomorrow's educators and policymakers. In sum, this prevention component is a missing piece that would help close the gap on a large scale. It would support the preschool and elementary school components in achieving a more sustainable and stronger effect.

What Educators Think

Following are some of their reactions that have been adapted from focus groups conducted locally. College students who also work in schools and the community reflect their insights concerning what adolescents need to know.

Educator 1

Once parents are educated in ways conducive to developing smarter children, we may begin to see progress take shape. Parents must make and adhere to the decision to become active parts of their children's lives. In most circumstances, children will not reach their maximum potential if the parents are not an active part of the growth process.

A growing number of today's children live in single-parent homes. In families structured as such, it would be helpful to form extended relationships to help socialize the children. Many parents spend very little time with their children and then wonder why their child causes so many problems during the adolescent and young years; these are inactive parents.

Once the parents realize that they are, in fact, the primary teacher of their child, they should begin to recognize and avoid the behavior patterns that causes such great risks to children. They can begin by making up for lost time with their children, and one hopes they will not miss out on any more teachable moments. With the knowledge that time is short will come the passion to give positive experiences to the children. With the knowledge that time is fleeting will come the selfless self-control to pick up children when they are down instead of allowing them to fall down further. With the knowledge that our children are only children for a precious few years will come the longing to help children become all they are meant to be. The parents should recognize that their children need them now more than any other time in their lives, and this will lead the parents to the pursuit of knowledge of ways to help and encourage their children as they develop.

The majority of children with school-related problems come from homes where the parents did not and do not invest time in their children's lives. These children often do not believe in themselves or their abilities because of this. The problem of under-and over-parenting must be remedied, or the result will be a continuous cycle when these children grow up and have children of their own.

Educator 2

Children are constantly growing and, therefore, like any other living thing, require nurturing and tending. Growing into adolescents, children still need to be nurtured and guided. At times, an adolescent will need to learn things on his or her own by trial and error, because experience in itself is a part of learning and quite often a great teacher. From the parent, trial and error should be allowed to an extent: if that exploration becomes life threatening or potentially dangerous, the parent should intervene. It is a parent's "job" to challenge his or her own self and the adolescent to learn new skills and to expand knowledge in certain areas of interest.

Adolescents can still be challenged on a daily basis. Doing volunteer work or working at a part-time job is constantly learning. It may not be math skills or science experiments, but they are learning to better themselves on the job and in their personal life. They learn how to deal with people and how to manage their time. If they work, earning a paycheck is a great way to become more responsible. They may be able to buy a car, clothes they have wanted, or save up for college. A parent can help by opening a checking or savings account for their teen and helping them balance it each month. By volunteering, working, or helping around the house, the adolescent is learning responsibility. Working teens have to show up at a specific time and stay for a certain number of hours, and teens helping around the house have to have specific tasks finished by a certain time. Some adolescents may babysit for a younger sibling or neighbors in order to fulfill their wants. The parent is a very important role model in these situations. If the adolescent sees the parent going to work on time every day and keeping a checkbook balanced, they will want to do the same, and it will come more easily to them. These activities demonstrate a good work ethic and money management skills.

It is very important for a parent to have an active role in his or her adolescent's life. Parents who ask know what's going on in their child's life. Teenagers are not often likely to admit needing structure and boundaries in their life, but a parent is responsible for giving guidance and support throughout their child's life. What a person learns as a child helps to shape his or her life as an adult.

Educator 3

During adolescence, children begin to search more definitely for their identities and see how they fit into the world. As children enter this stage of life, it is known that they become more difficult to reach, but that doesn't mean it's impossible. As important as it is to continue to reach out to them, it is also necessary to remain cognizant of areas of learning (in all aspects of their life) that they are ready to pursue. Since adolescence is such a time of physical and cognitive change, one can expect a period of storm and stress. It is a time of striving for more independence. It is the parent's job to help their teen find ways into the world while offering assistance when it is needed. By being as supportive as possible and looking for the positive in the child, parents help to bolster their child's self-esteem. There needs to be clear expectations and boundaries in the parent-child relationship. The parent's goal should be to help the teen define who he or she is as an individual while continuing to develop and broaden intellectually. It is important to think of ways to encourage adolescents to think about social issues in developing their potential. At the same time, this should propel them toward continued intellectual growth. It is the parent's responsibility to treat issues as an opportunity for intellectual growth and not avoid them altogether.

The above reflections by school counselors and educators suggest some of the topics for discussions with teens as they "pretend" to be parents. By discussing "as if" they were parents and what they might do to support their children's development, a foundation is laid for greater parental involvement in the future.

Summary and Conclusions

The strategies in this adolescent component call for a radical change in secondary education and a re-conceptualization of our social policy and educational goals. A human development "spiral curriculum" class organized for all students is proposed before they become parents. The primary prevention target is the yet-unborn child. Adolescents begin to prepare family context beforehand, using critical thinking skills that involve vocation, economics, healthy relationships, and self-regulation. The key to primary prevention and a cultural historical approach is to help adolescents master basic concepts and critical skills, particularly those important in backing out of the cycle of poverty.

The methodology consists of organizing the activity settings, operations, context, goals, and tasks that assist the development of children placed at risk. In this curriculum, a student-centered space is created to discuss (as it were) a variety of problems and solutions concerning family life, adolescent issues, violence and hate, addictions, identity concerns, and the consequences of teen parenting, among others. It would include social history, and knowledge about family functions, how some manage to break out of the cycle of poverty, and how our society is organized politically and economically.

Primary prevention calls for treating everyone before symptoms or problems emerge in children through the co-construction of know-how skills. If the problem concerns the student placed at-risk—who is generally doomed to a lower quality of life by virtue of her parents and a "situation" that includes attitudes, values, expectations, and knowledge that interact with educational institutions—then many of the goals of a prevention effort can be anticipated.

In this new curriculum, students learn about effective parenting: infant care, abuse, neglect, attachment, behavior management, and how to maximize their children's motivation and chances of success in school. Also included are effective decision-making, group work, and planning skills connecting the present to the future. This curriculum is generally more available for advantaged students and delivered informally. However, much can be accomplished for all students within a formal curriculum. Achievement motivation, self-regulation, communication skills, conflict resolution, and self-efficacy topics are among the many topics to be included.

Each component proposed in the plan, once in place, helps the others work much more effectively. As future parents are educated in this adolescent component, preschool education, and K–12 are also being indirectly supported. The gap is prevented from emerging in elementary school through the other components. Academic assistance can be organized in and out of school for all SPARs as the gap is reduced for those most left behind.[13] Eventually, as adolescents have children, that child then participates in the other components and a full cycle is completed for one generation. Our premise is those children are more likely to succeed in school and life when their parents are prepared with more social capital or resources. Over a few generations a significant effect at the group level may finally be observed.

The problem in a nutshell is not just then about distribution of economic capital or resources, or school leadership or teachers' content expertise. It is not just about partnerships or Head Start. It is not only about after-school programs or school reorganization. It is about all of these and the sharing of tools and information. Information can amplify and guide power. Knowledge maximizes development. Lack of cultural knowledge constrains development at various levels. Given that economic redistribution in our society is unlikely, the next best strategy is perhaps a developmental, educational primary prevention approach to assist those left behind. In it, educational excellence and a more sane society can be organized and achieved without violence. The costs are not more than those being paid for today through prisons, welfare, the "justice" system, and social work-related band-aids.[14] Primary prevention calls for profound change more than educational initiatives, being presently

Table 5–2: The Present and the Anticipated Secondary Life Skills Curriculum: A Sampler

2005–Present	2015–Anticipated
■ Not enough professionals ready	■ 50–100% of educators prepared to close the gap
■ No primary prevention curriculum	■ Shared curriculum in higher education for counselors, teacher education, students, and administrators
■ No parenting skills	■ Primary prevention curriculum in secondary schools
■ No informal teaching methods	■ Socio-drama, service learning, etc.
■ No components in counseling programs	■ Specific training in primary prevention
■ Gap not included in ethics courses	■ Gap included in ethics courses
■ No assessment plan	■ Formative and longitudinal studies
■ Minimum focus on parent education	■ Focus on parent education
■ Continued progress by underrepresented SPARs not made	■ Grade-level gaps do not emerge
■ Socio-cultural issues remain ignored	■ Dealing with stress
	■ The psychology of eating disorders: obesity, anorexia, bulimia
	■ Identity development
	■ Human relationship building

delivered in a fragmented, inconsistent fashion. The strategy also would be in line with early detection. Who will be at-risk before birth is already known. The knowledge that could be co-constructed in the future parents' mind may have long-term positive impacts on new SPARs and society.

Higher-level thinking skills are socially constructed. Thus far, some of these skills are offered in some programs, some of the time, for some students under a variety of short-term initiatives (e.g., character education, life skills, health classes). The difference for the field of education is that this approach needs to be systemic, policy based, reliable, and provided by knowledgeable educators.

At a time when families are too stressed to fulfill many socialization functions, and teachers are under-prepared and already over-extended, this approach seems timely (see Table 5–2). As adolescents are prepared for family life, they can also serve as mentors to younger children in elementary school. This chapter addressed some of the implications that a theory-based rethinking of the problem might have in changing current practices and policies. The general lack of a developmental, integrated approach now found across numerous initiatives can be addressed by a comprehensive, coordinated strategy.

Endnotes

1. The needs are based on the criterion of establishing equity in educational outcomes. As long as parent involvement in education is left to chance, poverty will continue to discourage parent involvement in SPARs' development.
2. The gap becomes manifest in the schooling process but is actually already present much earlier in terms of the development of "school readiness."
3. It is believed that poverty compounds the gap by limiting not only economic but also informational channels. Few SPARs have parents who, in spite of poverty, have the "know-how," concepts, and practices, that help support their child's development. It is argued that what has been referred to as the middle-class hidden curriculum—that is, that knowledge regarding how the system works institutionally, how the mind of the child works in terms of human development, and how to be responsive to the child's potential in general—is largely derived from education. This education or knowledge is generally shared and also bought. It is a form of capital that is linked with social class. However, if there is truly a wish to close the gap in educational outcomes and establish equity as soon as possible, then this knowledge must be shared. It must generally be shared with those in certain class or ethnic cultures, with those who most need it being least likely to be aware of it. This intentional maneuver, even at the collective level, would take some time to decrease the number of underrepresented groups in higher education and various professions.
4. Primary prevention consists of intervention programs that are delivered to all those susceptible to a problem before the problem develops further and symptoms emerge. Today, our approach to promoting parent involvement is ineffective because it begins too late and is not systemically applied.
5. This can be illustrated by Abraham Lincoln's 1859 account in a letter to Jesse Fell ("Lincoln on Education," 2003). "There were some schools, so called; but no qualification was ever required of a teacher beyond 'reading, writin and cipherin' to the Rule of Three. . . . There was absolutely nothing to excite ambition for education."
6. We believe this is important lest this whole initiative becomes diluted and whitewashed as another health or home economics curriculum. It is conceptualized as incorporating both areas and extending far beyond with a focus on promoting future parent involvement and health promotion.
7. The education of first-generation immigrants is viewed as a special case, separate from that of second- or third-generation immigrant students who are identified with groups subject to GBI.
8. It may be argued that schools provide for both areas given extra-curricular activities. It is believed that the latter are not only of secondary importance but geared toward different purposes than in our model.
9. See Mehan, Hubbard, & Villanueva, 1994; 1996; Levin, 1988.

10. This is because we would begin with eleventh and twelfth grade now to catch generations before they leave school. Over time the essentials of the curriculum could be introduced in earlier adolescence. In time, the next generation begins effective preschool and obtains academic support from K–12. Theoretically, SPARs who master life skills might soon have children. Those children would be identified and assured access to early childhood and preschool programs such as those pioneered by Dunham, Miller, Gray, Ramey, Weikart and others (Consortium for Longitudinal Studies, 1983; P.R. Portes, 1982). Again, once they enter K–12, they should have access to after-school academic assistance and collaborative relationships or partnerships as described in the lifespan model in Chapter Four and the subsequent ones.

11. See international comparisons in Stevenson and Stigler's *The Learning Gap* (1992).

12. This is based on a socio-historical analysis of culture and mediated action (Vygotsky, 1978), a concept that is fairly new in counselor and teacher education.

13. Those most left behind are students from groups subject to GBI, many of whom have been re-segregated in the schools (Orfield, Frankenberg, & Lee, 2003).

14. Critics may note this strategy amounts to a sort of social therapy. The response is indeed "yes," and a wise one to deploy relative to attempts to re-socialize when it is perhaps too late through social work, psychiatric, criminal justice, or health actions.

6 The Preschool Component

Roles of Community, Schools, and Government

"A capacity, and taste, for reading, gives access to whatever has already been discovered by others. It is the key, or one of the keys, to the already solved problems. And not only so. It gives a relish, and facility, for successfully pursuing the [yet] unsolved ones."

—FROM ABRAHAM LINCOLN'S ADDRESS BEFORE THE WISCONSIN STATE AGRICULTURAL SOCIETY, SEPTEMBER 30, 1859

Overview

This chapter describes the second preschool component. It is an essential part of the sequence proposed in the primary prevention plan. With socially competent parents in the future, both preschool and K–12 programs lend more robust support to SPARs. The chapter provides policymakers and practitioners an understanding of what needs to be done early in the development of SPARs beyond present measures. What needs to be done is to extend effective preschool programs to 100% of SPARs, which is not the case now. In order to reduce or close the achievement gap in school, gaps in preschool learning experiences and conditions need to be addressed. Far too many poor children grow without the literacy-related supports needed to succeed in school. While Head Start provides one year of support to approximately 60% of children, the great majority of children in poverty enter school already behind. Of the four components in the overall plan, this is the one that has received the most research attention and may be easiest to address fully (Ramey et al., 2000; Weikart, 1995). The reason is due largely to earlier preschool intervention program research after the War on Poverty was declared (Consortium for Longitudinal Studies, 1983). That research and resulting policy (see Lazar & Darlington, 1982; Dunham, Kidwell, & Portes, 1988; Schorr, 1988; Zigler, 1986) are still relevant in informing current discourses regarding educational inequality and excellence. The history of that research seems to have been partly forgotten along with lessons that remain important with respect to the timing and intensity of early childhood education. However, the good news from recent longitudinal reports points to what might be accomplished with seamless levels of support (Ramey et al., 2000; Weikart, 1995).

Counselors, teachers, principals, and parents have a limited role during this period, except as early childhood educators themselves of children in their communities. For these reasons, it is proposed that all educators share a strong conceptual knowledge base and professional identity with expertise in human development.

Early childhood educators and health and family services personnel also have a limited role and understanding about this period in shaping the achievement gap. In mounting a frontal attack to close the gap, the professional education of early childhood educators should be included in our needs assessment. A parenting knowledge base for both educators and also (future) parents—who are considered to be the most important and influential educators of all—is important. The education of new professionals and parents on how to provide SPARs with optimum conditions can be only briefly illustrated. For parents, it is essential to understand how to establish intelligent ways of interacting with their child and how to begin preparing an intelligent context for the coming years. However, the main idea of the chapter is to extend preschool education to promote the school readiness for 100% of SPARs. Secondly, some aspects of the knowledge base needed to assist children's development are emphasized.

Introduction

The main issue concerning the role of early education in closing the achievement gap that appears later in school is no longer one of whether such programs work or not. After years of research, it is clear that early age educational programs can be effective in promoting school readiness. They assist children from low-income families to develop in ways that reduce differences in literacy acquisition. Some programs can actually raise the measured intellectual level of participants to middle-class norms (P.R. Portes, 1982), although not for long without continued support. As discussed earlier under

Table 6-1: Rubric for Estimating Risk Status of Children Living in Poverty Hypothetically Across Contexts (1–4)

SPARs Context	Risk Increases	Risk Decreases
Home Environment 1st	Presume 50% have low parental involvement	Presume 50% of SPARs have adequate support
Day Care 2nd	50% poor quality or does not have	50% good quality (age 0–3 years)
Preschool or Head Start 3rd	40% poor quality or does not have	60% has effective program for 1–2 years
K–12 School 4th	80% schools with most SPARs below grade level	20% schools with SPARs at grade level
Effect	Risk is compounded	Risk is reduced

the critical period hypothesis, unless favorable intellectual development supports are maintained, the gains from these programs tend to wash out in elementary school. Thus it seems that early age education is necessary but not sufficient in closing the gap.

A key issue is not only that of early care for children living in poverty but also providing preschool experiences of high quality and ensuring parent involvement as well. Quality is defined here as experiences that are school compatible and that promote school-required literacy development. Some preschools, including Head Start, prepare children so that at the end of kindergarten and first grade, gaps in academic literacy areas are practically non-existent. However, this is not enough. Unless the home environment is also "involved" through effective parent-child interaction practices or other support functions, the child is placed at risk later by increased academic demands in the public school system. Sometimes, both the school and the parents collaborate to reduce risks for the child, such as staying behind grade level when they are most capable of learning. In other cases, both schools and the home environment together place the child at risk and undermine this development. The typology above illustrates these problems (see Table 6–1).

It has been noted earlier that those one in five children lives in poverty and is thus placed at risk for educational failure. Poverty is the primary cause of the achievement gap and poverty again increased in 2003. For groups subject to GBI, almost half of their children live in poverty and tend to be placed at-risk by an accumulation of factors. Illustrated in Table 6–1 are estimates according to the current level of support provided by Head Start in serving children of poverty. These estimates—made for illustrative purposes only—also reflect what public schools achieve in terms of ensuring that these SPARs perform at grade level according to current educational standards. The effect of daycare is estimated similarly to that of the home environment to be positive for half of the children in poverty. Let's assume both are positive or supportive of these children's development. A key question here is what is the probability of a child being poor (20%), growing up in a positive home environment (50%) and having a good-quality daycare experience (50%) then having access to an effective preschool (60%) and going to a top school (20%) making it to college?

What can be seen is that the majority of children in poverty are, in effect, cumulatively at risk when the factors are considered together. Those who have effective preschool, parent support, and responsive schooling manage to succeed more often than others but are rare. By fourth grade a two-year gap in math and reading is generally established; by eighth grade the gap is three years (Haycock, Gerald, & Huang, 2001). Only a few schools in the nation are able to keep large proportions of SPARs at or above grade level. (The characteristics of those rare schools are examined in the next chapter.) It should be noted at the bottom right cells that even if children attend effective Head Start programs, an undetermined number of them may not have sufficient academic supports at home to do well at school. The risks encountered by children of poverty are amplified over time, so that by middle school it is unlikely they will do well. This underlies the importance of having extra supports when these children enter elementary school (see the next chapter) as well as involved parents (see the previous chapter). To increase the number of SPARs who will complete school at or above grade level, multiple sources of support need to be tapped simultaneously for sustained interaction and long-term impact. Single-focus solutions such as leadership training or reducing school/class sizes are unlikely to counter the effect of preschool, home and school experiences.

A key goal of education is to make sure that every student has a chance to excel; children's early success in school determines later success as adults. Many factors prevent education from serving this role as "the great equalizer." This is because schools serving low-income students receive fewer resources, face greater difficulties attracting qualified teachers, face many more challenges in addressing student's needs, and receive less support from parents. This inequality of school quality interacts significantly with the inequalities facing children before they enter school. SPARs begin kindergarten with significantly lower cognitive skills than their more advantaged counterparts. These same disadvantaged children are then placed in low-resource schools, magnifying the initial inequality according to the US Department of Education's Early Childhood Longitudinal Study,

Kindergarten Cohort (ECLS-K), a recent comprehensive analysis of kindergarten students. In general, before even entering kindergarten, the average cognitive score of children in the highest SES group is 60% above the scores of the lowest SES group. Moreover, average math achievement is 21% lower for blacks than for whites, and 19% lower for Hispanics. According to Lee and Burkam's summary (2002), race and ethnicity are associated with SES. For example, 34% of black children and 29% of Hispanic children are in the lowest quintile of SES compared with only 9% of white children. Cognitive skills are much less closely related to race/ethnicity after accounting for SES. Even after taking ethnic differences into account, however, children from different SES groups achieve at different levels.

Family structure and educational expectations have important associations with SES, ethnicity, and with young children's test scores, though their impacts on cognitive skills are much smaller than either race or SES. Although 15% of white children live with only one parent, 54% of black and 27% of Hispanic children live in single-parent homes. Similarly, 48% of families in the lowest SES quintile are headed by a single parent, compared to only 10% of families in the highest quintile.

Socioeconomic status is quite strongly related to cognitive skills. Of the many categories of factors considered—including race/ethnicity, family educational expectations, access to quality child care, home reading, computer use, and television habits—SES accounts for more of the unique variation in cognitive scores than any other factor by far. Entering ethnic differences are substantially explained by these other factors; SES differences are reduced but remain sizeable.

Low-SES children begin school at kindergarten in systematically lower-quality elementary schools than their more advantaged counterparts. However school quality is defined—in terms of higher student achievement, more school resources, more qualified teachers, more positive teacher attitudes, better neighborhood or school conditions, private vs. public schools—the least advantaged US children begin their formal schooling in consistently lower-quality schools. This reinforces the inequalities that develop even before children reach school age.

The point here is to emphasize the importance of a unified approach to the problem, one that would have most SPARs enter school ready to learn as well as those not suject to GBI regardless of class. As the above authors point out, the schooling process should not magnify initial inequalities.

Inequality from Start to Finish

Americans' beliefs about education are inconsistent. What is recognized on the one hand is that children neither begin nor end their education on an equal footing. On the other hand, Americans simultaneously believe that schools are places where social inequalities should be equalized, where the advantages or disadvantages that children experience in their homes and families should not determine what happens to them in school—in essence, that school is a place where children should have equal chances to make the most of their potential. There is widespread faith among Americans in the value of education for social betterment, for both individuals and the nation. Among the many institutions in US society, schooling is seen by most Americans as the embodiment of a meritocracy. They believe—or at least hope—that children's experiences in our nation's elementary and secondary schools allow them to succeed without regard to their family circumstances, their ethnicity, or their gender.

Despite widespread faith in the role of schooling to address or ameliorate social inequalities, what should be recognized is that the nation's schools actually play a major role in magnifying such inequalities. For example, it is common knowledge that children's school performance, including scores on standardized tests of academic achievement, is associated with their family background, particularly ethnicity, and socioeconomic status. Several social scientists have written about how schools structure inequality, so that social differences in achievement actually increase as a result of children's participation in differentiated educational experiences as they move through school. (Bourdieu & Passeron, 1977; Rank 2004). Social differences in academic competence among young children must be explored at the point at which they begin before school. The need to document and understand these differences has become increasingly clear in recent years.

Two ways to assess the success of a modern society are the level of literacy of its children and youth and the extent of disparities in literacy skills among children and youth with differing characteristics and family backgrounds. These indicators are markers of how investments of material, social, and cultural resources made during the past decade have been translated into skills and competencies in the present generation: they reflect the relative success of families, schools, and communities in producing a literate, cultured society.

Relevant Theory and Research

Children's early experiences in school represent an "especially critical but generally neglected period in research on child development" (Alexander & Entwistle 1988, 1). Among those who do investigate early schooling, there is considerable and long-standing debate about whether social background differences in school performance are a result of "cultural deprivation" (also called "social deprivation") or "educational deprivation." Other current language includes descriptors such as "at-risk" and "educational disadvantage."

But casting the debate in these terms may actually inhibit individuals from fulfilling their potential. Factors marking risk or educational disadvantage include race and ethnicity, poverty, single-parent family structure, poorly educated mothers, and limited English proficiency. Although a study of Baltimore schoolchildren found few racial differences in children's performance at entry into first grade (Entwistle, Alexander, & Olson 1997), other research using data from the National Assessment for Educational Progress (NAEP) has documented substantial differences by race for elementary school children (e.g., Applebee et al., 1986), and at least one study documents substantial cognitive differences between black and white children at as early as three and four years old (Jencks & Phillips, 1998).

Although large numbers of children have trouble learning to read, such difficulties are much more likely to occur among poor ethnic children. (Snow, Burns, & Griffin, 1998). Virtually all researchers agree that social background is associated with school success. Moreover, there is general agreement that social stratification in educational outcomes increases as children move through school (Entwistle et al., 1997; Phillips, Crouse, & Ralph, 1998). Social inequalities in school increase as children advance through school mainly because of differentiation in educational experiences that begin as early as first grade (with reading groups, special education placement, and retention), extend through elementary school (as ability grouping, special education, and gifted and talented programs continue), and are well recognized in high school (with formal and informal tracking, advanced placement, and so on).

Despite many studies that have resulted in widespread agreement that social background influences children's educational experiences and successes, the association between family background and cognitive performance at the point where children enter school has received less empirical scrutiny. Many studies have evaluated the efficacy of preschool programs designed to enhance the cognitive and social competence of disadvantaged children (such as Head Start and state-financed preschool programs for low-income children). Many other studies have targeted children in elementary school who have already demonstrated educational problems.

Social background and young children's development
A few carefully designed studies have focused on very young children's development of language skills (e.g., Hart & Risley, 1995). Such studies often require repeated and regular observations in children's homes to investigate family dynamics that are associated with infants' and toddlers' vocabulary development. These studies demonstrate quite conclusively that mothers' speech (its frequency, elaboration, and verbal interchanges with children) is closely linked to young children's vocabulary development.

Moreover, early vocabulary development is strongly associated with later school performance. One study, in which researchers observed mother-child interactions every month for the first two years of children's lives, concluded that the elaboration of mothers' language interactions with their young children was strongly differentiated by social class (Hart & Risley, 1995). Moreover, socially linked language development observed in very young children was found to be quite stable throughout elementary school (i.e., schooling did not ameliorate these socially based language differences developed in infancy). Intergenerational transmission of language was substantial.

Several relevant articles in a recent international and multidisciplinary volume explore the strength and variation in socioeconomic gradients or slopes (see Brooks-Gunn, Duncan, & Britto, 1999). Countries with high average literacy scores among youth tend to have shallow gradients, that is, youth from lower socioeconomic backgrounds also demonstrate relatively high literacy. A key link between SES effects and context (including family, community, and schools) results from segregating low-status groups from mainstream society by using their place of residence as a filter for distributing educational resources.

Brooks-Gunn and her colleagues report other associations between family income and children's attainment:

> Most noteworthy is the importance of the type of outcome being considered. Family income has large effects on some of the children's ability and achievement measures, but large effects on none of the behavior, mental health, or physical health measures represented by the dozen developmental studies (1999, 107).

Moreover, they contend that very poor children are especially disadvantaged, far more than children at or just above the poverty threshold.

Early Experience

Differences exist in the quality of childcare (Clifford et al., 1998) regardless of the background of children. Higher-quality practices were compared with medium- and low-quality care in a longitudinal study for the national Center for Early Development and Learning. Better language, reading, and math skills were found over a three-year period that lasted through kindergarten. Head Start programs also vary in their quality and, as a whole, promote readiness more effectively for children than no programs at all do.

The first three years of life are critical in determining the child's intellectual development (Hart & Risley, 1992; White, 1982). It is further known that by age four, children's intellectual development can account for about two thirds of the difference in intellectual development at age seventeen

(Bloom, 1964). From this perspective, it appears that childcare and preschool programs may be failing to impact significantly children who are placed at risk in public school. Perhaps they do have a positive impact, but the gap is caused by the lack of continuity and efficacy of the support lent to children living in poverty after they enter school.

So how can the main issue regarding the significance of pre-kindergarten period be crystallized in terms of what educators need to know to close the gap? Early childhood educators need to be included along with teachers, counselors, and principals in a national effort to eradicate the achievement gap, along with their college and university educators. An integrated lifespan perspective and approach in terms of human development is needed to facilitate the joint effect of various components in the model (sketched in Chapter Eight). Yet it seems clear that policy that supports early childhood education is well directed. This component is necessary but not sufficient in dismantling the ethnic achievement gap.

Preschool is divided into two periods that helps make clear what seems necessary to prevent the achievement gap in K–12 education. From prenatal care to up to three years of age, development proceeds at a rapid rate—and is mostly under biological control—but still requires healthy nutrition, stimulation, and care. Ensuring all parents are educated in critical parental involvement practices as part of their own high school education plays a major role for helping children living in poverty. In effect, what we argue is that it is already unfortunate enough for children to endure poverty. The least that can be done in our society is to have an educational system that prevents some of the effects of poverty on human development. The system's organization and its outcomes must become less correlated with social class per se and independent from it. In other developed countries, poverty is less correlated with school literacy.

The period from childcare and preschool to kindergarten requires mainly promotion of the child's development of school readiness. The minimum requirement for advancing children's emotional and intellectual development calls for extending Head Start to all eligible children for a sufficient period. (Ramey et al., 2002) Engaging SPARs in meaningful literacy experiences and supporting low-income parental involvement efforts is necessary for a family oriented policy if a society is seriously motivated to close the achievement gap and promote educational excellence at the same time. In fact, the latter cannot be achieved without equity.

A related aspect of the preschool strategy concerns activating and sustaining parent involvement effects by infusing child development concepts and skills not only in secondary schools but also in other contexts. This does not preclude the promotion of family literacy with young SPARs. The "dos and don'ts" of effective childcare, language development, discipline, neglect, and parental conflict—along with nutrition and healthcare basic knowledge—need to be broadly disseminated as children participate in preschool. This is a most critical intervention point. Public service announcements can serve to promote assistance for young SPARs.

This period is subtle since developmental gaps are practically impossible to identify before age four. Well-informed parents who have sound, basic skills in child development represent key players in this critical period of children's development. In making children's early experiences and socio-cognitive environments more compatible across SES groups, a primary constraint is removed in preventing a school achievement gap in the future. This investment in the infrastructure of society is cost effective since reading readiness can be economically promoted in preschools.

The most important aspect of this component offers effective childcare and preschool education to children whose development is being placed at risk. The primary prevention target ideally is the child with parents who have graduated from the curriculum proposed in the last chapter. This will take time and a major social commitment to bring about. However, this does not mean it can only be done after those cohorts graduate with the new human development knowledge base. The plan is to extend effective preschool programs to all eligible children as soon as possible. There are a variety of ways to achieve the goal of countering cumulative disadvantages with cumulative supports for development. A main goal then is federal calls for full funding of Head Start centers with well-trained staff and models that have been evaluated as effective. It is also one for which hard evidence now exists in achieving positive outcomes. (Ramey et al., in press; Weikart, 2002).

Federal Support for Community Preschools

Since closing the achievement gap is a national concern and merits national support, the support level should be commensurate with the problem. It should not be limited to what is now allocated for Head Start and Title 1 programs. As with the postal, military, transportation, and similar services, the costs can be shared by all to assist children living in poverty to develop in areas valued in schools. This strategy is also consistent with leveling birth rates for poor parents through education. Colleges and universities can help develop service learning operations to assist in this, as well as other, K–12 components in serving communities. Community clubs and businesses can also help adopt and lend support to child care and preschool programs in churches that need assistance. In building a sufficiently large effect size, many of the current costs can be reduced. Grade retentions and learning and behavior problems can be diminished while the gap is prevented from occurring at grade level. Again, this and the other components represent the foundation not only for closing the gap but in allowing for greater success in the educational system and its outcomes.

In promoting school readiness and preventing the gap, the essential issues for policy are:

a. Serving all those eligible children from underrepresented groups early with effective preschool programs
b. Sustaining the effect over time and
c. Ensuring SPARs, once in school, are not allowed to fall behind through the means outlined in Chapter 7.

The rest of this chapter focuses on preschool issues and also part of the knowledge base for parents and educators. They need to be on the same page in their socialization of preschool children. Much of this material complements the last chapter's goals for future parent education and provides a primer for use in parenting workshops and training of educators. The main issues and goals for educating professionals and parents in preschool to provide SPARs with optimum conditions are discussed.

Activating the Parent-Involvement Effect in At-Risk Students and Families

A large body of evidence pointing to family interaction exists that predicts student academic success or achievement. SPARs leave high school unmindful of this important knowledge. Differences in family interaction patterns account for many of the reasons why early childhood experiences and social class are important constraints in later development. (P.R. Portes & Vadeboncoeur, 2003). As a consequence of massive disparities in experiences and opportunities, a sustainable set of supports needs to be structured for all SPARs when they are still young. Fortunately, how they can enter elementary school as ready as others is already known. This is a must.

The main issue lies in identifying effective preschool programs and practices in the community and extending them to all eligible children. Such preparation for public schooling can no longer be optional. For SPARs it must be regarded as part and parcel of human civil rights, given a documented history of disadvantages compounded by tracking in schooling. Educators in elementary school need to be aware of the learning readiness of such students beyond current testing and tracking practices. They need to provide instruction that is responsive to what students are ready to know.

Early childhood and elementary educators can help SPARs enter school ready to learn and help develop effective programs in the community. As part of their preparation they can support local community preschool programs through field-based work before and after kindergarten. At present the proportion of SPARs participating in effective preschool activities that support literacy development is unknown. Not all at-risk children have access to effective programs in Head Start, although these programs "graduate" up to 60% of SPARs.

A new function for educators lies in preparing elementary school counselors and conducting diagnostic dynamic assessments of SPARs once they complete preschool. The goals are to create and expand learning areas for future development. When all SPARs enter school sufficiently prepared, schools will be able to teach students at grade level. Educators can find out what percent are served effectively by Head Start programs and help others who are not, as time allows. At later grade levels it becomes more difficult so the investment must be early. First grade educators, for example, might focus on SPARs at the bottom of the kindergarten group. Second grade educators may, in turn, begin working with low-performing SPARs until 100% are served by preschool programs of high quality and reach proficient levels of performance.

Children from low-income groups generally become low achievers in disproportionate numbers unless they have effective after-school or home cognitive supports. Research in this area of educational equity is relevant because ethically it is not prudent for a democratic society to place in jeopardy the futures of perfectly able children simply because of their sociocultural background or scarcity of effective preschool programs. What are the consequences of choosing to abandon the 20% of school-age children who are stranded in the cycle of poverty with little hope of overcoming the barriers imposed by the task demands of school? The answer is already known to us, particularly for African, Latin and Native American children, who are twice to three times further behind in their developmental readiness for school relative to majority children (14%). What happens if we try again and again but keep falling short of the necessary means to establish equity in education? Essentially, this is the case at present. The alternative is to invest in a system to produce more equitable outcomes gradually each year from preschool to post-secondary education. Once SPARs function at grade level, a second generation of ethical questions can be anticipated. Let's decide from what is known can be accomplished and remind all that while many other scientific and social problems have been addressed, the four-year gap that originates at this early age has not been diminished by even half a year since 1971.

Effective Preschool Programs

Head Start helps most participating young children achieve greater school success and avoid crime as they grow up. Lawrence Schweinhart and David Weikart present encouraging findings from a seventeen-year follow-up study of 622 young adults twenty-two-years-old in Colorado and Florida who were born in poverty and did or did not attend Head Start as young children (Schweinhart & Weikhart, 1998). The study found evidence of important effects on school success and crime. For females (but not males) at one study site—after adjusting for background differences—only about one-fourth as many Head Start participants as non-participants (5% versus 19%) failed to obtain a high school or GED diploma, and only one-third as many (5% versus 15%) were arrested for crimes.

New evidence finds the High/Scope model improved performance on fourth-grade achievement tests at ten schools; six schools increased the percent of students passing state tests by a mean of eleven percentage points in reading (p < .01) and 26 points in mathematics (p < .001). In some schools, standardized achievement test means increased by eight normal-curve-equivalent (NCE) points in reading and six points in mathematics.

In the one to five years since High/Scope Educational Research Foundation support ended (the model has continued). Two High/Scope schools with relevant data improved a mean of 33 percentage points in reading and 51 points in mathematics, outdistancing comparison schools by a mean of 20 points in reading and 47 points in mathematics. High/Scope at four schools decreased discipline referrals by 48 percent. Other preschool programs may be similarly effective but have not been studied as carefully.

In sum, Head Start students in programs using the High/Scope approach had a significantly higher grade point average throughout their schooling and experienced fewer than half as many criminal convictions by age twenty-two. A recent national survey found that 37% of today's Head Start programs use the High/Scope approach. Edward Zigler and Sally Styfco (1993) noted "The findings confirm that we are on the right track in deploying comprehensive interventions and advocating for high-quality services." It seems then that the main task before the nation is to extend these quality Head Start Programs to all eligible children as part of a no-nonsense strategy to close the achievement gap as defined earlier. Yet, this is not enough. Such investments must be ensured with adequate support in public education.

Table 6–2 presents school performance on fourth-grade achievement tests for High/Scope schools and their matched comparison schools in the time since High/Scope support ended, at the end of the period of High/Scope support, and this year (five years later for site one, four years later for sites six and ten, and three years later for site nine). These statistics show how much test scores continued to improve during the years after High/Scope provided support but the model continued to be practiced, an indicator of how well the school staff remained motivated in their effective use of High/Scope in the aftermath of direct support. The findings for percentages of students passing state tests are as follows:

a. In reading, 89% of the students in High/Scope schools passed the test, nine percentage points more than the 80% at the end of High/Scope support (6.39, $p < .05$) and for two of the schools, a total of 33 percentage points from baseline to this year (27.52, $p < .01$).

b. In mathematics, 86% of the students in High/Scope schools passed the test, ten percentage points more than the 76% at the end of High/Scope support (6.84, $p < .01$) and for two of the schools, a total of 51 percentage points from baseline to this year (77.32, $p < .001$).

Table 6–2 also presents the percentage of students passing state tests at the High/Scope schools in comparison with the matched comparison schools for these High/Scope schools at the end of High/Scope support.

a. In reading, the three High/Scope schools had improved by six percentage points more than their comparison schools since High/Scope support ended (89% vs. 82% = 4.14, $p < .05$), making the total improvement for two of them 20 percentage points more than the comparison schools (7.44, $p < .01$).

b. In mathematics this year, the three High/Scope schools had improved by 12 percentage points more than the comparison schools since High/Scope support ended (86% vs. 74% = 8.29, $p < .01$), making the total improvement for two of them 47 percentage points more than the comparison schools (19.05, $p < .001$).

Table 6–2 also presents mean NCE (normal curve equivalent) scores for one site's standardized achievement tests give at grade four. On reading, the mean NCE score of students at the High/Scope School was 43—14 points higher than at the end of High/Scope support. On mathematics, the score was 47—21 points higher than at the end of High/Scope support. Versus the comparison school, the High/Scope School improved another 19 points in reading and six points in mathematics in the time since High/Scope support ended. The good news is that this is but one model with proven success, and a sound empirical foundation has been established (Weikart et al., 2002; Ramey et al., 2000) for this launching this component nationwide.

Summary

This section concerned extending current effective Head Start programs and research on early childhood programs for children placed at risk. The main points centered on:

Table 6–2: Grade Four Achievement Test Performance of High/Scope Support (2000–2001)

Site	# of Cases	High/Scope School			Comparison School			Difference Between Increases
		2000 Support	2001	Increase	2000	2001	Increase	
Percent Passing State Test								
Reading								
1	98	55.4%	72.9%	17.5	38.9%	41.0%	2.1	15.4
6	179	91.0%	95.3%	4.3	88.9%	90.5%	1.6	2.7
9	136	83.0%	96.0%	13.0	88.0%	93.0%	5.0	8.0
Mean[a]	141	79.7%	88.8%	9.1	78.4%	81.5%	3.1	6.0
Mathematics								
1	98	66.1%	84.7%	18.6	63.9%	48.7%	-15.2	33.8
6	179	91.0%	95.5%	4.5	77.8%	82.3%	4.5	0.0
9	136	57.0%	69.0%	12.0	71.0%	80.0%	9.0	3.0
Mean[a]	140	75.6%	85.8%	10.2	72.7%	74.1%	-1.7	11.9
Site 10: Mean NCE Score on Stanford Achievement Test								
Reading	87	29.0	43.0	14.0	55.0	50.0	-5.0	19.0
Math	96	26.0	47.0	21.0	39.0	54.0	15.0	6.0

[a]Means are calculated by numbers of cases per group and cannot be calculated from the information presented in this table.

a. Extending services to the eligible children not being served today
b. Ensuring that those services are effective in promoting school readiness
c. Discussing ways educators can mobilize resources.

This second component concerns delivery of intense stimulation early in the socio-cognitive developmental sequence of young poor children from underrepresented groups. It needs to equal or exceed normal standards during preschool since it is known that, once in school, the cognitive supports will be weakened. The goal should be that of early overcompensation and the maintenance of that level as long as possible. To increase the effect of preschools, a number of strategies are called for which include involving high school and college students and voluntary groups such as the elderly and the extended family.

In conclusion, the preschool is the most advanced component in the model. It has an established knowledge base with respect to effective programs. Evidence exists that when SPARs have successful and positive early experiences, schools can educate more successfully. In the last part of the chapter, some samples of a general knowledge base for early childhood, preschool education, and parents were illustrated. The purpose was to show the natural connections that exist in preparing educators as well as future parents in this area of human development. The premise in this chapter is that knowledge and practices associated with subsequent academic success need to be shared particularly with groups that have the least opportunity generally. Offering the nation's most vulnerable children cover during a critical point in their development is essential. Until the other components in the model are well in place in particular, it is crucial that effective preschools serve to offset the massive disadvantages children from poor underrepresented groups face.

Text Box 6–1: Some Applications

In terms of what educators and parents need to know, a report from the Mid-Continent Regional Laboratory suggests the following in helping children develop thinking skills (Marzano, 1998):

- When teaching new material, ask students to compare it with information they already know by such methods as categorization.

- Teach students to ask four questions about a statement: Is it unusual? Is it common knowledge? If, not, what is the proof? If there is proof, is it reliable?

- Help students develop a good problem-solving framework that helps them to understand the problem, design a plan to solve it, carry out the plan, and decide if the plan worked.

- Use "guided imagery" to help students actually imagine an event or experience.

- Teach students to elaborate, to expand on information not necessarily stated.

- Encourage students to create new information or products based on the lesson content.

- Be sure students know how and when to use a good procedure or formula.

- Encourage students to set goals.

The Elementary
School Component

Roles of Educators, Counselors, Colleges, and Universities

"Education, then, beyond all other devices of human
origin, is the great equalizer of the conditions of
man—the balance-wheel of the social machinery."

—HORACE MANN

Overview

This chapter centers on preventing the washout effect generally produced when children placed at risk, many of whom have been served by Head Start enter elementary school. It focuses on the components needed during elementary school to prevent a one- to three-year gap from emerging for SPARs' academic learning. While the earlier preschool and parent education components are critical in maximizing the success of the educational system (as noted earlier), significant progress can also be made in reorganizing elementary education in two major ways: First, increase academic learning in school to support SPARs after school. This component requires instituting college mentors and after-school programs for SPARs with an academic focus. Second, it requires transforming the school culture and its pedagogical practices to ensure SPARs do not fall grade levels behind.

What can be learned from the few elementary schools that have already reduced the achievement gap? They keep SPARs at grade level while challenging all other students. Whether these effects are sustainable at the district level is not known.[1] This chapter centers on the analyses (of changes) in schools serving high numbers of SPARs that might prove effective across the nation. Along with preschool preparation and parental involvement, a two-pronged way to help schools achieve equity—and thus, higher test scores—is presented. Key variables in the school culture influencing effective teaching for SPARs and mainstream students are also examined.

Introduction

A teaching and learning gap that originates early in elementary schooling, regardless of SPARs' preschool experience, maintains the massive and persisting inequality found today in education. While group differences in school readiness obviously exist upon entering public school, as a whole, public schools are ineffective in leveling the differences students bring with them. There is evidence that schools exacerbate disadvantages through an educational system that has been designed primarily for the more advantaged. Most SPARs attend low-quality schools with the least-qualified teachers.

When SPARs enter first grade, they are only slightly behind, but a four-year gap emerges in reading and other areas by the end of high school. For example, a thirteen-year-old mainstream student performs at the same level as a seventeen-year-old of African American background in reading, science, writing, and so on (*Condition of Education*, 1998). This gap has not diminished for over a quarter of a century, ever since programmatic efforts were first established to help children of the poor. Part of the problem is due to how poverty impacts on the quality and amount of parental involvement. Not knowing how to promote effective parental involvement remains a major problem for both developmental theory and educational policy and practice.[2]

Family literacy and parental involvement programs usually begin too late and are rarely geared towards establishing the interaction patterns necessary to provide assistance in academic areas, unlike those available to middle-class students (P.R. Portes, 1988). As noted in the previous chapter, too few SPARs participate in effective preschools. Parental involvement requires attention to culturally relevant practices that promote participation aligned with—and rewarded in—school. A developmental approach is thus necessary in sustaining learning supports over SPARs' formative years. The latter ensures new students remain at grade level or above. The extra supports are essential for SPARs in co-constructing the necessary concepts and tools required for academic success across literacy areas. To close the gap, the educational system must structure extra assistance each year, in and out of school. However, certain current premises will be challenged next before outlining a strategy for assisting the academic development of SPARs in general.

Premise #1: Head Start Can Close the Gap

In spite of major advances in early childhood education programs and programmatic efforts such as Early Start, Head Start, and Even Start, only a fraction of eligible children actually find access to effective programs. One premise is that those served will not be placed at risk for academic failure. Another premise is that if all SPARs were served, the gap would close. Unfortunately, this is not the case. It is becoming increasingly clear that earlier expectations for early age intervention efforts to fix the problem—or fix the child so that schools could then work more effectively—were based on faulty analyses of the problem. As noted recently (Bruer, 1999), stimulation aimed at developing more and stronger synapses is as much a myth as notions regarding a critical period in mental development (Bloom, 1964). Rather than criticize why such programs have failed to close the gap, a preferred alternative is to understand how such programs are helpful and are a necessary part of a solution but are still not sufficient to close the gap. Head Start's argument, for example, is that it does work, but it can't be held accountable for what happens later in schooling. This appears to be correct to a great extent. So, even if all SPARs were served by effective preschool, the gap would emerge within the first few years of school. The notion that schools can close the gap is generally faulty since they actually serve to generate it.

Premise #2: Parental Involvement Programs Can Close the Gap

Parental involvement involves a complex of parental attitudes, competencies, social capital, and other characteristics such as routines, activities, beliefs, and goals that vary systematically by class and culture. Parental involvement may be regarded as a regulating mechanism that constrains or assists development in areas that may be connected to school success and other areas. Parental involvement is not a dichotomous variable but varies along a continuum. It is not simply parents being involved in PTA groups. Parental involvement reflects directly on the quality and continuity of family interactions from which children's (in and out of school) knowledge and learning readily emerge and are sustained. It varies in the degree to which its characteristics match external academic demands and expectations. Current programs for family literacy and parent education are generally limited in scope and reach and ineffective in closing the gap.

The main influence on children's school success remains parental involvement, particularly when it is compatible with school goals and task demands. Such compatibility is associated generally with:

a. modeling positive behaviors, attitudes, and affect related to learning,
b. devoting time to reading and related literacy tasks, both individually and in group activities,

    c.   monitoring and rewarding of curiosity and effort,

    d.   showing interest in children's school-related efforts and activity,

    e.   adapting consequences to school related efforts, and

    f.   making school success a priority in the value system of the family.

The assumption that schools, parent involvement programs, or family literacy programs can overcome or compensate for class-related differences is erroneous. While schools organize teaching and learning in ways that do not compensate for lack of parental academic supports, there is little evidence that current strategies to promote parent involvement close the gap.

Premise #3: Schools Can Close the Gap

While most of the gap is constructed in and by schooling, on occasion schools can adapt to and educate SPARs at or above grade level. Schools are generally organized in ways that are subtly hazardous to SPARs while they are advantageous to others. Most SPARs fall further behind the longer they stay in school due to a complex of disadvantaging practices that invariably depend on support. This suggests that the gap depends on school and outside assistance for SPARs or they are penalized and gradually get the message that they are less able (Comer, 1980). In some exceptional cases[3] some schools manage to educate many SPARs at grade level. The premise thus must be explored that they may be effectively compensating for parental involvement and preschool through greater delivery capacity than usual. In other cases poor SPARs manage to adapt to schools. In a third case, both contribute to keep the SPAR at or above grade level overcoming the constraints of poverty and cultural history.

Preschool can make a positive contribution to school performance. The main reasons effects of preschool wash out in the elementary grades concern the following:

    a.   The intellectual/academic demands upon the child begin to increase, and such demands are organized in a cumulative fashion. Weak academic support or delays in any one area become amplified over time. Social class differences in literacy development usually become manifest and predictive of school performance by the first two years of school.

    b.   As homework and projects increase in complexity, the resources of low SES home environments are outstripped relative to those of the middle-class home where differences in social capital, parental involvement and cognitive supports are substantial.

    c.   Even when low-SES parents attempt to help, schools' demands on the at-risk child become overwhelming to both parent and child (P.R. Portes & Zady, 2002). Formal schooling requires (implicitly) a certain amount of informal social as well as cognitive support outside school for academic standards to be met.

d. A small gap in the early grades can become a formidable impediment in children's academic success because of the organization of learning experience and sequential nature of many academic skills. The activities those children are involved in after school become increasingly important in supporting academic success. Generally, the top 20% of students generally achieve three-quarters of an academic grade edge over the lowest 20%.

What Is Needed

The main goal of the elementary school component is twofold: to extend family and community resources to help SPARs academically after school and to improve teaching and learning opportunities for them in school. After-school assistance can be mobilized and activated in ways that can help keep SPARs at grade level regardless of limited support available at home. Preschool effects need to be sustained for SPARs by mobilizing resources in and out of school. Both areas will be addressed next, along with the affective and motivational factors necessary in attaining a significant effect size in academic areas.

To accomplish the goal of mass mobilization of resources in children's cognitive environments, a strategy must be able to address two issues:

a. It must organize and coordinate the necessary assistance for learning to achieve a significant effect in children's school success. This requires a longitudinal design or "pipeline" of volunteers to help support the work of educators at school. SPARs require assistance in and after school. Most programs today have not sustained assistance to SPARs. Without help, teachers alone cannot often make up for the gap created outside their control; With after-school mentoring of SPARs, the effects of class size may be indirectly reduced.

b. The strategy must also be organized in ways that allow for it to be integrated with the local community long after the initial novelty and effects of funded programs end. The strategy must adapt academic support within Big Brother/Sister, Boys and Girls, church clubs, college-based service learning, and similar initiatives. At present, some of these efforts have been initiated in particular communities (e.g., some professional athletes, philanthropists, foundations, and colleges of education have helped launch individual programs). What seems most needed then is a systemic plan to provide all SPARs with academic assistance on a regular basis after school and extend what is now available in some schools to others.

From a primary prevention standpoint, the goal of the elementary component is to remove the risks that are responsible for placing the low-income student at a disadvantage in learning normally at school. "At-risk" is a relative term that is dynamic and future oriented. "Disadvantaged" is a more pessimistic, albeit realistic, term that also denotes what will happen based on what has already happened. By organizing new social settings where interactions with personnel other than overburdened teachers take place regularly to support academic goals, after-school programs (ASP) can replace the less academically focused alternatives available to SPARs. Secondly, they can help provide the affective and cognitive supports that educators in schools cannot extend individually to SPARs on a regular basis. Considerable evidence exists that after-school programs are effective (Weisman & Gottfredson, 2001; Shann, 2002). The question is how to ensure all SPARs have full participation as part of their educational package.

Schools That Work for SPARs: One Swallow Does Not Make a Summer

What is known about schools where high proportions of SPARs do exceptionally well in meeting minimum performance standards? Even though these schools are extremely rare, they offer an opportunity to test various hypotheses. For example, what proportion of those SPARs who tested at or above grade level participated in Head Start or live in single-parent homes, compared to others or those in low-performing schools? What are the characteristics of the instruction, teachers, and curriculum that contrast most sharply between high- and low-performing schools? How is teaching organized so that high test scores as well as meaningful learning result? How is the school climate changed? These are critical questions. It is already known that even when preschool education programs level differences in school readiness for students living in poverty upon entry to first grade, a gap emerges by the third or fourth grade. This wash-out cancels the effect of early childhood or preschool programs.

Few schools have closed the gap, and it would seem to some that no clear formula has been found that can work for all schools and SPARs. Exhorting all schools to be like the rare exceptions is a fallacy in logic that is presently misleading educators away from a sustainable strategy. It is important to understand what produces and sustains equity in the few successful schools. What must be unraveled is how various persons, artifacts, goals, beliefs, and actions come together to produce exceptional outcomes before the effect can be replicated across schools in a reliable fashion.

In Louisville, Kentucky, for example, one elementary school beat the odds,[4] showing remarkably high scores for SPARs compared to schools with lower proportions of poverty-level students. It might help illustrate what works so that other schools might follow suit. Do such schools manage to attract a critical mass of educators and community members to ensure SPARs learn more than is generally the norm? Perhaps, since educators know SPARs lose ground over the summer in a phenomenon called "seasonality" (Alexander, Enwistle, & Olson, 2001), measures can be taken. At Englehard Elementary in Louisville, the principal was able to gain consensus from most of her faculty to go on a year-round schedule with the same number of school days in the year spread over the twelve months. She explains that teachers who did not like the arrangement were transferred out and replaced. Fridays were left open for field trips, since the school week was four days. Other options for teachers existed so that they were not obligated to work Fridays, yet most did so. An after-school program offered SPARs academic help regularly. The community was involved with parents helping to pitch in on the school's cultural Fridays and other activities. Teachers collaborated and monitored students' progress across content areas. High expectations and attendance rates were valued. The principal protected teacher and student academic learning time. Employing expert itinerant resource teachers and cooperative learning groups also reduced class sizes for SPARs. Long before test scores accounted for the effectiveness of these and many other related practices, a sense of community seemed to have been established and built around the challenge of learning and teaching at optimum levels each day.[5] Years later, the school remains well above average in spite of a change in leadership.

What kinds of teaching promote learning that reduces the influence of poverty? What types of arrangements and relationships prevail in such schools that set them apart from average or failing schools? As these issues are analyzed, a conceptual insight emerges that centers teaching in the students' most sensitive areas for learning (Vygotsky, 1978). When teaching is organized to tap into students' readiness level on a steady basis, across grade levels, successful schools are found.

It is clear that exceptional schools are local phenomena. They sometimes do not depend necessarily on funding so different from that of other schools or on a particular instructional method. These phenomena are not the result solely of state-legislated policies or accountability reform mandates. While reform policies have been initiated nationwide that attempt to claim credit for the few school outliers that exist, the truth of the matter is that these exceptional schools are not necessarily their result and are not well understood[6]. They cannot be claimed by any one approach or model. If they were, there would be more consistency across schools with similar populations across districts or states. The few elementary schools where most SPARs perform at grade level must still show both sustainability and exportability[7] year after year. Other elementary schools in Louisville have reduced the gap over the past three years.[8] Those educators may perhaps display certain collaborative characteristics to a higher degree than in other contexts. What is the necessary level is not yet known for sure, but what is known is that many fine educators share these characteristics across settings. Key questions then are:

a. To what extent do commitment, values, methods, content expertise, and other personnel characteristics play a major role in ensuring that students learn at grade level regardless of parental SES?

b. To what extent must the above interact with new routines or learning opportunities structured in and out of school?

c. To what extent is this due to the increased educational activity created by a sufficiently large critical mass of educators?

d. Are there critical quality and/or number of educators necessary to produce collaborative activities in school?

e. What roles and actions seem essential for the principal, counselor, and teachers in elementary school that vary or are similar to those needed in secondary school?

f. What are the characteristics and practices of these school cultures and educators relative to those in other sites? For example, are there reduced class sizes for SPARs or year-round schools?

g. How do these characteristics translate into actions that maximize student learning? For example, if in fact the school culture in each of these exemplary elementary schools is different, how does it invite success week after week, month after month so that by year's end, students make significant progress?

h. Let's say that these educators appear to be more committed in assisting SPARs and collaborate specifically toward that end, what precisely are the most salient variables activated that promote engagement or on-task learning time?

i. Relative to less successful schools, are the differences more likely to be of degree or type? That is, if a minimum but not unique set of factors were to be found, such as the collective level of faculty experience and content expertise for each school, how do static factors such as per-pupil expenditures or class size interact with dynamic, sociopsychological processes based on shared goals, beliefs, and expectations?

j. Finally, what activities and routines are students experiencing regularly that differ from those of students in comparable settings? Or, to what extent is success founded on sheer increases in academic learning time spent around engaging activities?

The School Culture Puzzle

It might be presumed that the main answer to this puzzle lies in the school (personnel and their actions). Could it be otherwise? Perhaps certain interactions between students, parents, and district and state demands come together by chance in some schools differently than others. Surely most schools and districts are trying to organize such interactions to produce an improvement in SPARs' school performance. Yet, very few are tapping the key variables, ensuring each reaches a necessary level for a prolonged period, and counts on the educators and students who can bring about a significant effect each year. Statistically, it may be that 1–5% of the time a variety of factors happen to coalesce in producing more academic learning time and sensitive or effective teaching on content that is tested. How is it is possible to organize schooling so that SPARs and teachers work well together more often? Perhaps this is like the gifted and talented student population where only the top 3–5% of students succeed under current conditions.

Rather than purport to know all the answers and propose an explanation based on a particular viewpoint such as leadership, teacher expectations, cooperative learning, class-size reduction, vouchers and such, educators must be honest and realistic. It is still not known how sustainable these factors and arrangements are even if they are associated with test scores. However, the belief is that that there are no single-barrel explanations. Secondly, even if research-based answers were found, it is still unclear if what accounted for success in one context can be exported to another. It is easy to reason post hoc (or after the fact) and claim that our favorite variables were responsible. Research suggests otherwise. Models and successful programs have to be adapted locally (Goldenberg & Gallimore, 1991; Tharp & Gallimore, 1988) until a desired outcome can be produced. In our model, the first phase requires all SPARs to perform at or above grade level over time without fail. This means schools begin by identifying those who should not fall behind and organize school change. What are the main categories and key factors within each that must be adapted locally by less-successful schools? Fortunately, theory suggests that the usual suspects or factors can be found in the activity-setting unit (see Tharp and Gallimore, 1988):

a. Personnel (at school, after school, at home, and in other settings),
b. Salient cultural values, beliefs, and attitudes brought into various activities by the learners, educators, and others,
c. Task demands and operations (particularly those related to literacy),
d. Scripts for routine behavior,
e. Purposes, motives, intentions guiding action.

Each of the above must be optimized before SPARs' development can be maximized. The school, home, or other settings combine to constrain or promote various developmental outcomes. It may be that under the current press for equity and excellence in educational outcomes, there is particular interest in those few exceptional cases that perhaps have been proactive in aligning activity settings with learning outcomes. Let's suppose that just as the top three or five students in a hundred are considered exceptional, that one school in a hundred combines the personnel and other factors above to produce higher-performing students from all backgrounds. Even if this were a random event, this does not mean that it cannot be made to occur elsewhere or more frequently. While we are still at a prescientific stage, the best bet is to organize school activity settings in ways that activate the factors found associated with higher learning for SPARs and all students. As noted before, the beauty of this venture is that in the process of addressing the ethical issue of equity for groups left behind, actually all students' development is assisted, not only in test content but in other related areas of learning. Once this is achieved, the next issue to be considered is if more is better or how much more is needed and why, particularly before continuing to increase standards or task demands on educators and students.

Maximizing SPARs' ALT (Academic Learning Time)

Elementary school represents a different type of critical period for preventing inequality in educational achievement precisely because:

a. This is when the gap becomes manifest through annual assessments,
b. It is when public resources are generally distributed unfairly for the education of SPARs (at the gate),
c. This is when cumulative learning gaps and increased academic task demands test the mettle of students' home environment and the family's social capital.

Even if closing the gap in a poor school is only a rare happenstance, activating key mediating factors may improve instruction for SPARs.[9] A main organizing principle for school performance is time: time "on task" by the student and adult and time spent making meaning with students on content related to test success in everyday experiences. Tests measure how much has been taught and learned in a specific amount of time. Success results generally when there is a match between learning activity and testing activity. Time spent on learning after school makes a difference in explaining success.[10] Time spent on particular activities allows for effort and skills to develop. The amount of time learning with a more capable peer—or even with comparable and less advanced peers—on activities related to test content matters relative to less time spent. This is why after school programs and in-school mentors are important to breaking out of the poverty cycle.

A vaccine for preventing school failure is ensuring SPARs education meets the conditions for learning. Tests are linked with success and admission to college in ways directly related to socialization patterns and opportunities related to academic learning. Hence, the arrangement of external conditions that predict success and admission to college becomes a central means for establishing equity. Development may be promoted then not only by performance standards but by a system that assists SPARs in ways that parallel more advantaged populations.

In California and other states, the removal of affirmative action criteria in college admission has led to a set of frantic measures to identify promising underrepresented minority students for college admission.[11] Just as access to facilities was built for the physically challenged or academically talented, so must they be built for SPARs to move though the K–12 education system successfully in order for equity to be accessed. Once sustainable conditions for learning are activated for SPARs, a new reorganized structure can aim for the success of all. After a certain point, unlike physical, intellectual, and emotional exceptionalities, certain strategically organized scaffolds can be removed. This is because scaffolds are culturally co-constructed tools, just as prior barriers effected unequal conditions. After a few generations, between-group differences can be eliminated through new structures and activity, leaving only individual differences within groups.

A new cultural change must be orchestrated in organizing academic success. While the organizing principles may appear to center on time dedicated to promoting academic development and motivation, just as important perhaps is the agency or the will to effect changes at each of the proposed levels. When collaboration and commitment are found among a core of competent educators in a top school, the quality and number of activities are changed so that SPARs' time in school is used to learn more test-related skills and content. If it is found that in these rare top schools, educators develop a positive climate that attracts parent involvement, it would be noted that such involvement works because it promotes SPARs' potential for learning more of the time, relative to lesser involvement. Similarly, various modes organizing class sizes or grouping students for cooperative learning—or direct or activity-based instruction—make a difference again because of this organizing principle.[12] Whether it is parent involvement, adult-child ratio, or year-round schools, the factors work because they serve to advance students' potential for development in areas that are meaningfully associated with what is valued by the educational community. This functional interpretation may appear circular in logic yet may help shed light on this puzzle. What occurs by chance in perhaps one in a thousand schools is that educators organize and/or have conditions that obtain desired results more often than expected within the constraints of time.

Table 7–1: Dynamic Assessment Model for Estimating Time and Assistance Needed to Meet Performance Standards for Various Groups of Students

(Academic Development Area)	(Conditions)	
Performance Standard (Z)	Engaged Time (x)	Student Development Level (y)*
Z_1 = Content and Grade Level (e.g., 3rd Grade Math)	Very Short	Level 1 Very Advanced (1 grade level advantage)
Z_2 = Prior Knowledge Needed	2 Short	2 Advanced (.5 grade level advantage)
	3 Average	3 Normal (grade level)
A–Z	4 Long	4 Some Gaps (below grade level)
External Assistance to Reach Grade Level	5 Very Long	5 Many Gaps (>1 grade level behind)

*= Model assumes effective pedagogy, content expertise, and preparation of teacher

Part of the challenge is connecting activities in ways that students are more likely to understand, care more about, and better remember certain concepts and skills through experiences and practices. The school climate and interaction patterns can also make huge differences in terms of attitudes and motivation that promote academic learning time. To educate future educators *better*, essential factors must be identified and coordinated in organizing routine activities with SPARs.

In Table 7–1, SPARs may be generally at levels 4–5 (y) that require increased engaged learning and teaching time (x) in mastering various performance standards that, in turn, depend on mastering of prerequisites. For some SPARs in certain settings, sufficient learning and teaching are ensured to reach a proficient level of performance while for the majority, insufficient conditions are institutionalized that become impossible or most difficult to overcome over time. What is needed is a way to develop an individualized learning plan for each SPAR so that teachers and mentors can tell what the student knows or does not know well or at all across content areas and the current grade level performance standards. Without attention to the conditions and time needed, SPARs predictably fall years behind in the present system.

Text Box 7–1: Englehard Elementary: A Case Study

Mrs. Theresa Jensen, ex-principal of this exceptional school, candidly reflected that there is no magic bullet or single factor to close the gap. Rather, it seems as if various forces coincide when prior efforts mature at about the same time both in and out of school to bring about high test scores. She is a calm, optimistic, can-do, aware person, who is a respected leader, yet she suspects it is her effect on others and theirs on her that made the school special. She reports *helping* set up an established set of practices, beliefs, and expectations based on listening and collaboration. This school still ranks at the top of the district's elementary schools in standard performance measures two years after turning the school around. In spite of having a larger proportion of SPARs (70%) compared to other schools in the district, educators at this school experimented and worked collaboratively until all students began to gain ground. Theresa noted that while the "phenomenon" was being documented, various educators came to see it and walked away convinced that their particular explanation was correct. Some who were partial to organizational approaches in educational administration believed it was her effective leadership, while others thought it was the after-school programs and/or extended learning time (year round) available to students. Others believed it was mainly due to parents' involvement in the school, its open and friendly climate, and volunteers. Still other experts believed the effect was primarily due to the teachers, who were a special bunch of dedicated, able professionals who worked together to build a collaborative school culture and had high expectations for all students.

In studying these and other factors more carefully, their interaction in context may help explain the exceptional outcomes. In another context, the interaction may be different in terms of the factors themselves and the levels of each required to make significant gains in academic achievement. Across contexts, how the various ingredients come together can affect what is taught, how it is taught, and the very definitions of success. It thus seems advisable to rely on a variety of measures rather than a single indicator of educational progress. Each is essential in defining equity in the pursuit of happiness and opportunities to learn. Comparative studies are needed in determining local and general factors that result in educational progress. In other schools, many of the same factors may be operating at similar levels, and the outcomes may not be as positive. Ms. Jensen was not concerned as much about test scores as about establishing positive conditions for work

Text Box 7–1 continued

and student learning. She describes the following characteristics in particular.

What Educators Need to Keep in Mind

- Students feel connected, valued, and included. This occurs when a positive climate prevails and is part of the educators' agenda. Positive affective relations with students, humor, caring by "with-it" teachers who make good use of learning time across classrooms help produce a school-wide effect.
- Educators share the goal of taking on the challenge posed by SPARs and feel united in their common "social" purpose as change agents. In contrast to low-performing schools, there appears to be a larger critical mass of conscientious, prepared, demanding professionals who have no intention of giving up on SPARs.
- The change occurs gradually as educators collaborate, have a shared understanding and commitment to assist all students, particularly those who need more assistance. Educators do not work insulated from others but rather come together regularly to share concerns, ideas, and monitor students' progress. School counselors help teachers and SPARs gain allies.
- Principals and counselors lead by example in assisting teachers to excel in their jobs. They protect academic learning time and help promote morale by encouragement and gaining logistical support for students. They assist in managing and preventing problem behaviors and seeking external supports for SPARs.
- A major function in the collaboration of educators is to prevent social promotion. Through early identification and resource allocation, each student's progress matters and failure is not an option. The group implements strategies that assist SPARs in and after school.
- Another function is taking a proactive approach to involving parents through notes, mail, calls, meetings when necessary, and using counselors' skills and outside community resources to sustain continuous progress. (Personal Communication, 2002)

The Elementary School Component: After-school Mentoring and Academic Clubs

At the policy level, compensatory education efforts and services are facing budget cutbacks. Many such programs have shown limited results. Title I is not closing the gap (Borman & D'Agostino, 1996), yet it is clear that services need to be extended in ways that not only serve more SPARs but also assist their learning directly and over time. While the US Department of Education and state and district policies focus on accountability and identification of failing schools, proactive measures are needed to supplement SPARs' learning, such as reducing class sizes and providing academic tutors in after-school clubs regularly within a coordinated system or during the school day.

Two major steps are proposed that would help close the achievement gap: restructuring educational practices and culture within the school as noted earlier and developing and coordinating of after-school programs and extra learning opportunities for SPARs. The second part of this chapter concerns how to build architecture capable of improving the school performance of at-risk elementary school students after school and during school with extra mentors guiding SPARs. This calls for new roles to be played by educators, particularly counselors, principals, and others in higher education.

Among key factors influencing educability and achievement in education are on-task academic-related learning time, student-adult ratio, and family involvement, and yet each converges on a common area. One key is the intensity of the person's participation in activities related to what tests value. This plan calls for new efforts for sealing a college mentoring (CM) and after-school program initiative that are based on best practices research. Positive results have been found not only for young SPARs but also college volunteer students in this literature.

Educators can play a lead role in organizing school academic mentoring relationships with volunteers. However, both in- and after-school programs need to be institutionalized alongside schools and involve every SPAR in the school. A mentor, working along with teachers in the school, assists each SPAR. The plan calls for each to have a mentor throughout the elementary school year precisely when the achievement gap generally begins and widens. One major goal is to prevent these students from entering middle and high school with learning gaps. Another purpose is to help sustain and develop motivation, work habits and an academic identity that may resist peer pressures, resistance, stereotypes, violence, aggression, and other risks later.

The overarching goal for this component is to develop and refine a sustainable delivery system that serves to:

a. develop, extend and link university service learning programs, courses, training, credits and incentives in extending the local school districts' after-school (safety net) programs
b. study the effects of extending at-risk elementary students' learning time with volunteers coordinated by regular teachers

   c. evaluate the progress of after-school efforts as at-risk students are served across the first years of public school in the district

   d. design sustainable models for assisting homework/school perform-ance directly and studying the long-term effects of this initiative across districts

   e. develop effective workshops for participants in exploring and infusing technology through after-school mentoring activities, and also scal-ing the model to other school district–university collaborations. (For example, see the Department of Education's Safe and Smart After-School Programs: http://www.ed.gov/pubs/afterschool/3what-works.html.)

Rationale for the Elementary School Component

The after-school model is focused on developing and maintaining the cognitive supports required to avoid the "wash-out" effect now affecting SPARs served by Head Start and similar preschool programs. It is also aimed to assist those not ready for elementary school and who have not had effec-tive preschool education. The latter may be effective in developing school readiness. There is ample evidence that elementary schooling creates and amplifies the achievement gap. Since many children living in poverty are not served in effective preschool programs, a significant difference exists by third grade in both literacy outcomes and academic identity relative to students not living in poverty. Living in poverty translates into a different—yet still disadvantaging—set of socialization conditions that constitute the "missing half" outside schooling that define the home environment. The critical ingre-dients of parent involvement and related sociocognitive supports that are aligned with school success and compatibility for students not at-risk are often missing. This call for a systemic plan to activate the most significant predictors of school success includes involvement and relationships with adults around activities designed to assist learning in academic task demands related to performance objectives of schooling. The time spent on such tasks with caring others also helps improve self-esteem, a positive student identity, and motivation (Comer, 1980). This new "adopt a SPAR" initiative, even for a few hours a week, can make a difference, particularly in urban areas sur-rounded by colleges and universities.

A new directive to expand the delivery capacity is needed to increase compatibility between SPARs' learning and schools' teaching. It would call for the mobilization of resources to ensure volunteers serve SPARs, particu-larly in schools where they are most concentrated. College and high school students in particular and also retired volunteers under the direction of university-school district-community partnerships would serve regularly toward this national effort. Volunteers would sign up for a time period or tour of service to work with a particular SPAR.

The model could be implemented across the nation to target SPARs specifically so that a significant proportion performs with a mentor connection. Along with new collaborative practices modeled in schools, academically oriented after-school programs would complement the regular education of SPARs in elementary school.[13] The plan helps reorganize many activities that are already occurring across some schools in the nation. Efforts to establish in- and after-school partnerships that assist SPARs' school performance under various arrangements can attract community support from retired and social organizations. To connect available human resources to each school leadership would be required not from the school alone but from the state and federal levels, business and sports communities.

Many districts have programs that only serve a variety of purposes that often exclude a focus on academic outcomes. What is needed are for existing programs to be focused on areas where SPARs need most improvement in school. It is most difficult to sustain such programs over time unless they form part of a larger, comprehensive framework. The proposal links universities, colleges, those in the social services, firemen, retired persons, businesses, and college students—particularly those in teacher education—with school districts' efforts to extend at-risk students' learning time. To coordinate mentoring activities with teacher recommendations, new structures are needed to drive change.

University-school district partnerships are needed to create local pipelines of volunteers sufficient in number to mentor SPARs each year in sustaining grade-level performance. Federal and state programs can offer college tuition assistance in ways similar to Peace Corps and VISTA volunteer programs to serve across communities. Many philanthropists are looking to contribute toward school equity and excellence. Students in colleges and universities, for example, might be required to complete a minimum service-learning requirement for this purpose. Students might receive tuition credits, loans, or stipends to work with one SPAR during one or two semesters. Big Brothers and Big Sisters and other community clubs might also join along with similar community programs. Counselors and principals would work with the community in launching these partnerships. Retired teachers and education faculty could also help train mentors and coordinate with teachers. The goals would be set for every SPAR (to have a mentor) during each year in elementary school. College-bound high school seniors might also be recruited to serve along with college students. Once the gap is prevented in elementary school, teaching as a whole and in later grades particularly is facilitated.

In effect, what is being proposed is a reliable network of after-school programs for SPARs to prevent the gap from persisting in another generation. We know these programs are effective (Beck, 1999; Posner & Vandell,

1999). Presuming preschool education is provided for all SPARs, this strategy component would target "test-related" literacies so that once minimum standards are met, broader aspects of development could be included. As with Head Start, the design and field tests of pilot programs would be part of research collaboration between school districts and college faculty and graduate students. This research would be helpful for scaling effective approaches to new school districts serving at-risk elementary students. A district plan to identify the SPARs most left behind would help initiate the concentration of resources. This strategic assistance does not have to be rejected by conservatives since this resource allocation has multiple economic benefits that are unlike social welfare. In building greater capacity for those at risk, savings from a lower retention ratio and other special services would be considered. On the other end of the spectrum greater equity in access to current

Figure 7.1: Blueprint for Dismantling the Achievement Gap for SPARs

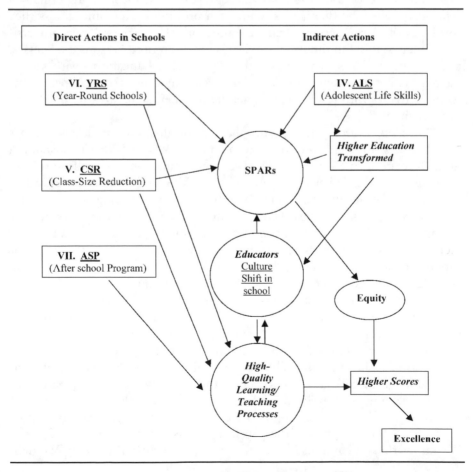

opportunities would be supported. What is clear is that the current NCLB strategy underestimates the problem of capacity and is minimally concerned about equity. Situating the problem solely in schools and teachers is misguided.

After the initiative in elementary school is established, middle schools would also be served as well as high schools. Mentoring relationships could be sustained for SPARs entering middle and high school for those performing below grade-level standards. Secondary and middle school students would also serve in mentoring younger peers as part of everyone's experience in the educational system. This enlistment of human resources from the community helps educators and society as a whole in more than one way. This component calls for a teaching and learning society and a social movement that would parallel other health and economic campaigns of the past. Businesses and corporations would be asked to join in contributing in some measure so that the time and supports required for learning could be organized strategically. Teachers and low-income parents need help in assisting SPARs.[14] Teachers and counselors would assist mentors with individual educational plans for each student to maximize their learning potential.

In sum, the overall academic elementary component (see Figure 7–1) of the model requires attention to:

a. Cellular change in school culture where well-prepared educators collaborate to close the gap as a primary goal,
b. Extra mentors in and after school,
c. Year-round schooling,
d. Reduced class sizes for SPARs (<15),

> Extended Learning Time

e. Assessing and developing academic zones of proximal development in addition to individualized educational plans (IEPs),
f. Educators savvy in effective instructional practices, diagnostic assessment, and their own content area, and
g. Administrative supports for both teachers and counselors in expanded roles.

A model for all elementary schools serving SPARs requires a corps of (volunteer) mentors from nearby high schools and colleges. College students and volunteers would serve a four- to seven-month tour of duty with brief training. As new roles are established in the preparation of educators (see Chapter Eight), this aspect of the restructuring plan would become part of the transformation experienced by future generations of SPARs. As counselors, principals, and teachers become certified, they will have mastered the necessary competencies to close the gap (i.e., establishing collaborative programs, primary prevention, and applied human development and learning).

A major concern in establishing a sustainable after-school program is to explore how new university and community-based programs can help the district's efforts to close the gap and ultimately improve K–12 education overall. A central goal is to promote literacy, including literacy in math and science, by constructing activity settings after school during these formative years. At-risk students' participation in after-school academic clubs over time may be conceptualized largely as part of the "missing half" that accounts for the increasing literacy gap. Recruiting this level of assistance from a steady, qualified source represents a formula for a major educational policy shift. The impact is potentially at a level comparable to Head Start. The difference between the two delivery systems is substantial in terms of costs, yet the two initiatives are interrelated and together provide continuity.

Conceptualizing the Social Basis of the Problem

There are at least two ways to understand the problem of successfully educating students from low SES backgrounds. Each focuses on the reason(s) why schools are unable to narrow or prevent the gap after a quarter century of unsuccessful attempts. Schooling, as a cultural program that organizes specific literacy goals, requires or at least presumes certain conditions are met (e.g., compatibility between the family/community culture and school-based teaching and learning). The first viewpoint is that a massive gap is already established in the first three years of life that is largely language mediated. Socialization differences persist until their effects become evident generally by a one-standard deviation in school achievement, regardless of pre-, in- and after-school programs. It may be that performance differences that appear later during the elementary school years and beyond are largely a function of differences in early language-based interaction patterns, socialization practices, and values (Hart & Risley, 1992). These authors documented a three-to-one ratio differential in the linguistic-based measures observed in children across professional, working-class, and poor families in the first three years of life. While preschool programs attempt to address this cumulative difference in literacy and may be necessary, they are not sufficient in sustaining school readiness.

A second perspective is that this early gap can and has been narrowed by some early interventions, including a few Head Start-like programs that are effective. The gap, however, is widened in elementary school mostly due to disadvantaging schooling practices and the removal of prior institutionalized supports and structures that are most compatible with middle-class group values and their literacy-related practices (P.R. Portes, 1996; Portes & Zady, 2002). Current practices tend to transform and amplify cultural differences in development into deficits in school adaptation. It is at this juncture (K–4th grade) that literacy demands and expectations in school interact with family and community culture in constructing an increasing, cumulative gap. The latter compromises the success of middle and high education efforts. In effect, schooling—as it is generally organized—is not and cannot be considered independently of students' learning and development outside school. Schooling is organized in ways that explicitly and implicitly impose demands and sanctions founded on certain assumptions concerning the student's family/community culture-based program. Incompatibility (Tharp, 1989) in the latter transforms cultural differences quickly into literacy/performance deficits that undermine SPARs' potential for full development. A counter initiative or program is needed.

Even with early intervention (see Schweinhart, Weikart, & Lerner, 1986; Zigler & Styfco, 1993), not all children at-risk develop school readiness, and those who participate in effective preschool practices typically begin to slide in the early grades. Culture and SES based differences result in pervasive effects that generally are founded on a sustained gap in delivery capacity (Dunham et al., 1988), variables such as those inherent in parental involvement, time on task, adult-child ratio, and mediated activity. School's effects on human development are not generally independent of the family/community culture. In fact, their interdependence grows over time and before long, the consequences become further etched via tracking programs, expectations, identities, and a host of non-academic factors. It seems most plausible that both mechanisms are partly correct and in fact act together to explain the massive GBI confronting multicultural societies. Yet evidence exists that extended learning time and effective pedagogical practices can make a significant difference.

Research Context and Merit of the After-School Program Component

Current practices—along with teacher–student ratios, pedagogical limitations and family/community variables—tend to amplify differences in sociocognitive development in early elementary school. By middle and high school, both teachers and SPARs are flustered. Given a growing literacy gap, it becomes less likely that at-risk students can make a successful transition from school (*Condition of Education*, 1998, 2003). Perhaps new institutional efforts that have a strong empirical and theoretical base can address the problem. The "school-constructed" part of the literacy gap may be a result of an institutionalized socialization program that tends to be more adaptable and compatible with middle- rather than low-income families (Hixson & Tinsmann, 1990). Several literatures are relevant to understanding the elements required for a successful systemic approach that centers on activating parental involvement (Funkhouser, Gonzales, & Moles, 1997; Epstein, 1991), extending learning time and bridging research and practice (Donovan, Bransford, & Pellegrino, 1999).

So why is the educational research and policy community today not using this new knowledge in reducing the gap? The evidence suggests initiatives involving after-school programs for at-risk students are effective in reducing the gap across the country (Posner & Vandell, 1994, 1999). The growing literature on service learning programs in the last two decades shows school-community-based partnerships can become integrated into the early school life of SPARs.

The bad news is that no one knows exactly what works across contexts, why it works, when it works, how long it takes to work, what the cost/benefit and long-term gains are, or if such efforts are scalable. Many demonstration projects have no long-term support. To eradicate this culture-based literacy gap, it must first be shown that extensions in learning time, family involvement, and mediated learning arrangements can be scaled widely. Many well-intentioned efforts go on without longitudinal evaluations, although some address key parts of the problem. Efforts such as those organized by the National Center for Literacy, CREDE, CRESPAR, Accelerated Schools, Success for All, America Reads, Even Start, Title I, and Fifth Dimension provide important support to teaching and learning, but as in many other projects, long-term effects, cost effectiveness, and sustainability remain unknown. In sum, chunks of district, state, private, and federal budgets are committed to these efforts without a programmatic research and development (R&D) component that aims to effect changes in the educational system as a whole for the nation. Process and outcome evaluation feedback is also critical to build and institute an effective "antidote" to the school-based part of the gap. Schools alone cannot eradicate cycle-of-poverty effects that are essentially social and historical in origin. Yet, they can educate SPARs better when ASPs are in place. The scope, focus, and operation of such programs need to be integrated within a comprehensive plan.

In fact, it is the relative difference in literacy experiences before and after school that is linked to reading and related deficits. The fact remains that, while many at-risk children become successful readers, most do not. Much of the current research on the achievement gap implies a deviation from a culture and class-based norm of factors such as:

a. literacy enriching practices, reading readiness activities;
b. parental involvement in the educational sequence during the formative years;
c. assisted or metacognitive support/exposure by peer and adult;
d. time on tasks related to school achievement (i.e., reading, modeling);
e. social learning of attitudes, values, motives adaptive to school;

f. peer and adult support of academic and social competence;

g. access to educational tools (i.e., technology, museums, travel), and;

h. responsive in-school education and peer cohort effects related to tracking or grouping practices.

Fortunately, the educational research community is finally at a point where many quasi-experimental advances in the knowledge base are becoming evident and may be ripe for scaling to wider sectors in schooling (see Slavin, 2002a). According to a recent RAND report (Grissmer et al., 2000) that utilized NAEP data, lowering pupil–teacher ratios for students in "lower grades in states with low SES . . . has very large predicted effects." The authors note that preschool has much stronger effects for students at risk with respect to student achievement (which would seem to also support extended learning time programs). In contrast to a long history of limited research investments, now is the time to mount larger-scale projects that have policy implications for the nation's school districts. Rather than waiting for years of failure to overcrowd schools with vouchers, the answer seems to lie in evidence-based research and primary prevention. Both can produce larger effects and tax savings.

Summary

In sum, the elementary component calls for establishing academic after-school programs for all SPARs, reducing their class size, and providing year-round schooling. The key areas are: to organize after-school, university-based mentoring pilot models to be sustainable, technology rich and beneficial to both college/community mentors and SPARs. Extending educational programs after school for SPARs to provide individualized academic help can bolster school effectiveness and prevent the achievement gap. A mentoring pipeline needs to be established as part of the educational system, mostly with urban college students who may receive tuition or course credits. Once these partnerships become the norm in a district, the gap can be lessened.

In this chapter different types of actions in transforming elementary and secondary education were considered and new ones proposed. First, directions for change in the school culture and practices that best capture the qualities found in outstanding schools (i.e., reduced class size, year-round schooling, leadership in changing school culture and instruction, and scaffolding in target areas such as reading) were examined and integrated within the overall strategy. Second, in- and after school programs focused on academic development were proposed as an integral part of the educational program for SPARs. An extended school year with increased guidance and mentoring for SPARs also ensures that assistance is sustained from preschool to the later grades and is critical for a large-scale population effect. Policymakers and educators can help by organizing this multifaceted, technology-rich component in and after school to increase academic learning time.

The main focus of this component is to build architectures capable of improving the school performance of SPARs through increased mediated activities in and after school, By reducing the current adult–child ratio, learning can be promoted in areas most sensitive to change. The strategy is to deploy extra personnel or mentors on a regular basis in a program based on best practices research. Positive results are expected not only for elementary and college students but also for teacher recruitment and education. We know the key factors influencing achievement in school are academic learning time, student–adult ratio, and family involvement. The plan requires certain intermediary steps (such as evaluating current and new efforts, designing and piloting an effective model, and incorporating technology), and scaling the model to university/school district sites nationwide. A mentoring pipeline as part of the educational system requires federal support yet involves a broader sector of society. This component can also be facilitated by changes in higher education (see Chapter Eight), where college–district collaborations may set up a steady pool of mentors for SPARs.

Educators can play a lead role in organizing after-school academic clubs and setting up mentoring relationships with volunteers. In particular, the plan calls for each child subject to GBIa to have a support system at a time when the achievement gap generally begins to widen. One major goal is to prevent these students from entering secondary schools with serious literacy lags. Another is to help develop motivation, work habits, and an academic identity that may resist peer pressures, bullying, and alienation. Finally, involving others besides educators is essential in preventing the gap in elementary school and helps make this initiative a societal responsibility rather than just a school-bound problem. As Thomas and Bainbridge (2001) note, it is a fallacy to believe "that all children can learn the same curriculum, in the same amount of time, and at the same level. The problem with such an unexamined belief is that it may be used to deny differential. . . support for those who come to school with environmental disadvantages" (p. 3).

Those placed at risk may be defined as those in the lowest third of standardized achievement who are in living in poverty. In essence, this approach considers that children should not be doomed largely on the basis of their parents' background or current characteristics. Any child should be assured a chance to compete fairly in working towards meritocracy in our society. Educators would break from past tradition in considering that regardless of whether parents may be held responsible, their child's development should not be compromised by how current barriers in the educational system are organized.

Endnotes

1. Some effective programs that have proven effective in closing the school achievement gap may be sustainable (Levin, 1988; Slavin, 1990), yet students may attend other schools that later neutralize or fail to support earlier gains.
2. In a sense, our model may be seen as a programmatic strategy to promote and at the same compensate for differences in socialization (P.R. Portes & Vadeboncoeur, 2003).
3. See programs noted by Borman & D'Agostino (1996).
4. An effective, exceptional school is one that reduced GBI. (The odds for a school with greater than 50% SPARs in the student population are that it will score below the mean for the district.)
5. These observations were based on conversations with local educators.
6. Schools, as units of analysis, may be distributed normally for all we know.
7. Exportability refers to applying what has proven effective in one project and extending it to others.
8. Again, closing the gap is defined by criteria based on the unusually high percentage of SPARs served by each school who are performing at or above grade level.
9. Equity can be measured by the proportion of SPARs performing below grade-level standards across groups. In the present case SPARs should have a comparable percentage above grade level as the mainstream population. Only then is it likely that a sufficient pool of high achievers can be sustained throughout middle and secondary school.
10. The literature in this area consistently points to improved performance by SPARs.
11. These are generally average minority students who meet minimum grade level standards (see Mehan et al., 1994).
12. Recent research (Borman et al., 2002) points to the different models that have proven effective in raising SPARs' test scores by focusing on basic skills: Success for All, Accelerated Schools, and Core Knowledge. It may be that each performance standard requires x amount of teaching and learning by y student (see Table 7–1).
13. While after-school programs are considered crucial for the elementary school component of our approach, they are not excluded from the strategy during middle and secondary school. Rather, we would propose they be organized for sustaining continuity after they are firmly established as part of the elementary school program. SPARs struggling at the end of elementary school should most definitely remain adopted by capable mentors. Even with low test scores, what matters most is maintaining a presence and social capital in SPARs' academic journey.
14. A conceptual problem here in closing the gap is that SPARs are not and have not been considered as having special needs.

Part III

Transforming the Education of Educators and Policy Makers

8 The Higher Education Component

Transforming Educators' Professional Preparation in Higher Education

"We must not believe the many, who say that only
free people ought to be educated, but we should
rather believe the philosophers who say
that only the educated are free."

—EPICTETUS, *DISCOURSES*

Overview

A comprehensive, multilevel plan to eradicate the educational achievement gap must include changes in higher education. Not only does higher education continue to motivate efforts to assist SPARs from underrepresented groups with improved instructional strategies and multicultural curricula for teachers, but more importantly, higher education requires transformation in the ways it prepares all professional educators and the extent to which it commits itself to promote excellence through equity in the public school system. One way to accomplish this challenging task is to view higher education as that link in the socialization process that not only prepares educators but also future policymakers from a variety of other disciplines. Hence, a twofold function appears justified. Not only must we prepare future educational leaders to work collaboratively in K–12 schools to "move" achievement with a focus on principals, teachers and counselors. This is a current initiative supported in many quarters by groups such as the Wallace Foundation. We must also include in undergraduate education sufficient exposure to other majors about human development, learning, culture with respect to the achievement gap, current and proposed solutions and models. Educators, in particular, need to have a common knowledge base in this area, including how to improve current practices through leadership, know-how, and collaboration. Today we miss a critical opportunity in higher education to prime changes in our schools and communities. This chapter sketches some of the directions for change in what college graduates ought to know about the problem.

In order to differentiate between cosmetic, sporadic solutions and more substantive, theory-driven actions to end inequality in education,[1] the understanding and education of the public, policy makers, and educators need retooling. Few educators know, for example that the gap has widened for black children since 1979 (Jencks and Phillips, 1998) or that their level of poverty has increased recently, (Lee & Burkham, 2002; Rank, 2004). Even fewer understand the ramifications of placing 20% or 40% of children at-risk and raising standards. While they confront the consequences of increasing gaps for students, few understand the ways the system ensures the majority of SPARs are left behind. Instead, they are led to believe that it is their fault that they can close the gap across the board or that others can through vouchers and charter schools.

There is also a gap between what educators know and are not able to do professionally, relative to other types of professionals who enjoy higher status and income. In fact, an excuse for the lower status and power of educators lies precisely in the view that they have fewer skills and less knowledge than other professionals about what works in learning and teaching. Whether this perception is accurate or not depends largely on definitions and the extent to which higher education constructs their professional identity, dispositions, and skills. A variety of gaps emerge in great part from the manner in which educational structures have been organized. To reorganize such structures in any given area—such as linking elementary education with mentoring SPARs academically—requires institutional changes in and outside schools, colleges, and universities. In this chapter, the focus is on strategic changes within higher education, particularly on preparing educators and future policy makers. The focus lies partly on identifying conceptual aspects of a knowledge base that is needed for educators to close the gap. Much more emphasis on developmental principles and practices needs to be shared in higher education, although specific preparation for each type of professional role is obviously needed and desirable. Also, educators need to become increasingly knowledgeable in primary prevention and promotion. Yet this remains an area limited mostly to medical research doctors dealing with health care and some psychologists. For the sake of illustration, the primary focus here is on counselor education to illustrate some of the areas that need to be integrated into the knowledge base of all programs in higher education that prepare educators. Many of these can be shared across disciplines and in an effort to disseminate knowledge and skills to close the gap in undergraduate study. While this chapter focuses only on one strategic area of preparation that has to become more proactive in closing the gap, others will require similar attention in the future.

A central rationale for a higher education component is that it makes sense within a cultural-historical approach to focus on mediating activities that can direct development. If it is known that both in and out of school factors need to be addressed jointly in closing the gap and that collaboration centered on closing the gap amongst educators is essential, then:

a. transforming the preparation of educators in higher education offers a window of opportunity to facilitate collaboration in the future (just as it does for adolescents before they become parents).
b. help could be provided to promote a common core of knowledge, pedagogical strategies, and concepts pertaining directly to dismantling the gap; and
c. new roles and functions for educators can begin to be structured and carried out across school districts.

The strategy of maximizing the academic development of SPARs before a gap emerges through the organization of and a pipeline of assistance (pre K–12) in and after school illustrates the point.

The contexts and activities SPARs encounter from preschool to high school are crucial targets in reorganizing the educational system. Closing the achievement gap can serve as a central organizing theme in preparing professional educators. It serves as a perfect social science problem around which the education of counselors, teachers, and administrators can be designed in advantaging all students.

While educators may assume specific roles as teachers, principals, and counselors in the system, they also need to be on the same page when it comes to defining the problem and having a general strategy to reduce GBI in education over time. After graduation, educators should enter the field of education with a common vision and set of prevention and developmental practices around which critical collaborations become routine in each school. This is not the case now. With a common understanding of excellence through equity as an indispensable principle, new generations of educators[2] can apply a growing knowledge base to promote the development of those now left behind. This new type of professional preparation would be sustained over the next few generations until all students meet current standards and GBI ceases at that level. In higher education, educators would learn and teach not only how inequality is structured and defined but also their own roles. A second piece of the higher education component lies in promoting greater participation and leadership of SPARs completing the prior components. Some recommendations for activating this last component are noted later in the chapter.

Introduction

Precisely what must educators understand about the gap? How different will their roles and professional practices be in a multi-level reform in education? For example, how is the academic gap to be interpreted by educators? The gap reflects not only students' learning or educators' expertise but also societal conditions that are imposed and maintained subtly in the educational system (see Haberman, 2002). Regardless of role, educators would need to understand that—while standards are necessary—they must be developed reasonably without practices that ensure a certain number of students will fail to attain them. Another issue lies in understanding the advantages and problems with tests in relation to instructional and educational goals. The focus on instruction that meets standards is preferable to feedback based on norm-reference tests that only provides relative information about where students and schools stood relative to each other. However, the advantage of understanding how tests assess the extent to which standards-based instruction and content knowledge and skills are mastered (by grade level) is of little value if how the achievement gap is constructed is not understood. Educators need the feedback provided but must avoid misuses of that information. The feedback should serve to support significant restructuring and provide the assistance necessary to close the gap for SPARs in every school rather than to bash education. Other important concepts for empowering the preparation of educators are noted.

The Speed-Up

Many educators are prepared without fully understanding the relation between organizing SPARs' academic learning time and achieving higher standards through guided performance opportunities. Those opportunities can be organized in and after school through reliable delivery systems. Raising the bar in terms of higher standards demands more time and effort from students and educators. This amounts to a general speeding up of the teaching and learning rate without corresponding structural changes in the means for guiding and supporting SPARs' academic performance. This imbalance exposes the shortsightedness of placing tougher task demands on an already failed system for SPARs without substantial corresponding measures to prevent the gap from widening.

In speeding up the rate of instruction and learning through standards-based tests, many SPARs are left without reliable academic support and become alienated while others are challenged above grade level. This type of excellence comes at a cost that, thus far, most are unwilling to recognize. Without programmatic and strategic investments, the system fails in assisting those left behind. It succeeds in making it seem as if the gap is being addressed while the gap remains well sustained. With a host of international problems related to security in past years, the focus on closing the gap has been diverted.

From an intellectual perspective, it is fortunate that this speeding up[3] is occurring because it exposes the internal contradictions inherent in the system and shows its unfairness that much better and sooner. This current reform might just also speed up the need to rethink the No Child Left Behind (NCLB) policy now being pursued that will sustain group-based inequality. Second, the question that needs to be asked is who benefits? The reform seems geared toward higher test scores for the nation and preparing not-so-diverse minorities for college. In fact, some advanced courses help accelerate students bound for college so they do not need to take certain first-year college courses. This savings suggests that the current system actually pays some of the costs of college for a few who tend to be already privileged. Those who exceed the standards can skip basic college coursework. The irony here lies in that while there is a lack of resources to close the gap in basic skills for SPARs, this very system provides free college-level education to some[4] of the more advantaged. Educators rarely question what reformers really mean by equity or closing the gap.

The goal of education is not only to prepare some for college, but all for life and to do so as fairly as possible. Standards-based reform can serve as a mechanism for change as long as there is an awareness of the ways and purpose(s) for which it is being used. To reduce the achievement gap, standards cannot be manipulated but must instead be kept at a level commensurable with not only the educational systems of developed nations but also the cultural and economic diversity of their student groups. Many of the top educational systems in the world do not have large multicultural populations or severe group-based inequality as found in the United States, Latin America, and other developing countries. With the exception of the latter groups, the present system seems to work quite well for the majority of students. In effect, the segmented educational system works well for majority (Berliner & Biddle, 1995) and most immigrant students.

Educators need to understand that what is at stake is the challenge of designing a casteless[5] educational system capable of producing minimum standards-based learning outcomes equitably for all groups. The most urgent educational and professional priority remains establishing a minimum level of equity in learning outcomes because these are the primary means toward existing opportunities. By employing what is learned by such transformation, social inequality might at least be held in check. This and other related concepts are important in the preparation of educators in higher education. The benefits of eradicating the achievement gap, even at the modest level being proposed, may bring about improvements in learning and teaching that extend far beyond educating the least advantaged.

Higher Education to Better Prepare Educators

Educators in particular remain uninformed about the origins of "at-risk" students and how they are involved in producing it, although they could be instrumental in bridging the achievement gap. The professional preparation and roles of educators are not directly designed for promoting equity and excellence. Their training is limited—and often focused—on goals that are not aligned within an overall strategy to reduce the massive inequality in learning outcomes. Much of their time is spent dealing with problems produced by the failure to educate SPARs to grade level in the first place. Many educators begin their career in failing schools where they remain undersupported year after year. For many the problem lies in the earlier grades where SPARs' gap was allowed to extend. The premise of the current reforms is that if counselors and teachers do their job well, both excellence and equity will be achieved. Unfortunately this is not the case. Reform after reform has failed largely because of three prevailing limitations: (a) knowledge about the root causes of the problem, (b) tools and strategic actions with which to promote academic development, and (c) power to implement the latter.

Most educators specialize in a context or developmental area that is not concerned directly with closing the achievement gap. The latter is only dealt with superficially in multicultural classes. The rhetoric implies that if they are committed enough, work hard enough, and are culturally sensitive, the problem may be solved within the existing system. This myth remains ingrained in higher education and government.

Educators and policy-makers enter their fields missing essential competencies for closing the gap in educational outcomes. For example, do most understand how the present system reproduces the gap by the way practices, routines, and professional roles are organized? Generally, they believe it is the individual's problem or parents' that causes low achievement. They miss the interaction of cultural history, status, and achievement. But let's assume for the sake of the present argument that most school districts in the nation were truly willing to work toward equity in achieving minimum proficiency for all groups' educational outcomes. Let's assume that they were willing to move beyond current programs and practices that have been unsuccessful in curtailing the achievement gap for SPARs. What would be their next step?

To promote systemic change, new roles and functions for educators are needed in launching a sustainable model to close the gap as defined in this book. An overhaul of the educational system and its practices in K–12 is needed in transforming local school culture and practices. For example, the levels of support and collaboration in structuring experiences for SPARs outside school that help close the gap in school are now insufficient. Educators need well-informed, cooperative leadership that also understands the developmental nature of the problem (and of the present plan). But this is not the case, nor is the preparation sufficient in higher education for those who shape policy and practices.

Professional education programs must offer theoretical knowledge and applied expertise in order for educators to play significant roles in the schools as leaders in prevention-oriented restructuring efforts. Society—including colleges—must become a part of the solution. Educators should be prepared to provide skills and leadership to others in addressing the achievement gap as it is manifested locally. In so doing, many related consequences, such as domestic violence, drug abuse, and a host of social risk problems that affect future SPARs can be mitigated.

Teachers, counselors, administrators, and policymakers need to share a conceptual plan for dismantling the achievement gap. Teacher and counselor education offers a unique opportunity to increase literacy development in special and regular populations. What new support systems need to be in place for at-risk students to increase academic skills? This is where counselors' hands have been tied and their activities limited, thus diminishing an ideal partnership with teachers. That is, counselors need to lead in areas related to students' overall growth, development, and motivation outside the classroom, helping to construct positive school cultures that promote excellence through greater equity. Counselors can help coordinate and organize various support systems and workshops for students at-risk in areas that indirectly contribute to school learning and prevention at the same time. They are, with proper training, the natural ally of SPARs and their teachers, leading to an overall positive effect for the whole school. Much depends, however, on the extent of collaboration with principals and teachers. This is why it is crucial that all educators understand the GBI problem at various levels and share a vision for its solution. In sum, most counselors have been teachers who often become principals. All depend on higher education having a capability that actually remains to be developed.

In transforming higher education, areas must be defined in regard to what various discourses found in the reform educators would need to become knowledgeable about and also be able to analyze. It is imperative that SPARs are not allowed to fall grades behind, particularly in elementary school. That is yet not clear. Some educators protest testing and the market economy approach reflected by vouchers, charter schools, and school reward and punishment measures. Policymakers often place the total responsibility for closing the gap on educators without a complete understanding of the cultural and developmental bases of inequality. The majority of educators agree with the use of tests to measure the extent to which student learning meets standards. Yet the public generally does not want the schools punished but rather assisted to help their children. While tests are important, how they are used is what matters most.

Lending assistance to educators and students is the key to curtailing the achievement gap from a developmental perspective. To leave the present system unaltered structurally and to place the whole of the burden of reformed standards on K–12 educators is both unrealistic and unreasonable. For improved results, causal structures must be improved and others changed. Reforms continue to be institutionalized across states without constructing effective structural changes. Higher education rarely shows educators how policymakers (inside and mostly outside of education) can hold the system hostage, often keeping it from educating SPARs equitably. Educators need to know that the main problem is not simply how to close the gap, which is already known under certain conditions. What is not known is how to integrate those conditions within the whole system of education by restructuring some of its rules.

Since higher education prepares those who ultimately educate our children and eventually organize our schools, it serves to launch a major strategic window in transforming the educational system. Ultimately, it is a key avenue to sustain changes and direction over time. What needs to be done to close the gap may already be known to some extent. Yet, most educators remain unaware of how various initiatives might impact on educational outcomes or how they may be interwoven to produce substantial, lasting improvements in learning. The gap cannot be eradicated without a full view of the system's interconnected levels. It extends beyond preschool to postsecondary education in college. Launching specific initiatives at one level without coordinating connections to other levels simply cannot dismantle the gap.

The current situation is not new with respect to standards-based teaching and evaluation. Just a few decades ago, instruction was designed in accordance with learning theory and well-defined objectives (see Gagné, 1970; Mager, 1975; Gronlund, 1988). Effective instructional practices such as cooperative learning (Slavin, 2002b) have been well researched and found useful for many educational goals and groups. Unfortunately, research-based practice has not generally been well mastered and disseminated in higher education. Few educators develop the theoretical learning based on applied experiments. Unlike the fields of business, industry, and the military—which generally employ knowledge—educators graduate with only a superficial understanding of research-based learning. The results are obvious.

Figure 8–1: Blind Spots and Fragmented Explanations of the Achievement Gap

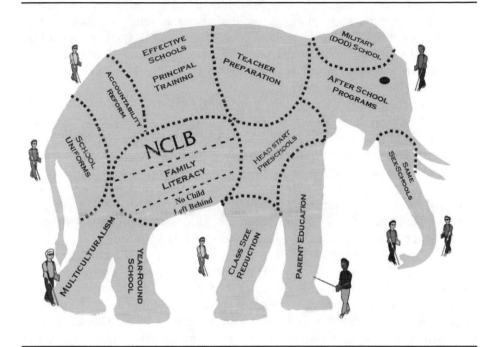

Higher education is fragmented by design, discouraging collaboration across disciplinary boundaries. It continues to prepare educators in traditional ways that are remote from ending GBI in educational outcomes. Aligning professional preparation with this clear purpose offers a way to reduce fragmentation and promote excellence in a consistent fashion. Instead of more emphasis on test content, multiculturalism, expectations, and accountability alone, expertise in eradicating the gap systemically is needed. Current transformation proposals for counselor and teacher education, supervision, and administration are mostly disjointed. As noted in Figure 8–1 (see the elephant figure), the focus seems to be on molecular rather than molar changes in the system. One community of educators emphasizes leadership, professional development schools, or family literacy factors; another community believes instructional factors come first, while another focuses on teachers' content expertise. In some instances, contradictions can be observed across the political spectrum that tend to neutralize any real effort to alter the system. For example, requirements related to teacher content knowledge expertise and testing are offset by the recruitment needs for teachers (especially minority) during a shortage that is likely to last a decade or more. One group suggests that the educational system be turned over to a market economy, taking the millions dispensed by the Elementary & Secondary Educational Act (1968) for vouchers. Other groups may stress leadership (Childs-Bowen, Scrivner, & Moller, 2000), finance, or organizational factors. Another current group emphasizes the importance of reforming science and mathematics teaching (Laws & Hastings, 2002) to close the gap. Scores of articles focus on teacher beliefs, racism, expectations, student learning styles, counselor transformation, and teacher reform that vary in their emphases on multiculturalism or accountability.

While recognizing that the very notion of a university education is antithetical to sharing a singular view (as it should be), an effective way to attack the problem of educational inequality and excellence lies in a concerted interdisciplinary and complete preparation of educators in colleges and universities. In addressing equity, teachers and counselors—as well as administrators—need to develop a core specialty with respect to closing the gap that is based on the study of human development. The proposal is that of sharing a common strategic plan, a set of goals, a knowledge base, and organizational principles in all of higher education that can support those in K–12 education.

How would educators need to be prepared differently and empowered to close the gap? Rather than tinkering with the system at cosmetic levels (school uniforms, block scheduling, resource centers), perhaps educators might start by transforming the organization of learning time, resources, educators, parents, and those who will soon become parents. This might follow with an analysis and understanding of programs, prevention, and learning opportunities.

Educators must also study and help guide the direction and priorities of actual reforms in education. Whether a common conceptual framework can be approximated in coordinating practices for achieving excellence through equity has yet to be decided. In short, if educators and policymakers are expected to reach consensus with regard to establishing educational equity, it seems that the educational research and policy community also must try coming together.

A central issue then is how to amplify the delivery capacity[6] of educators at various levels by restructuring the educational system in ways that maximize SPARs' academic development directly. The restructuring described in the last three chapters depends to a great extent on a transformation that determines "how" educators are professionally being prepared in higher education and for "what purpose."

The next three sub-disciplines that now need the most integration and redefinition are: teacher and counselor education and educational leadership. Other communities in higher education are to be also included (e.g., special education, early childhood, psychology, human services, law). Faculty development in these professional areas is critical in transforming the present sys-

Figure 8–2: Hypothesized Sources that Produce a 3–5 Grade Level Gap in Educational Outcomes between Groups

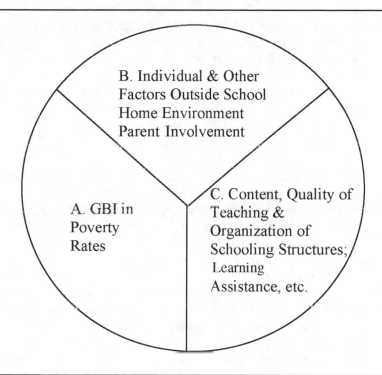

tem. Higher education is pivotal in narrowing the gap and sustaining excellence in public education.

As poverty remains imposed on some students subject to GBI, both educators and parents of those shortchanged continue to believe their schools are treating their children fairly. As a distinguished teacher educator notes:

> In my own city we tolerate a high school which had 18% graduation rate in a district that has an overall 36% high school graduation rate for African Americans, which is a higher rate than many urban districts. . . . The function of public schools in urban districts is to maintain the bottom half. Urban schools function as custodial institutions rather than as places where learning is the primary activity. The "pedagogy" offered in these "schools" is a set of cultural rituals that bears no resemblance whatever to the knowledge base in teaching and learning. (Haberman, 2002, 2)

Major problems are not only malpractice and negligence[7] stemming from poor preparation and lack of a knowledge base for establishing equity but more importantly:

a. The knowledge base pertaining to the gap remains vague for educators as a whole.

b. Faculty preparing educators under-prepare them in human development and learning and the content and pedagogical principles of a knowledge base focused on development, equity, and excellence. The knowledge base (in teaching and learning, evaluation, counseling and administration) is extensive, yet it is not utilized or understood well in professional programs. Part of the reasons why research and practice remain disconnected may be found in the limitations in *our social knowledge* (P.R. Portes, 1996; Stanfield, 1985; Cordova, 1997) that is further reduced by specialization.

c. Our knowledge base is incomplete, fragmented, and not well articulated in the professional preparation of educators. As such, the determination of effective strategies is compromised. A general interdisciplinary strategy for closing the achievement gap is not evident in higher education. In fact, what should count as knowledge is often disputed across academic communities (Berliner, 2002; Erikson & Gutierrez, 2002; Slavin, 2003; Stanfield, 1985). Yet, educators in the field, unsurprisingly, remain apprehensive and diffused given the disparities between their university learning experiences and the more traditional interpretations found at the district level regarding what kinds of knowledge and practices count. The confusion exacerbates powerlessness and conformity in the field.

d. Assuming most educators' knowledge base was more complete and shared upon certification, it is still difficult for new educators to have much influence since they must conform to local pressures and standing practices. Educators cannot afford to wait for external social and school conditions to be fixed before closing the gap.

e. Educators are the ones who in the final analysis must do it and, in some cases, have done it. They need help from those outside who govern education, strategy, and new tools in effecting change proactively. Educators are not being prepared to change and improve the system. Rather, the system prepares them to serve it in its current operations and goals.

f. A historical perspective (Vygotsky, 1978) on how societal change has and does occur may be established in higher education. However, learning how such changes are brought about through mediated actions is even more important, and that requires learning theoretical knowledge (Karpov & Bransford 1995);

g. Secondary-level educators may not be able to close the achievement gap directly for those already grade levels behind. However, they can help close the gap for future generations of SPARs through a different type of pedagogy content and goals besides scoring well on high-stakes tests.[8] Preschool and elementary educators can prevent the gap from emerging once the system reaches certain equilibrium independent of parental SES.

In sum, preparing future professionals in higher education for excellence through equity is the most important priority in the formation of the social conditions necessary to restructure the system.

Expanding a Common Knowledge Base for Educators

For educators, knowledge regarding the relation between sociopsychological development and learning is as important as teaching in their academic content area. Their thinking skills and professional know-how need to extend beyond the basic skills tested by PRAXIS types of basic competency exams. For example, as they master the concept of aptitude-treatment interaction (Snow, 1992) in the traditional sense, educators can be challenged to see beyond a narrow field or literature.[9] A broad professional education would help them understand that our present educational system, as a whole, is the treatment, and the aptitude interaction concerns developmental status, class, and culture. That is, the current programs offered in the educational system generally benefit one group more than others. If educators are to promote thinking skills in adolescents, they also need to promote them in higher education.

In higher education, a valuable opportunity is lost if there is no sharing of a common understanding or approach to the problem of educational inequality and how it is organized socially. Without a sound developmental understanding of cultural mediation (Cole, 1996), educators remain constrained by traditional instructional and grouping practices that benefit some students more than others. They may be swayed by cosmetic solutions (e.g., diversity training) that may not be necessary or sufficient to improve SPARs' achievement. In effect, educators need not only content expertise but also pedagogical concepts in mediating learning. For example, teaching students along theoretical learning lines is more effective than traditional methods guided totally by hands-on trial and error empirical learning (Karpov & Bransford, 1995). Yet, educators prepared in higher education today rarely master this type of teaching, and similar approaches guided by research (see Kozulin, 2003; Tharp et al., 2000). Few institutions that prepare educators are actively involved with reducing the gap.

How can colleges and universities prepare educators with the tools and knowledge with which to approach the problem locally? A conceptual knowledge of the problem of educational inequality as well as the goals and nature of field-based applications of best practices is essential. At present, most educators take courses that present them with some aspects of the problem in some fashion. Much is left to chance. Higher education might consider addressing curricular issues that include:

a. A common thorough knowledge base with respect to how schools can establish new practices to help SPARs meet minimum standards (see Mosteller & Boruch, 2002);

b. Education's higher and humanistic educational goals are hinged on the dismantling of inequality in academic outcomes.[10] Like the justice system, education must be blind to class, ethnicity, gender. Like health policy, it must be proactive in prevention and removing risks;

c. Effective approaches for SPARs need to form part of the curriculum beyond choral responses and drills centered on texts. Rather, organizing new structures and modifying existing ones improve meaningful learning to meet minimum levels of proficiency in underperforming schools;

d. For the educational system to serve all students equitably, it must be supported politically in promoting the components outlined earlier. Higher education mediates political support.

Educators alone generally cannot reorganize the major factors for change but must work within the resources and organizational plans established locally. Sometimes a few schools succeed when allowed to put research into practice and practice into theory. Hence, the question becomes what must 99% of educators know and do that the 1% of schools serving high proportions of SPARs apply in closing the gap?

Schools vary considerably in the quality and quantity of key factors such as faculty, student body, climate, schedules, goals, community, parent support, and leadership. Schools and districts vary in the extent to which educators have the knowledge, resources, and support needed to improve instruction directly and the effect of teacher unions. Educators working under the most challenging conditions need assistance in organizing successful practices, particularly during key transitions.

The literature points to some models that purport to close the gap. For example, the Mid-continental Regional Laboratory suggests that educators design an effective involvement plan to promote family involvement (e.g., teach parents to help kids with homework), have culturally sensitive staff, and high expectations of students in order to close the gap. Educators may read about schools that segregate students by gender, employ direct instruction, or have an "adopt a SPAR" program to improve in test scores. The literature also contains anecdotal evidence and case studies (Maeroff, 1998b; Thernstrom & Thernstrom, 2003). At the local level, educators under pressure must often gamble on which variables might work, often without the conceptual knowledge necessary that may best guide their school. In effect, what is encountered in the literature are educators who are essentially urged to try any number of modifications without structural changes in the system as a whole. Little progress can be made with fragmented approaches that ignore the issue of continuity in scaffolds in SPARs' development (see Figure 8–1).

The majority of schools could close the gap if the system were to be reorganized as a whole in the first place. For example, if the research community influenced district and state policies in ways that have been shown to close the gap (preschool, reduce class size for SPARs, collaborative approaches,[11] mentors, year-round school schedules, knowledgeable professionals) simultaneously, more schools might be considered exceptional and effective even when SPARs constitute the majority of the student body. Low-performing schools generally have the highest risk factors and the least social and economic capital. They often serve low-SES populations that move their children for economic and other reasons. SPARs attend them increasingly with low literacy in both English and Spanish, often taught without enough competent veteran educators, and face discipline or school climate problems. Truancy, suspensions, and expulsions all take away from academic learning time (ALT) that SPARs desperately need to progress in school. Schools that educate predominantly SPAR communities today are being compared with those that serve more advantaged groups. SPARs' risk is cumulative and pro portionate to poverty rates.

The achievement gap must be defined conceptually, but at the same time precisely, if a sound plan is to be implemented. A suggestion would be to begin with a plan to have all SPARs perform at grade level as long as proficiency at that grade level predicts success at the next level. How could stable standards be set that are meaningful in real life? It seems they must be partly defined in terms of the level of competence required in the work force and the jobs available in an economy linked to the future. It might also be defined humanistically in terms of the level of education needed to meet basic needs and provide for self and others. One might ask what is the point of an educational system that ensures all SPARs perform and graduate at minimum grade level when mostly minimum wage jobs are available which do not allow altering of their poverty status? Yet, a greater proportion of students within some underrepresented populations needs to overcome poverty but, just as importantly, to attain minimum standards of proficiency in academic areas. In short, the economic system may require a certain level of poverty. Yet, the political system insists it is not biased against particular groups nor enforced by withholding a grade-level education and higher wage.

Learning at a minimum level of functional literacy might enable individuals a choice out of the cycle of poverty, or it may not. However, that option appears crucial for groups placed economically and historically at-risk to meet current higher standards. It generally vanishes in districts and schools where teachers and student populations are segregated by the public school system, (Orfield, Frankenberg, & Lee, 2003). When this segregation is not possible, private schools provide for a back door to meet the needs of the more privileged students first.

A restructured system places SPARs in a position to continue learning and earning if and when they have the opportunity to do so. What is currently available is a system that ensures poverty status for those it places at-risk directly by not meeting even minimum proficiency standards. Most SPARs remain at-risk for life, bound by prior cultural constraints in spite of their potential. In other words, poverty is reproduced for certain sectors of poor students precisely by leaving them behind relative to others.[12] We do know GBI may be altered by educating SPARs up to grade level. But after decades of failure and demographic changes, it may no longer be an option to address the problem systematically (Miller, 1995).

Higher education can play a vital part in the solution for closing the gap by preparing educators well beyond current theories of diversity, test-driven instruction, or expectations. Tougher questions, such as what are the expectations of the current reform movement and its goals, need to be considered in terms of resource use and the present organization of school failure (Foley, 1991; Neisser, 1986). Educators must be prepared to become agents in human development rather than just respond to accountability standards. For example, almost 30% more white than African-American students perform proficiently in math and reading in the reports cited earlier. It seems educators need to understand how promoting best practices in instruction across all levels might not close the gap in the long run. The problem suggests the need for multi-level, integrated changes in the present system from pre-K to post-secondary schooling.

If poverty is a given in the developed nations of the world, and educators are not permitted to reorganize structures that govern allocation of means and best practices to reduce poverty's impact at school, then understanding the meaning underlying reform seems important professionally. The gist of the message today is that the gap is due to educators' mediocrity or malpractices. Yet, the effect of poverty on schools' capacity to educate SPARs to grade level is at least as great as that of schooling and the structures it applies of those students (see Figure 8–2). In Maslow's (1954) needs hierarchy, deficiency needs are more extreme in SPAR groups than those of the more advantaged in terms of nutrition, safety, belonging, and self-esteem needs that need to be met before development in intellectual and related areas is possible. What is seen then is that for children born in poverty (A), two major consequences await that sustain group disparities in the future. As Figure 8–2 shows, three basic pillars or sources are critical in producing and sustaining the gap directly and indirectly.

First, instructional practices are surely different and important but represent only part of the problem. They operate according to the parameters set by the structures that allocate school-based capital. The initial disparity reflected in A assures consequent disparities in both B (home life) and C (quality of schooling) under present conditions. Since A can't be changed directly, restructuring C offers some hope of improving B and leads to the prediction that over time there could be some reduction in GBI. However, different sets of structures are proposed to be instituted at higher levels to govern the practices through which C can help SPARs academically and socially. Unfortunately, those at the bottom of the grade level hierarchy will remain most prone to poverty. There may be no absolute minimum grade level standard that guarantees escape from poverty. It is presumed that achieving at grade level will alleviate poverty but relative differences in literacy will still prevail in relative terms. As Haberman (2002) notes:

> . . . the (gap) is not an aberration of American society nor is it an unintended consequence. Quite the contrary. It reflects the will of the overwhelming majority of Americans who believe that education is a personal not a common good and that the highest quality education is a scarce resource. Schooling is the means we use to produce winners and losers. Who gets into the prestigious colleges is the critical question at the top achievers' level. Who goes to other colleges or to post secondary institutions reflects the competition at the next levels down. Who gets training for a decent job or any job at all is the next level and so on. When we get to the poor and diverse children in urban schools the lofty mission of knowledge, citizenship and self-actualization we want for our children has been narrowed down to get a job and stay out of jail. At this lowest level of the bottom half there is no longer any competition for a future of any substantial value. (1)

The ethical problem arises when certain groups of SPARs are left behind at twice or usually three times their representation in the general population in terms of performance at grade level. Many educators gradually come to understand the educational system's role within the broader political economy and may become more flustered. Even in higher education, many professors are not aware of the savage inequalities documented by Kozol (1992, 2000) and others. However, knowing more about the problem is not sufficient; part of the change needed in higher education requires knowing more about reducing inequality in opportunities to learn. There are other fundamental aspects of a knowledge base pertaining to equity that are important for educators to consider before buying into a particular model for closing the gap. For example:

a. Educators would need to understand how various communities define the gap and equity. Closing the gap is not the main priority of the current reform. For example, policy-makers generally do not distinguish students subject to GBI from others and do not know the difference nor demand real change in the system.

b. Equity in terms of educational outcomes can be defined in various ways. Completing high school or college, taking advanced courses or meeting grade level performance standards serve as different indicators that lend themselves to further comparisons by ethnicity. The last-named is adopted in this book.

c. Eliminating group differences in test scores may be viewed as a gradual process that can be estimated by the proportion of students performing at grade level, at least initially. If education is responsible for providing students with the latter regardless of background, this becomes the newest frontier since the Civil Rights movement led to desegregation of schools. A new Children's Bill of Rights (Clinchy, 2001) would include the right to a grade level education and the end of segregation by schooling processes and outcomes.

d. By offering advanced college prep-work for some and not others, a mechanism exists to advantage the already advantaged with public funds earmarked mainly for all students to reach performance standards. The present system spends scarce resources for college-level instruction when it locks them to help SPARs reach grade-level proficiency.

e. While poverty is not an educational problem, it contributes to schools placing students at risk for it. K–12 education remains instrumental in constructing the gap by tolerating below-grade academic development today.

f. By insisting on a minimum level of equity where all students are prepared to meet grade level standards first, new solutions may be found indirectly to help in reducing GBI and poverty and promote excellence for all in the system.

g. Educational excellence, as defined by higher test scores, may be regarded as a by-product of equity as educators are allowed to educate more of the time and to SPARs in particular.

h. Higher standards can be met more effectively in schools where all students perform at grade level under a restructured system designed to promote the development of the least advantaged.

i. In preparing students not only academically for college but also socially for family life, a societal transformation can gradually take place that helps remove some of the present barriers. Rather than focusing education only on tomorrow's workforce, educators understand the mission of education more broadly and its developmental and ethical goals more fully.

Summary of Knowledge-Based Component for Higher Education

It may be that education will remain as a personal, scarce resource, as it is particularly likely to remain in higher education. However, some resources need not remain scarce or finite. Perhaps as more resources are developed (such as human capital), eventually more material resources and jobs that pay above poverty level can be created. Perhaps poverty can be reduced or distributed more fairly by extending new health, housing, and economic policies outside education. In order for this to occur, education still must first be reorganized beyond accountability driven by tests and vouchers that, along with increased college costs, serve to keep disempowered groups behind.

College admission practices represent another field that is strategic in transforming the system. Some colleges, for example, may value more than just SAT and ACT scores and provide assistance to SPARs even when they are not athletes. Higher education can contribute in many yet-unexplored ways to reduce inequality, particularly for the least advantaged groups. In sum, higher education and the educators it prepares must understand not only the causes of the achievement gap. More importantly, they must act and be able to understand that in tackling inequality in education, society benefits as a whole locally even before lasting change can be effected in the educational system.

Developing Educators' Professional Identity

A new educational approach that integrates actions at various levels (see Chapter Four) may produce a more equitable system and, in fact, help piece together various current initiatives. Educators must be allowed greater breadth in their preparation and freedom to pursue equity and excellence. Jobs involving fast food or making beds are not a scarce resource, perhaps because a good education is. Perhaps the problem is not just only about school-to-work transitions for SPARS but countering the debilitating effects of poverty generally imposed on students lacking proficiency in basic skills.

Educators need not collaborate in the sorting and reproduction (of inequality) functions that schools organize so reliably. Viewing education as a limited resource to be extracted from the system in unfair competition is neither inevitable nor necessarily desirable. Education has historically helped create surpluses and new resources by investing in human development. There is evidence that oligarchies that stifle growth are not good for a society's economy. Education is a right without which pursuit of happiness is trumped, and it can mitigate some of the unfairness imposed by poverty and how it is distributed today.

It may be that educators need to transform their own identity and development in the process of helping eradicate GBI in educational outcomes. Counselors concur that a lack of consistent identity and legitimization, along with limited involvement in reforms and the imposition of non-counseling responsibilities, have historically curtailed the profession. But that may not be enough. Even when an adequate and effective approach is discovered, society and those most empowered must be willing to act in dismantling or reversing GBI-producing structures that are indexed by the teaching and learning gap. Many new teachers are thrown into the worst working environment and eventually leave the profession in the first few years, fueling a teacher shortage.

Inequality in education is the most complex social problem and paradoxically both a cause and an effect of school failure. Educating all SPARs to grade level, preparing more qualified teachers and reducing class size do not have to be ever-distant options. Education in rare cases manages to succeed in preparing SPARs to meet standards by teaching directly to the test, in itself a dubious definition of excellence. The need is for a less superficial reform. Ironically, it is through a more complete education, including that for higher-education and policy circles, that remains the most effective way to promote excellence through equity in the long run.[13]

External Conditions of Learning

Given that considerable external support is needed for the structural changes to reverse a system that reproduces the gap, how can higher education best contribute to this social project? For example, support ranges from serving SPARs early and reducing class sizes to employing proven models and extending the school year to promote meaningful learning. However, even if educators could close the gap with a comprehensive approach, would society have the will and offer the support needed to restructure the educational system and itself? This collective will is reflected by how students are now being educated. Establishing an equitable educational system is a cultural value in itself that determines the extent to which supports and resources are allocated for particular goals. It requires teaching that is distributed equitably and that includes equity as a national goal that preserves democracy.

Public support is needed in extending the secondary curriculum beyond basic academic goals. A broader approach serves to promote not only parent involvement in education and prevention but also a means toward a broader educational mission. It must transcend tyranny imposed by "teaching to the test" and move toward learning to learn and the development of critical thinking skills across a variety of areas. However, tests and grade level standards are necessary, particularly for equity to become established at the group level in a higher-stakes environment—even if relative gaps still remain above grade level. The basic right to be educated equitably (to grade-level standards) would have to be inalienable. This may be as far as education can go in eradicating inequality. Poverty eradication is a much larger societal problem that extends well beyond education as noted elsewhere. Our professional and ethical obligation is mainly to extricate the educational system from achievement gap-producing structures and organized practices.

Once society activates the means necessary to deliver a grade-level education to SPARs, the system can more easily move beyond meeting the current standards. The transformation needs to include critical analyses of the ever-changing "more–is-better" mentality standards that ultimately favor the already advantaged. Today 20% percent of the richest families send over 85% of their children to college while families at the bottom 20% send 4% of SPARs to college. A well-reasoned, basic rule is that while all students must meet standards based on education, it is the responsibility of those who set them to ensure the means and assistance necessary are also in place to meet them and gradually end GBI in educational outcomes.

What Educators Need to Know

Bringing teacher or counselor education into major educational reform efforts is far from new. The calls for extending and changing the roles of counselors to support educational reform—as well as improve the profession—have been heard time and again in past decades (Herr, 2002). It seems that in spite of claims to the contrary, school counseling tends to follow rather than lead reform efforts. It reflects roles and practices that have generally been in the service of practices in the administration and instruction sectors.

Educators, regardless of their specific role, also need to know more about social and economic trends that impact directly on their practice. For example, how often are educators prepared to work effectively in schools serving high concentrations of SPARs? How is their preparation differentiated so that the achievement gap can be addressed early in their career? At present, educators are not prepared specifically to assist those left behind. To what extent are they expected to master knowledge pertaining to the best practices and data found in research? For example, part of the massive inequality found in schools pertains to finance, with few schools serving SPARs receiving the same level of funding found in high-performing schools. What does it mean to have two or three thousand dollars less per student annually for schools that serve mostly SPARs in a school of one thousand students? In just a few schools, millions are at stake that could be directed, in part, at the problem.

What is being suggested here is that a more equitable system of education is not necessarily going to bring about a more democratic and just society. Poverty may still be imposed on working families and disproportionately on minority populations. For example, in Boston, the minimum wage would have to be close to twenty-four dollars an hour in order to afford minimum standard housing. So why focus on minimum standards if economic poverty is likely to await SPARs who might meet them?

Counselors understand their joint roles as educators in guiding and assisting SPARs for life. This is a critical difference between how educators are currently being prepared and the proposed transformation for professional educators. There is a system in place now that limits a broader professional preparation in favor of training to conform to narrow practices in an unfair system. Counselors and school psychologists are constrained in fixed roles that reproduce or even amplify inequality. This situation produces part of the potential crisis in counselor and teacher education with respect to lack of preparation in narrowing the achievement gap. The new proposed approach would challenge educators in the frontlines at this level, not at the expense of teachers focusing on content skills but as part of a professional identity and set of interrelated efforts to educate the whole SPAR. Counselors and teachers would need to know how to function in troubled schools to avoid becoming part of the problem. To practice what is taught in higher education is difficult enough. However, it is even less probable to practice what is not known or has not been included in professional training. Higher education must share new sets of skills in leadership, instruction, and human development. Only when society defines higher standards in professional preparation including for policymakers—may sustainable progress be expected in K–12 public education. It is all interrelated.

The roles counselors fulfill today are unlike those required by the proposed (excellence through equity) framework. For example, educators today are more concerned with the roles at the left than those proposed at the right of Table 8–1.

In some cases, structured approach as to teaching pro-social skills can be found in the literature (e.g., Goldstein et al., 1980) along with others that attempt to extend the role of counselors in closing the gap. Programs that are developmentally based on the goal of prevention of primary, causal factors such as those defining effective parental "involvement" for teens are practically non-existent. Most calls for transforming counselor roles for leadership (e.g., Bemak, 2000) are generally heard only within that professional community without provisions for change in higher education as a whole. While it makes sense, for example, to have educators play leadership roles in promoting future skills and family involvement, this role is unlikely to be effected until a whole community becomes educated in prevention.

Table 8–1: A Typology of Functions and Roles for School Counselors' Current and Proposed Activities

Traditional Guidance Curriculum*	Transformed School Counseling**
Class scheduling	Group interventions
Developing academic year plans	Prevention of risk behaviors
Promotion /retention criteria	Promotion of parent education
Tests and testing	Teen pregnancy and its consequences
Registration, college and high school graduation	Violence and bullying
Bureaucratic paperwork	Suicide and depression
Crisis intervention	Prejudice and hate reduction
Referrals	Abusive relationships
Parent contacts	Eating disorders, health
Individual counseling	Schools failure—economics education
Drug education	Divorce adjustment
Exceptional child compliance	Conflict resolution
	Study skills
	Decision-making
	Use of data leadership
	Leadership
	Test-taking skills development

← Vocational guidance →

* Based on ASCA 20(11 Mode] for School Counseling Programs.
** These functions would be in the primary prevention curriculum in the Transformed Student Counseling Model.

What Do Educators Need to Consider?

Although it is well beyond the scope of the present book, a new curriculum needs to be developed in preparing educators so that their specialization links the above roles to reducing the achievement gap. For example, Sizer's (1992) typology of educational reforms is a useful tool through which constant calls for change may be better understood. It might be noted that our approach does not fit in his three strategies yet much can be learned from them in bringing about fundamental changes in the culture of schools (Herr, 2002; Timar, 1989). In counselor education, proposed changes have been made in several college programs across the nation (see The Education Trust, 1997, 2000) Counselor education programs have been funded to prepare educators specifically to play active roles in assisting schools to improve test scores. These efforts are clearly in the right direction, although this proposal would extend them differently. Counselors would play major roles in primary prevention with adolescents who have been left behind. Rather than the current reform's sole focus on higher standards and accountability, equity would become the cornerstone for excellence and ethical principles in professional programs for educators. Counselors would help organize assistance by developing sustainable support structures for SPARs in the K–12 community.

Educators require both the conceptual and practical knowledge necessary to be most responsive to SPARs. For example, why would an attorney work to ensure her client received the full benefit of the law? Why would an engineer ensure every floor and roof is safe? In our case, we argue for at least two reasons why SPARs should be educated well (i.e., not below grade level). First, because from a developmental perspective we understand that empowering the poor with a sound education might gradually change current social and economic conditions and policies. A more educated, ethical public might be closer than the current one to reducing poverty and healthcare and education costs for children or working families, regardless of occupation. It might take time but the proposed restructuring anticipates a more knowledgeable citizen with social competence. That is, we may not be able to solve the problem of class-based economic inequality in market-driven economies through education, but we might move it closer to a more ethical, and safer, solution. Economic inequality with minimal educational inequality is "better" than economic inequality with great educational inequality. Perhaps SPARs who are better educated, yet still poor, might seem worse than the present case, but it's not likely.

Secondly, in preventing a learning gap by achieving grade-level standards in all elementary and middle schools, educators move closer to improving the quality of education for all students. They also fulfill professional and ethical responsibilities. Schools would be organized to not only meet minimum standards that are valued by the dominant group but also help connect students to a variety of resources, models, apprenticeships, and service-based learning. The latter may be related to college or not.

So what kinds of programs are available that may be useful in preparing professional educators? Programs such as professional development schools (Abdo-Haqq, 1998), Accelerated Schools (Levin, 1988), AVID (Mehan, Hubbard, & Villanueva, 1994; Success for All (Slavin, Madden, Dolan,& Wasik, 1996), minority teacher recruitment efforts, school counseling transformation models (Hayes & Paisley, 2002; The Education Trust, 1997) and other models (Borman et al., 2002) offer valuable knowledge and mechanisms that can help reduce the gap. However, a more general approach is needed to integrate the latter and to reverse root causes for the gap. The above models form part of the internal and external changes needed to transform the educational system, including professional training. At the university or college level, expanding the professional education of those serving students is critical. What an educator does not know can hurt students (Krueger, Hanushek, & Rice, 2002). Shortcomings at higher levels can become amplified at other levels. Gaining greater community level support by promoting and maintaining service learning for college students, peer collaborations, employing retired persons, and promoting business, community and school partnerships also requires organizational knowledge and skills. In sum, changes in professional development are essential to dismantle the achievement gap.

Through collaboration, prevention, and promotion of human development, cultural changes required for closing the gap can be integrated in higher education programs. A common approach and vision in higher education help prioritize organizational and pedagogical strategies on closing the gap in pre K–12 education. Other important concepts in the preparation and retention of effective educators can be included.

Mediation, Guidance & Development

The human mind is guided by culturally mediated activities in particular. To develop skills in mediating the development of students, one must see that we are not only targeting the problems of students who are at risk but also their future roles as parents of SPARs and of society. Remediation from a cultural-historical perspective (Cole, 1996; Kozulin et al., 2003; Vygotsky, 1978, 1987) is different from traditional meanings associated with the "cultural" term. It involves co-constructing strategic tools with SPARs in order to circumvent the risks that are mostly social in nature. It includes concept development when and where SPARs are ready and creating zones for further development (Moll, 1992). Once a new concept or skill is mastered, future interactions with the environment are changed permanently after SPARs' acquire new reasoning skills, expectations, and goals. For example, when an adolescent identifies with a film or a play regarding teen pregnancy and its consequences, s/he may draw the conclusion that early parenthood may hurt everyone and thus alter a (risk) behavior. Or, perhaps following a counselor-led peer discussion, attitudes and concepts may change so that poor decisions are avoided. The re-mediation occurs when an idea, concept, or disposition derived from an activity leads to a change in attitude, emotion, or behavior. Without the mediated activity, some aspects of development would remain constrained or dormant.

Educators can work proactively with groups of students to promote strategic areas of social development (see Table 8–1) and to prevent certain extenuating risks. They lend their awareness and that of other experts and models. They collaborate with adolescent students who are negotiating their identities. In so doing, educators must be prepared for two new roles and be allowed to fulfill them. The first is to extend guidance activities by organizing and overseeing a new human growth and development curriculum in secondary education as noted in Chapter Five. They may help close the gap by organizing activities aimed to support academic development and college preparation in programs such as AVID, which aim to prepare SPARs for college. The latter fit the model well in providing for a seamless academic support system for SPARs.

Secondly, the role of the new educator in primary school focuses mainly on disallowing the gap (see Chapter Seven) by novel forms of collaboration and organizing mentors to assist SPARs. This component needs to be reflected in the elementary certification programs and supervised practice. Connecting all SPARs with the support systems required in and out of school is the gist of prevention and promotion strategies. Educators need to ensure collaboration across levels to maximize continuity in extracurricular activities and tutoring from Head Start and earlier through the elementary grades for each SPAR. In ways similar to special education students, each SPAR needs to have an Individualized Education Plan (IEP) to gauge the level of external support needed for academic learning. At the secondary level, educators continue to oversee and direct a prevention component in terms of the human development workshops described in Chapter Five.

Educators need new competencies to be aligned within restructured professional certification programs. The new educator must learn curriculum development and work with colleagues in designing district-level programs and evaluation procedures to close the gap. They need experience in program design, evaluation, and assessment of learning potential to help SPARs in particular. A strategy to assist teachers indirectly is by ensuring low-performing students have quality mentors and tutoring activities that can serve to upgrade the educational package now in place.[14]

Professional education also needs to contribute to defining the human development curriculum units and activities to be co-constructed with adolescent students, particularly SPARs. This is not difficult since human growth and development are already part of the field. However, growth-oriented activities adapted toward skills and knowledge are advantageous to future generations of SPARs (rather than already advantaged students). This curriculum, unlike others, must be values free and defined carefully to gain public support. It must be activity based, meaningful, and linked with the community. It may be partly integrated with other classes but must have a separate space in the curriculum and be aligned with basic developmental principles and curriculum standards. For example, adolescents might consider the effects of neglect, malnutrition, and abuse on learning. Another unit might entail vocational or budget planning and the consequences of financial stress on relationships and the family. A minimum set of units may eventually form part of graduation requirements. National and local models may be developed, assessed, and disseminated.

The school culture is often at odds with the culture of (at-risk) adolescents. This is because adolescents' identities generally are formed more in peer cultures that strive for differentiation from adults. Through a comprehensive prevention approach educators need to be prepared and empowered to prevent future generations of children and adolescents from being placed at-risk. Yet, professional education generally does not address the achievement gap directly but rather attempts to deal with some of its consequences. For example, most of the literature in this field is limited to simple discussions of multiculturalism or to secondary types of interventions that are unlikely to affect the gap in the long run (see Brown, 1999).

One way to address the gap problem in higher education is to include activities in college courses for educators (e.g., in adolescence or human development) that focus on the gap as a social science problem. This focus allows traditional content to be incorporated in theory and research more meaningfully and paves the way for including service-oriented mentoring with SPARs. Students can present different models, interventions, case studies, outcomes, and analyses. (See examples in the appendix to this chapter).

The school district and state must not only endorse this restructuring of secondary education but lead actively in its development. This implies that professional education needs to include information about current initiatives and how they came about. This dual role for the secondary school educator calls for empowering educators to develop activity-based workshops and experiences to help close the gap. Counselors need practice and support in adapting existing models and workshops into units for SPARs' present or future academic success.

At least three major problems appear before the field if educators are to play key roles in establishing equity in education:

a. *Theoretical and Practical Knowledge/Skills:* Counselor and professional education needs to have higher standards in the areas of primary prevention program design and evaluation, human development, learning theory, and research. Few programs provide guidance and preparation to promote SPARs' development directly. For secondary schools, adapting programs like AVID (Mehan et al., 1994), or SEER (www.seer.org) among others that help underrepresented minorities prepare for colleges (via funded university–high school partnerships) are important. For elementary school educators, directing after school programs such as those described in *Safe and Smart's*[15] (retrieved from http://www.ed.gov/pubs/parents/SafeSmart/) exemplary programs represent a new role that assists SPARs' academic progress. Educators also need to be prepared in social science well enough to not only understand but generate actions grounded in human development.

b. *Fidelity to the Profession:* Regardless of preparation and certification, educators remain at the mercy of supervisors who may not be committed to closing the gap or be aware of the problem, of existing alternatives, or of the strategic contributions that can be made insofar as collaborative school cultures, community-based mentoring assistance, prevention, and other areas are concerned. Often, they are not allowed to apply their professional skills and knowledge in the schools.

c. *Delivery Capacity:* Well-prepared educators must be allowed to be proactive and consistent in addressing various aspects of the gap. A primary mechanism appears relevant. As higher education programs become more interdisciplinary, the unique and shared roles played by each type of educator would be apparent to the others.

Educators need to understand SPARs constitute a group for special education—that is, an education that is special given the numerous and cumulative constraints on learning in their social contexts. It is one requiring both affective and academic support (Comer, 1995). Finally, even with individualized educational plans (IEPs), educators (including special education teachers) are rarely prepared to conduct dynamic assessments of learning potential (Kozulin & Presseisen, 1995). Educators in general need to be better prepared in applying developmental theory and interdisciplinary focus on the process of change.

From a higher education perspective, a new generation of educators needs to be prepared for key roles. A well-prepared school educator is an agent of change who is well acquainted with research grounded in existing prevention programs (Albee & Gullotta, 1997). They help students understand dilemmas and make life choices with care (Sloan, 1996). Part of their knowledge base includes mastery of principles for promoting social change (Wollman, Lobenstine, Foderaro, & Stose, 1998). They serve as mediators who use and model a variety of tools in teaching and learning activities such as socio-drama, theatre, film, and books to build positive identities and social skills (Newman and Holzman, 1996). They use the latter in fomenting collaboration amongst peers in the local school that is pivotal in closing the gap. Knowing that assistance is needed, counselors, like teachers, need to understand the stages of assisted performance (Tharp & Gallimore, 1988) in developing SPARs' potential development in academic areas. However, counselors' roles differ from teachers' and their contribution centers more in arranging extra assistance for SPARs through:

a. Organizing after school academic clubs for SPARs;
b. Recruiting and deploying community volunteers and mentors to SPARs;
c. Seeking corporate and state involvement to support SPARs development via training, and coordinating mentoring relations; and
d. Other group prevention and promotion activities.
e. Monitoring and using local data to drive actions.

Table 8-2: The Human Development Spiral Curriculum (HDSC)

AREAS OF DEVELOPMENTAL CONCERN:

Cognitive Skills Teaching	Affective Counseling	Psychomotor Vocational Education	Meta Cognitive Self-Regulation
SCHOOL SETTING			----------Clinical setting

Examples:

Developmental Competencies	Preventative Knowledge	Education and Secondary	Adjustment
1. Nutrition	1. Drugs	1. Career intervention	1. Depression
2. Study Habits	2. Sexual abuse	2. Academic concerns	2. Stress management
3. Exercise	3. Alcoholism	3. All psychological and developmental concerns	3. Anxiety
4. Learning styles	4. Physical abuse	4. Decision making	4. Neglect
5. Communication skills	5. Youth and law	5. Self-assessment which might require long-term therapy and external help	5. Abandonment
6. Learning disabilities	6. Suicide	6. Careers and values	6. Anger
7. Self-concept	7. Violence preventions in family	7. Occupational orientation	7. Guilt
8. Thinking skills	8. Health risk reductions	8. ACT/SAT	8. Children of alcoholics
9. Life goals	9. Loss of love	9. Study skills	9. Racial concerns
10. Overcoming shyness	10. Anger control	10. Time management	10. Divorce
11. Sexual values	11. Teenage pregnancy	11. Military	11. Stepfamilies
12. Conflict resolution	12. Violence in school	12. Orientation moral values	12. Single parent families
13. Social skills	13. STDs	13. Parenting	13. New schools
14. Giftedness	14. Sexual harassment		14. Moving
15. Multicultural awareness	15. AIDS		15. Fear
16. Behavioral awareness	16. Marital relations		16. Parenting
17. Time management	17. Smoking		
18. Self-help	18. Micro-skills		
19. Economics	19. Rape		
	20. Child abuse		
	21. Gun risk		
	22. Parenting		

Starting Point: Pre-adolescence ——— Mid-adolescence ——— Late Adolescence

Nature of Counseling: Group Counseling ——→ Individual Counseling

In Table 8–2, a general model from which to understand the educators' roles in primary prevention and promotion of life skills is presented. Note that in contrast to current efforts to transform education for educators with test scores as the primary focus, root causes for low scores are the focus here. Life skill units are listed below to show how certain themes can be used to promote students' concept development. An underlying premise here is the use of non-traditional methods for making the units meaningful to students, using group activities, special guests, field experiences, student writing, and service projects. Guided participation allows skills and competencies to develop and gradually be self-regulated. A critical element in this curriculum lies in developing competencies for family life.

New Roles

Educators in secondary levels have new roles with respect to prevention and promotion activities. Their preparation as specialists in human development, vocational, family, health, and other domains makes them the ideal leaders in spearheading change. Given they are few in number, counselors must help organize activities at the group level by collaborating with other prepared professionals and volunteers (Seely, 1985). Even so, they must enlist community support in helping SPARs enter college, develop self-confidence, motivation, and social and parenting skills. A human development curriculum requires educators to organize, supervise, and evaluate novel ways to co-construct life skills with SPARs. Their task is multifaceted because in empowering SPARs' development in both academic and social areas, they help promote parental involvement or support in future generations of SPARs. They are working to close the gap at the primary and secondary levels of preparation simultaneously.

Continuity in support of development is a critical area for educators to keep in mind, from preschool to university. Organizing a seamless pipeline of support from elementary to beyond secondary school for SPARs promotes development at the collective level. Arranging significant mediating activities is thus a key role in applying social learning in non-academic areas that promote thinking skills. At the state level, educators and the public may advocate that SPARs attend college free if they maintain a certain grade level average (e.g., in Indiana). In some communities, wealthy sponsors offer similar support. The plan to connect all SPARS with mentors throughout their education is not solely educators' new responsibility. In other developed nations, for example, low-income students receive considerably more support (Slavin, 1997). In the United States, educators generally do not lend SPARs sufficient support.

Envisioning Primary Prevention & Promotion in Action

Adolescence is the optimal period in which to target[16] the co-construction of formal operational or higher-level thinking both in and outside academic learning. In extending the curriculum to promote competencies in cognitive strategies and socio-emotional health, both short and long-range goals remain well within the traditional parameters of education. However, what is different here are the multiple purposes involved. For example:

a. Students might receive academic credit and/or grades in this curriculum, particularly if it is to be valued formally.

b. Even if SPARs remain poor—and struggle in academic learning—they can be competitive in other human development areas. This may be achieved by activity-based, performance-oriented (Holzman & Newman, 1993) interventions geared toward quality of life goals independent of income. Finally, it must promote the rights of others. It must teach not values but choices of values and their consequences.

c. Working with SPARs and others in a space that promotes human growth and development requires a different type of pedagogy that is important for educators to master in higher education. Content is acted out or performed in many instances. Activity-based classes that are student centered and include group work help promote development.

d. Social learning is a primary avenue for primary prevention objectives. It serves to promote motivation and learning as well. Models from the community, plays, visits to various facilities, and a host of non-traditional activities are envisioned as we re-think this aspect of the secondary school curriculum. Counselors' roles would expand considerably beyond the traditional vocational guidance functions of the past.

e. The counselor is also a mental health activist, in roles aimed to prevent child neglect, conflict, and violence. A range of purposes is served in this curriculum because as the adolescents' development is supported, the basis for reducing risks and expanding choices in the future is co-constructed. Modeling for future parents is also incorporated into the everyday lives of children. Exemplary models of resilient persons form part of the discussions and classes.

Adolescent students would obtain academic credit and grades for this life skills curriculum or class through a series of workshops in each school. It should be carried out separately from other classes since the aims differ from those of traditional content.

Much of what has been regarded as extracurricular and optional should instead fall squarely within the general mission of public education, particularly until academic success for SPARs is established. For those already behind, these human development goals seem important. The rationale is that both goals are needed. There is no compelling reason why the higher thinking skills of SPARs should remain untapped, regardless of how far below grade level SPARs may be in academic areas. Other vocational options in service, technology, art, sports, and entertainment are open that are independent of college preparation. Most SPARs' development of critical thinking depends on what is offered by the educational system.

Sustaining Democratic Values

Counselors and educators understand that achieving standards-based performance is a basic condition for establishing equity and excellence for the system of education as a whole. This is defined by a system capable of educating all children to grade-level standards. A spiral academic curriculum depends on sustained support of goals over time. Among the most compelling reasons for closing the gap is to address the under-representation of some minorities at the higher levels of test scores and college graduation. If this severe under-representation continues, the consequences endanger society (Miller, 1995). The decline in SPARs' performance since 1988 has been associated with a corresponding decline in their families' SES (Armor, 1996). Hedges and Nowell (1998) hypothesize that improving the educational attainment of SPARs' parents was responsible for the temporary improvement in low-income students' NAEP scores in the 1970s before the gap began to widen. Ten years from now, the data may show this pattern has held.

Without a systematic approach to close the gap, we not only waste effort and resources and blame others but undermine a democratic society. The issue then is not whether to reform the educational system or not. "Reform" is already ongoing as group differences in wealth and privilege become increasingly polarized. The irony is that as more wealth has been created in the past decades, the richest have thrived most and the groups living in poverty—in spite of effort and hard work—have generally lost ground. It is a democratic-like society we are placing at risk, not just others' children. Educators thus come to understand their work as meaningless efforts within the larger context of macro-level economic and historical factors over which they had little control. This is one way educators can begin to understand the implications of a cultural-historical approach that draws attention to how broad societal forces moderate education and development at the individual and group levels.

Summary and Conclusions

From a systems perspective, a change at one level triggers other changes across the contexts of education. Curricular and process changes aimed at eradicating inequality must be shared and co-constructed by various types of educators. Over time, this transformation contributes increasingly toward meaningful collaboration at the school level, regardless of new roles. Sharing of a conceptual framework for closing the gap in higher education may help curtail the trial-and-error patterns we now observe. Today, schools scurry to respond to higher standards. To close the achievement gap—and achieve excellence—the nation's public system of education requires transformation at some levels more than others. Some of the myths and information in the first three chapters serve to establish part of the content proposed in preparing future educators in higher education. Much more could be added beyond what has been referenced here. In Chapter Four, a cultural-historical approach was outlined that calls for action at several points in the development of SPARs. A cultural and historical model to understand development, learning, and teaching was presented. The most ambitious change lies in the way we prepare professional educators, school counselors, psychologists, and others. In this chapter some of the current efforts were noted and a guide in revamping various certification programs in higher education was explored.

In order to improve schools, we cannot wait for educators or districts to take action. Extending the goals and mission of schools with a human development curriculum is critical in preparing adolescents (see Chapter Five) to become involved parents in the future. This is a slow but important way to break the cycle of disadvantage. To implement primary prevention in the educational system, educators need not just training in designing and evaluating the various units and workshops suggested earlier. Most importantly, future (and present) policy-makers and educators require a more complete education than is now the case. Key principles of human learning and development in their social context and related practices help promote collaboration and positive changes in the culture of public school.

There is a need to examine how a common knowledge base and strategy can be co-constructed in higher education. A transformation of the way that educators are professionally prepared[17] requires synthesizing a common knowledge base in higher education. As with the secondary school component for adolescents, the new professional goals and identity may need to be constructed in certification as a specialist primary prevention educator.[18] The new content of this professional education needs yet to be specified.

Implications

It seems clear that educators must answer the call to close the massive achievement gap in several unique, new, and strategic ways. They must, in part, lead the system that leads societal change. Higher education needs to step up. Until now, education reforms have left higher education out of center stage. A transactional and developmental approach is needed to go beyond "the chicken or the egg" gridlock.

A principal role of educators is that of a proactive prevention expert. SPARs rely on what is offered at school much more than others who have more social capital or advantages at home. The new educator being envisioned in this plan will direct efforts to close the gap by ensuring that adolescents graduate with a set of critical thinking skills and social knowledge that would otherwise be absent. Secondary school educators often deal with SPARs when they are already well behind others academically. There is only so much educators can do at this point without a preventative approach espoused by the whole system. Consequently, their principal role may first lie in promoting development in areas that are not necessarily tested in current reforms.[19] Yet, it is precisely in these areas of social competence and life skills that the way can be paved for increased and lasting parental involvement in future generations. SPARs in most schools feel academically alienated and unmotivated to persist when tests just confirm cumulative gaps in instruction and learning. It is important to provide extra supports for SPARs academically. Adolescence is the critical period for developing higher-level thinking for social development.

Higher education programs are ideal for preparing experts in primary intervention. The challenge remains because few understand and support primary prevention as a long-term approach to a complex set of problems.

With increased knowledge—and skills in applying human development principles—comes increased power to improve schools. While current trends in economic greed, resegregation, and war weaken and neutralize efforts to improve the educational system, educators must endeavor to close the gap. In a sense, this endeavor is not only centered on assisting SPARs' development but also that of society.

Even if higher education were transformed, and a restructuring of roles and practices were now to be implemented, an obstacle that stands in the way of reforms is the resistance from local districts and states. The more substantial the change proposed is, the greater the resistance is to be expected. Thus, the plan will require sustained, bipartisan support before gradual progress can be achieved from changes in higher, preschool, elementary and secondary education. Policymakers and educators who understand how prevention promotes equity in educational outcomes are essential to restructuring the educational system as a whole.

Endnotes

1. To be precise in defining the achievement gap, I propose that operationally the gap be defined by the proportion of SPARs subject to GBI who perform at grade level or higher as measured by nationally defined standards such as Goals 2000. Test scores on NAEP and similar standards would be aligned to reflect a cut-off for marking grade-level performance that minimally meets those standards. The criterion to be used in defining "minimum" would be that of functional literacy. We may estimate scores that correspond to proficient levels. The initial goal in phase one is thus to close the gap in terms of providing the assistance necessary for SPARs to reach proficiency in reading, language, math and science principally. Regardless of changes in norm-referenced scores that compare students to each other, such as CTBS normal curve equivalents, grade-level equivalents would be held constant along with minimum performance standards. In phase one the goal would be to eradicate group differences in the proportion of students in each group above the novice level and attaining proficiency. This may correspond roughly to the 50% of norm reference tests. The norms are predicted to change and improve, as the bulk of SPARs are educated equitably. In phases to follow the upper quartiles might be targeted. As college costs mount, recruitment of SPARs likely to succeed academically needs to be assisted publicly and privately to achieve subsequent equity in postsecondary education. In short, grade-level standards must not be raised until equity is established first.
2. Their roles in ending inequality in education may differ but the goal and strategies are the same.
3. i.e. higher performance standards at each grade.
4. Perhaps a suggestion for reorganizing the system is that college-level coursework be reserved for college. Students ready for this level would simply attend college, pay tuition costs, and accumulate credits. The line between college-level and high school standards needs to be clear and maintained. Advanced students would enter college earlier. We view raising standards as partly subsidizing college costs for the few. We suggest those so advanced as to have completed high school-level standards be promoted out of the secondary school system and rewarded through a variety of options, including paid service opportunities. A top priority should be ensuring SPARs meet those new standards at all costs.
5. While lower, middle, and upper-class groups are likely to remain, we define casteless in terms of any one ethnic group not being over-represented at the bottom.
6. Delivery capacity refers to the extent to which persons, operations, routines, and other forms of social capital can be organized and mediated to promote children's development.
7. It is not uncommon to leave SPARs with the least effective, often inexperienced educators.
8. Preparing the parents of future generations of SPARs may be the most realistic and important goal for educators of SPARs who are already handicapped by past educational practices.
9. An aptitude-treatment interaction refers to situations where a treatment such as smaller class size or mixed-ability grouping has a different effect on students with different levels of academic aptitude or school achievement.

10. We consider the task of compelling changes in the educational system to achieve equity as most humanistic. Insisting that the system guarantee SPARs an education that meets minimum standards at least is the issue around which the educational community should unite. The system's current organization—rather than the behaviorism being imposed on educators by conservative, historical arguments—is what needs change. Rather than just exhorting educators to work harder and longer in a failed system, it is the system that needs to be upgraded, retooled, and restructured in terms of assisting those who educate work more effectively.

11. By collaborative we refer to teaching that is grounded the notion of educators working together to ensure SPARs stay at grade level.

12. i.e., behind three to five grade levels by age eighteen; at twenty-two most are seven to nine years behind college graduates.

13. As a community of educators divided and distracted, our definitions of equity and excellence have been dangerously close to a not too far cousin called "values education." As noted by others before, the question centers on "whose values" are educators teaching? And it is now a given that we are in fact teaching someone's values to a considerable, however subtle, extent.

14. This is a military term used here to show how the current package delivered to SPARs is designed to "degrade" or limit rather than promote or "upgrade" development as indexed by grade level performance.

15. See www.seer.org.

16. They become mature in early adolescence for formal logical thinking in terms of biological maturation and socio-educational expectations.

17. It seems unfortunate that so many are persuaded by faulty logic in trusting that simply because some very rare examples of mostly elementary schools have SPARs achieving well, that the answer lies totally therein. Reasoning from a concrete example of others in a district is highly useful but not necessarily the solution. We should not follow the mindless "Be Like Mike" slogans and expect everyone to be Einstein. Why then should we exhort schools to be like the outlier in some district when the conditions that can produce the outlier are ignored?

18. A title or name for those to be educated in higher education with expertise in closing the gap is needed.

19. This is where an approach centered on prevention and promotion differs from that found in the Dewitt-*Reader's Digest* initiative which is focused mainly on tests scores.

Appendix: College Student Mentoring Report (An Example)

Mentoring Report

I began my mentoring project with a student of mine, Tonya. Her mother approached me at the beginning of the school year about tutoring Tonya outside of school hours. Of course, I said yes, and 2 days a week for 2 hours, we review, talk, and study.

I didn't know much about Tonya at first. Her records were choppy and she had transferred several times to different schools. I knew she was on my "special needs" list, but her needs were non-specific. Therefore, I visited our special needs coordinator. She filled in the gaps where she could, but she too was unsure on some details of her background. As a result, I knew her home life was unstable. She lived with her mother in Louisville and her father and other siblings lived out of town. I figured that it must impact her to have her family split and affect her school and performance. I also learned that there were some financial problems. Her mother worked two jobs and her grandparents were paying the tuition money. Obviously, her mother was not at home much to help and encourage Tonya with her studies. Lastly, Tonya had previously attended The DePaul School. This information told me that she had some type of learning disability. However, the school would not release her records due to unpaid bills. I could only assume her disability. On a positive note, I was able to discover that she had ADHD.

After building my background knowledge of the situation I was dealing with, I began to formulate a plan. Tonya is an at-risk student since she comes from a low SES background and unstable home life. The special need also raised a red flag (all of this substantiated by her low grades). I decided that I would give Tonya all the support and help that I could, sensing that she was not receiving it at home, and help her raise her grades. I was also going to have to be very patient and include some activities other than drills.

For our after-school meetings, we started off working on Spanish vocabulary in her book. She was having problems remembering what the words meant. When applicable, we did word association with the vocabulary to help her remember. For example, the verb *escribir* means to write. She associated the word with *scribe*, whose job is to write. We also made flashcards with the vocabulary, including pictures. Putting pictures with words assisted her greatly. This was when I realized Tonya was an artistic person, and any activity that included drawing could only benefit. In class, I noticed that Tonya was improving her scores on her weekly vocabulary quizzes and also was participating more in class. Her confidence level seemed to be increasing. To this day, she is still scoring well on her quizzes and I see her hand often raised. I made it a point to write my homework assignments on the board so she could see them. I also emailed her other teachers asking that they do the same. From what I understand from the other teachers, her homework is now completed and turned in on time. When she enters my classroom, the first thing she does is write her homework down.

I still meet with Tonya, but we only meet once a week now. I can see the benefits of working with her. First, she is succeeding in school. Her grades in my class went from a D to a B+. From what I hear, she is doing well in all her classes. Second, her confidence has increased. She seems to interact better with the other students. She's not as quiet or shy. She also participates frequently. I feel that my spending time with her allows Tonya to see that people do care about her. Third, she understands the Spanish language much better! Our work after school has led her to appreciate the language and culture much more than she ever thought possible. You could see the pride on her face when she began to construct sentences on her own. She is also able to read and comprehend basic sentences and structures.

I can't help but feel proud as I watch Tonya blossom weekly. It's amazing to think about what a difference one person can make. I have a feeling that I am that parental figure that she so desperately needs in her life and is not getting. Working with Tonya has been one of the best things I've done this school year.

9 Conclusions and Future Directions

> "Unless it is possible for adults to manage their work
> and family lives without undue strain on themselves
> and their children society will suffer a significant
> loss in productivity, and an even more significant loss
> in the quantity and quality of future generations."
>
> KAMERMAN & KAHN (1981)

Overview

Part of the restructuring needed in higher education is continued in this last section. The main ideas of the book are summarized as part of a knowledge base necessary for the transformation of professional educators in the future. Essential issues pertaining to equity and policy action are noted for teacher and principal education along with some general recommendations.

Introduction

Although professional areas in (higher) education deserve a much more complete analysis than it is possible to provide here, a few directions and trends are worth noting in defining this last component. Change in one component is not sufficient. For example, parent support, instruction, tracking, and class size are key problems. While headlines link the worst teachers with

SPARs, the problem runs deeper. Simple solutions such as principals' leadership, reducing class size, or same-gender schools are short sighted. The problem lies in understanding the historical context and conditions of learning and teaching encountered at the segmented school and classroom levels, many of which generally stem from the tension created by various structures and practices that produce the gap in predictable ways.

Nevertheless, some important state-of-the-art trends in reforming teacher education are noteworthy. Outside of the model that has been sketched, the current trends may be classified under two broad categories (see Table 9–1). The first is humanistic, based on concerns about teacher expectations, social justice, critical pedagogy, multiculturalism, and citizenship in a democracy. The second is more behavioral and concerned primarily with raising test scores, accountability, and raising standards. The latter is more prevalent in current efforts to transform school administration and school counseling while the former is more salient in teacher education.

Today initiatives to reform teacher education vary in the extent to which eliminating the gap is regarded as a central goal or problem. For example, Professional Development Schools (PDS) and other initiatives for improving urban education and teacher preparation (Abdul-Haqq, 1998) respond to multiple purposes that are generally not specific to closing the gap relative to other programs that are, such as Success for All (Slavin, Madden, Dolan, & Wasik, 1996), The School Development Program (Comer et al. 1996) or Accelerated Schools (Levin, 1988). While efforts to cultivate professional learning communities are clearly important (Lieberman & Hoody, 1998), and focusing teacher education on diversity (Cochran-Smith, 2002; Ladson-Billings, 1998, 2001; Nieto, 2003) does target SPAR populations, it appears that a comprehensive paradigm is still missing because none can, or have, made a significant impact on the national level. The tension amongst different communities of practice promotes multiple alternatives to current practices that are disjointed. For example, the relatively small federal contribution to education and SPARs in particular (10% of the cost of educating students) has often been targeted in thirty-minute daily remedial sessions and such (Stringfield et al., 1997; Borman & D'Agostino, 1996) through Title I funds. However, to improve education for all children, much more can be accomplished if components are integrated with collaboration across levels, particularly when instruction is meaningful rather than drill and practice (Wong, Sunderman, & Lee, 1995). Nevertheless, a general paradigm includes the adoption of proven instructional models for whole schools that are generally at risk (Borman et al., 2002), that follow effective early intervention programs (Ramey, Campbell, Burchinal, Skinner, Gardner, & Ramey, 2000). Without an aggressive and coordinated approach, chances are too great that SPARs will remain tracked for failure. It is doubtful that current educational and social policy will ever achieve equity unless new initiatives can be coordinated at different levels of sustained support.

Table 9–1: Approaches Related to Closing the Gap: A Spectrum of Strategies and Ideologies—A Typology

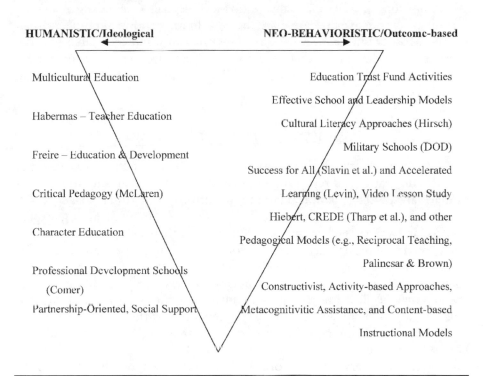

HUMANISTIC/Ideological   NEO-BEHAVIORISTIC/Outcome-based

Multicultural Education

Habermas – Teacher Education

Freire – Education & Development

Critical Pedagogy (McLaren)

Character Education

Professional Development Schools
  (Comer)

Partnership-Oriented, Social Support

Education Trust Fund Activities

Effective School and Leadership Models

Cultural Literacy Approaches (Hirsch)

Military Schools (DOD)

Success for All (Slavin et al.) and Accelerated

Learning (Levin), Video Lesson Study

Hiebert, CREDE (Tharp et al.), and other

Pedagogical Models (e.g., Reciprocal Teaching,

Palincsar & Brown)

Constructivist, Activity-based Approaches,

Metacognitivitic Assistance, and Content-based

Instructional Models

The current trends in reforming teacher education may be classified under several broad categories (see Table 9–1). One is humanistic and based on concerns about teacher expectations, social justice/critical pedagogy, multiculturalism and citizenship in a democracy. In this camp, the problem of the gap and inequality are not defined specifically in terms of test outcomes but in a broader set of interrelated concerns about power and the development of the whole child. Excellence is not necessarily defined only by higher score outcomes but also by child- or culture-sensitive approaches and processes. Process-oriented models aim toward developing a well-balanced learner and future productive, competent citizen.

On the right, concern about the basic curriculum, pedagogical methods, and standards related to both teachers' and students' achievement can be noted. The latter concern primarily raising test scores, accountability, and pragmatism in raising the productivity of schools. Excellence is defined along the latter lines more so than along equity across groups in a neo-behavioristic fashion. At the bottom of this figure, sociocognitive, developmental foundations are recognized in approaches that are cultural and developmental integrating both process- and outcome-oriented views. The figure is only for heuristic purposes.

Philosophical differences always divide the goals of education and the pursuit of various means. Some are more utilitarian and market driven than others. Most are not concerned directly with equity and the inability of the present system to educate each group fairly. Presently, there exists no cogent strategy to reverse group-based inequality as a means toward educational excellence.

Transforming Teacher Education

A number of influential communities within teacher education argue that teachers do matter and represent a fundamental aspect in closing the gap. As Haberman (2002), Darling-Hammond (2000), and others have noted, teacher characteristics count, particularly in terms of student learning, expectations, and values. Haberman (2002) contends that the teachers or "stars" (as he refers to those with a true vocation) we wish to prepare are those educators who take responsibility without making excuses. This view suggests that regardless of the context, or populations served and constraints found, the gap may be closed by the type of educator who walks the talk, refuses to fail, and avoids helplessness. In his suggestions for the transformation of teacher education, important points are made that might be incorporated in counselor and leadership preparation. While disagreeing with Haberman's depiction of teachers as either born stars or quitters, I agree that their worldview or perception can predetermine their failure long before they find excuses to abandon their career. Thus, the role of context in teacher education programs becomes critically important. However, neither transforming teachers and teacher education alone or the "No Excuses" approach proposed by some conservatives (see Thernstrom & Thernstrom, 2003) can close the gap without corresponding changes in other parts of the system.

In acknowledging that societal forces outside education conspire against equity in a system that compels it to reflect its iniquitous political economy, Haberman's position that teacher education can close the gap remains largely ideological in its analysis of the problem. It suggests that with the right teachers selected, SPARs could be taught well enough to close the gap. As with similar singular positions in the field, asserting that dedicated, multicultural, critical or ethically minded professionals can empower students enough to close the gap, the argument is flawed. Surely teachers must examine their values, beliefs, and expectations, and like counselors, must be authentic, caring and sensitive, but professional characteristics alone are not sufficient to dismantle or reverse structures and historical practices that maintain GBI. It is true teachers can make a difference for some SPARs some of the time (as a few schools do) but not sufficiently to outweigh the limitations structured in the system or to have a population effect.

Nevertheless, a highly valuable organizational implication that stems from the above position is that of identifying the necessary (if even not sufficient) elements in teacher education in general. For example, one is to prepare, assist, and maintain educators in a setting well, and long, enough to turn teaching and learning outcomes around. As a "star" himself, Haberman will make no excuses for the profession, showing educators what it may take to make a difference amidst the constraints of the system. Unfortunately, at present and amidst a teacher shortage, the average career in teaching lasts between six to eight years. This suggests that careful selection of teachers who have the vocation is essential but again improbable as with other single-issue approaches to closing the gap. What seems valuable here is the notion of educators developing a professional identity that is aimed toward educating all children equitably. However, they also need structural and organizational support for SPARs from a developmental perspective.

Critical Perspectives

A literature steeped in social justice education has emerged that seems to have increased leverage in teacher education programs across the country along with critical pedagogy (Apple, 2001; McLaren, 1994). The approach to closing the gap is centered on liberation and Freire's critique with respect to the "pedagogy of the oppressed" (Freire, 1993) and the whole genre of writing related to race and class it has spun in recent years (Berlak, 2001; Gamoran, 1987; Goodwin, 2002; Holt, 1990; Kozol, 2000; Nieto, 2000b). Related approaches are critical race theory (Delgado & Stephancic, 2000; Gordon, 1999) and teacher education programs centered on multiculturalism with respect to curriculum and instruction, untracking[1] and alternatives to testing in defining school success. In this category, ideological critiques prevail over researching practices that can be disseminated and evaluated in a process-product fashion. The gem in Freire's work and legacy is the clarity of analysis with respect to banking knowledge, poverty, and its reproduction in educational practices that conflict with the corporization of education in general.

Another force in teacher education centers on research-based inroads made by blends of constructivist and direct instruction methods in education from research on ability grouping to tutorial programs designed to assist SPARs. Research on a variety of methods in science, mathematics, language arts and related areas (Hiebert et al., 2002; Greeno & Goldman, 1998; Bereiter & Scardamalia, 1987; Knapp, 1995; Weinberger & McCombs,

2001) attempts to find ways to enhance student achievement and meaningful learning. Teacher education that expands on the concepts of cognitive apprenticeships (Greeno, Collins, & Resnick, 1996; Harpaz & Lefstein, 2000) and mediated and situated learning (Kozulin & Presseisen, 1995; Karpov & Bransford, 1995; Anderson, Greeno, Reder & Simon, 2000; Tharp et al., 2000) appears to be part of the solution insofar as the expansion of this knowledge base is concerned. Educators' knowledge about research on cooperative learning and ability grouping also seems critical (see Tomlinson, 2000; Fashola & Slavin, 1996). Along with self-efficacy (Bandura, 1986) and research on student learning characteristics, a rich literature has emerged related to predicting school achievement beyond social class (Jencks & Phillips, 1999; P.R. Portes, 1999). Unfortunately, most of the above research remains fragmented and unfamiliar to those who graduate from higher education.

Finally, a growing body of knowledge is emerging from compensatory education programs that are essential for teacher education. Head Start, Follow Through—and later, Title I programs—have been researched, uncovering a number of essential steps needed to make them effective (e.g. Wong, Sunderman, & Lee, 1995). Given that the latter have not been able to decrease the gap significantly as a whole, new generations of Comprehensive School Reform Programs have emerged from the existing knowledge and funding. Success for All (Slavin & Madden, 2001), School Development Program (Comer et al., 1996), and Direct Instruction (Adams & Englemann, 1996) are a few among several others (see Borman & D'Agostino, 1996). These models are important for educators from K–12 as part of a broad knowledge base that can help attain large effects on SPAR populations. They provide important insights on many of the within-school variables that must be coordinated to counter the many risks posed by poverty conditions.

Related to the above are standards-based reform, test-oriented teaching, instructional design and school accountability models. Included here are cases such as those focused on basic skills in Core Knowledge, or perhaps Modern Red School House (Kilgore, Doyle, & Linkowsky, 1996) or Accelerated Schools (Hopfenberg & Levin, 1993) and similarly oriented programs. However, a most visible element in the accountability-oriented field stems from the overarching Education Trust literature (see Haycock, 1998) as a whole. State-level reforms now seem to be most concerned about reducing the gap because of the adoption of higher standards. With these reforms, rewards for high performing schools are countered by sanctions for schools that fail to make continuous progress. From this view, the gap may be bridged by school-based teaching and educators becoming more effective and productive. Unfortunately, even with test-based instruction and drill and practice approaches to raise tests scores, the pattern of huge differences between ethnic groups would still be left intact.

Video Lessons and Other Technology

A new trend, also school-centered and multicultural in perspective, is emerging and involves the use of technology and video lessons. Teacher education has yet to systematically employ the resources offered by international initiatives and research. Lesson study videos of teachers actually engaged in effective practices for a range of standards-related lessons (Hiebert, Gallimore, Garnier, Givvin, Hollingsworth, Jacobs, Chui, Wearne, Smith, Kersting, Manaster, Tseng, Etterback, Manaster, Gonzales, & Stigler 2003) are being accumulated and developed as part of a virtual library of resources for teachers working on particular standards-based lessons with various levels of students across the world. Based on international comparisons of student data, Hiebert et al. (2003) have collected samples of lessons for a variety of grades and content areas across the world that may be shared for teacher education have been collected and developed. While this approach is still in its infancy, it promises to improve (teacher) education and offer effective means to improve the education of all students. Many other types of technology-oriented models may be found in the literature that aim to improve learning and test scores.

A Military Approach–DOD Schools

Another heuristic case relevant to closing the gap involves a different organizational and financing context for educating students from underrepresented populations. When the schooling of children from these groups is supported and organized differently, students are not placed at risk. Research teams at Vanderbilt University found certain military-operated schools educate children of service men and women well. African American and Hispanic students enrolled in schools operated by the Department of Defense (DOD) in the United States and abroad performed well above current standards on reading and writing tests. The Vanderbilt study, "March Toward Excellence," (Smrekar, Guthrie, Owens, & Sims, 2001) used 1998 data from the NAEP and was commissioned by the National Education Goals Panel. The research team believes that several key elements to the DOD schools' success can be applied to civilian schools to improve public education. The research found that gaps between white and minority students' NAEP reading and writing scores are considerably smaller in DOD schools than relative nationwide results. Some of the features, methods, and practices that promote success in DOD schools that could be applied in public school are: small schools, systematic measurement, empowered educators, rich and varied teaching methods, commitment to education and accountability, a strong sense of community, sufficient resources, and a clear mission. The DOD operates 227 elementary and secondary schools and serves 112,000 students. Minority student enrollment for elementary and secondary DOD schools is 40%, which is about the same percentage as the State of New York school system (Lewis, 2001). Unfortunately, while the education organized by the DOD is of heuristic value, its success may be explained by factors that are context bound. The student, teacher, parent, community characteristics are not typical of those confronting civilian schools. What is interesting is that here is a case of a public school system that is federally funded that is more committed to meeting standards than offering advanced programs or college-level courses.

While the DOD example may be didactic, the most important confound in this case concerns parents and the context in which they socialize their children. Children in DOD schools are not necessarily comparable to the SPARs in public school whose poor school performance defines the gap. As argued repeatedly, many who are classified by ethnicity into underrepresented minorities may not be at risk necessarily. It is possible that many of the DOD minority families would have children perform at or above grade level in regular public schools. We can't tell if it's the DOD model of instruction that is the critical factor or not. The reasons include:

a. Parents belong to an organization that is qualitatively different from those in the public sector. These are families who, by becoming part of the military setting, are selected into a system or treatment that provides academic supports and norms that neutralize a variety of risks.
b. While parents are expected to be involved in their children's schooling, support structures are available to prevent low performers from falling behind.
c. The moderating effect of parental income and education is minimized.
d. Military careers are based more closely on a meritocracy than is the case in the public sectors. In this context, GBI is less severe by design. The social contexts in and out of school are different.

While other differences might be noted, the main lesson here concerns the educational outcomes that stem from a system that is organized differently. The federal government may help neutralize inequality in finance (per-pupil expenditures), teacher quality, and similar factors. Defense department schools draw from various sectors of the population and yet provide a temporary refuge for many actually subject to GBI. The privileges afforded, of course, are tied to a different set of risks in time of war, particularly for groups who are less likely to be commissioned.

In sum, how different learning environments are organized and their relation to academic learning are general topics for analysis in higher education. While the above approaches contribute in alerting educators to parts of the problem (see Figure 8–1), they are not viable or complete enough to close the gap at the population level. The DOD example does not answer the call for a national policy change although it provides food for thought. Each approach remains limited by a respective ideology that is not aimed particularly toward ending GBI. Because each is lacking a cultural-historical understanding of a multifaceted problem, fragmented responses result that sustain the status quo. However, each one offers valuable elements to be considered in a more comprehensive model. Without a multilevel, interdisciplinary conceptual framework, educators chase after disjointed, quick solutions such as school uniforms, same-gender or smaller schools, and so on. A common framework is needed to unify mediated actions from each level in a historical, multifaceted model. The attempt is to help guide local successes to gradually produce a population effect. This effect is defined by a measurable difference from the 1971 NAEP gap between groups in scores reported by ethnicity. The latter provides only an indirect picture of the problem of equity in terms of how learning outcomes and opportunities are distributed. So what are some of the elements and principles for establishing a common general knowledge base in reorganizing higher education for educators? Let's examine how this component serves as a lynchpin in producing and sustaining a cultural change in a context that prepares those who would serve SPARs.

Principles for Reorganization

Academic learning time is a central concept for reducing the achievement gap. It stems from positivist research yet fits well within a developmental, cultural-context perspective (Cole & Cole, 1993). Most of the factors, solutions, and strategies that influence school achievement revolve around how much time the learner spends assisted—and then less assisted—on tasks, skills, and other types of learning that relate to test content. Class reduction is an example: the smaller the class (below sixteen), the higher the achievement because the learner has significantly more access to assisted performance than otherwise.

Smaller schools serve as another example of success that is related to alternative schools (Klonsky & Ford, 1994). Conceptually, more meaningful assistance can accrue in smaller classes. Similarly, family size, parent involvement, year-round schools, teacher experience, and expertise and expectations are among the most critical factors that predict achievement. Educators then need to understand that:

a. Academic learning is cumulative.
b. Academic socialization occurs across a variety of contexts (Bronfenbrenner, 1979; Whiting & Edwards, 1988; Weisner, 1984);
c. Attitudes (Steele, 1999) and affective factors are critical for encouraging academic learning that becomes interwoven across various areas related to literacy development.
d. The more vigorous the social interaction between learners, teachers, and peers, the more likely development is to advance (Portes, 1988; 1991).
e. Interactions with SPARs in zones of proximal development for grade-level standards and what tests value represent the essential target in closing the gap. Hence, organizing the activities necessary in settings that have the potential to support SPARs' development is of paramount importance.

Educators need to collaborate in increasing these interactions in the lives of all SPARs more so than is the case at present. To do so, the educational system must be restructured strategically and developmentally. Educators can maximize the learning opportunities that directly promote SPARs' academic progress, as well as prepare them to be more involved parents in the future. This one-two punch is a key organizing principle for closing a massive, resistant gap.

As noted elsewhere, some developed countries outside the United States spend more on low-income students' education as a democratic strategy within the system of education. While we obviously can learn from the rule that money can buy more assisted learning and performance, there is a related and more critical principle here. Too often money is employed for purposes that are not directly ensuring academic assistance activity or organizing prevention activities across settings for SPARs' participation.

Student resistance, dis-identification with academic learning, and similar concepts that stem from different genres of research are important (see Erickson & Gutierrez, 2002; Ogbu, 2002; Steele, 1992, 1997). They are valuable in thinking about the design of teaching and learning activities that not only take into consideration the interests of the school (test scores) but also the students' future development.

Recommendations for Organizing a Common Knowledge Base

As much as possible, higher education programs should share curricula and classes, as well as faculty, focused on collaborative work in closing the gap, not only diversity. Prejudice reduction is not enough. Collaboration is optimal when one knows what the educational system is doing and why. Each educator must understand the interwoven connections among personnel and goals. Their preparation includes strategies for developing partnerships in both undergraduate and graduate programs for educators, and a stronger, integrated curriculum should be developed around human development and learning. Rather than isolated required courses (e.g., philosophy and foundations of education, educational psychology, and methods courses), the integration should also be based on the relations among learning, instruction, development, and equity as essential to excellence in education with real world fieldwork for all college students.

The organizing theme and principles may be viewed as centered squarely on developing the necessary means for developing citizens equitably. Regardless of whether the aim is behavioral or humanistic, the goal of equity is shared at a basic level. The suggestion here is that this basic level be defined by teaching that results in student performance at or above grade level standards in launching a new national strategy. A moratorium might be placed on raising the standards now until the system is reorganized to meet minimum equity standards. The latter would center on assisting SPARs in ways necessary to avoid a form of cultural or academic degradation or decline relative to other nations that is, ironically, an underlying motive for the current higher standards (No Child Left Behind) agenda.

Specific Recommendations for Higher Education

■   One to two seminars on closing the achievement gap for current educators already in the field or in higher education are recommended. These may be organized in colleges of education by expert faculty and practitioners.[2] The seminars would join all types of educators (pre-service and veteran educators) whenever possible rather than segregating them into their respective leadership, counselor, teacher education, or other programs. One of the seminars could be linked to a national level, ongoing distance education project focused on curtailing the gap that is interactive and supportive. A technology-based network would support and lend coherence to the preparation of educators across colleges and universities as a contribution to professional development. Such seminars would serve to review and identify what works and why and provide scaffolds to instituting effective practices (Tharp et al., 2000).

■   In envisioning the future preparation of educators, we might extend recent efforts to develop a virtual library or resource center of effective educational practices now being collected internationally. Based on the work described by Heibert, Gallimore, and Stigler (2002), educators might be able to view and study how effective lessons can be co-constructed with different populations. Similar examples of proven practices for principals and counselors might be made available as part of a national strategy to close the gap.

- The first seminar would outline the knowledge base educators should have and an understanding of how different programs and approaches are connected conceptually, along with a theoretical foundation of human development. Readings would include research on successful programs and the corresponding mediated action that produced success across schools and districts. Other seminars might include program design and evaluation skills, collaboration and advocacy functions, and field experience in working with SPARs. This preparation of key personnel with a common goal of understanding and closing the gap is essential.

- Primary prevention for adolescents should commence as soon as possible, beginning with seniors and juniors who will soon become parents of new SPARs. Every effort should be made to invest in those children's development through the other components.

- In every district, the other two components should also be addressed simultaneously.

While the good news is that some parts of this strategy are already in place in various school contexts, only a few educators are prepared adequately. Their preparation varies in content and depth, and even when parts of the gap are covered, a sustainable, reliable delivery system is not well in place. Unlike schools of medicine, professional educators provide service often without the critical tools, professional conditions, capacity to teach well, or a system for closing the gap. While some are succeeding as a result of applying necessary and sufficient components and efforts, imagine what improvement might result at the population level as more and better-prepared educators enter districts that are also improving learning conditions for SPARs. The belief is that the gap is closed when SPARs' socialization is organized in ways that promote academic and socioeconomic literacy[3] with professionals who are well prepared.Needless to mention is the greater federal support and strategic assistance for SPARs directly.

Professional Concerns

Why train professional educators to enter careers in schools that do not support the roles they are trained for? After all, translating the recommendations from the educational research community in higher education into practices at the district and school level has been subject to various types of "error" or validity threats. First, the fidelity or internal validity of the intervention program may not have been preserved, and the results turn out to be disappointing. Second, the intervention program may be well implemented but does not produce the intended results because the "cultural validity" (Portes, 2000b) of the intervention research was flawed. That is, a new teaching approach, class size reduction, cooperative learning (Slavin, 2002b) or Accelerated Schools (Levin, 1988) may produce higher performance in one context with certain types of students, teachers, and schools than others. However, a model may not be necessarily helpful and actually may have a contrary effect in a different context.[4]

The gap is configured inter-generationally. A lag exists between the time new generations of students are socialized in new ways and the time their children can perform at grade level or above in the next generation. Consequently, a developmental framework aimed to disarm the ways class and power disadvantage SPARs' development each generation (relative to other children) is needed in the present strategy. In safeguarding a democratically inclined system, the following measures are also recommended.

a. In higher education, faculty must develop leadership with a clear strategy to help public schools close the gap and have equity or excellence at the top of their mission statement. School superintendents might also help ensure focused collaborations are sustained as urgent priorities. They must be among the first to form a variety of community partnerships (Seeley, 1985).

b. Educators, as well as others, may adopt a SPAR as part of their service, obtaining extra pay and/or tax credits. Private employers and the justice court system may also find ways to help provide staff assistance for SPARs in and after school.

c. College students and volunteers who mentor SPARs also receive tuition and other tax credits.

d. States, businesses, and universities may offer SPARs at-grade-level (free) tuition for college.

e. Class-size reduction and itinerant teachers become part of educational reorganization. Elementary schools are targeted first, followed by secondary schools in a systemic fashion to assist SPARs.

f. Finally, a needs assessment is carried out to help prioritize program elements. Some of the needed changes in counselor and teacher education are:

■ Human development theory and research focused on the achievement gap problem;

■ Impact analysis, along with political and economic analysis of related programs; and

■) Program evaluation tools to be included for process evaluation/feedback to change agents.

A new cadre of educators represents one of the links that would serve a new generation of underrepresented students who enjoy greater parental support as well as effective preschool experiences (see Table 9–2). Below the key points of the model are summarized in a schema for educators.

Conceptual and Political Issues for Educators in Higher Education

The predicament of the achievement gap is largely about literacy differences produced (paradoxically) through schooling. Schooling is regarded as democratic, but in practice, it is organized to be compatible with middle class-based experiences and lifestyles. The gap requires awareness of what decades of imposed poverty does to cultural patterns of adaptation. It requires a developmental understanding of how certain aspects of socialization vary by group and impact teaching and learning. There seems to be an unintentional complicity between schooling and the learning and development that occurs outside schools on a daily basis. This has been noted by critical theorists, sociologists, and others (Apple, 2001; Bourdieu & Passeron, 1977; Bowles and Gintis, 1976). Unfortunately, like approaches based on social justice, only parts of a solution are conceptualized in these writings. Each day, students at risk come home with less advancement in literacy relative to more privileged students. Each day, they return to school "less readied" by their experiences in and outside school. Counselors, teachers, and principals—as well as their university educators—are the only ones in a strategic position to make a difference. However, they need support from the community and colleges in terms of time, personnel, and mediated action. The creation of a strategic program of human development studies in adolescent students in preparing sound decision-making and parenting is long overdue. The prevention component may be the missing piece that—along with the other proposed components—achieves a sustainable positive effect in narrowing the achievement gap in future generations. The largest cultural difference or aspect of social capital lies precisely in this domain which remains conceptualized nebulously as parental involvement.

The Role of SES and Capital

The links among school achievement, cognitive development, literacy in general, and economic outcomes are undisputed in their recursive nature. Economic and social capital both predict achievement. Its cognitive developmental base lies in literacy. Statistically, the links are significant yet only

Table 9–2: Organizing Assistance to SPARs

WHEN		WHAT
Early Development		
	Birth–Three Years	Head Start— Extend to all SPARs
		—Extend services beyond current 60% of those eligible and up to kindergarten
		Extend programs such as Ramey and Ramey (in press) and Weikart (2002).
School K–12		
	Elementary	After-school Mentors
		Collaborative Practices
		Year-round schools (Seasonality), Class-size Reduction, etc.
		Track SPARs for Success (do not track teachers or students, or retain or resegregate as currently done)
	Secondary	Sustain the Above
		Professional Development for All Educators
		Deploy Adolescent Component
		Extend Programs Such As AVID (Mehan 1996)
College		
		Academic Assistance

account for a modest amount of the variance in each other. For example, in White's (1982) metanalysis of research on SES and school achievement, the variance accounted for by SES averaged about 5%. However, the range of factors generally considered is limited.

One argument is that relationship varies according to the population that is represented in the overall average. In a predominately wealthy society, the relation may be lower than in a context where a larger proportion of the population is poor. Yet, evidence suggests that even moderate investments for helping SPARs carry with them higher dividends than for non-SPARs. For example, smaller classes for SPARs improve achievement for SPARs more than for other students (Achilles, Finn & Bain, 1998). Academically focused after-school programs may also carry a similar impact.

Summary

In sum, higher education must be reformed as part of a comprehensive approach to close the gap. Current trends in teacher education were explored for their efficacy in dismantling the massive achievement gap found in our public schools, but as some approaches have been proven effective in raising scores or reducing inequality, no single-barrel approach has been sufficient thus far. Specific recommendations were offered in order to organize a common knowledge base for educators and professionals.

Endnotes

1. There is some evidence that untracking students does not help close the gap once tracking has been established.
2. In many cases, designated faculty may require retooling and professional development as part of a continually learning community. We foresee national and international collaborations that would have a common clearinghouse website. For example, designated faculty must be aware of current programs and monitor their progress as well as stay in contact with those of particular interest. For example, CREDE (Tharp et al., 2000), SEER AVID (Mehan et al., 1994), and various in- and after-school and preschool programs would be part of a general knowledge base as it evolves in practice.
3. The latter is defined by knowledge and some skill and self-regulation in social and economic areas.
4. This example is only used to illustrate the issue of cultural validity in translating research into practice. Theoretical learning and teaching (Karpov & Bransford, 1995) have shown positive effects and may be have cultural validity for all we know. What is tested and how it is evaluated needs to be considered in determining whether a new tool is effective for promoting SPARs' school learning. In urban centers such as Detroit less than 20% of high school students score at the proficient level, while less than 12% of Baltimore's students tested satisfactory (Stone, Henig, Jones & Pierannunzi, 2001). It remains to be seen if constructs such as self-regulated learning, self-efficacy, and such have similar relevance across groups.

10 Summary *and* Policy Recommendations

"A policy choice is an act of will and intention.
We must once in a while admit that the poor
have been impoverished intentionally."

—WILLIAM RYAN, 1981, p. 210

Let's close with some final reiterations of the main arguments and ideas in this book. Policy recommendations are to coordinate stronger support from federal, state, and local agencies in organizing new structures to address the problem of educational inequality. The achievement gap is defined in a way that differs from the current reform and the NCLB discourse. Rather than splitting the problem of educational inequality into a series of gaps and measures, conceptual unity is needed in defining ethnic gaps in learning outcomes as a cultural developmental issue. Test-score gaps in achievement reflect divisions of groups along ethnic and economic lines. In this book, the gap has been clearly defined by GBI in educational outcomes, particularly since 1971, when NAEP scores served to document an ethnic gap that unfortunately still prevails today. In fact, higher standards today only exacerbate a longstanding sorting of students by group as 2003–2004 reports have documented nationwide (*Condition of Education*, 2004).

I expressed caution against the insincerity of some proclaiming great concern about students left behind while imposing higher standards reforms, because such concerns have simply not been joined with the necessary resources to end group-based disparities in school learning. I have also argued against singular, if not fragmented, approaches to resolving the problem in favor of a comprehensive, developmental policy shift. Scolding educators (Tanner, 2000) in the public schools is not only misguided but also unjust, given past and existing practices outside of education. Educators do not control economic trends, wages, market forces, media, or technology, which all alter the roles and functions of the (American) family. I have desisted from the faulty logic of using the few exceptional schools educating high proportions of SPARs effectively as the primary strategy for addressing a massive, multi-faceted challenge involving thousands of schools across the nation, each with their own set of unique characteristics. Once in a while, a number of conditions coincide and produce such anomalies for a period of time. However, like chasing after yesterday's high-yielding stocks, such strategies are shortsighted. The folly of moving students to charter schools was noted as shortsighted and limited. Exceptional schools, of course, point to many useful practices that can serve low-achieving schools. However, they should not serve to bash educators either. They need to prove that a universal solution has been found that can withstand local tests (Gallimore & Goldenberg, 2001). By analogy, just as 3–5% of children are regarded as gifted and talented, the notion that the other 95–97% can also perform at similar levels is sanguine. However, I believe substantive changes in conditions for the socialization of low-income children that support their development can be organized and shared to a greater extent than is presently the case. In sum, the main point is not only to test for higher standards but rather to help achieve long-term improvements in learning outcomes at the population level for SPARs.

In the latest reports available, we must still extrapolate from poverty to achievement data available for each ethnic group to understand the gaps in achievement noted in Figure 10–1:

The data show between-group gaps that amount to about four school grade levels by high school. It is easy to see across for eighth-grade students a level that matches that of seniors for the other two groups! The scores for 1971 show relative differences between groups (twelfth grade—white 291, black 239, Hispanic 252) in a pattern unchanged. In eighth grade the differences were—white 251, black 222, Hispanic 232; while in fourth grade the point differences were—white 214, black 170, Hispanic, 183). Of course, the scores for low-income children would be dramatically different and alarming given the information below. This is because over 40% of children in the above minority groups live in poverty, while less than 15% of the majority groups experience it. Thus, the above graph must be interpreted carefully in reflecting averaged scores with regard to poverty rates, something which masks the extent of the problem. In the United States, children have a high poverty rate, affecting millions of students. The poverty rate

Figure 10–1: Average Reading Scale Scores, by School-Reported Race/Ethnicity,
Grades 4, 8, and 12: 1992–2002 (Adapted from *The Condition of Education*, 2003)

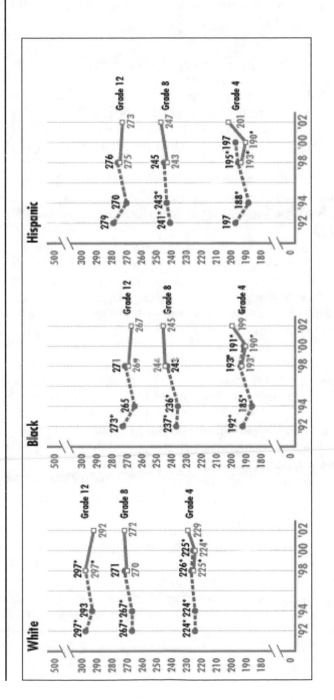

was lowest in 1974 and has increased significantly since the 1990s. Relative to other developed countries, these figures remain disconcerting given more children live in poverty now than before (Lee and Burkam, 2002; Rank 2004).

Family Poverty on the Rise

Between 2000 and 2001, poverty rose to 11.7% of the population, or 32.9 million people, up from 11.3% and 31.6 million. The poverty rate for 2002 was 13.9%, equaling about 35.1 million Americans living in poverty with over 14 million of those being children. In 2004, the poverty rate could average 14.2% or 35.8 million people (based on the US Census Bureau). The issue is not only that poverty depresses development, school learning, and is distributed unfairly, rather, it is the inequity added in school that is troubling and that exacerbates the gap for low-income children who are left behind two to four grade levels.

In spite of the current rhetoric, we remain a nation unwilling to invest in poor children and families. Many of the efforts initiated by the educational community are neutralized by the economic stress placed on families with school-age children. As long as students from poor minority groups experience poverty at three times the rate of the majority group, and schools continue to undereducate them, there will be an ethical and social dilemma. Non-Hispanic white families' poverty rate in 2001 was 5.7%, while African American and Latino families were 20.7% and 19.4%, respectively (Proctor & Dalaker, 2002) Eighth graders from the first group can already perform at the same grade level as seventeen-year-old high school students from the poorer minority groups. This achievement gap cumulates in the current educational system. Why defend an educational system that provides a high school-level education to the majority and a middle-school education to some minorities trapped by poverty? Evidence exists that SES interacts with intellectual development. Improvements in the educational environments often produce greater advantages for the poor than for the privileged (Turkheimer et al., 2003)

Social, as well as educational, equity becomes a primary concern in defining reform or excellence in education. From a privileged perspective, it is difficult to understand obstacles in children's learning, particularly when the effects and extent of actual poverty are underestimated. The manner in which poverty rates are presented is misleading, which tends to underestimate the levels of required assistance for students to learn at grade level. Yet, my premise is that despite economic poverty, an educational system can be redesigned to change the relative standstill of the past fifty years since the *Brown* decision. The current high-stakes reform is not adequate. A much more comprehensive approach is required, and American society as a whole has yet to grasp the consequences of flawed family and educational policies. The latter seems to be treated independently of economic policies not only nationally but at the global level, both of which impact on education indirectly and directly.

An initial policy recommendation is to focus resources within a developmental approach that would track SPARs for success upon entering the school system. The strategy would be to sustain assistance to more SPAR groups long enough (over the formative and adolescent periods) to prevent academic failure and degrading. Helping low-income students through magnet schools tends to average the below grade-level performance of the latter with the high scores from privileged, advanced students outside the neighborhood. This method is of limited value and allows resources to flow mainly towards a few who benefit from within-school tracking rather than SPARs. While current tracking practices place SPARs at greater disadvantage than more privileged peers, untracking is not necessarily the best solution (Yonezawa, Wells, & Serna, 2002).[1] Without a developmental framework, some strategies can be harmful.

Current tracking practices are unwarranted because their purpose is inherently unfair and inconsistent with reversing GBI. It is not that tracking can be avoided completely or should be. It can be a powerful tool in dismantling educational inequality in this plan. However, holding back advanced students is also unfair. Both issues require getting our priorities in order. In such a situation, what is more important? Given limited resources, do we focus on advantaging the already advantaged who cruise above grade level or help the needy achieve at grade level? It seems to make sense that perhaps we might focus on the latter and do better than not placing students three to four grade levels behind. As increased proportions of capable SPARs achieve at grade level, resources can be focused on challenging all groups, including those at higher-grade levels. This might cause flight to private schools initially for a significant number of well-to-do families as is already the case. After a few years, the impact analysis may be that more students are performing at or above grade level with this more equitable strategy. Yet, all learners must be challenged.

As the correlation between ethnicity and performing below grade level becomes insignificant, a number of benefits might be anticipated. For instance, innovative methods that improve student learning can become established in K–12 education. While inequality is being dismantled for those left behind, advanced students in the system would continue to be challenged. A cultural-historical approach calls for educating and stimulating students in their zones of proximal development (Vygotsky, 1978) regardless of age or grade. Students would have access to learning at whatever level they are ready for, regardless of background, age, or grade. It would not be uncommon for second graders to be in a class with third graders. This would help avoid within-school tracking practices and promote flexibility regardless of age as minimum grade standards are met. Nevertheless, the focus would remain on ensuring SPARs are educated at grade level by providing sufficient support.

In sum, large numbers of SPARs may need to be "tracked for success" in ways that do not allow them to fall behind academically with a comprehensive, reliable system. In fact, extra resources need to be focused in and after school, over time, if the cumulative gaps in learning are to be filled. The problem can be conceptualized then as that of resource deployment within a social policy that lessens constraints for poor families (Rauch, 1989). Once group-based inequality (GBI) begins to be reduced systematically, one grade level at a time, and score gaps decrease the condition of education may be truly sound for the nation.

For SPARs, the risk of remaining in the poverty cycle is well ensured by ignoring the actual conditions that cause them to fall grade levels behind, disproportionably each year. This is where the educational system has been most remiss and where it contributes more to the problem than to its solution. It is impossible to achieve a significant effect size at the population level unless larger numbers of SPARs are provided assistance in a sustained fashion. We know that "class effects" operate in such a way that an average student placed in a class with high-achieving students will perform better than if placed in a class with low-achieving students. The same holds true at the school level. The question here requires us to use existing knowledge in ways that not only end unfair tracking practices but also help higher proportions of those placed behind. More desegregation is needed now with peer and mentor assistance.

Since minimum performance standards do, in fact, index access to tools and means that permit the development of both economic and social capital, GBI could be reduced in part through prevention-oriented investments in those tools and related activities for groups most left behind. Economic and educational success at the group level may be seen as a precursor to a gradual release from risk status for some communities. In essence, this comes about through the cumulative development and redistribution of tools and social and economic capital.[2] GBI limits access to existing opportunities. Reorganization and alignment of the capital already being invested (like targeting smart bombs) aims multiple solutions at the problem when organized strategically over time (see Figure 10-2). Insofar as learning environments are concerned, there is growing evidence that students, particularly SPARs, do better when they encounter effective school practices for all ability levels (Slavin, 1990; 2002a).[3]

Figure 10–2 shows sustained assistance would count no matter how SPARs are distributed in the present system. This figure shows—hypothetically—a rough estimate of how SPARs are distributed along achievement in

Figure 10–2: Conceptual Approximations of SPAR and non-SPAR Student Distributions

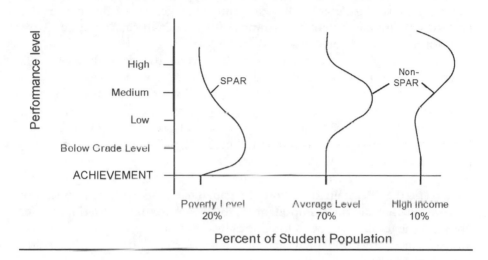

school tests relative to those not at-risk. Individual factors operate differently for students not at-risk and these factors—such as motivation or self-efficacy—operate differently for each group. For example, a SPAR would have to try harder and longer, and also believe differently, than his/her peer group when compared to a non-SPAR.

One hypothesis here is that the relationships among variables that predict achievement vary according to the area of the normal curve or populations involved (e.g., the first vs. third quartile). That is, the amount of resources spent at the district level on instructional improvements, class size, and other factors may have a weaker effect when spread across schools and classes than when targeted on those left behind. The implication is that to close the gap, generic solutions (e.g., school uniforms, year-round schools) aimed to treat all students the same are bound to be less successful than those aimed to assist learning more directly. The education of SPARs needs to be of higher quality, and sustained for longer periods, than is now the case. It calls for a sensitive type of special education, at least until greater balance is achieved in meeting grade-level standards by ethnic group.

Envisioning Fairness in Education

Excellence through equity—as an organizing principle—suggests focusing on helping the majority of SPARs to learn and remain at grade level as a top priority until the present disproportion between the largest minority and majority groups is reduced. This is necessary to bring sustained improvement in learning and higher scores (excellence). Current reform does not promote long-term changes in target populations (equity) directly. A primary target of this proposal is putting an end to the cumulative gap that originates in the current educational system and trumps efforts later in the life cycle. After that, loftier goals may be considered.

Another implication in the framework concerns the application of a sufficient number of means, concepts, and components of the model in actual practice at the state, district, and school levels. Some of the features recommended in the framework are already in operation in a few sites or being developed (e.g., reduced class sizes, after-school programs). On the other hand, the framework as a whole may be too intricate to implement completely in any one school, district, or state at one time. Given a developmental approach, one important implication is to ensure enough key components are advanced and sustained to close the gap. That is, given the impossibility of coordinating all the components (which may require a national-level effort), change may still be tailored locally as each component is developed and sustained. Recommendations for each major component have already been made explicit.

In effect, deploying this multi-level approach ensures that at the school, district, and state levels, several components are integrated or initiated and sustained to the greatest extent possible. As a broader understanding of the problem emerges, each community and district ensures all SPARs participate in effective preschools. Each community begins to prepare adolescents before they form families, not solely to score higher on tests but rather for critical thinking related to sound decision-making, parenting, and family life. Each district and school ensures young SPARs do not fall behind in elementary school by providing the necessary mediated experiences in and out of schools. Smaller classes, year-round school, and mentors become the norm. Colleges, universities, and community agencies pitch in, helping the school district close the gap. These extra academic supports are maintained as long as necessary in middle and high school. SPARs' development is protected, monitored, and assisted through the actions of a better-prepared educational community. Finally, higher education programs transform themselves in helping prepare educators and policy experts to dismantle culturally based disparities in educational outcomes. Perhaps what has been missing is a clear articulation of solutions based on a synthesis of the problem.

Each district and school would work in extending assistance to all SPARs who would already be entering school ready to learn. A focus on maximizing the development of those in the program is critical, particularly during the initial stages where many SPARs still enter school unready and without sufficient parental support to go the distance. The main difference between this socio-cultural approach and that found in the literature is that it is proactive in tackling the most limiting barriers that produce the gap by:

a. Promoting school readiness through effective preschools for all SPARs since development proceeds at the rate at which it is initiated (see Chapters Five and Six);

b. Establishing greater parental involvement for SPARs through primary prevention workshops with adolescents (Chapter Five);

c. Establishing more support for educators in confronting the gap early (Chapter Seven);

d. Implementing and coordinating a plan to stop SPARs from falling behind a grade level at the national level (Chapter Eight and Nine imply higher education impacts on both educators and policymakers).

Attention to research-based instructional programs and their dissemination remains important along with preparing educators, increasing learning time, and school-based reforms. Many of the in-school changes concerning climate, collaboration, and organization do not require great detail in my model because, fortunately, much is already available in the literature (e.g., Borman et al., 2002; Chubb & Loveless, 2002; Darling-Hammond, 2000; Gallimore & Goldenberg, 2001; Hiebert et al., 2002; Mosteller & Boruch, 2002; Tharp et al., 2000). The issue thus lies in ensuring that proven strategies and methods are brought together and implemented systematically over time and space. This will depend, to a great extent, on how the higher education components link with educators in the field. However, many of the above, including effective schools, leadership models urged by the Education Trust, and similar initiatives lack a deeper institutional reorganization outside and inside schools that would incorporate new means through which structural barriers can be altered directly to close the learning gap. This is where a clear definition of the gap is important to conceptualize the problem in terms of meeting minimum performance standards. The latter determine the extent to which new means and scaffolds are actually being extended to groups most likely to be left behind.

In closing, the primary aims of the book are centered on clarification of the achievement gap problem and integration of critical concepts in the field. Equity remains a vague goal unless there is a clear definition, and more importantly, a sound approach to achieve it. To advance—or up the ante—we might not only ask, "What plan would work?" but first, "What does work actually mean?" It does not only mean raising test scores for a few or undermining public education through vouchers and charter schools. It means eliminating a gap in grade-level standards among the most disempowered ethnic and class groups. Test performance indexes social progress with regard to addressing long-standing disparities. Once this occurs, excellence may begin to reach the whole of society. In being aware of the bias and narrowness that come with tests, a focus on sustaining the changes necessary for significantly raising the standardized test scores of students in NAEP, CTBS, SAT, or similar measures becomes essential for a variety of reasons. I believe excellence is to be defined by more than test scores and that in the final analysis this would require structural changes in time, space, and means for advancing learning. Excellence is a byproduct of achieving equity. When GBI becomes absent in a variety of basic academic performance measures, extending equity at higher levels of academic and socioeconomic achievement becomes possible. Without equity, excellence in education remains an oxymoron.

Syntheses and Recommendations

Schools and the higher education structures that inform them need to not only improve but to become redirected and less fragmented in transforming the whole pre-kindergarten–post-secondary system. Reproaching K–12 educators reflects part of the problem that is largely socio-historical in origin, and one of misunderstanding the bounds of inequality in present society. Some of the ways to avoid the latter—and for educators to become well informed—include the knowledge base here and in related writings (e.g., Jencks & Phillips, 2003). Educators can become more expert by applying developmental principles and practices for prevention and promotion. The current reform movement's trend toward standards-based instruction and testing is here to stay. It cannot be blamed for originating the problem of the achievement gap. One hopes it can contribute towards its solution. The trend marks the re-establishment and legitimacy of an often-interrupted cultural agenda. That every competent student should know enough to compete in a market-driven economy after twelve years of public schooling is not unrealistic. The trend also marks a return, perhaps, to a new behaviorism. Yet, a more sophisticated pedagogy may succeed with the integration of constructivist contributions and new advances in the field.

In order to increase the number of students from underrepresented groups ready for college and for middle-class professions, short-term solutions must be transcended. Programs that focus primarily on investing on those few SPARs in high school that achieve close to grade level ("creaming") are of limited value if pursued alone. While this strategy is part of the solution, the problem of eradicating GBI in education requires systemic, multi-level changes to focus on the lifespan and its contexts for learning. If the goal is developing a sustainable system that reliably produces sufficient numbers of college-ready students, strategic supports must be defined and integrated within and outside the educational system.

The change can be envisioned, organized, and sustained when sufficient numbers of SPARs enter all grades ready to learn in ways comparable to mainstream groups. It is fine to learn how in Montgomery County, Maryland, professional development and an extra reading block helped reduce the gap by 7% or how the consistent implementation of curricular programs is working, yet a molecular approach based on copying some practices needs to be transcended. Real progress can only be accomplished when some practices are altered and others sustained in a national system that not only tests but invests and employs dynamic assessments to focus on specific instructional activities. For example, tests might be used to guide mentoring activities more directly. Far too little of the assistance available goes to aid SPARs in areas where tests suggest that teaching and learning gaps exist. Title I funds often do not reach schools where SPARs constitute less than half of the student population. Currently, Title I is funded $6.1 billion below what it was authorized in the 2001 education law in the US Congress. Pell Grants for low-income college students still award only $4,050 at a time when tuition costs have soared. Similarly, only when sufficient numbers of SPARs enter the middle and secondary school levels equally prepared (at least by the criterion of performing at grade level) can existing opportunities be considered equitable. Only a small fraction of funds to help SPARs actually are employed to assist learning directly.

The resources for brokering greater equity are available. The gap between the wealthiest and the middle class has widened. Resources must be shared in avoiding socially constructed handicaps on children. Even without additional support, present resources can be targeted more directly at promoting equity in attaining a grade-level education. This proposal for equity in education may drive a children's Bill of Rights (Clinchy, 2001).

Countering the effects of the culture of poverty on children's schooling without changing the economic and social order substantially is the issue. If education and jobs were opened to underrepresented groups proportionally, society would be transformed toward equity and excellence, at least in education. Hence the issue is not that implied by Johnston and Viadero (2000) and similar reports about the US Department of Education (1996) or by Grissmer, Flanagan, Kawata and Williamson, (2000) about gains in Texas so that educators become convinced they need to tweak any number of factors before success is encountered. To avoid a piecemeal approach, successful schools need to be understood within a larger developmental framework.

The issue of raising the bar in terms of standards is not necessarily prejudiced against those silenced by poverty as long as adequate resources are contingent on need and employed wisely. This plan for equity in education simply calls for the mobilization of key resources in terms of structures for activities and social practices necessary and sufficient to meet minimum standards criteria. In other words, a no-holds-barred approach is needed in making any new reform such as the present one really accountable, but in a much different sense than what is observed today. While some hold schools and educators accountable for student learning by leaving no child untested, a developmental approach, in contrast, holds the dominant societal forces that control the current educational structures accountable.

Inequality in educational outcomes stems from how socialization practices are organized, yet these are not totally determined economically or by ethnicity. Schools are being asked to do more and more today to affect student development without the infrastructures necessary for academic socialization. We must build them well. Higher standards may be a blessing in disguise for advancing an educational agenda of excellence through equity! The latter make GBI more severe and salient, yet it is precisely because of this contradiction that the resulting conflict may draw serious attention towards meaningful change.

The educational system is bankrupt insofar as its mission of educating all children equitably. The old standards were not met even after half a century of equity-minded reform action.[4] The public and academic communities have seemingly settled for a market-oriented justification of the current system of inequality. To promote equity, the system would have to provide greater cognitive-developmental supports to SPARs over a period of time. It would have to make some sacrifices akin to those expected by developing nations. It would have to view all children as national resources.

Presently, schools are designed to provide support to those who already have considerable advantages or capital. By raising standards, policymakers may have to realize how they structure GBI by the very ways schooling remains organized. They eventually may note that a different approach to education is needed. It is not that higher standards should be lowered, but that support for SPARs should also meet higher standards nationally. Dewey (1938), Freire (1998), and others envisioned equity as central in their educational philosophy, ethics, and so must this frail ideal be safeguarded in the new century.

Who Benefits from Higher Standards?

Whether the Goals 2000 or No Child Left Behind model can serve to establish equity is questionable. Current estimates are that to reach them might require low-income high school students to remain in school an additional three to four years. This is about the term of a college education. It may be that higher standards and the inclusion of college-level coursework and standards in secondary education are problematic and currently exacerbate the gap. This internal contradiction is inherent in attempting to close the achievement gap through higher-grade level standards and serves to examine several concerns.

How exactly do SPARs benefit from a higher-stakes plan that is aimed to favor the college-bound population? A "trickle-down economics" logic seems at work. But regardless of others who are more advantaged reaping the most benefits, wouldn't this reform indeed promote greater equity? Retaining lower standards would also be unfortunate. How exactly would SPARs benefit from current reforms? Unless equity was to become a top priority, the failure the system is experiencing seems due to the low priority equity holds in actual practices.

While the type of equity advocated here is beyond the current high-stakes and accountability movement, it may be that indeed the achievement gap must grow wider before it can be narrowed at the group level. The gap remains a public concern because of work force concerns (Bowen & Bok, 1998, Miller, 1995). The paradox is that while equity is not the top priority of the current reform, accountability can serve indirectly as a first step toward assessing progress in bridging the gap. There is merit in raising standards if these were necessary for obtaining employment or access to additional education or to avoid poverty. However, if higher education is to be on the same page as K–12 educators in the future, there are some essential issues to be considered.

Poverty is not an educational problem but a societal one. However, education (or lack thereof) can and does cause some to have an increased probability of living in it. Hence, education's mission is to help students overrepresented in poverty avoid it. The first step would be to transform education so that all students meet and graduate at grade level even if some will remain in poverty afterwards. This requires we hold grade level standards steady for a period. It also requires mounting a comprehensive lifespan approach until all students meet proficiency for several generations. In addition, it requires ending social promotion and allowing more time for mastering valued concepts and skills for some while advanced students move on to college.

The difference between the present reform movement, which leaves equity on the back burner and what is proposed, is one of time and focus of resources. It will surely take longer to achieve equity with higher standards. But that is not the main issue for those who wish to "leave no child behind." Equity based on low standards is not really a solution for eradicating GBI. Neither is achieving higher test scores without equity. Standards are relative and essentially serve as a measurement aid to gauge improvements and troubleshoot problems in the system of education. One only has to envision what would happen if indeed equity were established with these standards. So, what really seems to matter is the extent to which equity becomes a standard through which to assess the effectiveness of education reform for the poor in particular as "canaries in the mine" (Singham, 1998). This requires greater awareness and understanding that establishing educational equity is instrumental in improving the educational system and its outcomes for the whole student population. When the educational system finally finds a way to ensure all student groups achieve at grade level regardless of class and ethnicity, teaching and learning can continue to improve for all. Regardless of whether the old or new standards are used, equity as so defined would have a salutary, beneficial, multiplying effect on the system.

The reorganization of an education that prioritizes equity does not require advanced students to remain unchallenged. The problem is developmental in nature. By assisting the teaching and learning of the least advantaged initially, the whole student population can move forward in terms of the nation's academic standing in the world. The labor force improves in quality. Social security becomes less threatened. The extent to which college-level standards and classes are retained in high school remains a local decision. However, the latter may be regarded as optional relative to the primary mission of ensuring all students perform at grade level. The order of priorities implied is not that of equity before excellence but rather excellence through equity. In realistic terms, we must transcend the zero-sum either/or mentality that has prevailed in the past that forces some to lose as others gain in terms of educational resources.

Given that this is a national cultural problem, I suggest that much of the start-up costs for establishing equity in grade-level performance for all students be assumed by an equity trust fund supported by federal and state funds and incentives for and from the private sector. It would help support the proposed restructuring plan. In sum, I agree with standards-based accountability but propose a new way to reorient the current reform in order to avoid the polarization it may otherwise bring. Erikson and Gutierrez (2002) warn about unintended effects of implementing new treatments without careful impact analyses, "Will our current desperate attempts to discover 'what works' to raise standardized test scores in the short run have analogous effects on our children and teachers in school (thalidomide), effects that are only apparent after much damage has been done?" As long as the system educates SPARs four grade levels below the norm, gaps in employment, pay, and crime and imprisonment rates seem justified.

As a last observation, this proposal is not only based squarely on major principles (i.e., primary prevention, promotion, early stimulation, continuity, parent involvement, developmentally sensitive instruction) but the best evidence is provided by history. Investments in human development and those left behind have paid off (e.g., women, immigrants, special populations, and others). Sustained inequality and social injustice promote conflict, violence, and waste. As the educational system evolves, so does our future.

Economic and Social Polarization

Concerns about the market economy's influence on education—and about education as a limited resource, a commodity, and a tool—demand further analysis. Rather than life imitating art (or vice versa), what we seem to have today is education-imitating business. This idea is not new. The view of Bowles and Gintis (1976) is that schools cannot help but reproduce the economic and political disparities in society in spite of leveling efforts since 1954. Schools were once centralized, factory-like organizations. Today, they require—instead of higher profits—higher test scores from the schooling that various communities of children undergo. The problem with this analogy is that too often the decisions made that have shaped the current educational system at the state and local district levels do not depend largely on what policymakers know, understand, and can do. However, it is the distribution of educational outcomes across populations that remains unfair and sustains the problem. Perhaps the best justification for higher standards is that employers and businesses require a better-educated labor force. Yet, there are only so many positions available in the economy, and an underclass of underemployed and unemployed appears important to have to keep labor costs down. A humanist, less corporate model for education needs to be considered.

The system of education we have has yet to profit from much of the best evidence that has been made available (Mosteller & Boruch, 2002; Slavin, 2000a; 2000b). A major problem is that of underutilization of knowledge and resources. Another is diverting resources in ways that compromise excellence and equity. Yet, gridlock in disseminating and sustaining new promising practices, particularly in using a scientific-humanistic approach in the design of a more equitable and sound educational system, remains an even larger difficulty.

The achievement gap was defined as a cultural and historical problem of differences in access to tools, opportunities and knowledge that produce better outcomes in some groups relative to others. This definition allows for a synthesis of conceptual and field-based applications today. In particular, the definition of the gap has been grounded here on equity in educational outcomes across groups independently of poverty rates and socio-cultural background. Because of the massive inequality that still remains, we have distinguished the primary source that lies beyond the control of the educational system (poverty) from the reproductive sources that lie, in fact, in schooling practices and related economic structures. We have alluded to the ethical dilemma that prevails today, with reforms that fail to reverse or at least end practices that place children from certain impoverished groups at considerable disadvantage in school and in life through no fault of their own. It seems the perpetuation of relative disadvantages in some groups sustains the social injustice of having three times the rates of poverty and below grade-level performance found for SPARs relative to the majority. This places the whole of society at risk, not just those students or victims.

This definition of equity serves as a criterion in assaying current reforms that purport to address the achievement gap. Discourses on leaving no child behind, saying "no" to drugs, "No Excuses," social justice, and critical pedagogy, among others, seem well intentioned but miss the target of ending group-based inequality as a socio-educational goal. From a historical perspective, this is a first step in revamping a system so that it can indeed produce a foundation for excellence. As the system learns to educate more diverse learners to higher levels, the old problems linked with limited resources change, particularly in an information age. The best evidence found from our cultural history suggests that as populations become more educated, cultural tools and technologies emerge that can solve many basic problems and also give rise to new challenges. If this rationale works for the billions NASA will spend exploring Mars, the policy implications for a more just, intelligent society are clear.

A major idea in this argument for restructuring the educational system seems paradoxical in nature. That is, in seeking ways to eradicate GBI in educational outcomes in education, the necessary tools, structures, pedagogies and new instructional practices will also benefit all students' development. In the long run, equity promotes excellence in the educational system's very own definition, based on current standards. It is perhaps at this point that a separate but often confounded issue—socioeconomic inequality—can begin to be addressed meaningfully and directly.

What We Have and What We Need

As Smith (2001) notes, poverty is a moral issue and whether or not it can be reduced or made more equitable across groups is beyond the scope of this work. But it is certainly related to it. The focus then is on that small segment that is within reach of the educational community were it to truly seek transformation in not reproducing GBI. Let's envision a united, informed, professional community of educators bound by a common purpose to use all the means at our disposal. They are willing to master the relevant skills and knowledge to close the achievement gap. We needed an operational definition for the gap, and now we have one. We needed a long-term strategic plan based on what works to reorganize the way we educate SPARs, and now we have one. We needed evidence that where the elements of the plan come together, the desired result is observed. We have several examples of schools where the gap has been closed for at least a window of time.

We still need support to extend effective early-childhood programs to all SPARs before entering school. We don't have that yet. We need support in building college/community volunteer pipelines of mentors for SPARs after school for every elementary school. We don't have it in most places, and where we do, it is not sustained. We need after-school programs that work, but these are not generally sustained or focused on academic learning. We need to transform school cultures in elementary and secondary schools with collaborative structures, principals, and counselors who assist teachers and SPARs simultaneously. Can it be done without transforming higher education and particularly specific professional programs? In order to promote parent involvement, we need an adolescent component in place led by educators prepared accordingly. To promote academic learning time, we need year-round schools, reduced class sizes, itinerant teacher specialists, and similar elements in a systemic plan. If too few schools move in the above directions without a critical mass, SPARs will remain trapped behind. We need all educators to be well prepared in development, learning, leadership, and culture.

Indeed, we need to transform the ways educators are prepared, and then colleges of education can play a pivotal role. The needed transformations are not even on the horizon, but rather exist in bits and pieces in some programs. The disciplines that underlie key professions remain divided, underprepared, underpaid, and consequently disempowered. We have advanced knowledge in improving the early education of SPARs (Ramey et al., in press) and how to transform teaching across student populations (Tharp et al., 2000), yet much of it is not applied. We know affective relationships must be firmly established with young SPARs before academic learning thrives (Comer, 1990), yet we often fail to design learning environments so this may happen. We know how leadership in instruction can drive achievement (Leithwood et al., 2004) and need to share it with all educators. We have an emerging technology that is promising to assist educators with experiences and videos of effective lesson studies across cultures (Hiebert, Gallimore, and Stiegler, 2002) that has yet to be disseminated where most teachers are to be prepared. We need colleges and communities to volunteer services to help SPARs and a different federal approach to assist them.

To reiterate the remaining critical points of the book, we need a primary prevention curriculum for adolescents to focus on human development and family skills that extends beyond traditional home economics parameters. Finally, we need to consider a system that is not simply organized around students' chronological age but more flexibly attuned to their socio-cognitive developmental readiness. What does it matter if variability in age becomes less restrictive so that instructional activities can be attuned more closely to students' developmental level? What if more advanced students went to college earlier and SPARs graduated later? Perhaps if more advantaged students meet standards sooner, SPARs can receive the extra attention needed and meet their peers later. Many successful persons bloom late.

An important point is that the strategy proposed here is not about elim-inating poverty, which is an oxymoron in a capitalist system. Rather, I argue for education to (at least) extricate itself from reproducing poverty through an inequitable system. If we wish our students to become self-regulated, just and motivated learners, at some level we must lead the way. In the process of establishing equity, at least at the minimum standard level, we might begin to discover a more direct route to excellence. And finally, in attending to the educational needs of culturally different SPARs, or any other special group, the great irony lies again in that we actually learn to improve education for all students in the long run.

Cultural Change and Self-Management

Current efforts to improve education lie within the much broader ques-tion of viable change in American culture. It requires we inevitably judge how far GBI can or should be reduced now relative to the latter part of the twentieth century. One of the principal themes to emerge from this book's analyses for ending the achievement gap is that of self-management. While it is crucial that the system as a whole is restructured in the ways described ear-lier, each community has to undergo internal changes according to its partic-ular problems and opportunities. Rather than awaiting directions from the top district and state policymakers or research and development labs, each school, district, or community needs to be proactive in developing its own needs assessments and development plan. The local school culture evolves from educators who share similar goals such as meeting the challenge of refusing student failure and promoting all children's development. School cultures have their own zone of proximal development (Vygotsky, 1978). With external, virtual, and peer assistance, schools can achieve much more through collaboration than in isolation.

Principles for Action

In order to establish equity in educational outcomes at the school level, a critical mass of educators must come together and lead change. This is unlikely as long as higher education remains the same. In the educational administration area, efforts to prepare leaders with the vision and the know-how to organize, support, and challenge educators in closing the gap are evolving (Bogotch, 2002). In the teacher education field, we find similar ini-tiatives centered on the nuts and bolts of everyday teaching and learning at the front lines (Darling-Hammond, 2000). Only recently has counselor edu-cation made closing the gap a priority. New initiatives are attempting to rede-fine the roles of counselors in helping to influence changes in the culture of local schools. Clearly a united approach is needed that interfaces roles, functions, and activities that must extend outside the school.

A second major principle noted is that a common knowledge base and strategic plan need to be shared by a critical mass of educators.

A third principle is that of not doing just more of the same but engaging in educational activity differently in terms of goals, actions, means, and expectations. Restructuring does not necessarily depend on doing more of the same except in some instances, such as supporting changes that have proven successful. Generally, it implies thinking out of the box in affecting key variables in the strategic plan. Some require district and state policy changes, such as the professional preparation of educators, rewards or raising salaries, hiring more educators to reduce class size, or extending learning time for particular students. Within-school restructuring, in terms of instructional methods, scheduling, grouping for instruction, management of academic learning time and professional development, can also make a difference.

Educators need to know more about the various ideological camps that advocate particular solutions. We still find a fragmented landscape of causes mixed with effects and various communities of practice attempting to amplify particular points of view. Educators need to transcend their professional identities in sharing a wider one. They need to understand how various programs and models address different parts of a much larger cultural and developmental problem.

Conclusion

Perhaps a societal transformation seems necessary first, before traditional structures can be reorganized and allow the present plan to be launched. The proposed plan may only be a heuristic for what it would take to produce population effects in academic outcomes. It differs from other models in linking mediated action to both the problem and its solution. It may appear impractical, too utopian, or troubling in other ways. I responded earlier to the issues of intervening in others' lives with a particular set of values (see Chapter Three). The first answer is that in order to achieve success in difficult endeavors (e.g., in science [penicillin], in space travel [rocket science], in reconstruction [Marshall Plan, Civil Rights]), one must invest in development long before a solution is in sight. One must experiment and launch combinations of actions or programs against the problem before the most essential elements are found and disseminated in a national effort. The second answer is that in not taking programmatic steps to deal with a historically constructed problem—given that we already know a great deal about how to succeed—is not only irresponsible but also unscrupulous. The current policy exacerbates the achievement gap for silenced SPAR, in spite of rhetoric to the contrary. The issue is not of imposing one culture over another but rather promoting a wider, transcultural identity for all.

Finally, how poverty plays the major role in shaping the gap was examined and also the ways it accounts for up to 50% of the variance in test scores (see Berlak, 2001). For every thirty-point increment on the SAT, a student gains an additional $10,000 in income. Schools that are excellent relative to others are most often in neighborhoods where families own homes, earn comfortable incomes, and where parents attended college. In 267 communities around one state with A-rated schools, only 21 had median incomes below $40,000. Most had median incomes of $60,000 to $100,000. Among the country's fourth-graders, 16% of poor students were proficient readers compared with 41% of more economically advantaged students.

Hence, we must examine how tests also indirectly sample the types of socialization contexts—such as values, beliefs, and practices—that money can buy. We must see that standing this argument on its head, devising tests that tap into income and related differentials, produces the very items that produce gaps in learning, teaching, and thus, academic test outcomes. As this problem becomes better understood, we see that it is more of an ethical problem than one that needs figuring out. In short, what kinds of conditions must be present for children to have a good chance of learning the necessary concepts required to answer a sufficient number of questions correctly and independently? In order to dismantle the gap shaped by such rules, the issue remains centered on the organization of the external conditions of learning and development in ways that are less dependent on relative influences exerted by family SES and cultural history.

A new, more equitable system of education will require an intelligent public in the future to be steadfast and confident that serious problems can be overcome. When astronauts lose their lives, newspaper editorials question the system employed by NASA. While both the public and Congress provide support and rarely hold decision makers accountable, their engineers point to lapses and room for improvement. Yet in education, each year, the majority of SPARs enter into a failed system that progressively places them behind and at risk for poverty and violence. The risks become actualized as the court system is overloaded and mostly SPARs fill prisons. We are the engineers who warn of the problems in the system that remains essentially unchanged. Let's do the math. The cost of failing to educate students placed behind by poverty can be as criminal and reproachable as preparing others for a space mission in a poorly designed system that fails to prepare 15–45% of them, depending on their social status and origin. My intent in this book has been to test the comfort level of the empowered in a society with a system designed to squander the potential of a significant number of children without regard to their rights, the nation's basic principles, and its best interests.

Perhaps the issue is not about money but the power to produce it and other forms of capital. I close with a simple message. The proposal for equity may scare conservatives, who fear losing their privileges and identity as a dominant group. Yet, the price for establishing equity for children of the poor does not require loss. It may scare liberals, who are afraid that a partic- ular set of values will be enforced upon the underclass. Yet neither outcome is necessary. The message is that in this proposal for leveling gross between- group disparities at basic minimum levels of literacy is the offer of a win-win option for those left behind—as it is for the more empowered, at least in rel- ative terms. If anything, it is still a timid call for equity that hardly threatens higher-level privilege because other types of GBI will still remain for other criteria. Nevertheless, a first step such as this is preferable to the default alter- native of continuing an unjust, divisive course regardless of its liberal or con- servative intent. Can we really afford paying the social costs of inequity and an emerging apartheid when a clear alternative is possible?

Endnotes

1. The above finding seems in contradiction of tracking having adverse effects on SPARs. However, it suggests that it is the system that needs to be untracked rather than the students.
2. As with the early days of desegregation, upper-class white flight results inevitably in more resources or tax dollars going to serve needy students. Before resegregation began in the 1990s (Orfield et al., 2003), a dramatic increase in NAEP scores could be noticed in the late 1970s.
3. The literature on ability grouping and instruction can be misleading in this regard. While average students and SPARs may do well, we do not know the extent to which high-income students in advanced programs benefit.
4. We refer to the 1954 *Brown* decision in this regard as marking the beginning of equity-minded reforms in institutional structures.

References

Abdul-Haqq, I. (1998). *Professional development schools: Weighing the evidence*. Thousand Oaks, CA: Corwin Press.

Achilles, C.M., Finn, J.D., & Bain, H.P. (1998). Using class size to reduce the equity gap. *Educational Leadership, 55*(4), 40–43.

Adams, G.L., & Engelmann, S. (1996). *Research on direct instruction: 25 years beyond DISTAR*. Seattle, WA: Educational Achievement Systems.

Albee, G., & Gullotta, T. (1997). *Primary prevention works*. Thousand Oaks, CA: Sage Publications.

Albert, L.R. (2002). Bridging the achievement gap in mathematics: Socio-cultural historic theory and dynamic cognitive assessment. *Journal of Thought, 37*(4), 65–82.

Alexander, K.L. & Entwisle, D.R. (1988). Achievement in the first two years of school: Patterns and processes. *Monographs of the Society for Research in Child Development 53*(2), Serial No. 218.

Alexander, K.L., Entwisle, D.R., & Olson, L.S. (2001). Schools, achievement, and inequality: A seasonal perspective. *Educational Evaluation and Policy Analysis, 23*(2), 171–191.

American Educational Research Association. (2000, July). *Position statement concerning the high-stakes testing in PreK–12 education*. Retrieved from http://www.aera.net/about/policy/stakes.htm. on 11/05/04.

American School Counselor Association. (1997). *The national standards for school counseling programs*. Alexandria, VA: Author.

American School Counselor Association. (1998). *The national standards for school counseling programs*. Alexandria, VA: Author.

Anderson, J. R., Greeno, J. G., Reder, L. M., & Simon, H. A. (2000). Perspectives on learning, thinking, and activity. *Educational Researcher, 29*(4), 11–13.

Anyon, J. (1980). Social class and the hidden curriculum of work. *Journal of Education, 162*(1), 67–92.

Apple, M. (1989). American realities: Poverty, economy, and education. In L. Weis, E. Farrar, & H.G. Petrie (Eds.), *Drop outs in schools: Issues, dilemmas and solutions* (pp. 205–224). Albany, NY: SUNY Press.

Apple, M.W. (2001). Markets, standards, teaching, and teacher education. *Journal of Teacher Education, 52*(3), 182–195.

Applebee, A.N., Langer, J.A., & Mullis, I.V.S. (1986). *Writing trends across the decade 1974–84.* Princeton, NJ: Educational Testing Service.

Argyris, C., & Schon, D. (1992). *Theory in practice: Increasing professional effectiveness.* San Francisco, CA: Jossey-Bass.

Armor, D. (1996). Hearing on legislative responses to school desegregation litigation–April 16, 1996. Retrieved from http://www.house.gov/judiciary/2189.htm on 11/05/04.

Aronson, E. (1999). *The Social Animal* (8th Ed.). New York: Worth.

Au, K.H. (2002). Communities of practice: Engagement, imagination, and alignment in research on teacher education. *Journal of Teacher Education, 53*(3), 222–227.

Baker, A.J.L., Piotrkowski, C.S., & Brooks-Gunn, J. (1998). The effects of the home instruction program for preschool youngsters (HIPPY) on children's school performance at the end of the program and one year later. *Early Childhood Research Quarterly, 13(4),* 571–588.

Baker, S.B. (1994). Mandatory teaching experience for school counselors. An impediment to uniform certification standards for school counselors. *Counselor Education and Supervision, 33,* 314–326.

Bandura, A. (1977). *Social learning theory.* Englewood Ciffs, NJ: Prentice-Hall.

Bandura, A. (1986). *Social foundations of thought and action: A social–cognitive theory.* Englewood Cliffs, NJ: Prentice-Hall.

Baratz, S., & Baratz, C. (1970). Early childhood intervention: The social science base of institutional racism. *Harvard Educational Review, 40,* 29–50.

Beck, E.L. (1999). Prevention and intervention programming: Lessons from after-school programs. *Urban Review, 31*(1), 107–124.

Bemak, F. (2000). Transforming the role of the counselor to provide leadership in educational reform through collaboration. *Professional School Counseling, 3*(5), 323–331.

Bereiter, C. (1994). Constructivism, socioculturalism, and Popper's World. *Educational Researcher. 23*(7), 210–223.

Bereiter, C., & Scardamalia, M. (1987). *The psychology of written composition.* Hillsdale, NJ: Lawrence Erlbaum Associates.

Bergin, D.A., Hudson, L.M., Chryst, C.F. & Resetar, M. (1992). An after school intervention program for educationally disadvantaged young children. *Urban Review, 24,* 203–217.

Berlak, Harold (2001, Summer). Race and the achievement gap. *Rethinking Schools, 15*(4), 10–11.

Berliner, D.C. (2000). A personal response to those who bash teacher education. *Journal of Teacher Education, 51,* 358–371.

Berliner, D.C. (2002). Educational research: The hardest science of all. *Educational Researcher, 31,* 18–20.

Berliner, D.C., & Biddle, B.J. (1995). *The manufactured crisis: Myths, fraud, and the attack on America's public schools.* Reading, MA: Addison-Wesley Publishing Co.

Bernstein, B. (1962). Linguistic codes, hesitation phenomena and intelligence. *Language and speech, 5*(1), 31–46.

Black, B., & Logan, A. (1995). Links between communication patterns in mother-child, father-child, and child-peer interactions and children's social status. *Child Development, 66(1)*, 225–271.

Blank, R.K., & Langesen, D. (1999). *State indicators of science and mathematics education 1999. State-by-state trends and new indicators from the 1997–98 school year.* Washington, DC: CCSSO, State Education Assessment Center.

Bloom, B. (1964). *Stability and change in human characteristics.* New York: John Wiley & Sons.

Bloom, M. (1996). *Primary prevention practices.* Thousand Oaks, CA: Sage.

Blustein, D., Phillips, S., Jobin-Davis, K., Finkelberg, S., & Roarke, A. (1997). A theory-building investigation of the school-to-work transition. *Counseling Psychologist, 25(3)*, 364–402.

Bogotch, I.E. (2002). Educational leadership and social justice: Practice into theory. *Journal of School Leadership, 12*, 138–156.

Bond, L.A., & Wagner, B.M. (1988). What makes primary prevention programs work? In L.A. Bond & B.M. Wagner (Eds.), *Families in transition: Primary prevention programs* (pp. 335–342). Newbury Park, CA: Sage.

Borders, L.D. & Drury, S.M. (1992). Comprehensive school counseling programs: A review for policymakers and practitioners. *Journal of Counseling and Development, 70*, 487–498.

Borman, G.D., & D'Agostino, J.V. (1996). Title I and student achievement: A meta-analysis of federal evaluation results. *Educational Evaluation and Policy Analysis, 18* (4), 309–326.

Borman, G.D., Overman, G.M., & Brown, S. (2002, November). *Comprehensive school reform and student achievement: A meta-analysis.* (CRESPAR, Report No. 59). [Online] Retrieved from: http://www.csos.jhu.edu/crespar/reports.htm on 11/05/04.

Bourdieu, P. (1987). *Distinction: A social critique on the judgment of taste.* Cambridge, MA: Harvard University Press.

Bourdieu, P., & Coleman, J.S. (1991). *Social theory for a changing society.* Boulder, CO: Westview Press.

Bourdieu, P., & Passeron, J. (1977). *Reproduction in education, society, and culture.* London: Sage.

Bowen, W.G., & Bok, D. (1998). *The shape of the river: long-term consequences of considering race in college and university admissions.* Princeton, N.J.: Princeton University Press.

Bowles, S., & Gintis, H. (1976). *Schooling in capitalist America: Educational reform and the contradictions of economic life.* New York: Basic Books, Inc.

Boyer, E.L. (1983). *High school. A report of secondary education in America.* New York: Harper & Row.

Boyer, E.L. (1990). *Scholarship reconsidered: Priorities of the professorate.* Princeton, NJ: Carnegie Foundation for the Advancement of Teaching.

Brand, S. (1996). Making parent involvement a reality: Helping teachers develop partnerships with parents. *Young Children, 51,* 76–81.

Bronfenbrenner, U. (1986). Ecology of a family is a context for human development: Research perspectives. *Developmental Psychology, 26,* 723–742.

Bronfenbrenner, U. (1979). Contexts of child rearing. *American Psychologist, 34,* 844–850.

Brooks-Gunn, J., Duncan, G., & Britto, P. (1999). Are socioeconomic gradients for children similar to those for adults? In D. Keating & C. Hertzman (Eds.), *Developmental health and the wealth of nations* (pp. 94–124). New York: The Guilford Press.

Brown, A.L. (1992). Design experiments: Theoretical and methodological challenges in creating complex interventions in classroom settings. *The Journal of the Learning Sciences, 2,* 141–178.

Brown, D. (1999). *Proven strategies for improving learning & achievement.* Greensboro, NC: CAPS Publications.

Bruer, J.T. (1999). *The myth of the first three years: A new understanding of early brain development and lifelong learning.* New York: The Free Press.

Bruner, J.S. (1966). *Toward a theory of instruction.* New York: Norton.

Bryk, A. & Thum, Y. (1989). The effects of high school organization on dropping out: An exploratory investigation. *American Educational Research Journal, 26,* 353–383.

Burns, S. (1996). *Parent involvement in children's education: Efforts by public elementary schools.* Washington, DC: National Center for Education Statistics, U.S. Department of Education, 26.

Buscemi, L., Bennett, T., Thomas, D., & Deluca, D.A. (1995). Head Start: Challenges and training needs. *Journal of Early Intervention, 20*(4), 1–13.

CACREP (1994). Accreditation standards and procedures manuals. Alexandria, VA: Author.

Campbell, F.A., Ramey, C.T., Pungello, E., Sparling, J., & Miller-Johnson, S. (2002) Early childhood education: young adult outcomes from the Abecedarian Project. *Applied Developmental Science, 6*(1), 42–57.

Caplan, G. (1964). *Principles of preventive psychiatry.* New York: Basic Books.

Capuzzi, D. (1998). Addressing the needs of at-risk youth: Early prevention and systemic intervention. In C. C. Lee & G. R. Walz (Eds.), *Social action: A mandate for counselors* (pp. 99–116). Alexandria, VA: American Counseling Association.

Carlson, E.A., Sroufe, L.A., Collins, W.A., Jimerson, S., Weinfield, N., Hennighausen, K., Egeland, B., Hyson, D.M., Anderson, F., & Meyer, S.E. (1999). Early environmental support and elementary school adjustment as predictors of school adjustment in middle adolescence. *Journal of Adolescent Research, 14*(1), 72–94.

Carnegie Corporation of New York. (1996). *Years of promise: A comprehensive learning strategy for America's children.* New York: Carnegie Corporation of New York.

Carnevale, A.P., & Fry, R.A. (2000). *Crossing the great divide: Can we achieve equity when generation Y goes to college?.* Princeton, NJ: Educational Testing Service.

Carolina Abecedarian Project, The. [Online]. Available at: http://www.fpg. unc.edu/ ~abc/embargoed/executive_summary.htm retrieved on 11/05/04.

Carpenter, W.A. (2000). Ten years of silver bullets: Dissenting thoughts on education reform. *Phi Delta Kappan, 81,* 383–389.

Center for Research on Education, Diversity & Excellence (CREDE). (2002). *Five standards for effective pedagogy and student outcomes, technical report no. G1.* Santa Cruz, CA: CREDE.

Childs-Bowen, D., Scrivner, J. & Moller, G. (2000). Principals: Leaders of leaders. *NASSP Bulletin, 84*(616), 27–34.

Chubb, J.E., & Loveless, T. (2002). *Bridging the achievement gap.* Washington, DC: Brookings Institution Press.

Clark, R. (1983). *Family life and school achievement: Why poor black children succeed or fail.* Chicago: University of Chicago Press.

Clifford, D., Peisner-Feinberg, E., Culkin, M., Howes, C., & Kagan, S.L. (1998). Quality child care: Quality care does mean better child outcomes. *NCEDL Spotlights Series, No. 2.*

Clinchy, E. (2001). Needed: a new educational civil rights movement. *Phi Delta Kappan, 82*(7), 492–498.

Cochran-Smith, M. (2002). Editorial: What a difference a definition makes: Highly qualified teachers, scientific research, and teacher education. *Journal of Teacher Education, 53*(3), 187–189.

Cochran-Smith, M., & Fries, M.K. (2002). The discourse of reform in teacher education: Extending the dialogue. *Educational Researcher, 31*(6), 26–28.

Cole, M. (1985). The zone of proximal development: Where culture and cognition create each other. In J.V. Wertsch (Ed.), *Culture, communication, and cognition: Vygotskian perspectives* (pp. 146–161). Cambridge, England: Cambridge University Press.

Cole, M. (1990). Cognitive development and formal learning. In L. Moll (Ed.), *Vygotsky and Education* (pp. 89–110). New York: Cambridge University Press

Cole, M. (1996). *Cultural psychology: A once and future discipline.* Cambridge, MA: Harvard University Press.

Cole, M., & Cole, S.R. (1993). *The development of children* (2nd ed.). New York: Scientific American Books, Inc.

Coleman, J.S. (1966). *Equality of educational opportunity.* Washington, DC: US Government Printing Office.

Coleman, J.S. (1987). Families and schools. *Educational Researcher, 16*(6), 32–38.

Coleman, J.S. (1990). *Equality and Achievement in Education.* Boulder, CO: Westview Press.

Coleman, J.S., (1994). Social capital, human capital, and investment in youth. In Anne C. Peterson & J. T. Mortimer (Eds.), *Youth Unemployment & Society.* New York: Cambridge University Press.

Coleman, J.S., Campbell, E., Mood, A., Weinfield, E., Hobson, C., York, R., & McParland, J. (1966). *Equality of educational opportunity.* Washington, DC: US Government Printing Office.

Coleman, M., Wallinga, C., & Toledo, C. (1999). Life-skills training within school-age child care programs: Patterns of delivery. *The School Community Journal, 9*(1), 71–82.

College Entrance Examination Board. (1993). *Summary statistics: Annual survey of colleges, 1992–93 and 1993–94.* New York: Henry Holt & Company, Incorporated.

Colton, A.B., & Sparks-Langer, G. M. (1993). A conceptual framework to guide the development of teacher reflection and decision-making. *Journal of Teacher Education, 44,* 45–54.

Comer, J.P. (1980). *School power: Implications of an intervention project.* New York: Free Press.

Comer, J.P. (1990). Home, school and academic learning. In J. Goodlad & P. Keating (Eds.), *Access to knowledge: An agenda for our nation's schools* (pp. 23–42). New York: College Entrance Examination Board.

Comer, J.P. (1995). *School Power.* New York: The Free Press.

Comer, J.P., Haynes, N.M., Joyner, E.T., & Ben-Avie, M. (1996). *Rallying the whole village: The Comer process for reforming education.* New York: Teachers College Press.

Condition of education, The. (1994). Washington, DC: United States Government Printing Office.

Condition of education, The. (1998). Washington, DC: United States Government Printing Office.

Condition of education, The. (2002). Washington, DC: United States Government Printing Office.

Condition of education, The. (2004). Washington, DC: United States Government Printing Office.

Consortium for Longitudinal Studies. (1983). *As the twig is bent: Lasting effects of preschool programs.* Hillsdale, NJ: Erlbaum.

Cooper, H., Valentine, J., Nye, B., & Lindsay, J.J. (1999). Relationships between five after-school activities and academic achievement. *Journal of Educational Psychology, 91,* 369–378.

Cordova, T. (1997, Fall). Power and knowledge: Colonialism in the academy. *Taboo, the Journal of Culture and Education* (Spring 1997) 209–234.

Cormier, S., & Hackner, H. (1999). *Counseling strategies and interventions.* Boston: Allyn and Bacon.

Cornell, D. G., Delcourt, M.A.B., Goldberg, M.D., & Bland, L. (1995). Achievement and self-concept of minority students in elementary school gifted programs. *Journal for the Education of the Gifted, 18*(2), 189–209.

Currie, J. (2000). *Early childhood intervention programs: What do we know?* Unpublished manuscript: UCLA and NBER.

Danish, S.J. (1996). Interventions for enhancing adolescents' life skills. *The Humanistic Psychologist, 24,* 365–381.

Darling-Hammond, L. (1993). Reframing the school reform agenda. *Phi Delta Kappan, 74*(10), 752–761.

Darling-Hammond, L. (1994). Developing professional development schools: Early lessons, challenges, and promises. In L. Darling-Hammond (Ed.), *Professional development schools: Schools for developing a profession* (pp. 1–27). New York: Teachers College Press.

Darling-Hammond, L. (1995). Cracks in the bell curve: How education matters. Myths and realities: African Americans and the measurement of human abilities. *The Journal of Negro Education, 64(3),* 340–353.

Darling-Hammond, L. (1996). The right to learn and the advancement of teaching: Research, policy and practice for democratic education. *Educational Researcher, 16*(6), 32–38.

Darling-Hammond, L. (2000a). How teacher education matters. *Journal of Teacher Education, 52*(3), 166–173.

Darling-Hammond, L. (2000b, January 1). Teacher quality and student achievement: A review of state policy and evidence. *Education Policy Analysis Archives, 8*(1). Retrieved May 19, 2004, from http:// epaa.asu.edu/epaa/v8n1/)

Darling-Hammond, L., & Falk, B. (1997). Using standards and assessments to support student learning. *Phi Delta Kappan, 79*(3), 190–199.

Davis, D.W., Burns, B., Snyder, E., Dossett, D., & Wilkerson, S. (2004). Parent-child interaction and attention regulation in children born prematurely. *Journal for Specialist in Pediatric Nursing (JSPN), 9*(3), 85–94.

Delgado, R., & Stephancic, J. (2000). *Critical race theory: The cutting edge.* Philadelphia: Temple University Press.

Delpit, L. (1995). *Other people's children: Cultural conflict in the classroom*. New York: The New Press.

De Vos, G. (1967). Psychology of purity and pollution as related to social self-identity and caste. In A.V.S. de Reuck and J. Knight (Eds.), *CIBA foundation symposium on caste and race: Comparative approaches* (pp. 292–315). London: J. & A. Churchill.

De Vos, G. (1993). A psycho cultural approach to ethnic interaction in contemporary research. In Martha E. Bernal and George P. Knight (Eds.), *Ethnic identity, formation and transmission among Hispanics and other minorities* (pp 235–270). New York: SUNY Press.

De Vos, G., & Suárez-Orozco, M. (1990). *Status inequality: The self in culture*. Newbury Park, CA: Sage.

Dewey, J. (1938). *Logic: The theory of inquiry*. New York: H. Holt and Company.

Dilg, M.A. (1999). *Race and culture in the classroom: Teaching and learning through multicultural*. New York: Teachers College Press.

Donovan, M., Bransford, J., & Pellegrino, J. (1999). *How people learn: Bridging research and practice*. Washington, DC: National Research Council.

Dreeben, R. & Gamoran, A. (1986). Race, instruction, and learning. *American Sociological Review, 51*(5), 660–669.

Dunham, R.M., Kidwell, J.S., & Portes, P.R. (1988). Effects of parent-adolescent interaction on the continuity of cognitive development from early childhood to early adolescence. *Journal of Early Adolescence, 8*(3), 297–310.

Dunham, R.M., Kidwell, J.S., & Portes, P.R. (1995a). Do the seeds of accelerative learning and teaching lie in a behavioral carrier wave? *Journal of Accelerated Learning and Teaching, 20*, 53–87.

Dunham, R.M., Kidwell, J.S., & Portes, P.R. (1995b). Effects of parent-adolescent interaction on the continuity of cognitive development from early childhood to early adolescence. *Journal of Early Adolescence, 8*(3), 97–130.

Education Trust, The (1996). *Education Watch: The 1996 education trust state and national data book*. Washington DC: Author.

Education Trust, The (1997, February). *The national guidance and counseling reform program*. Washington, DC: Author.

Education Trust, The (1997). Specific counseling skills necessary to transform the role of the school counselor for the 90's and beyond. Washington, DC. Retrieved June 29, 2001, from http://www.edtruct.orgmain/school_counseling.asp#specific

Education Trust, The (2000). *Achievement in America: 2000* [Computer diskette]. Washington, DC: Author.

Egeland, B., Jimerson, S., & Teo, A. (1999). A longitudinal study of achievement trajectories: Factors associated with change. *Journal of Educational Psychology, 91*, 116–126.

Ekstrom, R.B., Goertz, M.E., & Rock, D.A. (1986). Who drops out of high school and why? Findings from a national study. In G. Natriello (Ed.), *School dropouts: Patterns and policies*. New York: Teachers College Press.

Ekstrom, R.B., Goertz, M.E., & Rock, D.A. (1988). *Education and American youth*. Philadelphia: The Falmer Press.

Elmore, R. (1996). Getting to scale with good educational practice. *Educational Review, 66*, 1–26.

Entwisle, D.R., Alexander, K.L., & Karp, L. (1992). Summer setback: Race, poverty. School composition and mathematics achievement in the first two years of school. *American Sociological Review, 57*, 72–84.

Entwisle, D.R., Alexander, K.L., & Olson, L.S. (1997). *Children, schools, and inequality.* Boulder, CO: Westview Press.

Epstein, J. (1991). Effects on student achievement of teachers' practices of parent involvement, *Advances in Reading/Language Research,* 5, 261–276.

Epstein, J. L., (1995). School/family/community partnerships: Caring for the children we share. *Phi Delta Kappan,* 76, 701–712.

Epstein, J.L. (1999). *National Network of Partnership Schools.* Retrieved October 23, 1999 from http://www.csos.jhu.edu/p2000/index.html

Erford, B.T. (2003). *Transforming the school counseling profession.* Upper Saddle River, NJ: Pearson Education, Inc.

Erikson, E.H. (1968). *Identity: Youth and crisis.* New York: Norton.

Erickson, F. (1993). Transformation and school success: The politics and culture of educational achievement. In E. Jacob & C. Jordan (Eds.), *Minority education: Anthropological perspectives.* Norwood, NJ: Ablex.

Erickson, F., & Gutierrez, K. (2002). Culture, rigor, and science in educational research. *Educational Researcher,* 31, 21–24.

Fairbanks, C.M., Freedman, D., & Kahn, C. (2000). The role of effective mentors in learning to teach. *Journal of Teacher Education,* 51(2), 102–112.

Fashola, O. & Slavin, R.E. (1996). *Effective and replicable programs for students placed at risk in elementary and middle schools.* Washington, DC: Office of Educational Research and Improvement, U.S. Department of Education.

Felner, R.D., Brand, S., DuBois, D.L., Adan, A.M., Mulhall, P.F., & Evans, E.G. (1995). Socioeconomic disadvantage, proximal environmental experiences, and socioemotional and academic adjustment in early adolescence: Investigation of a mediated effects model. *Child Development,* 66, 774–792.

Ferguson, R.F. (1998). Teachers' perceptions and expectations and the black-white test score gap. In C. Jencks & M. Phillips (Eds.), *The black-white test score gap* (pp. 273–317). Washington, DC: Brookings Institution Press.

Fine, M. (1989). *Framing dropouts: Notes on the politics of an urban high school.* Albany, NY: SUNY Press.

Fine, M., (1994). *Chartering Urban School Reform: Reflections on Public High Schools in the Midst of Change* (Professional Development and Practice). New York: Teachers College Press.

Foley, D.E. (1991). Reconsidering anthropological explanations of ethnic school failure. *Anthropology & Education Quarterly,* 22, 60–86.

Fordham, C., & Ogbu, J. (1986). Black students' school success: Coping with the burden of "acting white." *Urban Review,* 18, 176–206.

Frawley, W. (1997). *Vygotsky and cognitive science.* Cambridge, MA: Harvard University Press.

Freeman, K. (1997). Increasing African Americans' participation in higher education: African American high school students' perspectives. *Journal of Higher Education,* 68(5), 523–550.

Freire, P. (1993). *Pedagogy of the oppressed* (Revised ed.). New York: Continuum.

Freire, P. (1998). *Pedagogy of freedom: Ethics, democracy, and civic courage.* Lanham, MD: Rowman & Littlefield.

Friedman, S.J. (2000). How much of a problem? A reply to Ingersoll's "The problem of underqualified teachers in American secondary schools." *Educational Researcher,* 29(5), 18–20.

Fullan, M. (1991). *The new meaning of educational change*. New York: Teachers College Press.

Fullan, M. (1993a). *Change forces*. London: Falmer.

Fullan, M. (1993b). The three stories of educational reform: Inside; inside/out; outside/in. *Phi Delta Kappan, 81,* 581–584.

Funkhouser, J., Gonzales, M., & Moles, O. (1997). *Family involvement in children's education: Successful local approaches: An idea book*. Washington, DC: Policy Studies Associates, Inc.

Gagné, R.M. (1970). Varieties of learning. In *The conditions of learning*, 2ⁿᵈ Ed. (pp .36–69). New York: Holt, Rinehart and Winston.

Gagné, R.M. (1977). *The conditions of learning* (4ᵗʰ Ed.). New York: Holt, Rinehart & Winston.

Gallimore, R. & Goldenberg, C. (2001). Analyzing cultural models and settings to connect minority achievement and school improvement research. *Educational Psychologist, 36*(1), 45–56.

Gallimore, R., Goldenberg, C., & Weisner, T. (1993). The social construction and subjective reality of activity settings: Implications for community psychology. *American Journal of Community Psychology, 21,* 537–559.

Gamoran, A. (1987). The stratification of high school learning opportunities. *Sociology of Education, 60*(3), 135–155.

Gamoran, A. (2000). High standards: A strategy for equalizing opportunities to learn? In R. D. Kahlenberg (Ed.), *A notion at risk: Preserving public education as an engine for social mobility* (pp. 93–126). New York: Century Foundation.

Gamoran, A. (2001). American schooling and educational inequality: Forecast for the 21ˢᵗ century. *Sociology of Education, 34,* 135–153.

Gans, H.J. (1995). *The war against the poor: The underclass and antipoverty policy*. New York: Basic Books.

Garet, M., Birman, B., Porter, Yoon, K., & Desimone, L. (2002). What makes professional development effective? Analysis of a national sample of teachers. *American Education Research Journal, 38* (3), 915–945.

Garmezy, N. (1985). Stress resistant children: The search for protective factors. In J. Stevenson (Ed.), *Recent research in developmental psychology* (pp. 213–233). Oxford: Pergamon Press.

Gauvin, M. & Rogoff, B. (1989). Collaborative problem solving and children's planning skills. *Developmental Psychology, 25,* 139–151.

George, P., & McEwin, K. (1999). High schools for a new century: Why is the high school changing? *NASSP Bulletin, 83,* 10–24.

Gerber, S.B., Finn, J.D., Achilles, C.M., & Boyd-Zaharias, J. (2001). Teacher aides and students' academic achievement. *Educational Evaluation and Policy Analysis, 23*(2), 123–144.

Gibson, M.A. & Ogbu, J.U. (1991). *Minority status in schooling: A comparative study of immigrant and involuntary minorities*. New York: Garland Publishing.

Giddens, A. (1992). *Human societies*. Cambridge: Polity Press.

Giroux, H., (1980). Critical theory and rationality in citizenship education. *Curriculum Inquiry, 10*(4), 329–66.

Giroux, H. (1983). *Theory and resistance: A pedagogy for the opposition*. South Hadley, MA: Bergin and Garvey Publishers.

Glassman, M., & Yang, Y., (2004). On the interconnected nature of interpreting Vygotsky: Rejoinder to Gredler and Shields: Does no one read Vygotsky's words (2004). *Educational Researcher, 33*(6), 19–22.

Glassman, M. (2001). Dewey and Vygotsky: Society, experience, and inquiry in educational practice. *Educational Researcher, 30*(4), 3–14.

Goffman, E. (1963). *Stigma: Notes on the management of spoiled identity.* New York: Touchstone.

Goldberg, M.F. (2001). A concern with disadvantaged students: An interview with Henry Levin. *Phi Delta Kappan, 82*(8), 632–634.

Goldenberg, C. & Gallimore, R. (1991). Local knowledge, research knowledge, and educational change: A case study of first-grade Spanish reading improvement. *Educational Researcher, 20*(8), 2–14.

Goldenberg, C. & Sullivan, J. (1994). *Making changes happen in a language-minority school: A search for coherence* (Educational Practice Report No. 13). Santa Cruz: University of California at Santa Cruz, National Center for Research on Cultural Diversity and Second Language Learning.

Goldenberg, C., Reese, L., and Gallimore, R. (1992). Effects of school literacy materials on Latino children's home experiences and early reading achievement. *American Journal of Education, 100,* 497–536.

Goldstein, A.P., Sprafkin, R.P., Gershaw, N.J., & Klein, P. (1990). *Skillstreaming the adolescent.* Champaign, IL: Research Press Company.

Good, T. (1987). Teacher expectations. In D. Berliner & B. Rosenshine (Eds.), *Talk to teachers* (pp. 159–200). New York: Random House.

Good, T.L. & Marshall, S. (1984). Do students learn more in heterogeneous or homogenous groups? In P. Peterson, L.C. Wilkinson, & M. Hallinan (Eds.), *The social context of instruction: Group organization and group processes* (pp. 15–38). New York: Academic Press.

Goodlad, J.I. (1983). *A place called school.* New York: McGraw-Hill.

Goodlad, J.I. (1999). Whither schools of education? *Journal of Teacher Education, 50*(5), 325–338.

Goodlad, J.I. & Keating, P. (1990). *Access to knowledge: An agenda for our nation's schools.* New York: College Board.

Goodwin, A.L. (2002). The social/political construction of low teacher expectations for children of color: Re-examining the achievement gap. *Journal of Thought, 37*(4), 83–104.

Gordon, L.R. (1999). A short history of the "critical" in critical race theory. *The APA Newsletter on Philosophy and the Black Experience, 98*(2), 23–26. Retrieved on 05 November, 2004 from http://www.apa.udel.edu/apa/ archive/newsletters/ v98n2/ lawblack/gordon.asp.

Green, P. (1981). *The pursuit of inequality.* New York: Pantheon Books.

Greeno, J.G., Collins, A.M. & Resnick, L.B. (1996). Cognition and Learning. In D. Berliner and R. Calfee (Eds.). *Handbook of Educational Psychology* (pp. 15–46). New York: Simon and Schuster.

Greeno, J.G., & Goldman, S. V. (1998). *Thinking Practices in Mathematics and Science Learning.* Mahwah, NJ: Lawrence Erlbaum Associates.

Grissmer, D., Flanagan, A., & Williamson, S. (1998). Why did the black-white score gap narrow in the 1970s and 1980s? In C. Jencks & M. Phillips (Eds.), *The black-white test score gap* (pp. 182–226). Washington, DC: Brookings Institution.

Grissmer, D., Flanagan, A., Kawata, J. and Williamson, S. (2000). *Improving student achievement: What state NAEP test scores tell us.* Santa Monica, CA: RAND.

Gronlund, N.E. (1988). *How to construct achievement tests* (4th ed.). Upper Saddle River, NJ: Prentice Hall.

Gronlund, N.E. (2002). *Assessment of student achievement* (7th ed.). Upper Saddle River, NJ: Pearson; Allyn & Bacon.

Gysbers, N.C. (1997). A model comprehensive guidance program. In N.C. Gysbers & P. Henderson (Eds.), *Comprehensive guidance programs that work–II* (pp. 1–23). Greensboro, NC: ERIC/CASS Publications.

Haberman, M. (2002, April 2). Can teacher education close the achievement gap? AERA Symposium Presentation, New Orleans. Retrieved on 05 November, 2004 from http://www.educationnews.org/can_teacher_education_close_the_.htm

Halpen, R. (1992). The role of after-school programs in the lives of inner-city children: A study of the "Urban Youth Network." *Child Welfare, 71,* 215–230.

Hamovitch, B. (1999). More failure for the disadvantaged: Contradictory African-American student reactions to compensatory education and urban schooling. *Urban Review, 3*(1), 55–77.

Hargreaves, A., & Fullan, A. (Eds.). (1992). *Understanding teacher development.* New York: Teachers College Press.

Harpaz, Y. & Lefstein, A., (2000). Communities of thinking. *Educational Leadership, 58*(3), 54–57.

Hart, B. & Risley, T.R. (1992). American parenting of language-learning children: Persisting differences in family-child interactions observed in natural home environments. *Developmental Psychology, 28*(6), 1096–1105.

Hart, B. & Risley, T.R. (1995). *Meaningful differences in the everyday experience of young American children.* Baltimore: Brookes.

Hart, P.J., & Jacobi, M. (1992). *From gatekeeper to advocate: Transforming the role of the school counselor.* New York: College Entrance Examination Board.

Haskins, R. (1989). Beyond metaphor: The efficacy of early childhood education. *American Psychologist, 44,* 274–282.

Haycock, K. (1998). Good teaching matters: How well-qualified teachers can close the gap. *Thinking K–16, 3*(2), 1–2.

Haycock, K. (2001, March). Closing the achievement gap. *Educational Leadership, 58*(6), 6–11. Retrieved from http://www.ascd.org/reaqdingroom/edlead/0103/haycock.html on 05 November, 2004.

Haycock, K., Gerald, C., & Huang, S. (2001, Spring). Closing the gap: Done in a decade. *Thinking K-6, 2,* 3–21.

Hayes, R.L., Dagley, J., & Horne, A.M. (1996). Restructuring school counselor education: Work in progress. *Journal of Counseling & Development, 74,* 378–384.

Hayes, R.L., & Paisley, P.O., (2002). Transforming school counselor preparation programs. *Theory into Practice, 41*(3), 169–176.

Heath, S.B. (1983). *Ways with words.* Cambridge, MA: Cambridge University.

Heath, S.B., & McLaughlin, M.W. (1987). A child resource policy: Moving beyond dependence on school and family. *Phi Delta Kappan, 68,* 576–580.

Heath, S.B., & McLaughlin, M.W. (Eds.). (1993). *Identity & inner-city youth: Beyond ethnicity and gender.* New York: Teachers College Press.

Hedges, L. V. & Nowell, A. (1998). Are Black-White differences in test scores narrowing? Pages 254–281 in C. Jencks and M. Phillips (Eds.), *The black white test score gap.* Washington, DC: The Brookings Institution.

Hedges, L. V. & Nowell, A. (1999). Changes in the Black-White gap in achievement test scores: The evidence from nationally representative samples. *Sociology of Education*, 72, 111–135.

Helderman, R.S. (2002, June 27). Committee sets goals to narrow achievement gap. *Washington Post*, p. LZ01.

Henderson, A.T., & Berla, N. (Eds.). (1995). *A new generation of evidence: The family is critical to student achievement*. Washington, DC: Center for Law and Education.

Herr, E.L. (2002, April). School reform and perspectives on the role of school counselors: A century of proposals for change. *Professional School Counseling, 5*(4), 220–235.

Herrenstein, R.J., & Murray, C.A. (1994). *The bell curve: Intelligence and class structure in American life*. New York: The Free Press.

Hiebert, J., Gallimore, R., & Stigler, J. (2002). A knowledge base for the teaching profession: What would it look like, and how can we get one? *Educational Researcher, 31*(5), 3–15.

Hiebert, J., Gallimore, R., Garnier, H., Givvin, K.B., Hollingsworth, H., Jacobs, J., Chui, A.M., Wearne, D., Smith, M., Kersting, N., Manaster, A., Tseng, E., Etterback, W., Manaster, C., Gonzales, P., & Stigler, J., (2003). Teaching mathematics in seven countries: results from the TIMSS 1999 video study. *Education Statistics Quarterly*, 5 (1), 7–15.

Hilliard, III., A.G. (2000). Excellence in education versus high-stakes standardized testing. *Journal of Teacher Education, 51,* 293–304.

Hirsch, E.D. (1996). *The schools we need and why we don't have them*. New York: Doubleday.

Hirsch, E.D. (1998). *Cultural literacy: What America needs to know*. New York: Vintage Books.

Hixson, J. & Tinzmann, M. 1990. Who are the at-risk students of the 1990's? North Central Regional Educational Laboratory Website. Retrieved on 12 November, 2004 from http://www.ncrel.org/sdrs/areas/rpl_esys/equity.htm

Holt, T. (1990). "Knowledge is power": The Black struggle for literacy. In A. Lunsford, H. Moglen, & J. Slevin (Eds.), *The right to literacy* (pp. 91–102). New York: The Modern Language Association.

Holzman, L., & Newman, F. (1993). *Lev Vygotsky: Revolutionary scientist* (Critical Psychology Series). Taylor & Francis Books Lt., UK.

Hopfenberg, W.S., & Levin, H.M. (1993). *The accelerated schools resource guide*. San Francisco: Jossey-Bass.

Hopping, L. (2000). Multi-age teaming: a real-life approach to the middle school. *Phi Delta Kappan, 82*(4), 270–272.

House, R.M. (2002, April). School counselors: Becoming key players in school reform. *Professional school counseling, 5*(4), 249–256.

Howes, C., Olenick, M., & Der-Kiureghian, T. (1987). After-school childcare in an elementary school: Social development and continuity and complementarity of programs. *Elementary School Journal, 88*(1), 93–103.

Hunt, J.M. (1961). *Intelligence & experience*. New York: Ronald Press.

Iverson, B.K., & Walberg, H.J. (1982). Home environment and school learning: A quantitative synthesis. *Journal of Experimental Education, 50*(3), 144–151.

Jencks, C. (1972). *Inequality: A reassessment of the effect of family and schooling in America*. New York: Basic Books.

Jencks, C., & Phillips, M. (1998). America's next achievement test. Closing the black-white test score gap. *The American Prospect, 9*(40). Retrieved on 11 November,

2004, from http://www.prospect.org/web/page.ww?section=root&name= ViewPrint&articleId=4656

Jencks, C., & Phillips, M. (1999). *The black-white test score gap.* Washington, DC: Brookings Institution Press.

Jencks, C., Smith, M., Acland, H., Bane, M.J., Cohen, D., Gintis, H., Heyns, B., & Michelson, S. (1972). *Inequality: A reassessment of the effect of family and schooling in America.* New York: Harper & Row.

Johnson, D.W., Johnson, R., Dudley, B., Ward, M., & Magnuson, D. (1995). The impact of peer mediation training on the management of school and home conflicts. *American Educational Research Journal, 32*(4), 829–844.

Johnston, R.C. & Viadero, D. (2000, March 15). Unmet promise: Raising minority achievement. *Education Week* [Online]. Retrieved on 11 November, 2004 from http://www.edweek.org/ew/ewstory.cfm?slug=27gapintro h19.

Jones, L.V. (1984). White-black achievement differences: The narrowing gap. *American Psychologist, 39,* 1207–1213.

Jordan, G.E., Snow, C.E., & Porche, M.V. (2000). Project EASE: The effect of a family literacy project on kindergarten students' early literacy skills. *Reading Research Quarterly, 35*(4), 524–546.

Kahne, J., & Westheimer, J. (2000). A pedagogy of collective action and reflection: Preparing teachers for collective school leadership. *Journal of Teacher Education, 51,* 372–383.

Kahne, J., Nagaoka, J., Brown, A., O'Brien, J., Quinn, T., & Thiede, K. (2001, June). Assessing after-school programs as contexts for youth development. *Youth & Society, 32*(4), 421–446.

Kao, G. & Tienda, M. (1998). Educational aspirations of minority youth. *American Journal of Education, 106,* 349–384.

Karpov, Y., & Bransford, J.D. (1995). L.S. Vygotsky: The doctrine of empirical and theoretical learning. *Educational Psychologist, 30,* 61–66.

Kilgore, S. Doyle, D. & Linkowsky, L. (1996). The modern red schoolhouse. In S. Stringfield, S. Ross, & L. Smith (Eds.), *Bold plans for school restructuring: The New American Schools Development Corporation designs.* Mahwah, NJ: Erlbaum.

Kim, J. (2004). Summer reading and the ethnic achievement gap. *Journal of Education for Students Placed at Risk, 9*(2), 169–188.

Klonsky, M., & Ford, P. (1994). One urban solution: Small schools. *Educational leadership, 51*(8), 64–66.

Knapp, M.S., (1995). *Teaching for meaning in high-poverty classrooms.* SRI International, Menlo Park, CA.

Kohn, A. (1999). Raising the scores, ruining the schools. *American School Board Journal, 186,* 31–34.

Kohn, M.L. (1977). *Class and conformity: A study of values* (2nd Ed.). Chicago: University of Chicago Press.

Konstantopoulos, S., Modi, M., & Hedges, L.V. (2001). Who are America's gifted? *American Journal of Education, 109,* 344–382.

Koretz, D. (1987). *Educational achievement: Explanations and implications of recent trends.* Washington, DC: The Congress of the U.S. Congressional Budget Office.

Kozol, J. (1992). *Savage inequalities.* New York: HarperPerennial.

Kozol, J. (2000). An unequal education. *School Library Journal, 46*(5), 46–49.

Kozulin, A., (2003). Psychological tools and mediated learning. In A. Kozulin, B. Gindis, V.S. Ageyev, & S.M. Miller (Eds.), *Vygotsky's educational theory in cultural context* (pg. 15–38). Cambridge, UK: Cambridge University Press.

Kozulin, A., & Presseisen, B.Z. (1995). Mediated learning experience and psychological tools: Vygotsky's and Feuerstein's perspectives in a study of student learning. *Educational Psychologist, 30*(2), 67–95.

Kozulin, A., Gindis, B., Ageyev, V.S., & Miller, S.M., (2003). *Vygotsky's educational theory in cultural context.* Cambridge, UK: Cambridge University Press.

Krashen, S.D. (1996). *Under attack: The case against bilingual education.* Culver City, CA: Language Education Associates.

Krueger, A.B., Hanushek, E.A., & Rice, J.K., (2002). In L. Mischel & R. Rodstein (Eds.), *The class size debate.* Washington, DC: Economic Policy Institute.

Kuhn, T.S. (1962). *The structure of scientific revolutions.* Chicago: University of Chicago Press.

Ladson-Billings, G. (1994). *The dreamkeepers: Successful teachers of African American teachers.* San Francisco: Jossey-Bass.

Ladson-Billings, G. (1998). It doesn't add up: African American student's mathematics achievement. In C.E. Malloy & L. Brader-Araje (Eds.), *Challenges in the mathematics education of African American children: Proceedings of the Benjamin Banneker Association leadership conference.* Reston, VA: National Council of Teachers of Mathematics.

Ladson-Billings, G. (2001). *Crossing over to Canaan: The journey of new teachers in diverse classrooms.* San Francisco: Jossey-Bass.Ladson-Billings, G., (2004) Landing on the wrong note: The price we paid for *Brown. Educational Researcher, 33*(7), 3–13.

Lapan, R.T. (2001). Results-based comprehensive guidance and counseling programs: A framework for planning and evaluation. *Professional School Counseling, 4,* 289–299.

Lapan, R.T., Gysbers, N.C., & Petroski, G.F. (2001). Helping seventh graders be safe and successful: A statewide study of the impact of comprehensive guidance programs. *Journal of Counseling and Development, 79*(3), 320–330.

Lapan, R.T., Gysbers, N.C., & Sun, Y. (1997). The impact of more fully implemented guidance programs on the school experiences of high school students: A statewide evaluation study. *Journal of Counseling and Development, 75,* 292–302.

Lareau, A. (1989). *Home advantage.* New York: Falmer.

Lave, J., & Wenger, E. (1991). *Situated learning. Legitimate peripheral participation.* Cambridge: University of Cambridge Press.

Laws, P., & Hastings, N. (2002). Reforming science and mathematics teaching. *Change, 34*(5), 28–36.

Lazar, I., & Darlington, R. (1982). Lasting effects of early education: A report from the consortium for longitudinal studies. *Monographs of the Society for Research in Child Development, 47*(2–3), 1–151.

Lee, J. (2002). Racial and ethnic achievement gap trends: Reversing the process toward equity? *Educational Researcher, 31*(1), 3–12.

Lee, V.E., & Burkam, D.T. (2002). *Inequality at the starting gate. Social background differences in achievement as children begin school.* Washington, DC: Economic Policy Institute.

Lee, V.E., A.S. Bryk, and J.B. Smith (1993). The organization of effective secondary schools. In *Review of Research in Education.* Washington, DC: American Educational Research Association.

Lee, V.E., Winfield, L.F., & Wilson, T.C. (1991). Academic behaviors among high-achieving African-American students. *Education and Urban Society, 24*(1) 65–86.

Leithwood, K., Louis, K.S., Anderson, S., & Wahlstrom, K., (2004). Executive Summary: How leadership influences student learning. Learning from Leadership Project, The Wallace Foundation.

Leonardo, Z., (2004). Part critical social theory and transformative knowledge: The functions of criticism in quality education. *Educational Researcher, 33*(6), 11–18.

Lerner, R.M. (1995). *American's youth in crisis: Challenges and opportunities for programs and policies.* Thousand Oaks, CA: Sage.

Levin, H. (1988). Accelerated schools for disadvantaged students. *Educational Leadership 44*(6), 19–21.

Levin, H.M. (1997). *Accelerated education for an accelerating economy.* Hong Kong: Hong Kong Institute of Educational Research, the Chinese University of Hong Kong.

Lewis, P. (2001, October 16). Military-operated schools may hold answers. *Vanderbilt Register.* Retrieved from http://www.vanderbilt.edu/News/register/Oct16_01/story3.html on 12 November, 2004

Lieberman, G.A., & Hoody, L.L. (1998). *Closing the achievement gap: Using the environment as an integrating context for learning.* State Education and Environment Roundtable [Online]. Retrieved on 11 November 2004 from: http://www.seer.org/pages/overview.htm.

Lincoln on education. (2003, February 12). Louisville, KY, *Courier-Journal,* A3.

Lorenz, K. (1952). *King Solomon's ring.* London: Methuen.

Loury, G.C. (2002). *The anatomy of racial inequality.* Cambridge, MA: Harvard University Press.

Lytton, H. (1990). Child and parent effects in boys' conduct disorders: A reinterpretation. *Developmental Psychology, 26,* 683–97.

Maeroff, G.I. (1998a). Altered destinies: Making life better for schoolchildren in need. *Phi Delta Kappan, 79*(6), 425–432.

Maeroff, G.I. (1998b). *Altered destinies: Making life better for schoolchildren in need.* New York: St. Martin's Press.

Mager, R.F. (1975). *Preparing instructional objectives.* Belmont, CA: Fearon.

Magnuson, K.A., Meyers, M.K., Ruhm, C.J., & Waldfogel, J. (2004). Inequality in preschool education and school readiness. *American Educational Research Journal, 41*(1), 115–157.

Mann, L., Harmoni, R.V., & Power, C.N. (1989). Adolescent decision-making: The development of competence. *Journal of Adolescence, 12,* 265–278.

Marshall, H.H. (1996). Implications of differentiating and understanding constructivist approaches. *Educational Psychologist, 31*(3–4), 235–240.

Marshall, N.L., Coll, C.G., Marx, F., McCartney, K., Keefe, N., & Ruh, J. (1997). After-school time and children's behavioral adjustment. *Merrill-Palmer Quarterly, 43,* 497–514.

Martin, D.B. (2000). *Mathematics success and failure among African American youth: The roles of sociohistorical context, community forces, school influence, and individual agency.* Mahwah, NJ: Lawrence Erlbaum Associates.

Marzano, R.J. (1998). Cognitive, metacognitive, and conative considerations in classroom assessment. In N.M. Lambert & B.L. McCombs (Eds.), *How students learn: Reforming schools through learner-centered education* (pp. 241–266). Washington, DC: American Psychological Association.

Marzano, R.J., & Hutchins, C.L. (1985). *Thinking skills: A conceptual framework.* Denver, CO: Mid-Continent Regional Educational Laboratory.

Maslow, A.H. (1954). *Motivation and personality.* New York: Harper & Row.

McCollum, H. (1996). Lessons for school-based reform: A study sponsored by the Department of Education. Washington, DC: National Academy Press.

McGee, G.W. (2004). Closing the achievement gap: Lessons from Illinois' golden spike high-poverty high performing schools. *Journal of Education for Students Placed at Risk, 9*(2), 97–126.

McInerney, D.M., & Van Etten, S. (Eds.). (2002). *Research on sociocultural influences on motivation and learning (vol. 2).* Greenwich, CT: Information Age Publishing.

McIntyre, A. (1997). *Making meaning of whiteness: Exploring the racial identity of white teachers.* Albany, NY: State University of New York Press.

McLaren, P. (1994). *Life in schools: An introduction to critical pedagogy and the politics of cultural studies.* London: Routledge.

Mehan, H., Hubbard, L., & Villanueva, I. (1994). Forming academic identities: Accommodation without assimilation among involuntary minorities. *Anthropology & Education Quarterly, 25*(2), 91–117.

Mehan, H., Villanueva, I., & Lintz, A. (1996). *Constructing school success: The consequences of untracking low-achieving students.* Cambridge: Cambridge University Press.

Meier, D. (1996). Supposing that . . . *Phi Delta Kappan, 78*(4), 271–276.

Metz, M.H. (2001). Intellectual border crossing in graduate education: A report from the field. *Educational Researcher, 20*(5), 12–18.

Mickelson, R.A. 1990). The attitude-achievement paradox among black adolescents. *Sociology of Education, 63,* 44–61.

Miller, L.S. (1995). *An American imperative: Accelerating minority educational advancement.* New Haven, CT: Yale University Press.

Moll, L.C. (1992). Billingual classroom studies and community analysis: Some recent trends. *Educational Research, 21*(2), 20–24.

Moll, L.C. (2002). Afterword. In G. Wells & G. Claxton (Eds.), *Learning for life in the 21ˢᵗ century: Sociocultural perspectives on the future of education* (pp. 265–270). Malden, MA: Blackwell Publishers.

Morris, D., Shaw, B., & Perney, J. (1990). Helping low readers in grades 2 and 3: An after-school volunteer tutoring program. *Elementary School Journal, 9*(2), 133–150.

Morrison, G., Robertson, L., Hardin, M., Weissglass, T., & Dondero, A. (2000). The protective function of after-school programming and parent education and support for students at-risk of substance abuse. *Evaluation and Program Planning, 23,* 365–371.

Morton, J.S., & Schug, M.C. (2001). *Financial fitness for life. Bringing home the gold. Grades 9–12. Teacher guide.* New York: National Council on Economic Education.

Moses, R.P. (2001). *Radical equations: Math literacy and civil rights.* Boston: Beacon Press.

Mosteller, F., & Boruch, R. (2002). *Evidence matters: Randomized trials in education research.* Washington, DC: Brookings Institution Press.

Mosteller, F., & Moynihan, D.P. (1972). *On equality of educational opportunity.* New York: Random House.

Mote, C.D. (2004, July 11). For higher ed, a graceful decline. Louisvile, KY, *Courier Journal,* D1.

Mulliken, D.G. (2003, January 22). Report: Segregation on rise: Harvard study finds schools increasingly divided by race. *The Harvard Crimson.* Retrieved on 11 November, 2004 from http://www.thecrimson.com/article.aspx?ref=261892

Murdock, T.B. (1999). The social context of risk: Status and motivational predictors of alienation in middle school. *Journal of Educational Psychology, 91*(1), 62–75.

Murname, R.J., & Nelson, R. (1984). Production and innovation when techniques are tacit: The case of education. *The Journal of Economic Behavior and Organizations, 5,* 353–373.

Murrell, P.C. (2001). *The community teacher: A new framework for effective urban teaching.* New York: Teachers College.

National Board for Professional Teaching Standards (1991). *Toward High and Rigorous Standards for the Teaching Profession* (3rd Ed). Detroit.

National Center for Education Statistics (1994a). *Access to early childhood programs for children at risk.* Washington, DC: US Department of Education. NCES 93–372.

National Center for Education Statistics (1994b). *Digest of educational statistics.* Washington, DC: US Department of Education.

National Center for Education Statistics (1999, August). ECLS-K data user's manual. Washington, DC: US Department of Education, Office of Educational Research and Improvement. (NCES 2000–070).

National Center for Education Statistics (2000a, January). America's kindergartners. Washington, DC: US Department of Education, Office of Educational Research and Improvement. (NCES 2000–070).

National Center for Education Statistics (2000b). ECLS-K base year data files and electronic codebook. Washington, DC: US Department of Education, Office of Educational Research and Improvement.

National Center for Family Literacy (2003). Take action! A guide to advocacy and raising awareness for family literacy [Online]. Retrieved on 11 November, 2004 from http://www.famlit.org/Publications/member-pubs.cfm

National Commission on Excellence in Education (1983). *A nation at risk: The imperative for educational reform.* Washington, DC: US Government Printing Office.

National Commission on Teaching and America's Future (1996). *What matters most: Teaching for America's future.* New York.

National Commission on Teaching and America's Future (1997). *Doing what matters most: Investing in quality teaching.* New York.

National Education Goals Panel (1997). *The National Education Goals report: Building a nation of learners, 1997* [Online]. Available: http://www.negp.gov.

National Education Goals Panel (1999). *Reading achievement state by state, 1999* [Online]. Available: http://www.negp.gov

National Institute on Student Achievement, Curriculum, and Assessment (1998). *The educational system in Japan: Case study findings.* Washington, DC: US Department of Education.

National Research Council (1989). Everybody counts. *A report to the nation of the future of mathematics education.* Washington DC: Author.

National Research Council (1999). *Improving student learning: A strategic plan for education research and its utilization.* Committee on a Feasibility Study for a Strategic Education Research Program. Washington, DC: National Academy Press.

National Research Council (2002). Scientific research in education. In R.J. Shavelson & L. Towne (Eds.), *Committee on Scientific Principles for Educational Research.*

Washington, DC: National Academy Press. Retrieved on 11 November, 2004 from http://www.nap.edu/books/0309082919/html/

Neisser, U. (1986). *The school achievement of minority children. New perspectives.* Hillsdale, NJ: Lawrence Erlbaum Associates, Inc.

Newman, F., & Holzman, L. (1996). *Unscientific psychology: A cultural-performatory approach to understanding human life.* Westport, CT: Praeger.

Nieto, S., (2003). *What Keeps Teachers Going?* ERIC Number ED474173.

Nieto, S. (2000a). *Affirming diversity: The sociopolitical context of multicultural education* (3rd ed.). New York: Longman.

Nieto, S. (2000b). Placing equity front and center: Some thoughts on transforming teacher education for a new century. *Journal of Teacher Education, 51*(3), 180–187.

Nisbett, R.E. (1998). Race, genetics, and I.Q. In C. Jencks & M. Phillips (Eds.), *The Black-White Test Score Gap* (pp. 86–102). Washington, DC: Brookings Institution Press.

No Child Left Behind Act of 2001, Pub. L. No. 107–110.

Noddings, N. (1996). Rethinking the benefits of the college-bound curriculum. *Phi Delta Kappan, 78*(4), 271–276.

Oakes, J. (1985). *Keeping track: How schools structure inequality.* New Haven, CT: Yale University Press.

Oakes, J. (1990a). Tracking and ability grouping: A structural barrier to access and achievement. In J.I. Goodlad & P. Keating (Eds.), *Access to knowledge: An agenda for our nation's schools* (pp. 187–205). New York: College Entrance Examination Board.

Oakes, J. (1990b). *Multiplying inequalities: The effects of race, social class, and tracking on opportunities to learn mathematics and science.* Santa Monica, CA: RAND Corporation.

Oakes, J., Quartz, K.H., Ryan, S., & Lipton, M. (2000). *Becoming good American schools: The struggle for civic virtue in school reform.* San Francisco: Jossey-Bass.

O'Connell, P.J., McGuire, C.K., Middleton, R., Thomas, A., Ruiz, R. Bellamy, G.T., Bornfield, G., & Ohanian, S. (2000). Agora: The impact of high-stakes testing. *Journal of Teacher Education, 51*, 289–292.

Odden, A., & Kelly, C. (1997). *Paying teachers for what they know and do: New and smarter compensation strategies to improve schools.* Thousand Oaks, CA: Corwin Press.

Office of Educational Research and Improvement. (1991). *Youth indicators 1991: Trends in the well-being of American youth.* Washington, DC: US Government.

Ogbu, J. (1978). *Minority education and caste: The American system in cross-cultural perspective.* New York: Academic Press.

Ogbu, J. (1992). Understanding cultural diversity and learning. *Educational Researcher, 21*(8), 5–14.

Ogbu, J. (1994). Racial stratification and education in the United States: Why inequality persists. *Teachers College Record, 96*(2), 264–298.

Ogbu, J. (1997a). Racial stratification in the United States: Why inequality persists. In A.H. Halsey, H. Lauder, P. Brown, & A.S.Wells (Eds.), *Education: Culture, economy, and society* (pp. 765–778). Oxford: Oxford University Press.

Ogbu, J. (1997b). Understanding the school performance of urban blacks: Some essential background knowledge. In H.J. Walberg, O. Reyes, & R.P. Weissberg (Eds.), *Children and Youth: Interdisciplinary Perspectives* (pp. 190–221). Thousand Oaks: Sage Publications.

Ogbu, J. (2002). Black-American students and the academic achievement gap: What else you need to know. *Journal of Thought, 37*(4), 9–34.

Ogbu, J., & Simons, H.D. (1998). Voluntary and involuntary minorities: A cultural-ecological theory of school performance with some implications for education. *Anthropology and Education Quarterly, 29*(2), 155–188.

Ohanian, S. (1996). Is that penguin stuffed or real? *Phi Delta Kappan, 78*(4), 277–284.

Ohanian, S. (1997). Some are more equal than others. *Phi Delta Kappan, 78*(6), 471–474.

Ohanian, S. (2000). Goals 2000. What's in a name? *Phi Delta Kappan, 81,* 345–355.

Olds, D.L., Henderson, C.R., Chamberlain, R., & Tatelbaum, R. (1986). Preventing child abuse and neglect: A randomized trial of nurse home visitation. *Pediatrics, 78,* 65–78.

Orfield, G., Frankenberg, E.D., & Lee, C. (2003). The resurgence of school segregation. *Educational Leadership, 60*(4), 16–20.

Orfield, G., & Yun, J., (1999). *Resegregation in American schools.* Cambridge, MA: The Civil Rights Project, Harvard University

Orpinas, P., Murray, N., & Kelder, S. (1999). Parental influences on students' aggressive behaviors and weapon carrying. *Health Education and Behavior, 26*(6), 774–787.

Osborne, A.F., & Milbank, J.E. (1987). *The effects of early education: A report from the child health and education study.* New York: Oxford University Press.

Osborne, J.L, Collison, B.B., House, R.M., Gray, L.A., Firth, J., & Lou, M. (1998). Developing a social advocacy model for counselor education. *Counselor Education & Supervision, 37,* 190–202.

Paisley, P.O., & Hayes, R. L. (2000). Counselor under construction: Implications for program design. In G. McAuliffe & K. Eriksen (Eds.), *Preparing counselors and therapists: Creating constructivist and development programs.* Alexandria, VA: ACES and Donning Publishers.

Palincsar, A.S., & Brown, A.L. (1984). Reciprocal teaching of comprehension-fostering and comprehension-monitoring activities. *Cognition and Instruction, 1*(2), 117–175.

Parish, R., & Aquila, F. (1996, December). Cultural wars of working and believing in schools: Preserving the way things are. *Phi Delta Kappan, 78,* 298–305.

Parker, I., & Spears, R. (1996). *Psychology and society: Radical theory and practice,* London: Pluto Press.

Peal, E., & Lambert, W.E. (1962). The relation of bilingualism to intelligence. *Psychological Monographs, 76,* 1–23.

Pedraza, P., & Ayala, J. (1996). Motivation as an emergent issue in an after-school program in El Bario. In L. Schauble & R. Glaser (Eds.), *Innovations in learning: New environments for education* (pp. 75–91). Mahwah, NJ: Lawrence Erlbaum Associates, Inc.

Peterson, P.G. (2003, June 22). Deficits and dysfunction. Louisville, KY, *Courier-Journal* (p. 7).

Phillips, M., Crouse, J., and Ralph, J. (1998). Does the black-white test score gap widen after children enter school? In C. Jencks & M. Phillips (Eds.), *The black-white test score gap* (pp. 229–272). Washington, DC: Brookings Institution Press.

Phillips, M., Brooks-Gunn, J., Duncan, G.J., Klebanov, P., & Crane, J. (1998). Family background, parenting practices, and the black-white test score gap. In C. Jencks & M. Phillips (Eds.), *The black-white test score gap* (pp. 103–148). Washington, DC: Brookings Institution Press.

Phillips, S. (1983). *The invisible culture: Communication in classroom and community on the Warm Springs Indian reservation*. New York: Longman.

Piaget, J. (1971). *Biology and knowledge*. Chicago: University of Chicago Press.

Pierce, L.H., & Shields, N. (1998). The Be A Star community-based after-school program: Developing resiliency factors in high-risk preadolescent youth. *Journal of Community Psychology, 26*(2), 175–183.

Pierce, K.M., Hamm, J.V., & Vandell, D.L. (1999). Experiences in after-school programs and children's adjustment in first-grade classrooms. *Child Development, 70*, 756–767.

Pinar, W.F. (1989). A reconceptualization of teacher education. *Journal of Teacher Education, 40*(1), 9–12.

Popham, W. (1997). What's wrong—and what's right—with rubrics. *Educational Leadership, 55*(2), 72–75.

Portes, A. (2000a). The two meanings of social capital. *Sociological Forum, 15*(1), 1–12.

Portes, A. (2000b). Doing high-stakes assessment right. *The School Administrator, 57*(11), 28–31.

Portes, A., & Rumbaut, R.G. (2001). *Legacies: The story of the immigrant second generation*. Berkeley, CA: University of California Press.

Portes, A., & Zhou, M. (1999). Entrepreneurship and economic progress in the nineties: A comparative analysis of immigrants and African Americans. In F.D. Bean & S. Bell-Rose (Eds.), *Immigration and opportunity: Race, ethnicity, and employment in the United States* (pp. 143–171). New York: Russell Sage Foundation.

Portes, P.R. (1982). *The effects of environmental processes on children's intellectual development: Longitudinal effects on family interaction through early intervention. Dissertation Abstracts International*. Tallahassee, FL: The Florida State University.

Portes, P.R. (1988). Maternal verbal regulation and intellectual development. *Roeper Review, 11*(2), 106–110.

Portes, P.R. (1991). Assessing children's cognitive environments through parent-child interaction: Estimation of a general zone of proximal development in relation to scholastic achievement. *Journal of Research in Education, 24*(3), 30–38.

Portes, P.R. (1996). Ethnicity and culture in educational psychology. In D. Berliner & R. Calfee (Eds.), *The Handbook of Educational Psychology* (pp. 331–357). New York: Macmillan Publishing.

Portes, P.R. (1999). Social and psychological factors in the academic achievement of children of immigrants: A cultural history puzzle. *American Educational Research Journal, 36*(3), 489–507.

Portes, P.R. (2002). Cultural historical processes and the educational achievement gap: Challenging policies for establishing equal educational opportunity. *Journal of Thought, 37*(4), 105–116.

Portes, P.R., & Dunham, R.M. (1988). Early age intervention and parent-child interaction: Their relation to student academic achievement. *Journal of Research and Development in Education, 22*(1), 78–91.

Portes, P.R., Dunham, R., Castillo, K.D., (2000). Identity formation and status across cultures: Exploring the cultural validity of Eriksonian theory. In A.L. Comunian & U.P. Uwe (Eds.), International Perspectives on Human Development (pp. 449–459). Lengerich, Germany: Pabst Science Publishers.

Portes, P.R., & Vadeboncoeur, J.A. (2003). Mediation in cognitive socialization: The influence of socioeconomic status. In A. Kozulin, B. Gindis, V.S. Ageyev, & S.M.

Miller (Eds.), *Vygotsky's Educational Theory in Context* (pp. 371–392). Cambridge, UK: Cambridge University Press.

Portes, P.R., & Zady, M.F. (2002). Self-esteem in the adaptation of Spanish-speaking adolescents: The role of immigration, family conflict, and depression. *Hispanic Journal of Behavioral Sciences, 24,* 296–318.

Portes, P.R., Dunham, R.M., & Williams, S.A. (1986). Preschool intervention, social class, and parent-child interaction differences. *Journal of Genetic Psychology, 147*(2), 241–255.

Portes, P.R., Zady, M. F., & Dunham, R.M. (1998). The effects of parents' assistance on middle school students' problem solving and achievement. *Journal of Genetic Psychology, 159*(2), 163–178.

Portes, P.R., Smith, T.L., Zady, M.F., & Del Castillo, K. (1997). Extending the double stimulation method in cultural-historical research: Parent-child interaction and cognitive change. *Mind, Culture, and Activity, 4*(2), 108–123.

Posner, J.K., & Vandell, D.L. (1994). Low-income children's after-school care: Are there beneficial effects of after-school programs? *Child Development, 65,* 110–156.

Posner, J.K., & Vandell, D.L. (1999). After-school activities and the development of low-income urban children: A longitudinal study. *Developmental Psychology, 35,* 868–879.

Poverty and Family Budgets. Frequently Asked Questions [Online]. Available: http://www.epinet.org/content.cfm/issueguides_poverty_povertyfaq. posted August 2001. retrieved 01/21/05.

Proctor, B.D., & Dalaker, J. (2002). U.S. Census Bureau, Current Population Reports, P60–219, *Poverty in the United States: 2001,* U.S. Government Printing Office, Washington, DC.

Promising practices. (1995). U.S. Department of Education.

Pungelloo, E.P., Kupersmidt, J.B., Burchinal, M.R., & Patterson, C.J. (1996). Environmental risk factors and children's achievement from middle childhood to early adolescence. *Developmental Psychology, 32,* 755–767.

Purcell-Gates, V. (1997). *Other people's words: The cycle of low literacy.* Cambridge, MA: Harvard University Press.

Purcell-Gates, V. (2000). Family literacy. In M.L. Kamil, P.B. Mosenthal, P.D. Pearson, & R. Barr (Eds.), *Handbook of reading research, vol. III* (pp. 853–870). Mahwah, NJ: Lawrence Erlbaum Associates, Inc.

Purcell-Gates, V. (2001). Emergent literacy is emerging knowledge of written, not oral, language. In P.R. Britto & J. Brooks-Gunn (Eds.), *The role of family literacy environments in promoting young children's emerging literacy skills* (pp. 7–22). San Francisco, CA: Jossey-Bass.

Purkey, S.C., & Smith, M.S. (1983). Effective schools: A review. *Elementary School Journal, 83,* 423–454.

Radcliffe, B., Malong, M., & Nathan, J. (1994). *The training for parent partnerships: Much more should be done.* Minneapolis, MN: Center for School Change, Humphrey Institute of Public Affairs, University of Minnesota.

Ramey, C.T., Bryant, D.M., Campbell, F.A., Sparling, J.J., & Wasik, B.H. (1988). Early intervention for high-risk children: The Carolina Early Intervention Program. In R.H. Price & E.L. Cowen (Eds.), *Fourteen ounces of prevention: A casebook for practitioners* (pp. 32–43). Washington, DC: American Psychological Association.

Ramey, C.T., Campbell, F.A., Burchinal, M., Skinner, M.L., Gardner, D.M., & Ramey, S.L. (2000). Persistent effects of early intervention on high-risk children and their mothers. *Applied Developmental Science, 4,* 2–14.

Ramey, S.L., & Ramey, C.T. (in press). The effects of early childhood experiences on developmental competence. In S. Danzinger & J. Waldfogel (Eds.), *Securing the future: Investing in children from birth to college.* New York: Russell Sage Foundation.

Ramirez, M., & Castaneda, A. (1974). *Cultural democracy, bicognitive development, and education.* New York: Academic.

Rank, M.R. (2004). *One nation, underprivileged: why American poverty affects us all.* New York: Oxford University Press.

Rauch, J. (1989). Kids as capital. *The Atlantic Monthly, 264* (2), 56–61.

Reese, L., & Gallimore, R. (2000). Immigrant Latinos' cultural model of literacy development: An evolving perspective on home-school discontinuities. *American Journal of Education, 108,* 103–134.

Reyes, P., Scribner, J.D., & Scribner, A.P. (Eds.). (1999). *Lessons from high-performing Hispanic schools: Creating learning communities.* New York: Teachers College Press.

Reynolds, G.M. (2002). Bridging the great divide: Broadening perspectives on closing the achievement gaps. Identifying and eliminating the achievement gaps: A research-based approach. *Viewpoints, 9,* 3–12.

Richardson, J. (1994). Few states require parent-involvement training. *Education Week,* June 6, 1994. Retrieved on May 15, 2004 from http://www.edweek.org/cgi-bin/texis/search?querystring=Few+states+require+parent-involvement+training&source=all&date=all

Robelen, E.W. (2002). *Taking on the achievement gap.* Retrieved December 13, 2002, from http://www.ncrel.org/gap/takeon/toc.htm.

Rose, M. (1995). *Possible lives: The promise of public education in America.* New York: Houghton Mifflin.

Ross, J.G., Saavdra, P.J., Shur, G.H., Winters, F., & Felner, R.D. (1992). The effectiveness of an after-school program for primary grade latchkey students on precursors of substance abuse. *Journal of Community Psychology (OSAP Special Issue),* 22–38.

Rotberg, I.C. (1993). *Federal policy options for improving the education of low-income students, vol. II, commentaries.* Santa Monica, CA: RAND.

Ryan, W. (1981). *Equality.* New York: Pantheon Books.

Safe and Smart After School Programs retrieved on November 12, 2004, from http://www.ed.gov/pubs/parents/SafeSmart/.

Sarason, S. (1966). *Revisiting "the culture of the school and the problem of change."* New York: Teachers College Press.

Scheurich, J., Skrla, L., Johnson, J.F. (2000). Thinking carefully about equity and accountability. *Phi Delta Kappan, 82*(4), 293–299.

Schinke, S.P., Orlandi, M.A., & Cole, K.C. (1992). Boys & girls clubs in public housing developments: Prevention services for youth at risk. *Journal of Community Psychology (OSAP Special Issue),* 118–28.

Schmidt, W. (2001, April 4). TIMSS press release. Retrieved on January 15, 2004, from http://USTIMSS.msu.edu/whatsnew.html.

Schorr, L.B. (1988). *Within our reach: Breaking the cycle of disadvantage.* New York: Anchor.

Schorr, L.B. (1997). *Common purpose: Strengthening families and neighborhoods to rebuild America.* New York: Anchor Books.

Schwartz, W. (2001). *Closing the achievement gap: Principles for improving the educational success of all students.* New York: ERIC Digest, ERIC Clearing House on Urban Education. Retrieved on November 12, 2004 from http://www.ericfacility.net/ericdigests/ed460191.html

Schweinhart, L.J., & Weikhart, D.P. (1988). The high/scope Perry preschool program. In R.H. Price, E.L. Cowen, R.P. Lorion, & J. Ramos-McKay (Eds.), *14 Ounces of prevention: A casebook for practitioners* (pp 16–34). Washington, DC: American Psychological Association.

Schweinhart, L.J., & Weikart, D.P. (1998). High/scope Perry pre-school program effects at age twenty-seven. In J. Crane (Ed.), *Social programs that work* (pp. 148–162). New York: Russell Sage Foundation.

Schweinhart, L.J, Weikart, D.P., & Lerner, M. (1986). Consequences of three preschool curriculum models through age 15. *Early Childhood Research Quarterly, 1,* 15–45.

Seeley, D.S. (1985). *Education through partnership.* Washington, DC: American Enterprise Institute for Public Policy Research.

Shanker, A. (1990). The end of the traditional model of schooling and a proposal for using incentives to restructure our public schools. *Phi Delta Kappan, 71,* 345–357.

Shann, M.H. (2002, July). Students' use of time outside of school: A case for after school programs for urban middle school youth. *Educational Administration Abstracts, 37*(3), 279–412.

Shartrand, A.M., Weiss, H.B., Kreider, H.M., & Lopez, M.E. (1997). *New skills for new schools: Preparing teachers for family involvement.* Cambridge, MA: Harvard Family Research Project (U.S. Department of Education Contract 43–31HA-7–40108).

Shaver, A.V., & Walls, R.T. (1998). Effect of Title 1 parent involvement on student reading and mathematics achievement. *Journal of Research & Development in Education, 31*(2), 90–97.

Sheets, R.H. (1999). Human development and ethnic identity. In R.H. Sheets & E.R. Hollins (Eds.), *Racial and ethnic identity in school practices: Aspects of human development* (pp. 91–101). Mahwah, NJ: Erlbaum.

Sheets, R.H. (2001). Whiteness and white identity in multicultural education. *Multicultural Education, 8*(3), 38–40.

Sindelar, P.T. & Rosenberg, M.S. (2000). Serving too many masters: the proliferation of ill-conceived and contradictory policies and practices in teacher education. *Journal of Teacher Education, 51*(3), 188–193.

Singham, M. (1998, September). The canary in the mine: The achievement gap between black and white students. *Phi Delta Kappan, 80*(1), 9–15.

Sizer, T. R. (1992). School reform—what's missing? *World Monitor, 5*(11), 20–28.

Slavin, R.E. (1990). Ability grouping and student achievement in secondary schools: A best-evidence synthesis. *Review of Educational Research, 60,* 471–499.

Slavin, R.E. (1998). Can education reduce social inequality? *Educational Leadership, 55*(4), 6–10.

Slavin, R.E. (2002a). Evidence-based education policies: Transforming educational practice and research. *Educational Researcher, 31*(7), 15–21.

Slavin, R.E. (2002b). Mounting evidence supports the achievement effects of Success for All. *Phi Delta Kappan, 83*(6), 469–471.

Slavin, R.E. (2003). A reader's guide to scientifically based research. *Educational Leadership, 60*(5), 12–16.

Slavin, R.E., & Madden, N.A., (2001). *Success for All and Comprehensive School Reform: Evidence-Based Policies for Urban Education.* Office of Educational Research and Improvement (ED), Washington, DC.

Slavin, R.E., Madden, N.A., Dolan, L.J., & Wasik, B.A. (1996). *Every child, every school: Success for All.* Newbury Park, CA: Corwin.

Sleeter, C. (1993). Advancing a white discourse: A response to Scheurich. *Educational Researcher, 22*(8), 13–15.

Sleeter, C. (1995). An analysis of the critiques of multicultural education. In J.A. Banks & C.A. McGee Banks (Eds.), *Handbook of Research on Multicultural Education* (pp. 81–94). New York: Macmillan Publishing Company.

Sleeter, C.E. (1996). *Multicultural education as social activism (SUNY Series, the Social Context of Education).* New York: State University of New York Press.

Sloan, T. (1996). *Life choices: Understanding dilemmas and decisions.* Boulder, CO: Westview Press.

Smith, F. (2001). Just a matter of time. *Phi Delta Kappan, 82*(8), 572–576.

Smrekar, C., Guthrie, J.W., Owens, D.E., Sims, P.G., (2001). March Toward Excellence: School success and minority student achievement in Department of Defense schools. A report to the National Education Council. Peabody Centre for Education Policy. Peabody College, Vanderbilt University.

Snipes, J.C., & Casserly, M.D. (2004). Urban school systems and education reform: Key lessons from a case study of large urban school systems. *Journal of Education for Students Placed at Risk, 9*(2), 127–142.

Snow, C., Burns, S., & Griffin, P. (1998). *Preventing reading difficulties in young children.* Washington, DC: National Research Council.

Snow, R.E. (1992). Aptitude theory: Yesterday, today, and tomorrow. *Educational Psychology, 27*(1), 5–32.

Soder, R. (1996). Democracy, education, and the schools. San Francisco, CA: Jossey-Bass.

Sorenson, S.B. & Rutter, C.M. (1991). Transgenerational patterns of suicide attempt. *Journal of Consulting and Clinical Psychology, 59,* 861–866.

Southers, C.L. (1991). Home economics teacher education reform. Prime time for a phoenix agenda. *Journal of Vocational Home Economics Education 9*(2), 56–69.

Spencer, S.J., Steele, C.M., & Quinn, D.M. (1999). Stereotype threat and women's math performance. *Journal of Experimental Social Psychology, 35,* 4–28.

Spring, J. (2001). *Deculturalization and the struggle for equality: A brief history of the education of dominated cultures in the United States* (3rd Ed.). New York: McGraw-Hill.

Stanfield, J.H. (1985). The ethnocentric basis of social science knowledge production. *Review of Research in Education, 12,* 387–415.

Starkey, P., & Klein, A. (2000). Fostering parental support for children's mathematical development: An intervention with Head Start families. *Early Education & Development, 11*(5), 659–680.

Stedman, L.C. (1987). It's time we changed the effective schools formula. *Phi Delta Kappan, 69,* 215–224.

Steele, C. (1992). Race and the schooling of Black Americans. *Atlantic, 269*(4), 68–78.

Steele, C. (1997). A threat in the air: How stereotypes shape intellectual identity and performance. *American Psychologist, 52*(6), 613–629.

Steele, C. (1999). Thin ice: "Stereotype threat" and black college students. *The Atlantic Monthly 284*(2), 44–54.

Stevenson, H.W., & Stigler, J.W. (1992). *The learning gap: Why our schools are failing and what we can learn from Japanese and Chinese education.* New York: Summit Books.

Stigler, J., & Heibert, J. (1999). *The teaching gap.* New York: Free Press.

Stone, C. (1998). Leveling the playing field: An urban school system examines equity in access to mathematics curriculum. *The Urban Review, 30*(4), 295–307.

Stone, C.N., Henig, J.R., Jones, B.D., & Pierannunzi, C. (2001). *The Politics of Reforming Urban Schools.* Lawrence, KS: University of Kansas Press.

Stringfield, S., Millsap, M., & Herman, R. (1997). *Special strategies for educating disadvantaged children: Results and policy implications.* Washington, DC: U.S. Department of Education.

Sullivan, J. (1994). *Producing change in an urban, second-language, elementary school.* Unpublished doctoral dissertation, Graduate School of Education, University of California, Los Angeles.

Tanner, D. (2000). Manufacturing problems and selling solutions: How to succeed in the education business without really educating. *Phi Delta Kappan, 88*(3), 182–202,

Teitel, L. (2001). *How professional development schools make a difference: A review of research.* Washington, DC: National Council for Accreditation of Teacher Education.

Teitel, L., & Abdul-Haqq, I. (2000). Assessing the impacts of Professional Development Schools. In I. Abdul-Haqq (Ed.), *The Professional Development Series* [Booklet]. Washington, DC: AACTE.

Tharp, R.G. (1989). Psychocultural variables and constraints: Effects on teaching and learning in schools. *American Psychologist, 44,* 349–359.

Tharp, R.G. (1997). *From at-risk to excellence: Research, theory, and principles for practice.* Santa Cruz, CA: University of California, Center for Research on Education, Diversity and Excellence.

Tharp, R.G., & Gallimore, R. (1988). *Rousing minds to life: Teaching, learning, and schooling in social context.* Cambridge: Cambridge University Press.

Tharp, R.G., Estrada, P., Dalton, S.S., & Yamauchi, L.A. (2000). *Teaching transformed: Achieving excellence, fairness, inclusion, and harmony.* Boulder, CO: Westview Press.

Thernstrom, A., & Thernstrom, S. (2003). *No excuses: Closing the racial gap in learning.* New York: Simon & Schuster Adult Publishing Group.

Thomas, D., & Bainbridge, W.L., (2001). All children can learn: facts & fallacies. *Phi Delta Kappan, 82,* 660.

Timar, T. (1989). The politics of school restructuring. *Phi Delta Kappan, 71,* 265–275.

Tomlinson, C.A. (2000). Reconcilable differences: Standards-based teaching and differentiation. *Educational Leadership, 58*(1), 6–11.

Towne, L., Shavelson, R., & Feuer, M. (2001). *Science, evidence, and inference in education: Report of a workshop (Washington, DC, March 7–8, 2001).* Washington, DC: US Department of Education.

Turkheimer, E., Haley, A., Waldron, M., D'Onofrio, B., & Gottesman, I.I. (2003). Socioeconomic status modifies heritability of IQ in young children. *Psychological sciences, 14,* 623–628.

Turner, S.E. (2000). A comment on "Poor school funding, child poverty, and mathematics achievement." *Educational Researcher, 29*(5), 15–18.

US Census Bureau (1970–1998). [Current Population Survey]. Unpublished raw data.

US Department of Education (1993). *The national educational goals report: A wake-up call.* Washington, DC: Author.

US Department of Education (1996). GOALS 2000: A Progress Report in GOALS 2000: *Building on a Decade of Reform* [On-line]. Retrieved on November 12, 2004 from http://www.ed.gov/G2K/ProgRpt96/build.html.

US Department of Health & Human Services (2001). *Early Head Start shows significant results for low income children and parents (press release)*. Retrieved January 13, 2003, from http://www.hhs.gov/news/press/2001pres/20010112.html.

Valentine, C. (1971). Deficit, difference, and bicultural models of Afro-American behavior. *Harvard Educational Review, 41,* 137–157.

Valli, L., Cooper, D., & Frankes, L. (1997). Professional development schools and equity: A critical analysis of rhetoric and research. In M.W. Apple (Ed.), *Review of research in education, 22* (pp. 251–304). Buckingham, PA: Open University Press.

Valsiner, J. (1989). *Human development and culture: The social nature of personality and its study.* Lexington, MA: Lexington Books.

Van der Veer, R., & Valsiner, J. (Eds.). (1994). *The Vygotsky Reader.* Oxford: Blackwell.

Varenne, H. & McDermott, R. (1999). *Successful failure: The school America builds.* Boulder, CO: Westview Press.

Viadero, D. (2000, March 22). Lags in minority achievement defy traditional explanations. *Education Week.* [Online]. Retrieved on February 17, 2004, from http://www.edweek.org/ew/ewstory.cfm?slug=28causes.h19.

Villegas, A.M., & Lucas, T. (2002). Preparing culturally responsive teachers: Rethinking the curriculum. *Journal of Teacher Education, 53,* 1.

Vygotsky, L.S. (1978). *Mind in society.* Translated by A.R. Luria. Edited by M. Cole, V. John-Steiner, S. Scribner, & E. Souberman. Cambridge: Harvard University Press.

Vygotsky, L.S. (1987). *Collected works of L. S. Vygotsky: Vol. 1: Problems of general psychology.* Translated by N. Minick. Edited by R. W. Rieber and A. S. Carton. New York: Plenum press.

Waters, J. T., Marzano, R. J., & McNulty, B. A. (2003). *Balanced leadership: What 30 years of research tells us about the effect of leadership on student achievement.* Aurora, CO: Mid-continent Research for Education and Learning.

Weikart, D.B. (1995). Early childhood education. In J.H. Block, S.T. Everson, & T.R. Guskey (Eds.), *School improvement programs that work* (pp. 289–312). New York: Scholastic.

Weikart, D.B. (2002). The origin and development of preschool intervention projects. In E. Phelps, F.F. Furstenberg, Jr., A. Colby, & M.F. Collie (Eds.), *Looking at lives: American longitudinal studies of the twentieth century* (pp. 254–264). New York: Russell Sage Foundation.

Weinberger, E.H., & McCombs, B.L. (2001, April). The impact of learner-centered practices on the academic and non-academic outcomes of upper elementary and middle school students. In *Integrating what we know about learners and learning: A foundation for transforming PreK–20 practices.* Symposium conducted at the annual meeting of the American Educational Research Association, Seattle, WA.

Weisman, S.A., & Gottfredson, D.C. (2001, September). Attrition from after school programs: Characteristics of students who drop out. *Prevention Science, 2*(3), 201–205.

Weisner, T.S. (1984). Ecocultural niches of middle childhood: A cross cultural perspective. In W.A. Collins (Ed.), *Development during middle childhood: The years from six to twelve* (pp. 335–369). Washington, DC: National Academy of the Sciences Press.

Weisner, T.S., Gallimore, R., & Jordan, C. (1988). Unpackaging cultural effects on classroom learning: Native Hawaiian peer assistance and child generated activity. *Anthropology & Education Quarterly, 19*(4), 327–353.

Weissberg, R.P., Caplan, M., & Harwood, R.L. (1991). Promoting competent young people in competence-enhancing environments: A system-based perspective on primary prevention. *Journal of Clinical and Consulting Psychology, 59,* 830–841.

Wenger, E. (1998). *Communities of practice: Learning, meaning, and identity.* New York: Cambridge University Press.

Wertsch, J.V. (1985). *Vygotsky and the social formation of mind.* Cambridge: Harvard University Press.

Whiston, S.C., & Sexton, T.L. (1998). A review of school counseling outcome research: Implications for practice. *Journal of Counseling and Development, 76,* 412–426.

White, B.L. (1975). *The first three years of life.* Englewood Cliffs, NJ: Prentice-Hall.

White, K.R. (1982). The relation between socioeconomic status and academic achievement. *Psychological Bulletin, 91*(3), 461–481.

Whiting, B., & Edwards, C. (1988). *Children of different worlds: The formation of social behavior.* Cambridge, MA: Harvard University Press.

Will, G. (2003, March 2). Making education change. Louisville, KY, *Courier-Journal,* D5.

Williams. B. (1996). *Closing the achievement gap: A vision for changing beliefs and practices.* Alexandria, VA: Association for Supervision and Curriculum Development.

Wilson, W.J. (1987). *The Truly Disadvantaged: The Inner City, the Underclass and Public Policy.* Chicago: University of Chicago Press.

Wilson, W.J. (1987). *The truly disadvantaged: The inner city, the underclass, and public policy.* Chicago, IL: University of Chicago Press.

Wollman, N., Lobenstine, M., Foderaro, M., & Stose, S. (1998). *Principles for promoting social change. Effective strategies for influencing attitudes and behaviors.* Washington, DC: Society for the Psychological Study of Social Issues.

Wong, K.K., Sunderman, G.L., & Lee, J. (1995). *When federal Title I works to improve student learning in inner-city schools: Final report on the implementation of schoolwide projects in Minneapolis and Houston.* Chicago: University of Chicago Press.

Yonezawa, S., Wells, A.S., & Serna, I. (2002). Choosing tracks: Freedom of choice in detracking schools. *American Educational Research Journal, 39*(1), 37–67.

Zigler, E. (1986). Assessing Head Start at 20: an invited commentary. *Annual Progress in Child Psychiatry & Child Development,* 669–677.

Zigler, E., & Muenchow, S. (1992). *Head Start: The inside story of America's most successful experiment.* New York: Basic.

Zigler, E. & Styfco, S. (1993). *Head Start and beyond.* New Haven, CT: Yale University Press.

Index